IN SEARCH

VOLUME 1 *Prentice-Hall of Canada, Ltd., Scarborough, Ontario*

IN SEARCH OF CANADA

OF CANADA

Ronald C. Kirbyson *assisted by* Elizabeth Peterson

To Cam Shepherd

Canadian Cataloguing in Publication Data

Kirbyson, Ronald C., 1937-
  In search of Canada

Includes index.
ISBN 0-13-453852-8 (v.1)

1. Canada—History. I. Title.

FC170.K57   971   C77-001060-1
F1026.K57

Prentice-Hall, Inc., Englewood Cliffs, New Jersey
Prentice-Hall International, Inc., London
Prentice-Hall of Australia, Pty., Ltd., Sydney
Prentice-Hall of India, Pvt., Ltd., New Dehli
Prentice-Hall of Japan, Inc., Tokyo
Prentice-Hall of Southeast Asia (PTE.) Ltd., Singapore

Design by John Zehethofer
Maps by James Loates

Printed in Canada
ISBN 0-13-453852-8
 2 3 4 5 THB 81 80 79 78

The author and publisher would like to thank the following for providing illustrations for this text.

Public Archives of Canada: p. 19, C-70249; p. 37, TC-305; p. 42, C-16336; p. 47, C-35415; p. 49, C-42126, C-42127; p. 50, C-86032; p. 52, C-25699; p. 58, C-6042; p. 105, C-19556; p. 107, C-11925; p. 116, C-5907; p. 131, C-13557; p. 145, C-2834; p. 148, C-6150; p. 168, C-46334; p. 171, C-17511, p. 183, C-2001; p. 195, C-276; p. 203, C-2771; p. 209, C-2146; p. 243, C-3305; p. 269, C-15017; p. 281, C-10671; p. 281, C-22744; p. 285, C-5655; p. 287, C-9790; p. 301, C-9001; p. 303, C-5795; p. 306, C-2404; p. 313, C-8166; p. 320, C-10379, p. 329, C-4552; p. 334, PA-22000; p. 337, C-23625; p. 341, C-8774; p. 343, C-24205, p. 350, C-18737; p. 354, C-2614; p. 360, C-11334; p. 369, C-733; p. 376, C-5811 and on pp. 17, 68, 69, 78, 83, 88, 98, 107, 131, 221, 246, 249, 262, 286. Royal Ontario Museum: pp. 35, 37, 40, 42, 88, 95, 99, 108, 112, 201, 222, 226, 235, 236, 237, 270, 274, 298, 301, 303, 306, 309, 310, 311, 312, 313, 315, 316, 317, 319, 338, 339, 340, 341. Confederation Life: pp. 159, 241. Committee for an Independent Canada: p. 164. Canadian Press: p. 19. Metropolitan Toronto Zoological Society: p. 85. Department of Indian Affairs: p. 60. National Film Board Photothèque: p. 60, first row, left, by Terry Pearce, August, 1968; right by Fred Ruggles, 1963; 2nd row, middle, Crombie McNeill, 1973; right, Terry Pearce, 1968; third row, left, Paul Baich, 1968; right, H. Taylor, 1963. Manitoba Archives: p. 213. John Ford: p. 252. National Parks, Historic Sites Branch: p. 128. Ontario Archives: pp. 259, 260. Manitoba Archives: p. 213. John Ford: p. 252. National Parks, Historic Sites Branch: p. 128. Ontario Archives pp. 259, 260. Page 5: © 1968. By permission of *Saturday Review* and Mr. S. Handelsman. Page 66: Reprinted by permission of NEA. Page 196: Reprinted by permission of Jules Feiffer.

Every reasonable effort has been made to find copyright holders of illustrations and quotations. The publishers would be pleased to have any errors or omissions brought to their attention.

Acknowledgements

The efforts of many people went into *In Search of Canada*. I shall be forever grateful for the support I received over the past three years.

To Elizabeth Peterson I must express special gratitude. She has been my colleague and friend throughout the enterprise. Not only did she contribute substantially to the writing, but she devoted thousands of hours to research, discussion and the myriad of tedious jobs that are involved in building such a book, including the typing of most of the manuscript in several stages.

Prentice-Hall of Canada supported me in the best way a publisher can: by providing talented personnel. As editor, Rob Greenaway has been a constant source of shrewd advice, ideas, helpful criticism and encouragement. His friendship and many kindnesses have been especially important during the difficult times when it seemed *In Search of Canada* would never be completed. Barb Steel has been much more than a production editor. She made countless suggestions for improving the writing. Not only did she supervise the research for pictures and illustrations, but she did much of the actual work. Without Barb's loyalty to the project, her talent for organizing, and her capacity for long hours of work, the preparation of *In Search of Canada* might have continued forever. John Ford, Executive Producer, Media Division, Prentice-Hall of Canada, Ltd., kindly made his extensive picture files available.

Many other people provided help along the way: Paul Hunt, who launched the project, in fact; Jim Burant of the Public Archives of Canada, who assisted with picture research; Ken Osborne, who read much of the manuscript in its early stages and offered much helpful advice; Cam Shepherd, who freely made his time available and helped me avoid many errors about economics; Janet Warren, who patiently handled many chores like preparing the bibliography; Janice Yeo and the staff of the Elizabeth Dafoe Library, University of Manitoba; Stephan Stankovic, with whom I so often discussed material in preparation.

My debt to my family cannot ever be repaid. My parents, Jean and Bill, helped me feel less guilty about spending so little time in their company. Dawn, Geoffrey and Jillian never wavered in their understanding, and they accepted "the book" with humour and patience as part of the household.

RCK

Contents

Introduction

Nobody reads introductions—well, almost nobody. But since you must be one who does, this introduction has a simple purpose: to point out the kinds of things you can find in *In Search of Canada*.

Not surprisingly, there is basic information in the form of narrative, description and explanation about Canadian history. But there is much more. Take, for example, the features. These appear in blue type in the book. They are designed to let you explore some topics which may be beyond the scope of a straight history course—things like problems in writing and interpreting history; ideas from the other social sciences like archaeology, anthropology and sociology; values analysis and choices; controversial events and people; and Canadian literature and how it reflects changes in society. On occasion, they also try to indicate how historical patterns repeat themselves—in other words, to help you appreciate how studying history can help you to understand what is happening in Canada and the world today.

Throughout the book, as well as within features, there are documents. These are drawn directly from primary sources—they give you the actual words written or spoken by people who played a part in Canadian history—or provide modern comments about people and events in the Canadian story. They have been chosen because they expand the basic narrative of the book, and make it more interesting, and they should help to develop basic inquiry and analytic skills.

Marginal notes explain points, define terms, identify people, raise questions—and introduce the lighter side of things on occasion.

Illustrations in the form of pictures, charts and maps are found in every chapter, of course, to help you get some visual impressions of the topics being discussed. But Chapter 14 in Volume 2 uses these visual materials in a different way. In this chapter, you will not find the usual pages of narrative and explanation. Instead, what you will be given are impressions of the many sides of important issues facing Canada and the world at present. You will not find solutions to problems since they are complicated problems; but you will find questions and ideas to help you clarify your thinking and points of view.

You can think of *In Search of Canada* as a history book. But look again. Included are ideas from economics; there are some from anthropology and sociology and other subjects you may be interested in. From time to time you can even find a poem or an excerpt from a novel or a short story. We hope *In Search of Canada* helps open some doors for you. It is intended to be a beginning, to encourage you to think about Canada and the world—and about yourself.

RCK

A Word to Help You Use This Book

The features, as was noted in the Introduction, appear in blue ink. They also start at the top of a page. Sometimes they may interrupt the text, but it is very easy to find where the narrative carries on, since you simply flip the pages until the black starts again. Then you can go back and pick up the features when you've finished your other reading. Sometimes, you'll notice words in **boldface** in the text; these will be defined in the margin, also in boldface, immediately opposite the spot where they appear. You'll also encounter asterisks (*) within the body of the text, and once again, these refer to specific notes in the margin which also begin with asterisks and can be found right opposite the material they refer to.

IN SEARCH OF CANADA

1

Discovery and exploration

Discovery: what is it?

Words like "discover" and "explore" are often used in modern advertisements to promote everything from soaps to trips. In history books, these words are associated with the romantic names of men from *Renaissance* times. These men crossed oceans in small boats in search of legendary places. Does a word like "discovery" have a different meaning in different times and situations or is discovery an experience that takes many forms?

"Discovery" is a familiar word, one that can be used whenever a person finds a place or thing that is *new to him* like a park, a restaurant, an idea. In this sense, discovery is subjective and personal, and whether it stems from a planned search or from chance, it is likely to be the result of curiosity, and the natural human need to know. So discovery is a kind of process as natural to a student now as to an explorer in past ages.

Varieties of discovery

> Sometimes by thought, more often by intuition, the Canadian people make the final discovery. They are discovering themselves.[1]

1

Discovery may mean finding the location of geographic areas on the earth's surface, and it may mean your own discovery of some object or place. There are many other kinds of discovery as well. What others can you think of?

For example, scientific discovery has enabled man to change his physical surroundings, especially in the last hundred years, in ways undreamt of for most of history. Whether using science to search for better ways to harness energy, safer and more efficient ways of travel, or for more sophisticated ways of exploring outer space, scientists have made discoveries without which our lives would be very different.

You may think that the scientist's method of discovery differs from that used by the explorer. How does a scientist work? In the first place there are, broadly speaking, two ways of approaching scientific research: the deductive and the inductive. In the deductive method, the scientist begins with an insight or viewpoint, puts it in the form of a *hypothesis*, conducts experiments, analyzes his findings, and draws conclusions about the truth of his hypothesis. In other words, he deduces facts and generalizations in the light of his original viewpoint. On the other hand, the scientist working inductively observes facts, questions and analyzes his observations, then induces, or draws general conclusions from the particular set of facts.

Consider the following paragraph about the invention of the storage battery. From the information given, which scientist would you say was working inductively? Deductively?

> Volta's discovery followed from a chance observation by a fellow countryman, Luigi Galvani, a Bologna anatomist, that dissected frogs' legs twitched when touched with certain metals. After a series of experiments Galvani concluded, wrongly, that there was a source of electricity in the muscle. Volta came to the right conclusion: electricity was produced when two different metals touched the leg simultaneously, and it came from the metals, not the frog.[2]

Notice that Galvani began with an observation, and having analyzed it, drew a conclusion. Volta began with an idea, or model, then tested it in order to draw his conclusion. In this case, it seems to have been the combination of inductive and deductive procedures, one scientist working deductively from the generalization developed inductively by the other, that produced the "discovery". No doubt a closer look at the methods of either Galvani or Volta would show that each one used a combination of the two approaches in his scientific discovery.

1. In using a map that showed the world to be round and indicated that Asia could be reached by sea, was John Cabot thinking deductively or inductively when he planned the route that led to the discovery of Newfoundland?

2. What similarities can you think of between the methods of the scientist and the explorer? Differences?

Medical discovery is closely related to scientific discovery. For most of history, there was no hope for a person who had tuberculosis, diphtheria or cholera. Because of medical discoveries we are now able to diagnose and cure many once-dreaded diseases or even to prevent them through immunization. Medical specialists are discovering ways of transplanting vital organs, of rehabilitating chronic drug addicts, and of prolonging man's life-span. Perhaps in the future, even such grim illnesses as heart disease and cancer will be eliminated. The medical frontiers to be explored are many and varied as the following passage shows:

> . . . in the Sixties [1960s], like a series of underground nuclear explosions, experiments began rumbling throughout the country that presaged perhaps the greatest medical discoveries of all time. . . .
>
> The simplest statement of the discovery is revolutionary: Given information about how any one of the internal physiological systems is operating, the ordinary human being can learn to control the activity of the system. It can be heartbeat, blood pressure, gastric acid, brain waves, or bits of muscle tissue. . . .
> ———————
> The discovery of this ability of mind is abbreviated in the term *biofeedback*. . . . The individual practices to control the action of the monitor by manipulating his mental and internal activities, and the result is a learned, voluntary control over the physiologic functions monitored. It is a technique for extending the capabilities of the mind to control the body—and the mind.[3]

It should be clear that thinking of discovery only in terms of things outside people would neglect an important kind of discovery —the *discovery of human nature*. The following two statements suggest why this may be the most important of all.

DEFINING THE QUEST

The harnessing of nuclear energy, the creation of cybernetic computers, the discovery of DNA, the development of the rocket— these, primary among a host of changes—have placed within man's reach the power to create life and nonhuman intelligence, to control evolution, to defer and perhaps abolish death, to destroy our species and our planet, to break out of our closed system into space.

The need to discover human nature is acute and urgent, because we have the capacity to alter or even extinguish it, and with it the whole baffling experiment. . . .

Poets, painters, dramatists, composers, novelists, historians, psychologists, anthropologists, archaeologists, sociologists, biologists, and philosophers—all are explorers in the field of human nature. Museums and libraries are crammed with strange and beautiful maps brought back by explorers since the beginning of man.[4]

CONSCIOUSNESS RESEARCH

As I survey the challenge facing humanity today, I see only one answer: *a transformation of consciousness.* Man must rise from his present ego-centered consciousness to find universal harmony, starting within himself and proceeding outward through his relations with other people and the environment to his relation with the cosmos. Otherwise, man will continue to move deeper into chaos and crisis toward a destruction of his own making.[5]

European discoveries of Canada

There is no known record of the first meeting between the original inhabitants and Europeans on voyages of discovery to Canada. In fact, not only did Indians not keep written records, but European evidence of pre-Columbus encounters with the land and peoples of Canada is sketchy, to say the least. People did not go on voyages of discovery in order to write history or to provide the documents from which history is later written. Nevertheless, historians, archaeologists and scientists continue to seek as much information as possible about the earliest events in the history of our country.

LEGENDS AND SPECULATION

The earliest accounts of discovery are legends (myths), which were sometimes passed on orally and sometimes in writing. Such literary sources often give clues that, when combined with the gleanings from monastic records, artifacts and other types of "historical" evidence, enable a modern researcher to speculate about what really happened. In other words, the true story is the one which appears to be most accurate according to the "circumstantial evidence". New evidence may show that the story believed to be true is no longer so. Now the proven record indicates that the Vikings were the first Europeans to

"Good. It's about time we had tourists in North America."

set foot on Canadian soil. Yet there are myths that Irish monks may have arrived 500 years earlier, and future research may force us to revise our historical "facts".

Norse voyages to North America

Contrary to popular belief, and despite the fact that Americans celebrate Columbus Day, Christopher Columbus was not the first white man to discover North America. If the right man were to be recognized, chances are there would be a Bjarni Herjulfson day, for that was the name of the Viking who may have been the first European to see North American coastline.

The possibility that Vikings were the first white men to discover North America was suspected for a long time before solid proof was found. According to legend, based on Norse sagas of the 12th or 13th century, Scandinavians—called Norsemen or Vikings—had travelled to North America around the year 1000. They were alleged to have visited, and even attempted settlement, in a region they called Vinland, located somewhere on North America's east coast. In 1898 the finding of the Kensington Rune Stone set off a lively debate about the possibility that Vikings had penetrated as far inland as Minnesota.*

* Runes are the straight-line letters of an alphabet used by ancient northern European nations. Stones having runic inscriptions on them are known as rune stones. The Kensington Rune Stone was found near the village of Kensington, Minnesota. Within a decade the rune stone had been examined by many experts American and Scandinavian, and declared to be a hoax.

Historians, archaeologists, linguists and other scholars continued to investigate, but not until the 1960s was there solid evidence for historical conclusions about the Vikings' discovery and exploration. Even the "Vinland map" published by Yale University in 1965 and thought by some to be authentic, has been challenged.

The Ingstads, a husband and wife team from Norway, began an excavation at L'Anse au Meadow in the early 1960s. This site on the northeastern tip of Newfoundland has yielded extensive evidence of a Viking village. The dating of the house sites and artifacts puts the time of settlement at approximately 1000 A.D. Thus the presence of Vikings in North America long before Columbus seems to have been confirmed, although the task of providing "absolute proof" may never be ended.

As far as it can be pieced together, the general account of why and how the Vikings came to North America begins with the early Middle Ages, when large numbers of Norwegians, Swedes and Danes left overcrowded homelands in search of places to settle. By the year 1000 they had travelled in their small open boats along much of Europe's coast and westward to the Shetland Islands, the Orkneys, the Hebrides and Iceland. From Iceland, the fearsome Eric the Red established a colony in Greenland in 985. Among the first settlers was a man called Herjulf. His son, Bjarni Herjulfson, also set out for Greenland, but overshot the mark. Storms carried his ships off course and he sighted land that was hilly and wooded, probably northern Newfoundland. Realizing that this was not Greenland and choosing not to stop to explore, Bjarni navigated northward. He passed the flat and wooded shorelines of Labrador, the mountainous and glacial Baffin Island and finally reached Greenland.

In such accidental fashion was Canada "discovered". Norse sagas tell further of travels by Eric the Red's son, Leif, in the year 1000. "Leif the Lucky", sailing from Norway to Greenland, seems to have reached the coasts of Labrador and Newfoundland. He may have ventured as far south as Nova Scotia, or even Massachusetts, for he named an area Vinland, where he reported finding wild grapes and wheat. Yet the location of Vinland and other places visited by Leif is still a matter of guesswork.

Similarly, little is known of Viking attempts at settlement. Within a decade or so of Leif's travels, one Thorfinn Karlsefni, a merchant, evidently tried to found a colony on the North American mainland. After two or three years the settlement was abandoned.

Regardless of where they travelled or tried to settle, the Vikings seem to have had little impact on North America and searchers have found scant evidence of their presence. Hopes for recovering more knowledge of Viking activities in Canada are likely to depend on archaeological finds like the one at L'Anse au Meadow.

What were the hazards of crossing the ocean in this ship?

The following news article appeared in the *Winnipeg Free Press* on February 6, 1974:[6]

To check the validity of a news story, you can note the news agency that is identified as the source—in this case, Reuter, a reputable operation, like AP (Associated Press), UPI (United Press International) or CP (Canadian Press). In a public library, you can read other newspapers to see whether they have carried the story. If several have done so, you can be more certain that the report is valid.

The reliability of the contents can also be checked. You can contact the organization mentioned and request copies of any statements presented. Short of actually interviewing the people involved, you can go to a *periodical index*, which lists articles by experts in the field which appear in journals.

Duped, Experts Admit

LONDON (Reuter) — With a scholarly chuckle and a hint of embarrassment, the learned members of Britain's Royal Geographical Society Monday night accepted scientific evidence and agreed they had been fooled.

But the question remained — by whom?

The cause of their discomfiture was the recent disclosure that the famed Vinland map, hailed nine years ago as "the cartographic discovery of the century" almost is certainly a forgery.

The map was thought to have been drawn by a monk in Switzerland about 1440. It shows a crude outline of the North American coast visited by Vikings some two centuries before that.

An anonymous benefactor paid $250,000 for the map and donated it to Yale University. But recent tests for Yale indicate the ink was made after 1920.

"A matter of obvious public concern," was how Dr. Helen Wallis, superintendent of the map room at the British Museum, described the affair at the geographical society meeting.

"It seems probable that the map is a fake," conceded Francis Maddison of Oxford's History of Science Museum.

One man was unyielding. George Painter, custodian of the British Museum's department of printed books and helped authenticate the Vinland map in 1965, said he still believes it "a product of medieval minds and hands."

Gerald Crone, who challenged the map from the outset, said even the non-scientific evidence showed it was 20th century.

Finally Dr. Walter McCrone, whose Chicago-based company detected the apparent forgery, presented his evidence. The conclusive factor, he said, was the presence in the ink of titanium dioxide, not introduced as a constituent until about 1920.

The identity of the possible forger may never be known. The man who first brought the map to light, Enzo Ferrajoli de Ry, an Italian who lived in Barcelona, is dead.

So is the British book dealer who marketed it, and so is British scholar R. A. Skelton, who helped authenticate it.

Laurence Witte, the New Haven, Conn., dealer who acquired it in 1957, has described details of the acquisition in a letter. But for discretion's sake, he says, it must not be opened for 9,000 years.

1. According to the article, why was the Vinland map once thought to be the "**cartographic** discovery of the century"?

Cartography means map-making.

2. What evidence leads to the conclusion that the Vinland map is a forgery? Has that conclusion been proved beyond all doubt? Why is it so difficult to prove the *facts* in this case, and in so many cases from centuries ago?

3. Historians are not the only ones engaged in historical research. What are some examples of other specialists who help historians decide whether information—data—is *valid*?

In writing history, the historian has many different jobs to do. One of the most basic, yet often difficult, tasks is to test the *validity* and *reliability* of his information, sometimes called data or evidence. In testing for *validity*, the historian tries to answer questions like the following: Is this piece of information authentic? Was this map really made in the 1400s, or could it have been produced at a much later time?

If he can prove that his information is valid, then he may ask: Is it true? Are the statements factual? Even though the map is several centuries old, does it provide information that is accurate, *reliable*?

In doing research, historians do not spend all of their time doubting nor do they prove over again every fact they use. What is important is a generally watchful, careful attitude; historians and any other investigators must use discretion in deciding what pieces of evidence need to be checked.

The same is true of the person in his everyday life. For example, did it occur to you to question the news article about the Vinland map forgery? Consider the following questions:

Could the article be a forgery? What are the chances that an editor, or even the author of this book, "planted" the story?

Could some or all of the charges of forgery be false?

What reasons might anyone have for such a practical joke?

How could you check to find out whether the article quoted is valid? How could you check to find out whether the article quoted is reliable?

The Renaissance as an age of discovery

The Renaissance, the period of European history from about 1450 to the early 1600s, was a time of rebirth in Europe. Europeans began making new discoveries in science, philosophy, religion and other areas of knowledge. An interest in knowledge, a spirit of questioning

9

about people and their world grew after centuries of dormancy. This climate of inquiry encouraged the European desire to stretch their knowledge of the physical world, through exploration and contact with faraway people. An ambitious mariner could find himself in the service of some king, probably of a country other than his own, perhaps destined to be the first white man in recorded history to explore a distant continent.

It may have been easier to sail an ocean in the 1500s than it was a century before, because of the improvements in navigational instruments—like compasses and sextants—and maps.

HÄGAR the Horrible   By Dik Browne

But ocean travel was still dangerous by modern standards, as this passage shows:

> Consider also the hazards of a sixteenth-century navigator exploring an unknown coast in a square-rigged vessel, incapable of quick maneuvering like a modern sailing yacht. With an onshore wind, the discoverers had to sail close to shore if they wanted to learn anything; yet it was always risky, especially on a fog-bound coast like Newfoundland. Submerged just below the surface, rocks capable of ripping the guts out of a ship were difficult to see in northern waters—dark green, opaque waters, not transparent like those of the Caribbean and the Coral Sea. Every harbor you entered added new risk, even if a boat were sent ahead to sound. Would your anchor hold, or was the bottom hard rock, eel grass, or kelp, along which your hook would skid like a sled, requiring quick and efficient action to prevent your ship's crashing? If the wind is offshore when you sight land, you might be blown seaward again and have to beat back, which could take weeks. . . . [7]

Besides, people thought the seas were full of monsters.

Why did they risk their lives on dangerous voyages knowing the odds were against them?

Their object was not discovery for its own sake—that was incidental—but the opening of ocean routes to distant India, China and Japan, countries known to exist and believed to be of commercial importance. The men who did the work were tough professionals, willing to serve any ruler who would employ them, ready to go anywhere and investigate anything if they were suitably rewarded. They were the maritime counterparts of the mercenary captains who made a profession of the land fighting of Europe. Skillful, imaginative and bold, they drew the map of the world we know.[8]

English voyages to North America

While the Viking voyages to Canada produced no lasting settlements, neither did the early ventures in the name of England. The main difference, however, was that the English expeditions—coming some 500 years later—made territorial claims which were eventually followed up. Ironically, England's claim to half the New World, as the Western Hemisphere was called, began with the incredible journey of a citizen of Venice, Giovanni Caboto (John Cabot), who received less than £100 for his trouble.

JOHN CABOT

In England, the news of the travels of Christopher Columbus and the benefits to Spain of New World exploration aroused great interest. On the southwest coast, the town of Bristol had for many years been the port of sail for fishermen and traders sailing to Iceland, the Azores and beyond. It was there that John Cabot found the financial backing to go with the royal authorization he had obtained from King Henry VII. In May, 1497, Cabot left Bristol in the ship *Matthew* with a crew of eighteen, and a little more than a month later landed, probably on the northeast coast of Newfoundland.

JOHN CABOT'S MOTIVES

It then occurred to him that England, being at the end of the spice line and paying the highest prices, would be interested in finding a short, high-latitude route to the Indies. Spices, especially pepper, cloves, and nutmeg, were household necessities in that era, for want of refrigeration; a liberal use of them disguised the flavor of spoiled meat. So to England went Cabot, and England was the one country where he was likely to gain support. Henry VII, in turning down the proposition of the Columbus brothers, had missed his chance to be "first"; he was not going to miss it this time, particularly since Cabot offered to sail on 'his own proper charges,' so it would not cost the crown a penny.[9]

The Matthew *arrives in Newfoundland. Based on this picture, what might Cabot have reported about his discovery?*

Deceived by the warm North American weather, Cabot reported back to England that he had reached Asia. He also noted that the seas were teeming with codfish. From Henry VII, impressed by the laying of an English claim to this new territory, Cabot received a small annual payment. Cabot's financial backers were sufficiently satisfied that they provided him with ships and supplies for another voyage. Setting out in May, 1498, the second Cabot expedition ended in mystery, for the ships never returned, and Cabot's fate is unknown.

Although the results of Cabot's efforts were disappointing and interest in further English exploration did not arise for more than a half century, the Cabot voyages were of considerable importance. He failed to find a short trade route to the Orient, but he did originate England's claim to the northeastern coast of North America. He opened the fishing areas off Newfoundland for England when the country needed a source of supply. Fish became an important article of English commerce on European markets. The fishing ships that crossed the Atlantic in increasing numbers were a good training ground for sailors at a time when the English navy was beginning to expand.

WHY DID MEN ENLIST?

It was not for money: the gold their captains sought would go to the Crown, and on a voyage of discovery there was little chance of loot or a division of prize money from a captured treasure galleon. Nor can the crusading motive have stirred the ordinary seaman, who was illiterate and uninterested in theology.

Since no common seaman left an account of the motives that led him to sign on, we can only guess about them. The pay was frequently somewhat higher than for an ordinary trading voyage in familiar waters, and it was certain, for exploration was soundly backed by a royal treasury or by a group of prosperous merchants. Moreover, all seafaring was hard and dangerous in that age. Voyages as long as any of those of Columbus (if not as chancy) were regularly being made from the North Sea to the Levant. It was an age when the average life expectancy was about 30 years, when even on land life was hard and uncertain; more farmers and tradesmen died of plague than did seamen of scurvy. So to Renaissance sailors the hazards of exploration did not present as lurid a contrast to ordinary life as they do by modern standards.[10]

THE "SEA DOGS"

During the reign of Elizabeth I, renewed interest in a Northwest Passage to Asia set off a wave of exploration. This resulted in additional English claims to parts of North America. In 1577 Sir Francis Drake sailed around the southern tip of South America and along the west shore of North America. He claimed the Pacific Coast of the northern part of North America for England. This claim proved important to England in the 18th century in negotiations with Spain and Russia regarding the sea-otter trade in northern Pacific waters.

Sir Humphrey Gilbert, another of Elizabeth's freebooting "sea dogs," renewed England's claims to Newfoundland in 1583. Although an attempted settlement by Sir Walter Raleigh failed, and men from rival countries fished adjacent waters, England's sovereignty over Newfoundland was continuous until 1949, when it joined Canada as a province.

The search for the elusive Northwest Passage continued. English efforts to find it resulted in explorations in the northern reaches of the Western Hemisphere. In 1576, Martin Frobisher's search ended tragically in what is now Frobisher Bay. John Davis, in 1586, ventured farther north into the strait that bears his name. In 1602, George Waymouth discovered Hudson Strait and Henry Hudson followed in 1610, continuing westward to discover Hudson Bay.

" . . . in 1610 Henry Hudson made the first trade with a Cree man in James Bay. This man, whose name is forgotten, must have been brave, for he approached the strangers' ship alone and exchanged his furs for a knife, a mirror, some buttons, and a hatchet."[11]

Portuguese voyages to North America

"This land is your land.
This land is my land.
From Bonavista to Vancouver Island. . . . "

Most Canadians would recognize these lines from a popular folk song, and they would identify "Bonavista" as a point on the eastern edge of Canada. But how many would realize that Cape Bonavista in Newfoundland was given its name by a Portuguese explorer nearly 500 years ago?

Gaspar Corté Real was the Portuguese explorer who gave the name Cape Bonavista to the south shore of Newfoundland. His expedition of 1501, and that of Joam Fegundes to Cape Breton twenty years later, were among the few Portuguese northern voyages. While many of their countrymen had sailed to North America in the 1500s to fish for cod on the Grand Banks, those in charge of major expeditions turned their attention southward. The rewards of gold and silver, and the prospect of finding the "fountain of youth,"* held far more appeal for kings and capitalists than did fish and fur.

"The Corte-Reals . . . in 1500 and 1502 took 60 Naskapi or Montagnais people to Portugal. One Inuit man kidnapped (with his kayak) by Martin Frobisher from Baffin Island gave an exhibition for Queen Elizabeth I, hunting royal swans on the palace pond."[12]

*Ponce de Leon, the Spaniard, was the most famous seeker of the "fountain of youth."

LIFE ABOARD THE DISCOVERY SHIPS

Conditions of life aboard during these lengthy voyages were appalling, not only by modern standards but by the standards of the time for life on shore. All the ships leaked; even with regular use of the pumps, water was constantly sloshing in the bilge which was further fouled by the casual sanitary habits of the age. Roaches and rats swarmed everywhere. No sleeping quarters were provided, save perhaps for the master and pilot: ordinary seamen slept on or below deck wherever they could find room. There was no water-proof clothing. . . .

Sheer discomfort and stench probably did not mean much to those who were used to the sea as traders or fishermen. But the voyages of discovery created major problems in the way of food supply. In part this reflected the large number of men needed to handle the sails of the early exploring vessels and for whom stores of food that would last for the whole voyage had to be carried. But there were other factors that added to the difficulties: the tendency of grain and ship's biscuit to become sour or to swarm with weevils; the speed with which even the best-made wine or water casks sprang leaks under the continual lurching of the ship. . . .

Shipboard menus consisted of dried or salted meat, salted fish, biscuit, rice, dried peas, cheese, onions, garlic, oil, vinegar, water and wine. . . . Eating at sea swung from frugality during voyages to gluttonous orgies after making a landfall, a pattern that corresponded exactly to eating habits ashore. The difference for the sailor lay in the terrible quality of the food during the times of scarcity: the putrefying water; the fresh food petering out after a few days; then a diet unhealthily salty; then a time when even salted and dried provisions turned into a slimy mess, undulating with worms.[13]

French voyages to North America

Like England, France in the 16th century was a developing nation-state, eager to compete with European rivals for land and possible riches in the New World. By 1500 French vessels were making frequent voyages to the fishing grounds off the coast of New-foundland. The ambitious King, Francis I, envious of the wealth Spain and Portugal were accumulating from their ventures in Central and South America, financed an expedition by Giovanni da Verrazano. In 1523 Verrazano crossed the Atlantic and explored from present-day South Carolina to Newfoundland, concluding that the land he had reached was not Asia but a landmass obstructing the way to Asia.

In 1534 and 1535, Jacques Cartier headed two voyages which explored the waters of the Gulf of St. Lawrence and took him up the river which he named the St. Lawrence. He met Huron Indians, like Chief Donacona, who told of a "Kingdom of the Saguenay"—a land of exotic people, fabulous riches and spices. Thus lured inland,

Cartier travelled as far as Hochelaga, an Iroquois settlement where Montreal now stands, to claim the land for France.

THE STORY OF CARTIER'S VISIT—1535

On Saturday, October 2nd, 1535, Cartier and thirty-three men arrived in their longboats at Montreal Island. Along the way the native Laurentians danced in formal welcome. At the landing-place a thousand natives assembled, and danced in three circles, one of men, one of women, one of children. Presents were exchanged, babies were thrust upon the Captain to be touched—this custom still prevails in our political world—and the hosts danced vigorously all night on the river bank. . . .

Cartier and his men were welcomed at the city's sole gate and ushered into the central square. 'At once,' he says, 'all the girls and women of the village, some of them had children in their arms, crowded about us, rubbing our faces, arms and other parts of the upper portions of our bodies which they could touch, weeping for joy at the sight of us and giving us the best welcome they could. They made signs to us also to be good enough to put our hands upon their babies. After this the men made the women retire, and sat on the ground round about us, as if we had been going to perform a miracle play. And at once several of the women came back, and each with a four-cornered mat, woven like tapestry, and these they spread upon the ground in the middle of the square, and made us place ourselves thereon. When this was done, the ruler and chief of this tribe, whom in their language they call *Agouhanna*, was carried in, seated on a large deerskin, by nine or ten Indians, who came and sat him down on the mats near the Captain, making signs to us that this was their ruler and chief. This *Agouhanna*, who was some fifty years of age was in no way better dressed than the other Indians except that he wore about his head a sort of red band made of porcupine quills. This chief was completely paralyzed and deprived of the use of his limbs. When he had saluted the Captain and his men, by making signs which clearly meant that they were very welcome, he showed his arms and legs to the Captain, as if he expected thereby to be cured and healed. On this the Captain set about rubbing his arms and legs with his hands. Thereupon this Agouhanna took the band of cloth he was wearing as a crown and presented it to the Captain. And at once many sick persons, some blind, others with but one eye, others lame or impotent and others so extremely old that their eyelids hung down to their cheeks, were brought in and set down or laid out near the Captain, in order that he might lay his hands upon them, so that one would have thought Christ had come down to earth to heal them.' . . . [15]

Problems of writing history: what did Jacques Cartier really look like?

Jacques Cartier is one of the best known names in Canadian history, but other than the record of his voyages, not a great deal is known about him—that is about Cartier the person. Born in the seaport of St. Malo just about the time of Columbus's voyage of 1492, Cartier grew up in a town from which fishing boats sailed to the Grand Banks. By the time he was married in 1519 he was a veteran sailor and master pilot in St. Malo, but little is known of his activities for the next fifteen years. Similarly, the last fifteen years of his life, following the expeditions to North America, are lost to history.

"Jacques Cartier, as much perhaps as any man of his time, embodied in himself what was highest in the spirit of his age. He shows us the daring of the adventurer with nothing of the dark cruelty by which such daring was often disfigured. He brought to his task the simple faith of the Christian whose devout fear of God renders him fearless of the perils of sea and storm."[14]

The picture above is a copy of a painting of Cartier painted in the nineteenth century! The sketches, prints or other evidence from which this painting was made are no longer available. In other words, there is probably no way of knowing what Jacques Cartier really looked like.

1. Might a painter in the 16th century have portrayed Cartier any differently than the 19th century painter did?
2. What is meant by saying that a portrait or painting is a *subjective* interpretation of history?
3. From the painting, what kind of a person do you think Cartier might have been?
4. From the manner in which he portrays Cartier, do you think the artist would have agreed with the author of the quotation?

The rugged land and the treacherous Lachine rapids prevented further inland exploration. During the severe winter, when many of the crew died of scurvy, Cartier's expedition was turned into a nightmare. Nevertheless, upon his return, he had much to report, and his story was made more impressive by the presence of Donacona and four other Indians.

In 1541, Cartier undertook another expedition. Intending to establish a settlement, Cartier set out with five well-supplied ships and reached a point a few miles upstream from Stadacona (Quebec City). The endeavour was hampered by a severe winter, and the settlers were disheartened by the failure of a supporting expedition to arrive. Cartier and his people abandoned the settlement the following year and, in spite of meeting French ships on the way, returned to St. Malo.

Though Cartier did not reach the Orient or found a French settlement in Canada, he did discover and explore the great highway into the continent, the St. Lawrence River. His contact with the native peoples revealed opportunities for religious groups to do missionary work—and for traders to deal in furs, which later became the economic basis of the French empire in North America.

The 16th century was an age of many discoveries of North America, both recorded and unrecorded. For the nations on whose behalf they sailed, explorers made claims to vast undefined areas of the New World. However, they did not leave behind any permanent settlements in the part of North America from which Canada was to emerge. Not until the 1600s were conditions in Europe more favourable to the establishment of French and English colonies—and to the colonial rivalry which would ensue.

1. When Neil Armstrong set foot on the moon's surface he said, "One small step for a man, one giant leap for mankind." John Cabot's words on sighting North America or landing on Newfoundland are unknown, but would he have been right in saying the same thing?
2. One historian, Samuel E. Morison, writes:

"There is no basis of comparison between the astronauts who first landed on the moon on 20 July 1969, and discoverers like Columbus, Cabot, Verrazano, and Cartier. Those four were men with an idea, grudgingly and meanly supported by their sovereigns. The three young heroes of the moon landing did not supply the idea; they bravely and intelligently executed a vast enterprise employing some 400,000 men and costing billions of dollars; whilst Columbus's first voyage cost his sovereigns less than a court ball; and Cabot's, which gave half the New World to England, cost Henry VII just fifty pounds. The astronauts' epochal voyage into space, a triumph of the human spirit, was long prepared, rehearsed, and conducted with precision to an accurately plotted heavenly body. Their feat might be slightly comparable to Cabot's if the moon were always dark and they knew not exactly where to find it—and if they had hit the wrong planet."[16]

Do you agree with his viewpoint? According to the historian, what are some of the ways in which the early navigators like Cabot had a more difficult time than the modern astronauts?

Future discovery

"A wanderer is man from his birth.
He was born in a ship
On the breast of the river of Time."[17]

"In human affairs there is no snug harbor,
no rest short of the grave. We are forever
setting forth afresh across new and stormy
seas, or into outer space."[18]

More than any other event of the "space age," the landing of men on the moon in July, 1969, aroused the imagination of people around the world. Not since the Renaissance have people wondered so much about man's place in the universe, and the outer limits of his existence as a species.

In the 16th century, the impetus for discovery was the possibility of reaching areas of the earth previously unknown, at least to Europeans. In the 20th century, there are no more continents wholly unexplored and no more land to be claimed on earth. What then lies behind the urge to keep discovering and exploring? Consider the explanation by the noted science writer, Arthur C. Clarke, of our need to find new areas to explore, in his comments about exploration in the book *Profiles of the Future*:

In all the long history of man, ours is the first age with no new frontiers on land or sea, and many of our troubles stem from this fact. It is true that, even now, there are vast areas of the Earth still unexploited and even unexplored, but dealing with them will only be a mopping-up operation. Though the oceans will keep us busy for centuries, the countdown [has] started even for them. . . .

There are no more undiscovered continents; set out toward any horizon, and on its other side you will find someone already waiting to check your visa and your vaccination certificate. . . .

The road to the stars has been discovered none too soon. Civilization cannot exist without new frontiers; it needs them both physically and spiritually. The physical need is obvious—new lands, new resources, new materials. The spiritual need is less apparent, but in the long run it is more important. We do not live by bread alone; we need adventure, variety, novelty, romance. As the psychologists have shown by their sensory deprivation experiments, a man goes swiftly mad if he is isolated in a silent, darkened room, cut off completely from the external world. What is true of individuals is also true of societies; they too can become insane without sufficient stimulus. . . .

Though the planets can give no physical relief to the congested and impoverished Earth, their intellectual and emotional contribu-

tion may be enormous. The discoveries of the first expeditions, the struggles of the pioneers to establish themselves on other worlds—these will inspire a feeling of purpose and achievement among the stay-at-homes. They will know, as they watch their TV screens, that History with a capital H is starting again. The sense of wonder, which we have almost lost, will return to life; and so will the spirit of adventure.

It is difficult to overrate the importance of this—though it is easy to poke fun at it by making cynical remarks about 'escapism.' Only a few people can be pioneers or discoverers, but everyone who is even half alive occasionally feels the need for adventure and excitement. If you require proof of this, look at the countless horse operas now galloping across the ether. The myth of a West that never was has been created to fill the vacuum in our modern lives, and it fills it well. Sooner or later, however, one tires of myths . . . and then it is time to seek new territory. There is a poignant symbolism in the fact that the giant rockets now stand poised on the edge of the Pacific, where the covered wagons halted only two lifetimes ago.[19]

Another writer speaks of the relationship between discovery in space and man's sense of purpose:

Life, as we know it within the terms of our earthly prison, makes no ultimate sense that we can discover; but I cannot, myself, escape the conviction that, in terms of a larger knowledge than is accessible to us today, it does make such sense. Our position is simply that of the intelligent creatures confined to the ocean deeps. Now, however, that we are at last beginning to escape from our native confines, there is no telling what light we may find in the larger universe to dissipate the darkness of our minds. There is also the possibility that we may begin to populate new planets as, after 1492, we began to populate a new continent. Suddenly man's future seems boundless.[20]

Philosopher Bertrand Russell reminds us that discovery may or may not be beneficial to mankind:

There is something which might almost be called impiety in the ruthless disregard of everything already existing, which characterizes those in whom a mechanistic outlook is unchecked by imagination and contemplation. It is not the whole of what should make up human life, to cause changes, however vast and however clever. Contemplation, also, must play its part. If we allow it to do so, some element of wisdom in human affairs may be reflected into our lives from the contemplation of the heavens. But, if we think of the heavens only as something which we can change, until the

universe is degraded to the level of the most trivial of human concerns, we shall only widen the sphere of folly and shall deserve the disasters which it will bring upon us. We need less ruthlessness and more respect.[21]

1. Considering the varieties of discovery about which you read on pages 2-4 which areas of discovery do you feel will become most important to mankind in the future?
2. What are some of the considerations Russell and others like him would want us to ponder before we pushed on toward new frontiers of discovery?
3. Assuming people need opportunities to make discoveries for themselves, what kinds of personal discoveries do you think may be important in your future?

THE CHALLENGE OF FUTURE DISCOVERIES
Robert Stanfield, former leader of the Progressive Conservative party (1967-1976), commented in 1970 about the future use of discoveries:

The last fifty years have established Man the Scientist and Man the Technician. We have been to the moon, and doubtless will go beyond. The next half century will test our capacity as Man in Society. Our challenge will not be so much to make new discoveries—we know we can do that, and we shall—but rather to make good use of the tools and the resources which our discoveries provide.[22]

1. Is Robert Stanfield making a plea for a more humane use of technological discoveries?
2. What do you think he would want us to do concerning the discovery of new oil reserves, for example?

What can Canadians discover?

Canadian history offers many opportunities for discovery for those who are willing to inquire, use their imaginations, analyze and reason. As you explore the pages that follow, you may profit by keeping in mind the words from writer, journalist and historian, Bruce Hutchison:

"Sometimes by thought, more often by intuition,
the Canadian people make the final discovery. They
are discovering themselves."[23]

2

The first Canadians
and the land

A group of British Columbia Indians found this joke very humourous.

"In a white community several Indians lived nearby. One day an old Indian's horse died. Since it was winter, he pulled it near a creek which provided the town with water. Since spring was nearing, the community was concerned with the dead horse polluting their drinking water. A member of the white community was delegated to talk to the old Indian and ask him to move it. He agreed and three days later the delegate from the community saw the old Indian's son move the horse five feet. It of course did not solve the problem. The result was that the white delegate moved the horse. Several weeks later, a second horse of the old Indian also died. He pulled this dead horse onto a hill near a Catholic church. Each day the priest would ask the old man to move it and he would agree but things always kept coming up which prevented him from moving the horse. Each week the stench grew greater so that after church services one Sunday, the priest and several white men moved it two miles out of town."[1]

Do you get it? Probably not, if you did not view it from the point of view of the Indian. The joke is that the old Indian was able to get white men to do his job.

The purpose of this story is not to differentiate between the humour of two cultures, but rather to point out that people tend to

"Culture" means the way of life of a people. Children become part of their culture as they learn to do things the way others of their culture do. Language, mannerisms, clothing styles, attitudes of all sorts—these and many other kinds of behaviours are learned from our cultural surroundings.

The word "culture" has a popular, or everyday, use. How often have you heard people described as "cultured" because they attend the symphony regularly, prefer caviar to sardines, and read books instead of watching wrestling on T.V.? However, everybody is "cultured" according to the social scientist (the anthropologist, the sociologist, the psychologist

and others who study people and how they behave) since we all have characteristics that identify us with a certain way of life.

In other words, in studying how Canada's first inhabitants lived, we are learning about the cultures of the Indians and Inuit.

The anwers to the following questions tell us something about our culture—

(a) What is the accepted greeting for two adult males who are introduced to one another?

(b) What do we give children on Halloween?

(c) What is the proper behaviour for a maitre d' or host in a restaurant?

(d) How long must children attend school before they are allowed to quit?

(e) Who is the "breadwinner" in the family?

How might these answers differ in another culture?

look at things only from their own point of view. This tendency can make it very difficult to understand other people, especially those whose backgrounds and experiences are different from our own. In the case of people who lived in the past, the differences—and thus the problems of understanding—are likely to be even greater.

This chapter tries to give you an idea of Indian and Inuit culture before the coming of the white man. As you read it, you should try to "put yourself in the shoes" of these early people.

THE BEGINNINGS

Most of us divide the past into at least two parts. One is what we can remember personally and the other is the part that precedes our own memory. We have trouble thinking in terms of "centuries ago" and thus of the order in which things happened long before our time. Yet we are interested, generally, in our origins. To study the origins of Canada, or at least to find out about the first Canadians and the land they occupied, we need to realize that Canada's original inhabitants, ancestors of present-day Indians and Inuit, arrived more than 20 000 years ago!

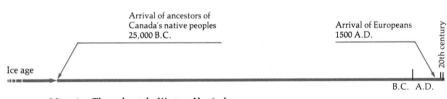

Migration Throughout the Western Hemisphere

An unusual character in Canada's earliest years was Marc Lescarbot—adventurer, historian, dramatist. He was a lawyer in Paris when he became dissatisfied with political confusion and corruption in France. In 1606, Lescarbot decided to immigrate to Port Royal. Though he stayed only a year, he befriended native people of the region, even involving them as participants in plays which he produced. His account of life and events in the early days of New France was later published in France.

It is now known that Canada's native peoples are descended from a race who migrated from Asia. They crossed the Bering Strait and spread, during the course of several centuries, throughout North America. The Eskimo, or *Inuit*, because of their marine/hunting economy, migrated east, eventually all the way to Greenland, rather than south. The ancestors of the Indian moved slowly southward, where, in time, many different Indian cultures evolved.

Information on what the first Canadians were like is very sparse. We have the accounts of Cartier and Champlain as well as the descriptions of Marc Lescarbot. But probably the most detailed accounts were those written by the Recollets and Jesuits, both groups of French missionaries who travelled to New France to bring Christianity to the natives. The Jesuits in particular painted a vivid picture of the land, its geographical features and vegetation as well

24

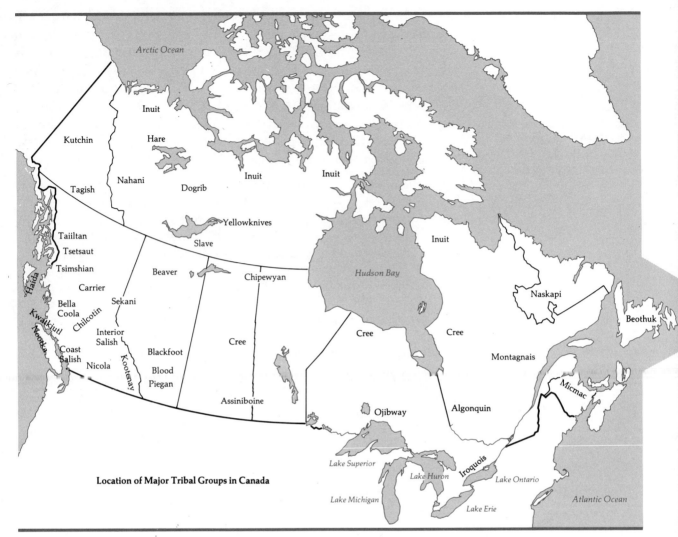

Location of Major Tribal Groups in Canada

What native groups inhabited your province?

as of Indian traits, manners, customs and living conditions. Each Jesuit missionary was required to document his experiences and send these reports back to France yearly. These reports, known as the *Jesuit Relations*, have been translated into several languages. They remain one of the most valuable clues to the way the Indian lived when the first white men came to this land.

first-hand information, for example the actual words written by the Jesuit priests.

The *Jesuit Relations* are certainly a most valuable **primary source** for research about the period, but just how objective were these accounts? Consider this information:

> Such accounts could not be absolutely objective, in view of the corporate and personal interests of the writers.... Even though the Jesuits tried honestly to write the truth, it was as they saw it....
>
> The inaccuracy and incompleteness of the Relations arose from the circumstances of missionary expansion. At first, in a rush to capture the essence of the Indian character, the Jesuits set down whatever they saw; without thought or discrimination they mingled bland generalizations about the whole race with precise comments about members of tribes whom they knew intimately. Biard, for example, attributed traits of the Acadian tribes to Indians in general. Later, as the missionaries ventured deeper into the forests and met other tribes, their observations became more exact. They rarely generalized, except to contrast the distinguishing marks of one tribe with those of another that they already knew.... Where evidence was slight, as with the Sioux, the tendency to generalize persisted; then the Relations presented merely a blurred image. On the other hand, the Relations were packed with detail about tribes among whom the missionaries had long sojourned; here it was not vagueness but a profusion of facts, sometimes contradictory, that impeded accuracy.[2]

1. How do each of the following detract from the accuracy of the *Relations*:
(a) missionary fervour or desire to convert as many natives as possible to Christianity?
(b) hasty generalization from a few characteristics of one tribe?
(c) many facts all gathered together, some of which were contradictory?
2. The accounts of Cartier and Champlain were probably no more objective than the *Jesuit Relations*. How do you think the following might have affected the objectivity of their reports:
(a) economics (encouraging further financial assistance for voyages of exploration)?
(b) honour or status (how they would be looked upon by their fellow countrymen)?
(c) credibility (how believable their reports were)?

How do we know what happened? The study of prehistory

In order to understand what occurred before men began to record histories of people and events, we make use of the talents of a variety of people. Archaeologists, who study remains of ancient civilizations such as bones, arrowheads and pottery; geologists, who study rocks, soils, volcanoes, and fossils; and botanists, who study plants and plant life all help us to make sense out of the time known as prehistory.

Prehistoric analysis is a relatively new and highly complex task which is similar to doing a puzzle with some of the parts missing. We are continually learning new facts and piecing together newly-found evidence about the people and the land of ancient times. With more scientific discoveries and sophisticated methods, we may eventually have a more complete picture of life on earth in prehistoric times.

CARBON—14

The latest and most accurate method for learning the age of rocks and fossils and thus for determining what forms of life lived in a given area at a particular time is called Carbon—14. All living things contain amounts of radiocarbon which disappears at a constant rate after death. Scientists can measure the remaining amounts of this substance in ancient rocks and bones, and thus determine their age.

An archaeological dig. Note the way the ground is marked off for digging and the earth is sifted for fragments of pottery, bones and tools.

1. Suppose archaeologists find an ancient Indian burial site with some remnants of Indian tools. What kinds of things might be learned from this find?

2. Why could this information be of interest to modern scientists and social scientists?

If there is a museum in your city, you may want to visit it to see if there are any displays of early civilizations.

Problems of writing history: whose truth? Bias in historical research

Each of the following cases gives a situation in which the "whole truth" is not present. Each illustrates practices which, if used by historians, would interfere with the accuracy of their work.

SITUATION 1

An advertisement for a new car recently appeared in a national magazine. The advertisement made the car sound very appealing. It got good gas mileage, was compact yet spacious, set records for safety and above all was reasonably priced. Many prospective car buyers went to dealers to look at the car because of this ad. What they found out after they talked to a dealer, though, was that many of the safety features were "options" and thus added significantly to the cost of the car. There were few cars in this line made without at least several of these "options" and thus the original price was not low. Replacement parts were difficult to obtain when service became necessary.

SITUATION 2

The only daily newspaper in a sizeable eastern city consistently strikes out against what it sees as the increased tendency toward violent behaviour in our society. Its editorial columns and editorial cartoons frequently cite examples of the increase in violence today. In addition, its news stories, although they are more objective, very often deal with violent acts, or people who act violently in ordinary situations. The sports editor has been waging a campaign against violence in sports, and other columnists have written about studies on the effects of violence in the media.

SITUATION 3

Mr. Sage, an employee of the personnel department of a large company, is about to interview a candidate for a job. While waiting

for the young man to arrive, Mr. Sage reads through the written application. He finds several incomplete sentences and a number of errors in grammar and punctuation. He thinks to himself, "This man is supposed to be a high school graduate, yet he is obviously illiterate. If he writes this badly, he likely can't read very well either. This company has no place for people who cannot read and write."

When the applicant arrives, the secretary tells him that the job has already been filled. Mr. Sage is busy in his office writing a memorandum to his supervisor. "The graduates we are getting from the high schools these days," he writes, "are not well enough educated to qualify for employment with our company."

1. What problems can you identify in each situation?
2. In each situation a type of distortion can be found. See if you can locate examples of:
(a) bias in omission of information
(b) overgeneralization
(c) use of biased information
(d) hasty generalization

From the above situations, you should be able to see that bias— slanting information usually with the intention of influencing someone unfairly—is a common occurrence in our lives. It is also true, however, that total objectivity in research or reporting is not possible. Historians, like scientists, attempt to be as objective as possible. That is, they either seek evidence and then draw conclusions, or make hypotheses ("educated guesses") and then seek evidence to test them. However, two important processes, perception and communication, often work against total objectivity.

In order for historians to record or report events, they must first perceive them. Several senses plus mental processes must be used to become aware of these events, and each person who is aware of an event may perceive it differently. Thus if we "see" things differently, we may record them differently.

Even if we all perceive the same things the same way, we could have a problem communicating them the same way. Written language, tone of voice, word choice, word meanings and even gestures all help us communicate our messages.

Then too, since communication is a "two-way street", even if we all perceive identically and transmit identical messages, those receiving our information may receive it differently. If they are influenced by their feelings toward the communicator, the subject matter, their mood that day or some future event, they could receive a message that differs from the one sent, or from what another "receiver" might get.

All in all, bias is probably impossible to eliminate unless computers are communicating with other computers (and even then, there could be bias because of what each computer has been programmed to "do"). We must not assume, however, that bias is necessarily negative. Could the newspaper's bias against violence, for example, be considered positive?

1. Under what circumstances do you think bias is acceptable?
2. When can bias be harmful?

Why are we biased? An introduction to values analysis

Earlier you read about the Jesuits and about the writing of the *Jesuit Relations*, a historical example of bias. Now you have just read about modern cases: the newspaper advertisement for a new car, the newspaper editors who wrote about violence in society, and the personnel man who rejected the "illiterate" student. Each of these situations involved a person's or group's bias for or against someone or something. Why do these people hold these biases? Why can't we be as objective as computers?

The answers to these questions lie in the study of values. Throughout the book, you will find activities which allow you to observe, analyze and judge the values of yourself and others. To do this, however, you must know that *values* are beliefs, attitudes or principles which are formed over time and which guide our behaviour. More strongly held than opinions, values influence every decision we make.

See if you can answer the following questions:

1. What did the Jesuits value?
2. How did their thoughts and actions express these values?

Values have great influence on people. Our perceptions and actions are influenced by our values.

1. How did the values of the Jesuits influence how they perceived the Indians?
2. How did their values bias their writings in the *Jesuit Relations*?

Of course, the Jesuits are not the only people who have values and who are influenced by them. Could you list the five most important values in your life at the present time? What order of importance would you give them? (Rank order them with number one being most highly valued and number five least highly valued.) Now can you list at least two specific actions or ways you behave

Some values are more strongly held than others. You may value playing baseball over soccer, but this may not be a "life-or-death" issue for you. You may also, however, value your right to speak out against a government's policies, and you may not be so willing to give up this privilege. Then there are values which are so important that you feel you will hold them forever—the value of human life is an example. You may say that life is so important that no one has the right to take it away, and you may think you will always hold this value. You may, of course, change your mind at some future time, but this value is certainly more important to you than your preference for a particular sport. In other words, there are degrees of importance in what we value.

which are caused by each value? For example, if you value equality, you may try to treat all your friends and acquaintances equally, or you may insist that your brothers or sisters share equally in the household chores.

Every one of us has a set of values. At this time, you are being asked to think about what you value. Later in this book you will be given opportunities to analyze those values and compare them to the values held by others. In addition, values analysis will be an important part of your study of people and events throughout this text.

THE LAND LONG AGO

The land we now know as Canada was, of course, very different thousands of years ago. Everyone is aware that there were no cities, large buildings and landscaped property. But there were even more significant differences—differences which we probably never even consider. For example, scientists have told us that for millions of years a thick blanket of ice covered much of Europe, Asia and North America, so that during this Ice Age, much of these continents was uninhabitable. As the ice slowly melted, people were able to migrate from Asia into North America, as the ancestors of the Canadian Indian and Inuit did.

Many of the animals which are hunted today lived in this new land, but there were also species which are extinct today. Long-horned bison, mammoths and mastodons were plentiful, as were caribou, beaver, bear and moose.

Once the ice melted, the geography of the land was probably similar to what we see today. Forests, plains, rivers and mountains all helped to determine the kind of lifestyle the inhabitant would lead. The culture of each Indian group was influenced by the geographical features of the part of the country in which the tribe settled. Thus the Iroquois, for example, who settled along the Great Lakes as far east as the Hudson River became farmers. The Algonquins (of the Eastern Woodlands) settled in heavily wooded or barren areas and became hunters and fishermen.

The land has been described by various authors; the following documents explain what it was like to live in this **virgin land**:

Virgin land is a term meaning land which has not been cultivated or used in any manner.

FOREST AND TUNDRA REMAIN THE SAME

"Both the northern forest and the barrens have probably changed very little during the past 500 years," remarks historian Keith Crowe:

If you were able to fly over the north as it was in those days, before any Europeans came, you would see a land without cities,

31

roads, mines, airstrips, or other large evidence of people. In summertime you might see the flash of canoe or kayak paddles on water, or the wakes of moving boats. The colour of meat and fish on drying racks, a file of people and dogs moving over the tundra, or the smoke of fires might catch your eye. In winter the tracks of snowshoes or sleds and the stained snow of villages might be visible, but the snow-banked lodges and domed snowhouses would be hard to see.

There would be stone fishing weirs and caribou ambushes of stones or brush, but the works of people would be very few and far between in the vast land. Wildlife would show itself far more —immense flocks of summer birds, the walrus jostling in water or hauled out like brown sausages on ice-pans, bison and caribou in great herds with their breath in winter following like a cloud. Beaver dams would span waters in the forest country, and everywhere in the north ancient game trails would groove the turf.[4]

1. What is said in this document which could give you the idea of the harmony between man and nature?

THE VIRGIN FORESTS

Author Morris Bishop gives a picture of the land at the white man's coming.

Picture this land as an endless forest coming down to the riverside, broken only by rare meadows, swamps, and clearings. Here was the forest's edge; from hence it rolled away to the Mississippi, to the Great Lakes, to Hudson Bay. All of eastern North America was a forest, and its inhabitants were woodsmen, living in perpetual shadow, seldom seeing the full blaze of sun. . . .

It was a transition forest; Cartier mentions oak, elm, ash, beech, walnut, willow, maple, chestnut, as well as the evergreens. There was much less underbrush than one would see today. The battle for light was fought high above; little life stirred in the duff formed of the droppings of pines, spruce, and hemlock. Even the dead trees, sheltered from normal winds, stood on their feet until they crumbled. Champlain said that all the region of present Montreal was open woodland. . . .

The trees were taller than they are today. . . . Cartier . . . speaks of 'grounds as full of as faire and mighty trees as any be in the world.'

Here at Hochelaga the oaks, he says, were 'the most excellent that ever I saw in my life.' Though he may have exaggerated, to advertise his discoveries, his report is exact and detailed. His walk through the woods, from the landingplace to Hochelaga, was on a path 'as well-trodden as it is possible to see.' This was a veritable highroad. The trails were seldom more than eighteen inches in width, for the Indians travelled in Indian file, appropriately. Europeans shouldering guns found the trails all too **exiguous**. They often began as tracks made by deer and other animals in their seasonal migrations between feeding grounds.... The trails kept to the high ground.... They avoided rough, stony ground, destructive of moccasins.... [5]

Exiguous means scanty or small.

WERE THE WINTERS COLDER AND LONGER THEN?

Early Canadian explorers and missionaries reported on the climate:

In 1608, at Quebec, Champlain reports a white frost on October 3rd; the leaves began to fall on the 15th.... Father Le Jeune describes the hard winter of 1632-3 in Quebec, when the snow lay four to five feet deep, when trees froze and split with a sound like gunshots, when ink froze before the fire, when he had to keep a pan of hot coals by his inkstand when writing. (Yet the Indians ... came to visit, uncomplaining.) ...

What about long summers?

Occasionally a warm season would confound all expectations. In 1609−10 there was scarcely any winter. In 1646−7 one seldom needed a fire for morning mass. Such untimely warmth upset the economy of the colony. One could hardly capture moose, which snowshoed hunters must tire out as they plunged through heavy snow. Any meat, deep-frozen by being hung in trees in winter's onset, would inopportunely defrost.

The melting came suddenly in mid-April, with the snow lingering later in the woods. Champlain summed up his observations in 1623, saying that from one year to another there were hardly two weeks of difference. The norms were from November 20th to April, with a usual winter depth of snow of a foot and a half.... [6]

THE PROBLEM OF INSECTS

The insect life has hardly changed since those days. Black flies, deer-flies, mosquitoes, ticks, no-see-ems, feasted on the tender white meat of the Europeans, and deposited their novel poisons in bodies unconditioned by inheritance. 'The flies do not let you rest day or night,' said Father Le Jeune. 'During certain summer months they attack us with such fury and so continually that no skin is proof against their sting, and everyone pays his blood as tribute. I have seen persons so swollen after being stung by them that one would think they would lose their eyes, which can scarcely be seen. This annoyance can be dispelled by smoke, which the flies cannot bear.' The mosquitoes' attack is worse than that of wolves, says Brother Sagard, for wolves are satisfied with a single sheep, whereas these creatures are not sated by a single sting. This missionary, fearing that he would lose his sight, contrived a veil, the first mosquito-net in American records.[7]

33

The following documents are intended to give you a picture of the people and their land as the first white men in North America saw them. Various aspects of native culture have been included, although the picture must remain incomplete because of the limited sources available. Nevertheless, you should be able to gain some insight into the lives of the first people to inhabit this land.

What Do Eskimos Want To Be Called?

Certainly not *Eskimo* or *Eskimos*, says Louis-Jacques Dorais of the department of anthropology at Laval University, Quebec City. They want to be called *Inuit* (in-new-it) as they call themselves in the plural, and *Inuk* (Inook) as they refer to themselves in the singular. *Eskimo* comes originally from an Algonquin word meaning 'eaters of raw meat', which the Inuit feel is not an adequate description.

The terms *Inuit* and *Inuk* are catching on in Canada, but as the term *Inuit* becomes popular and with the term *Eskimo* still current, some persons mistakenly believe there are two groups of people in the far north. In fact, all Eskimos living in Canada, Quebec, and Alaska, call themselves *Inuit*. The *Inuit* community and the *Eskimo* community are identical. But the community wants to be called *Inuit*.[3]

THEY CALLED THEMSELVES *PEOPLE*

We may call them Indians or Eskimos, Iroquois or Inuit, but, according to author Keith Crowe who has spent much of his life living and working with these people—

Long ago ... the northern people did not think of themselves as part of a great language group, or even as a tribe. They lived most of the time in little bands of a few families. Once or twice a year they might gather to hunt caribou or white whale and to trade, dance, and feast. At such meetings there might be a few hundred, perhaps a thousand people. ...

Those who shared a common territory, the same dialect and customs, called themselves *People* and still do among their own kind. The names used now such as Indian, Eskimo, Athapaskan, Algonkian, Copper, Dogrib, and Cree and all 'foreign names', that is, given to the people by 'outsiders', native or European.

... smaller bands of people would be called by their neighbours 'People of the Mountains', 'People of the Painted Coats', or similar names. Those whose language and customs were different and with whom there were fights would be called by rude names such as 'Bad People', 'Stinkers', or 'Louse-eggs.'[8]

1. For whom might it have been a problem if all the northern people had insisted upon being called "People", rather than by different tribal names?

2. Would you rather be identified as a Canadian or a resident of your province? Why?

HEROIC STATURE

Father Le Jeune describes the physical attributes of the Montagnais:

If we begin with the gifts of the body, I shall say that they possess them in abundance: they are tall, upright, strong, well proportioned, agile, nothing feminine appears in them. Those little dandies who are seen elsewhere are just caricatures of men in comparison with our savages. Once I almost believed that the pictures of the Roman emperors represented rather the idea of the painters than men who had ever existed, so great and powerful are their heads; but I see on the shoulders of these people the heads of Julius Caesar,

Pompey, Augustus, Otto, and others that I have seen in France, drawn on paper, or in relief on medallions.[9]

1. What is the compliment Father Le Jeune is paying the Montagnais?
2. Looking at the picture, would you agree with the priest? Why or why not?

Pierre Biard, another Jesuit priest, concurred:

[Biard could] not find a potbellied, hunchbacked, or deformed man among them; they do not know what it is to be leprous, gouty, afflicted with gravel, or insane; those among us who have some defect, like one eye, squint eyes, a flattened nose, etc., are noticed right away by them and generally laughed at, especially behind our backs and when they are by themselves.[10]

Father Bressani describes the Iroquois:

. . . first their senses which are most perfect; although they pass almost six months without seeing outdoors anything but snow and in their cabins anything but smoke, they have with all this very acute vision; an excellent and musical ear; a rare sense of smell, different from ours only [in] that they consider musk stinking and are unconcerned with the odors of things that are not edible, and with this sense they often discover fire long before seeing it, especially at night. They have a most delicate touch and skin. . . . [11]

. . . they have an admirable fortitude in hardships; they suffer from hunger for ten or fifteen days, sometimes out of superstition, more often out of necessity; [they suffer] fire without crying out, to which the youths accustom themselves at the age of ten or twelve years, two of them binding their arms together and then putting a coal between the two arms to see who will shake it off first and be despised for it; [they suffer] cold, heat, pain, illness without complaining, and although among pains the sacred scripture considers that of childbirth the greatest, the women to set an example of courage bear their children without giving any sign of pain, for if they cried out they would be deemed cowardly and be despised, and they would not find husbands again.[12]

1. According to the Father, how would the Iroquois define bravery?
2. What might have been the merits of training young children as the Iroquois did?

EXAMPLES OF GENEROSITY TO OTHERS

Father Le Jeune tells a story of some unknown Indians who are starving and lost during one severe winter. They come to a village where the Indians have just returned from a successful moose hunt:

Indian Chief. How would you describe this man?

"It was vital for the missionaries that strangers should be received and offered protection as new friends. Then as a matter of course the savages willingly led them into their villages, inside their cabins, and around their stew-pots. Many a wandering, half-frozen missionary was welcomed to some isolated hut after he had abandoned the hope of ever seeing a human face again. Even if the . . . hospitality meant wriggling under ill-cured skins to lie beside some filthy children in a reeking, smoke-filled den, the guest was grateful. . . . [15]

Now please admire the love which these barbarians bear toward one another; no one asked these new guests why they came onto our boundaries, if they did not know well enough that we were in as great need as they, that they were coming to take the crumbs from our mouths; but on the contrary they were received, not with words but with deeds, without external courtesy, for the savages have none, but not without charity: they threw them some large pieces of the freshly killed moose, without saying another word to them but *mitisoukou*, eat . . . while they ate a feast was prepared, at which they were treated generously. . . . [13]

Biard tells about the Micmac:

Among themselves they are marvelously liberal; no one may enjoy any good fortune by himself without giving away the largest part of it to his neighbors, and whoever holds a *tabagie*, as they say, that is, whoever asks others to a feast, does not himself sit down with the rest but serves, and sets aside no part of the food for himself but distributes it all, so that the host is forced to suffer hunger that day, unless one of the guests takes pity on him and gives him back some from what remained over from his share. [14]

FAMILY RELATIONSHIPS

While living with the Montagnais, Le Jeune wrote:

On the 12th of November winter advanced, beginning to besiege us with its ice. Having been for a long time that day in a large cabin of the savages, where there were many men, women, and children of all conditions, I remarked their admirable patience; if there were as many families together in our France, there would be nothing but disputes, quarrels, and insults; the mothers do not get impatient with their children, they do not know what it is to swear, their only oath consists in this word *taponé*; in truth there is no jealousy among them; they aid and support each other magnanimously because they hope a return of the favor; this hope failing, they do not respect whoever it may be. [16]

1. What clues here tell you that the Montagnais were a closely-knit group?

SONGS AND DANCES

Music was life to the northern people. Using voices, drums and other hand-fashioned rhythm instruments, Indians sang about sad times, happy times, conquests and defeats. Here are some examples of Indian songs:

Indian Bear Dance

The Bear's Song

(Whoever can sing this song is
admitted forever to the friendship of
the bears)

I have taken the woman of beauty
For my wife;
I have taken her from her friends.
I hope her kinsmen will not come
And take her away from me.
I will be kind to her.
Berries, berries I will give her from
    the hill
And roots from the ground.
I will do everything to please her.
For her I made this song and for her
    I sing it.[17]

Lightning Song

See the destructive lightning
   Going to kill the distant tree.
It is going, my younger brother,
   To split the distant tree.

Around the mountain I carry
   My poor younger brother:
Carry him around the mountain
   And then stand before it.

The lightning like reddish snakes
   Tries to lash and shiver the trees.
The lightning tries to strike them,
   But it fails and they still stand.

Through the roaring darkness I run,
   Carrying my poor younger brother;
From the top of the sky the lightning
   Shoots, and strikes nearby.[18]

1. Different priests have commented on the generosity and kindness of the early Indians. How are these qualities reflected in these songs?

WIGWAMS

Describing the dwellings of the Indians of the Gaspé, Father Le Clercq writes:

Their wigwams are built of nothing but poles, which are covered with some pieces of bark of the birch, sewed one to another; and they are ornamented, as a rule, with a thousand different pictures of birds, moose, otters and beavers, which the women sketch there themselves with their paints. These wigwams are of a circular form, and capable of lodging fifteen to twenty persons; but they are, however, so made that with seven or eight barks a single one is constructed, in which from three to four fires are built. They are so light and portable, that our Indians roll them up like a piece of paper, and carry them thus upon their backs wheresoever it pleases them. . . . It is the business of the head of the family, exclusively over all others, to give orders that camp be made where he pleases, and that it be broken when he wishes. This is why, on the eve of departure, he goes in person to trace the road which is to be taken, and to choose a place suitable and ample for the encampment. From this place he removes all the useless wood, and cuts off the branches which could be in the way. He smooths and opens out a road to make it easy for the women to drag over the snow on their toboggans, the trifle of furniture and of luggage which comprises their housekeeping outfit. He marks out, also all by himself, the plan of the wigwam, and throws out the snow with his snowshoes until he has reached the ground, which he flattens and chops in pieces until he has removed all the frozen part, so that all of the people who compose his family may lodge in the greatest possible comfort. This done, he then cuts as many poles as he considers suitable, and plants them in a circle around the border of the hollow which he has made in the earth and the snow—always in such a manner, however, that the upper ends come together in a point. . . . When this is finished, he makes preparations for hunting, from which he does not return until the wigwam has been completely put in order by the women, to whom he commits the care thereof during his absence, after assigning to each one her particular duty. Thus some of the women go to collect branches of fir, and then they place the barks upon the poles; others fetch dry wood to make the fire; others carry water for boiling the kettle, or in order to have supper ready when the men return from the hunt. The wife of the head of the family, in the capacity of mistress, selects the most tender and most slender of the branches of fir for the purpose of covering all the margin inside the wigwam, leaving the middle free to serve as a common meeting-place. She then fits and adjusts the larger and rougher of the branches to the height of the snow, and these form a kind of little wall. The effect is such that this little building seems much more like a camp made in the spring than one made in winter, because of the pleasing greenness which the fir keeps for a long time without withering. . . . The women occupy always the first places near the door, in order to be all ready to obey, and to serve promptly when they are ordered. There are very great inconveniences in these kinds of wigwams; for, aside from the fact that they are so low that one cannot readily stand upright in them, and must of necessity remain always seated or lying down, they are moreover, of a coldness which cannot be described, whilst the smoke which one is necessarily obliged to endure in the company of these barbarians is something insufferable.[19]

LIFE IN A MONTAGNAIS WIGWAM

Like Father Le Clercq, Father Le Jeune described the Indian wigwam:

Converging poles are planted in the snow, and rolls of bark wrapped upon them, with a skin to serve as a door. Fir branches make the floor. 'You cannot stand upright in this house, as much on account of its low roof as the suffocating smoke, and consequently you must always lie down, or sit flat upon the ground, the usual posture of the Savages. . . . This prison has four other discomforts—cold, heat, smoke, and dogs. As to the cold, you have the snow at your head with only a pine branch between, often nothing but your hat, and the winds are free to enter in a thousand places. . . . Even if there were only the opening at the top, which serves at

Interior of a Wigwam

once as a window and chimney, the coldest winter in France would come in there every day without any trouble. When I lay down at night I could study through this opening both the stars and the moon as easily as if I had been in the open fields. Nevertheless, the cold did not annoy me as much as the heat from the fire. A little place like their cabins is easily heated by a good fire, which sometimes roasted and broiled me on all sides, for the cabin was so narrow that I could not protect myself against the heat. You cannot move to right or left, for the Savages, your neighbours, are at your elbows; you cannot withdraw to the rear, for you encounter the wall of snow, or the bark of the cabin which shuts you in. I did not know what position to take. Had I stretched out, the place was so narrow that my legs would have been halfway in the fire; to roll myself up in a ball and crouch down in their way was a position I could not retain as long as they could. My clothes were all scorched and burned. You will ask me perhaps if the snow at our backs did not melt under so much heat. I answer, No; that if sometimes the heat softened it slightly, the cold immediately turned it to ice.

'I will say, however, that both the cold and the heat are endurable, and that some remedy may be found for these two evils. But as to the smoke, I confess to you it is martyrdom. It almost killed me, and made me weep continually, although I had neither grief nor sadness in my heart. It sometimes brought low all of us who were in the cabin; that is, it caused us to place our mouths against the ground in order to breathe. For although the Savages are accustomed to this torment, yet occasionally it became so dense that they, as well as I, were compelled to prostrate themselves and as it

were to eat the earth, so as not to drink the smoke. I have sometimes remained several hours in this position, and especially during
the most severe cold and when it snowed; for it was then that the
smoke assailed us with the greatest fury, seizing us by the throat,
nose, and eyes. How bitter is this drink! How strong its odour!
How hurtful to the eyes are its fumes! I sometimes thought I was
going blind; my eyes burned like fire, they wept or distilled drops
like an **alembic**; I no longer saw anything distinctly.'

a vessel which distills or purifies

As to the dogs, 'these poor beasts, not being able to live outdoors, came and lay down sometimes upon my shoulders, sometimes upon my feet, and as I had only one blanket to serve both as
covering and mattress, I was not sorry for this protection, willingly
restoring to them a part of the heat which I drew from them. . . .
These animals, being famished, as they have nothing to eat any
more than we, do nothing but run to and fro gnawing at everything
in the cabin. Now as we were as often lying down as sitting up in
these bark houses, they frequently walked over our faces and
stomachs, and so often and persistently that, being tired of shout-
ing and driving them away, I would sometimes cover my face and
give them liberty to go where they wanted. If anyone happened to
throw them a bone, there was straightway a race for it, upsetting
all whom they encountered sitting, unless they held themselves
firmly. They have often upset in my gown my bark dish, and all
that it contained.'[20]

1. At the beginning of this chapter you read that we often see things
from only one perspective. Is this true of the Europeans who
complain about the wigwams? Can you sympathize with them?
What could have been the Indians' response to European complaints?

GAMES AND AMUSEMENTS

*Many of the games and sports which we enjoy today were played by the
Indians of long ago:*

Prominent among the amusements of men were athletic contests
such as wrestling, running . . . archery, hoop and stick, and a peculiar form of spear-throwing called snow-snake, practised in winter
on the snow. Lacrosse, now so popular in America, had its home in
the eastern section of the continent from Hudson bay to the gulf of
Mexico, and the Micmac and Malecite Indians of the Maritime
Provinces played an indigenous form of football. The Eskimo also
enjoyed football, played in a slightly different way, and by women
as strenuously as by men. . . . For indoor amusement there were
quieter pastimes like juggling, cat's cradle, and the ring-and-pin
game.

More popular than any of these distractions were games of
chance or guessing. . . .

Inordinate gambling connected with one game or another was

Indian Ball-Play. What similar game do we play in the 20th century?

almost universal in Canada, and the traditions of the Indians contain many stories of men who lost all their possessions. It was a fertile source of quarrels and bloodshed, particularly when the opponents in the games belonged to different tribes or bands. Some tribes played much more recklessly than others. In British Columbia the natives occasionally gambled away not only their clothing and other property, but even their wives and children. The Piegan Indians, on the other hand, 'have some things which are never gambled, as all that belongs to their wives and children and in this the tent is frequently included; and always the kettle, as it cooks the meat of the children, and the axe as it cuts the wood to warm them. The dogs and horses of the women are also exempt.'[21]

RELIGION AND THE SPIRIT WORLD

The religion and spirit-worshipping of various Indian tribes often seem unusual to outsiders:

All tribes firmly believed that prayer combined with fasting and ceremonial purity exercised a powerful influence on the unseen world. ... Almost inevitably [the Indian] would be granted a vision that would bestow on him supernormal powers, or give him one or more supernatural protectors. The type of vision varied tribally according to traditional patterns. On the plains an Indian would hear a voice, or behold a strange being, human or animal, that would promise its help in the crises of life. Among the Carriers and other tribes of British Columbia the spirit of a dreamer might journey to some distant cavern in the mountains, where it would hear the beating of a drum and the noise of singing. . . . So throughout nearly the whole of Canada, boys, and sometimes girls, passed days and even months in partial solitude, striving under the direction of parents and relatives to obtain a guardian spirit. Such experiences always aroused feelings of the deepest awe, and few Indians dared to reveal their visions afterwards from fear of offending the spiritual world and forfeiting its blessings.[22]

1. What parallels can you think of between early Indian religion and religions of today?

THE ORIGINAL "RED MAN"

The Beothuk Indians described here are now an extinct tribe which originally occupied Newfoundland from the time of the glacial retreat until the last Beothuk woman died in 1829:

. . . there are reasons for believing they might have come from different stock [than the mainland tribes such as the Micmac, Malecite and Naskapi]. They had neither dogs nor pottery and, though their boats were made of birchbark, the design was unique on the continent. So was their routine practice of smearing themselves from head to foot with **red ochre**. This was the basis of the Micmac nickname for them that meant "Red Man." This in turn gave rise to the European myth of a "Red Race" in the Americas, and the designation has recently been revived in the phrase "red power."[23]

a reddish substance obtained from clay

ALGONKIAN MAGIC

Shaman, or medicine men, were common to all Indian groups. The shaman employed a different technique for different problems:

In an Algonkian band there might be several kinds of shaman. Most popular was the *jossakeed* who divined the whereabouts of a missing article or person. Within a small cylindrical pole structure, walled with bark or hide but open at the top, the *jossakeed* communed with his *manito* [a lifetime guardian or protector] while the tent shook with what witnesses invariably described as superhuman violence. Meanwhile, voices could be heard above the opening—various supernatural beings and fellow shamans speaking from a hundred miles away—'just like a radio,' as one informant has explained. Reliable observers have testified to the accuracy of the information obtained by these 'tent-shakings.' The practice was used not only to find missing articles and people, but also to injure or destroy the enemies of a client.

Nearly as widespread as tent-shaking was the Algonkian belief in mysterious beings with magical power who made their home in solid rock, usually in a high rocky outcrop of the sort found everywhere along the shores of lakes in the Shield. Descriptions of these *Maymaygwessiwuk* (an untranslatable name) vary from region to region. For the Woods Cree they were little people, which Scottish employees of the Hudson's Bay Company confused with the fairies of Europe. In the southern woodlands they were thought to be the same size as humans. Everywhere they were ashamed of their faces: in the northwest because they had no noses, in the east because their faces were covered with hair.... In some areas they were said to possess a highly valued 'rock medicine' which gifted shamans could obtain by dreaming their way into the living rock where [they] dwelt.... [24]

1. How does the idea of the exorcist compare to the idea of the shaman?

INDIAN WARFARE

Like many of the other facets of Indian culture, methods, tactics and reasons for warfare differed from group to group. Consider these statements:

Iroquoian Warfare

The Iroquois were exceptionally good warriors and they had such an efficient organization that their enemies could seldom resist them successfully. There was a separate series of chiefs and leaders for warfare, and they planned their expeditions with great skill, taking advantage of every imaginable scheme and ruse. Their tactics included ambush and surprise attacks and other methods which were not often used by the European troops who fought against them....

The Iroquoian warrior travelled light. Bows and arrows and a wooden club were their principal weapons, and these they nearly always carried with them in peace as well as in war.... Many of them carried a light braided cord with which to tie their prisoners. The cord was hardly strong enough to hold a man, but it was the custom for a prisoner tied in such a way to admit that he was captured, even though he knew he might be tortured when he reached the village of his captors.

The Iroquoians practised ferocious cruelty towards some of their prisoners, making them suffer as long as they could, reviving them when they fainted, and even stopping the tortures to feed them so that they might live longer. It was considered the proper thing for the prisoner to suffer in silence or else to sing loudly, insulting and scorning his tormentors. Even women and little children were sometimes tortured, but most of these, most prisoners in fact, were adopted into the tribe of their captors.

War parties were made up of volunteers, and there was no such thing as compulsory military service. A man could join a war party if he wished and leave it when he wanted to, and nobody would think anything of it unless he was obviously afraid. Then he would have to face the contempt and ridicule of everybody.[25]

Prairie Tribal Warfare

Scalping was fairly common among the prairie tribes, though the custom apparently did not start there but in the valley of the St. Lawrence, and it seems to have been the white people who carried the idea west and introduced it to the people of the prairies. It was because bounties were paid for dead Indians that the white men valued scalps; the Indians on the other hand valued them as proof of triumph over an enemy. Scalping was the act of taking a square or round patch of skin, often with a scalp lock of hair attached, from just behind the crown of a man's head. It was painful, of course, but by no means fatal, and many a man has been scalped and then let go, even white men. Much more frequently the man was killed first and then scalped. Many Indians used to grow a special lock of hair, which they wore braided and decorated with beads, for the convenience of the enemy as a sort of act of defiance. Sometimes quite a large piece of the scalp might be taken, which was later cut up into smaller pieces for decorating a war shirt or for some other purpose.[26]

1. What evidence is there in these documents that the Iroquois and prairie Indians were:
(a) a primitive people
(b) a humane people, and
(c) a fair people?

THE ORGANIZATION OF COMMUNITY LIFE AMONG INDIANS

Social organization remained at an elementary level among the Indians and rested upon blood ties traced, according to the varying customs of the tribes, through male or female lines of descent within the framework of the family. The families expanded into clans, the clans into tribes. Since their survival in most cases depended entirely upon hunting and fishing, the tribes took over definite territories which they claimed as their exclusive property and which were, in effect, their sources of livelihood. These grounds belonged collectively to the tribe and were not divided among the members: the rights of all were exactly equal and foreigners were wholly excluded.

These peoples had no system of writing and no laws other than traditional customs frequently of esoteric origin, which were stored in the memory of elders who thereby became the lawmakers and enforcers. Political organization was limited to special meetings called with a view to reaching a common decision as to collective action or to debating topics which affected common interests.

There were no recognized chiefs. There were no bodies whose duty it was to maintain order and respect for rights. Redress for any injustice—from theft to murder—was left to the family or to the individual concerned. The guilty party could pay for his crime by offering gifts to the injured party, but if he did not choose to do so the family to whom he had brought harm were quite free to do away with him altogether. The tribe never intervened, save in those cases involving an exceptional injury to the community as a whole or a violation of sacrosanct custom.

Even in time of war, the commander exercised no absolute power: though they elected chiefs, the warriors reserved to themselves their own freedom of action, so that it often happened that the more hotheaded undertook forays despite express orders to the contrary from the chiefs.[27]

1. Does this description of Indian life seem more like democracy or anarchy? How do you think the system met the needs of the Indian at that time?

CLOTHING, ORNAMENTS, AND PERFUME

Clothing style and "fashion" varied from one Indian tribe to the next:

...the Canadian aboriginals depended on furs and skins for their clothing. Except on the Pacific Coast a basic garment—a sleeveless tunic reaching below the waist for men, below the knees for women—was supplemented by long leggings and moccasins. Variations occurred from tribe to tribe, with the women sometimes converting the tunic into a blouse and skirt, and introducing an apron worn either outside or beneath the skirt. In winter detachable sleeves were added to the tunic and a blanket or over-robe, partly for warmth and partly as a status symbol, was draped about the shoulders. Double tunics, with the fur of the inner garment against the skin, were worn by the northern tribes. Caps, usually the pelt of a small animal with the tail retained, were common on the Atlantic Coast and in the Arctic. Sometimes they were attached to the tunic in parka fashion.

In summer many of the Pacific Coast Indians were quite modern for they wore next to nothing. They went barefoot throughout the year.... For outerwear in rough weather the poncho, a blanket with a hole in the centre through which the head might be slipped, was in common use. The Coast tribes also had loose gowns of fine fur for both sexes, with mittens to match. For ceremonials they wore conical hats of cedar bark or spruce root which they adorned profusely. They were indebted to other lands for such garments—the poncho belonged to the Spanish Main, the conical hat to the Orient, the wrap-around robe to India and the Mediterranean....

In spite of the dearth of materials and the primitive tailoring facilities—bone bodkins and needles, a stone or native copper

Indian ornaments. Why do we wear jewelry today?

knife, sinews or twisted hair as thread—the Pacific Coast tribes greatly developed the arts of ornamentation, both of the body and of dress. The males...shaved their heads either in whole or in part; in the east and on the plains they retained the scalp-lock. Tattooing was almost universal, some of the tribes employing as many as ten colours. Feathers denoted status—a single plume for a brave, a flowing mane for a chief. Necklets, bracelets and anklets varied in composition from region to region; they were valued according to their intricacy and rarity and in due course they emerged as currency in belts of **wampum**...; the take of the chase, such as bears' teeth, wildcats' claws and wolves' ears, were sewn on headbands or on garments; comprehensive collections of such trophies sometimes were displayed on trains which hung from the headdresses. Bodies were anointed with oil, the more **rancid** the better; as a young buck stalked past his smell was as exciting as his finery.[28]

Wampum was beads which were strung and then used as money in trading.

offensively strong

1. What do we have to compare to the Indians' practice of:
(a) tattooing
(b) feathers
(c) charms or "trophies"?

AMULETS: "GOOD LUCK CHARMS" OF THE NATIVES

Indian people believed in amulets or charms which they could wear on their persons, but each of these symbols was important only in that it represented or stood for a spirit or magic of the spirit world. Consider this example of an Algonquin Indian's belief:

47

An Algonkin Indian lovingly preserved a hair, which he worshipped as a little divinity. 'It is a hair,' he said, 'that I have pulled from the moustache of the Manitou [the most important spirit to the Algon-quins]. That hair saved my life a thousand times, when I have been in danger of losing it. I would have been drowned a hundred times had it not been for this hair. It is this which has enabled me to kill moose, has preserved me from sickness and has made me live so long. I have cured the sick with this hair; there is nothing that I cannot do with it. To ask me for it is to ask for my life....'[29]

1. Explain the significance of the following of our amulets:
(a) rabbit's foot
(b) religious medals
(c) favourite numbers or colours.
2. Can you think of other things we use as amulets?

NOT JUST ICE, IGLOOS AND SEALS

Just as there are incorrect pictures of Indian life, there are also distortions of the Inuit's lifestyle. Here are some facts about their traditional lifestyle:

In his public lectures, the arctic explorer Vilhjalmur Stefansson continually emphasized the fact that Pacific air currents moderated temperatures in the western arctic, so that minimum winter temperatures there were no lower than on the Saskatchewan and Dakota prairies where he grew up. Igloos were unknown to some bands, and were used only for winter travel by others. Far more typical was the caribou-skin tent that all the bands used in summer. And while the majority of Inuit were coast people, depending for their food on sea-mammal hunting, they moved inland during the summer to hunt the caribou, one of the most important natural resources of their way of life.

Arctic survival required light, warm clothing, and the hide of the caribou was ideal for this. When the tough, lightweight hide was sewn into clothes with the hair inwards, the slivers of air trapped within each filament provided excellent insulation. As a bonus, a caribou carcass produced meat, sinew thread, and a kind of spring salad of half-digested green fodder that was found in the stomach. This latter food was an Inuit delicacy that he could get in no other way, for the high arctic provides few edible plants.

If starvation threatened a band, caribou hide could be eaten. On one occasion, Stefansson reported, his party had nothing to eat but a bag of seal oil, which they had difficulty keeping down and which had little effect on their hunger. To give it "body," they tried various combinations: tea leaves, ptarmigan feathers, and caribou hair. "Most commonly," he said, "we took long-haired caribou skin (boiled with the hair on), cut it into small pieces, dipped the pieces in oil, and ate them as a sort of salad." "Fresh raw hide," he

Inuit woman in parka

added, "is good eating, it reminds one of pigsfeet if well boiled."
And the Anglican missionary, Bishop Bompas, is celebrated for
having survived one crisis by eating his boots![30]

'A MAN IS THE HUNTER HIS WIFE MAKES HIM'

*This saying conveys how important clothing is to the hunter. Clothing is
always made to resist the elements, as this document suggests:*

Air is a poor conductor of heat and when it is possible to create an
insulating layer of air it is not difficult to keep warm. This is the
point of double windows, and the clothing of the Eskimos is made
on the double-window principle, i.e., it consists of an inner and a
separate outer layer. In warm weather the underclothing alone is
worn. In the skins of the Arctic animals they have an invaluable
material for clothing. On the whole, so many skins are available
that they can afford to be particular in their choice. Seal skin is
strong and to a certain degree waterproof; but in very cold weather
it is not warm enough. Bear skin is exceedingly warm, and one can
fall into the water wearing a pair of tied bear-skin trousers without
getting wet; but they are tremendously heavy. Musk-ox skin has

49

points to the roof; the cover of the smoke-hole is removed and the evil spirit which has caused the sickness escapes amid the beating of drums and the triumphant cry, 'He is gone! Ugh! Ugh!' and the old woman, her task accomplished, collapses into a mass of rags on the floor. It is the third spirit driven out of this patient—how many more dwell within him nobody can tell; if it was the last he will soon mend, but on the other hand, . . . there will be more chanting, more drumming, more cuffing, and more payments to the cunning tungaks, until the sick man either dies or can pay no more.[34]

1. What does the shaman believe has caused the man's illness?
2. If the treatment does not cure the person, how can the shaman justify her failure to cure him?
3. What is the danger in using these primitive treatments to cure ailments like fever and rheumatism?
4. If, in fact, the treatment *did* work and the patient were cured, how might you account for the cure?

INUIT LEISURE

Peter Pitseolak, an Inuit from Cape Dorset on Baffin Island, is a native historian. This is his description of Inuit celebrations of long ago:

At the time of celebration a lot of people used to sing together. In the large igloo they had a kudluk—a seal oil lamp. The snowblocks were piled up and the kudluk was on top. These people would sing and look at the lighted kudluk. The song would be a hunting song, made by a hunter. Many women would sing along with the men; they had learnt the words.

They would play games—gambling games. One game was Noo-lootak. They would make a piece of string taut to the ground. In

An artist's impression of Inuit children dancing, c. 1824.

the middle they'd put a piece of ivory with a hole in the centre. People had to try and get a stick in. On the string were tied the teeth of walrus. They were made like beads and made a noise like bells. The sound was fantastic when the people were pushing at the ivory. Whoever hit the hole first was the winner and he got a prize. Just as today we pay to go into the community centre when we go to a movie, these people did the same. They threw their gifts down in the kagee when they arrived.

The winner of the game would lead the song. The winner would stand by the kudluk. The snow blocks were piled up so the height was right for the ordinary man. Those who were taller would look down. An ordinary man would look straight at it....

Also there were acrobatics. Ropes were twisted and attached through the walls of the igloo with toggles. The rope was quite high; a man couldn't reach it without jumping. I've seen my father swing on the rope; even when he was old he used to do it. Once my uncle Kiakshuk went in a sealskin boat and Inukjuarjuk in his wooden boat to play games with the people in Arctic Quebec. The people from Baffin Island won everything. One of my father's people could cross his arms in his sleeves and fall sideways or backwards and bounce right up without using his hands. That's why the Quebec people gave up. Unukjuarjuk asked them for a return match on Baffin Island but they never showed up.[35]

$150–$200 FOR A FAMILIAR SPIRIT

In the past, Inuit would trade what would seem to us very valuable items for simple items which held special powers. Today, hundreds of dollars are sometimes spent to buy amulets or charms which will bring these people good fortune. But, as this document points out, this only seems unusual if we observe this practice from the viewpoint of our own culture:

A Diomede islander showed the author a blue bead about the size of a marble, which would not be valued at more than a fraction of a cent among us; yet because of its imputed power as an amulet it had been traded for a large skin boat, which is about the equivalent of an automobile in our own country. The word 'superstition' is too weak. Primitive spiritual beliefs are not to be thought of in terms of black cats and the number thirteen. An Eskimo of the Iglulik group purchased a few magic phrases, which had been handed down for generations, for the promise that he would supply the former owner with food and clothing for the rest of her life....

A native of the Mackenzie River is willing to pay the equivalent of $150 or $200 for a familiar spirit. A large price, it cannot be denied, for an intangible 'power'! ...

It might be asserted that the value of $200 placed upon a familiar spirit cannot have been determined through logical reasoning. But to study the Eskimo religion with the aim of finding everywhere an underlying foundation of rationality and consistency is to lose one's self in an empty maze. . . . For the religion is based not so much upon reason as upon emotion. Spiritual beliefs which by the very nature of the mystery surrounding them cannot be tested through reason are supported by powerful emotional convictions.[36]

When two cultures meet—the interaction of Indians and Europeans

"When the White Man came, we had the land and they had the Bibles, now they have the land and we have the Bibles."
CHIEF DAN GEORGE

An old Indian was watching a mine working and said,
"First, white men come and take all the beaver, then come back and take all the trees. This time they're even back for the rocks!"[37]

These statements, both made by Indians, characterize native attitudes toward the coming of the white man. Perhaps they are not entirely true, but there are certain inevitable things that occur when two cultures meet.

From your readings in this chapter, you will have noted that the Indian customs, traditions and lifestyles—no matter which tribe is described—were very different from those of the Europeans who journeyed across the seas. When two cultures interact or come together, each is affected by the other. The degree to which each is affected, however, varies. It is usually true that the dominant or stronger culture will have a greater influence on the other culture.

When Europeans first met Indians, this is exactly what happened. The first white men to settle here needed to learn a great deal in order to survive in the new setting. The Indians taught them survival skills such as hunting, trapping, snowshoeing and canoeing. The Europeans also patterned their clothing after that of the natives in order to adapt to the climate.

In exchange for this Indian technology, the Europeans had technology to trade. The Indians were at first interested in, and curious about, the white man's tools; later they were eager for all the "inventions" the white man would trade. Thus the Indian obtained iron instead of stone weapons, metal instead of wooden pots and cooking utensils, and many other items which made their way of life easier.

It would be nice to think that the meeting of two cultures brings

"Technology" refers to the tools with which a group of people make their goods and change their natural environment. Thus technology may refer to stone implements or an iron forge, a mill wheel or a computer. It may also refer to the techniques for using the tools, such as making clothes from animal skins, or glass-blowing or operating a loom. You can learn much about a culture by studying developments in its technology and the effects on people and their surroundings.

Ideas from the social sciences: what is anthropology?

Anthropology may be defined as the study of human differences and similarities. As a discipline, or organized form of studying human behaviour, anthropology is a fairly new subject, like the other social sciences. Yet it has come a long way from being regarded, a century ago, as the activity of eccentrics interested in strange and exotic practices.

Anthropology is an attempt to blend the sciences and the arts in an objective study of human nature. Philosophers and historians had long been interested in why people acted in certain ways, but the investigation of human origins required the study of physical evidence, such as the remains of skeletons, tools and dwellings. This required the use of procedures not normally available to "established" experts.

In trying to identify the basic characteristics of man as a species, anthropologists focused on primitive cultures.* Only by studying the Samoans of the South Pacific or the Kwakiutls of British Columbia could they be satisfied they were dealing with people unaffected by modern civilization.

*See marginal note, p. 23.

For Canadians, anthropology can provide clues into the origins of their country. The first people—or aborigines—may have arrived in Canada as far back as 25 000 years ago. Anthropology is a means of reconstructing evidence about the earliest Canadians and how they lived. The *physical anthropologist* can examine artifacts that tell us about the appearance and size of people who once inhabited the country, and the environment they had to cope with. The *cultural anthropologist* can reconstruct the ways of life of simple cultures and study basic human relationships.

Working with fragments of evidence, anthropologists must first make sense of the pieces. Even if they are quite successful in getting the "picture" of a culture together, they face difficulties in interpreting its meaning. They are themselves products of their own cultures and are inclined to think of their own as "normal" and other cultures as "strange." To understand another culture, especially one that is very different from theirs, they must try to see it through the eyes of a member of that culture.

For example, in all Inuit cultures, killing newborn infants and old people who were infirm or no longer productive was common, especially where poverty was a problem. It was often against the wishes of friends and relatives, but as is shown in the following document, the relatives, even young children, respected the ultimate wish of the aged.

A hunter living on the Diomede Islands related to the writer how he killed his own father, at the latter's request. The old Eskimo was failing, he could no longer contribute what he thought should be his share as a member of the group; so he asked his son, then a lad about twelve years old, to sharpen the big hunting knife. Then he indicated the vulnerable spot over his heart where his son should stab him. The boy plunged the knife deep, but the stroke failed to take effect. The old father suggested with dignity and resignation, 'Try it a little higher, my son.' The second stab was effective, and the patriarch passed into the realm of the ancestral shades.[40]

1. How do you feel about the episode described in this document? Why do you feel the way you do?
2. What does the episode reveal about Inuit culture? About the difficulty of viewing a culture "through the eyes of a member of that culture"?
3. Is the Inuit attitude toward life and death different from ours? Could it be the same attitude expressed in a different way?

Anthropologists do, of course, make comparisons between the customs of one culture and another, including their own. However, as much as temperament and training permit, they must avoid judging another culture by the standards of their own. This is important whether they are studying cultures of the past or cultures, primitive or complex, of the present.

In the age of the "global village," the research of the anthropologist may very well be more urgent than at any time in the past. The question "What is the basic nature of man?" may not be answered, if indeed it is answerable, but at least the attempt may increase the emphasis on the similarities in human behaviour from culture to culture.

---

benefits to both and losses to neither. Unfortunately, when one culture meets another, there are often negative effects as well. It is usually the smaller or weaker group which is the loser. Although the Europeans brought improvements to the lifestyle of the aborigines, they also brought "negative payoffs."

Disease, alcohol and guns are the three things usually mentioned in any discussion of the effects upon Indians of contact with the Europeans. Although the Europeans did not mean to bring such diseases as smallpox, typhus and measles to the natives, they carried microorganisms to which their bodies had naturally become immune. These were completely new to the Indians. Because they had no natural immunity and no vaccines, the Indians fell prey to these diseases. Epidemics wiped out whole tribes.

Alcohol, unknown to the Indians before the arrival of the white man, had a profound influence on them. The fur traders first began to give the Indians whisky and brandy in return for furs. The white trader, eager to get more furs, exchanged greater volumes of liquor with no thought of moderation, in spite of the objections from missionaries. Alcohol, it is said, contributed to the moral, spiritual and physical decline of many native people.

Probably as serious a problem as alcohol was trading for guns. At first, the Indian was surprised and impressed just by the loud noise the guns made. This alone was often enough to frighten off enemies. Later, however, the value of the gun was fully realized. Bows and arrows were no match for its power and accuracy. Tribes which were able to trade for guns and rifles were too strong for their enemies and became superior in any struggle for power among various tribes.

Consider some of the following statements made about the problem:

INDIAN DEPENDENCE ON EUROPEAN GOODS

Nicolas Denys, a leading figure in Acadia, wrote in 1672 on the effect of European goods on the Indians:

... They have abandoned all their own utensils, whether because of the trouble they had as well to make as to use them, or because of the facility of obtaining from us, in exchange for skins which cost them almost nothing, the things which seemed to them invaluable, not so much for their novelty as for the convenience they derived therefrom. Above everything the kettle has always seemed to them ... the most valuable article they can obtain from us. ...

The musket is used by them more than all other weapons, in their hunting in spring, summer, and autumn, both for animals and birds. ... With the arrow it was necessary to approach the animal closely: with the gun they kill the animal from a distance with a bullet or two. The axes, the kettles, the knives and everything that is supplied them, is much more convenient and portable than those which they had in former times, when they were obliged to go to camp near their grotesque kettles, in place of which to-day they are free to go camp where they wish. One can say that in those times the immovable kettles were the chief regulators of their lives, since they were able to live only in places where these were.

With respect to the hunting of the Beaver in winter, they do that the same as they did formerly, though they have nevertheless nowadays a greater advantage with their arrows and harpoons armed with iron than with the others which they used in old times, and of which they have totally abandoned the use.[38]

1. Nicolas Denys made his comments in 1672. What does he say was the effect of European goods on the natives?

Three Indian chiefs. What does this painting tell you about the contact between native peoples and whites?

Trading between Inuit bands and fur traders began as early as 1697. By 1817 trading was constant, and one ship's officer recorded the following "trade":

One sealskin coat—one steel knife
One pair sealskin pants—one needle
One pair sealskin boots—one saw
One wooden eyeshade—one bullet
One pair birdskin gloves—two buttons
One fishing spear—one file[39]

Here is another view of trading among natives and Europeans:

"Exchanging beads for gold is a fantastic idea.
We'll go and get our beads."

1. What thoughts do these two items bring to mind about trade between the native people and the Europeans?

The future of the first Canadians

We have looked at some aspects of the way of life of the first Canadians before the coming of the white man. In later parts of this book, you will be able to study and investigate contemporary issues involving the native peoples. Meanwhile, perhaps this final document can give you some idea of the future for these people.

ONE FOOT IN EACH CANOE

The past few years have been full of mixtures of the very old and the very new. A hunter going up the Eastmain River may use his skin drum in a ceremony to find caribou and his transistor radio to

listen for news. A hostess at Eskimo Point will cut potatoes with her ulu, but slice the caribou roast with an electric carving knife.

At Pangnirtung, people move out of their houses each summer into tents, but wires run from house to tent so that electric guitars and tape recorders, both part of the modern Inuit culture, can be plugged in. Only one year-round group of hunters lives near Pangnirtung. They come to visit the town on powerful snowmobiles, but heat their tents with kudliks of ancient form, burning a wick of moss. There is another twist even to this, for the kudliks are made from old oil barrel metal, and the seal-oil is carried in plastic jugs.

A young Indian delegate bound for his tenth conference that year may board a jet airplane and fasten the seat-belt around a moosehide jacket scraped, smoked, and beaded by his mother.[41]

FACING PAGE: *the interaction of cultures. How has twentieth century technology changed the ways of life of the native peoples?*

3

Fur trade, exploration and settlement

The Community of Habitants, formed in 1645, was the first "co-op" in Canada. Organized by the colonists themselves, it persuaded the financially troubled Company of One Hundred Associates to hand over the monopoly to the fur trade. In its first year, the Community made a profit of nearly 100,000 livres on the sale of furs. If one livre was worth some $2.00 in present-day Canadian money, the profit was approximately $200,000![1]

The settlement of New France is a major theme in Canada's first 150 years. But the keys to French success in our early history are the fur trade and exploration. From a hardy start at Port Royal and Quebec, the French empire in North America reached out through the next hundred years to the Prairies, Hudson Bay and the Gulf of Mexico. Building on Cartier's discovery of the St. Lawrence, Samuel de Champlain and his successors took advantage of the access to major continental water routes provided by this "gateway" to North America. While the English settled on the coast, between the sea and the Appalachian barrier that extends the length of the Atlantic seaboard, the French used their geographic advantage to explore the heart of the land mass.

Among the French were missionaries anxious to spread the power of the church. Other explorers looked for adventure and dreamed of French influence spreading far and wide. Early explorers did hope to find a Northwest Passage that would permit their ships to reach the Orient. But in the long run, the fur trade—especially the trade in beaver pelts—was the main motive for exploration.

As the fur trade spread, a network of French traders and Indian suppliers covered much of the interior of North America. From their trading posts and forts, the French engaged in a century of competition and warfare, first with the Dutch and then with the English, and their Indian allies. For the whole of that time, and even for many years after the end of French power in North America, the fur trade was vital to the region that would become Canada.

A DIFFERENT VIEW OF THE REASONS FOR EXPLORATION

The exploration of Canada, and the fact that the nation today does not terminate at Windsor—or Lakehead, or Winnipeg, or Calgary— are almost entirely by-products of the fur-trade. A quaint Victorian assumption colours some of our earlier history books, equating the exploration of Canada somehow with the spread of the Empire or the spread of the gospel; but this hardly deserves serious notice today. Canadian exploration has been sometimes represented also as a romantic 'search for the western sea'; and this may have confused generations of Canadian school children into thinking of Canada's mainland explorers in terms of Balboa or the searchers for the Northwest Passage, always looking for something, not at hand, but beyond. This approach among most historians seems fortunately at last to have given way to a purely economic interpretation, that Canadian exploration and the fur trade are practically one and the same thing.[2]

1. The author seems to be saying that the only *real* reason behind the exploration of Canada was the hope of economic gain. Do you believe this is the real motive behind most things people strive for?

The Value of the Beaver

The European market for the beaver trade is suggested by the following:

. . . it was the hat-makers who became the stimulators in Europe of a demand for beaverskins which for the first time came at all near to reciprocating the Indian demand for European goods. The precise requirements of the hat manufacture were somewhat technical, but the basic consideration was that the downy hairs of beaver fur possessed in unrivalled fashion the gift of natural coherence into an extremely durable felt. So durable was it that in the late seventeenth century beaver hats made at La Rochelle were returned there after their French wearing to be re-made for sale in Spain, whence they were again returned to be prepared for Brazil and for the last time to be used for trade purposes by the Portuguese in Africa.[3]

Features of the fur trade

Why did furs, particularly those of the beaver become the **staple** of the economy of New France? The answer is found in the economic principle of *supply and demand*. Canada was the home of millions of beaver, and they were easily located and trapped. Indians not only obtained the beaver pelts, but in many cases "processed" them by greasing them and wearing them fur side in. The result was the soft, valuable fur known as "greasy beaver", which attracted greater and greater numbers of customers in Europe.

Since the beaver was plentiful, the cost of production was low enough that other potential North American products could not

basic product

What is economics?

How is it that a certain product becomes important? Is it because the product, or what it is made of, just happens to be handy? Is it because some group of people expresses a need? The answer is that both the *supply* and the *demand* are necessary; yet, to explain how the combination of supply and demand leads to the making of a product, we need to dig deeper into other questions.

THE BLUEBERRY STAND

One summer day, two nine-year-old sisters decide to set up a stand to sell wild blueberries. They think they can make some *money* picking the berries on the edge of town, washing them and selling them to passersby. Their mother gives them a table and helps them make a sign advertising blueberries for sale.

After two hours they make 90¢ and decide to continue their business the next day. However, the *supply* of blueberries on the edge of town is nearly exhausted, and the other places where they know wild blueberries grow are too far for them to reach by bicycle. They ask their mother if she will drive them to pick more berries, and she agrees. However, in order to teach the girls something about money, she suggests that they spend some of their *profits* on the gas it will take to operate the car. The girls agree to pay part of the *costs* for gas, and they drive to the new berry patch where blueberries are plentiful. They return, thinking their "business" will now prosper.

However, down the street, a brother and sister have set up a rival blueberry stand, selling their berries for two cents less.

1. What influenced the decision about "what was to be produced"?
2. What *risks*, or chances, were the girls taking?
3. How might the girls have dealt with the *competition*?

In your answers to these questions, you might have noted the following:

For question 1, the availability of blueberries probably influenced the girls' decision to sell this item. Yet the *resource* is *scarce*—there are not as many blueberries as are needed to stay in business. In other words, blueberries do not "grow on trees"; the girls must choose to pay a *price*.

For question 2, when they decided to sell blueberries, the girls took risks that: (a) there would be enough different passersby who would want blueberries; (b) they could sell their berries cheaper than a supermarket would, (c) the cost of business expenses—e.g. the cost

64

of gasoline—would not cancel their profits, and (d) it would not rain during the day.

For question 3, the competition could be met in several ways. They could reduce their prices to maintain their sales, but their profits would shrink. They could threaten to break up the rival stand, but they would be inviting retaliation. They could become more *efficient*, by eating fewer berries while picking them, thereby increasing the quantity of berries they bring home, or they could stamp on the berries to get the juice and sell blueberry juice drinks. They could persuade the mothers to divert the other children into other activities, and permit the original "blueberry sellers" a kind of *monopoly*.

BASIC IDEAS OF ECONOMICS

Economics is the study of how a society organizes the provision of goods and services and their distribution to consumers. In every society people have needs and choices to make about using their resources to satisfy those needs. Though the ways of making decisions about "what, how, and for whom" vary from one society to the next, certain things are basic to them all.

"The Blueberry Stand" illustrates some of the basic ideas of economics:

money: anything generally accepted in exchange for other things—a medium of exchange

supply: the quantity of an economic good that will be offered at a certain value at a particular time

profits: the return on the sale of goods or services above and beyond all operating costs

costs: total amount of overhead or outlay for equipment, labour and other expenses involved in production

competition: the situation where there is more than one seller dealing in the same product or service, and no one is able to dominate the market

resources: wealth, or the means of producing it—natural resources, human resources and capital resources (equipment, financing)

scarcity: the idea that there is never enough of an economic good (resource, product) to satisfy all who want it

price: an item's money value

demand: the quantity of an economic good that will be bought at a given price at a given time efficiency: increasing the amount of output from a given amount of input; eliminating waste, improving procedures

monopoly: the situation where a single seller controls the market and may determine supply and prices

THE ECONOMICS OF THE FUR TRADE

In studying the fur trade of New France, you can apply these ideas in order to answer such basic questions as:

1. What influenced the decision about "what was to be produced"?
2. What risks were involved? What costs?
3. What influenced the choice of emphasizing the fur trade at the expense of settlement?
4. How did the operation of the fur trade have to change (a) when competition arose; (b) when resources (beaver) became more difficult to obtain?

FRANK AND ERNEST   by Bob Thaves

DRINK UP AND GET OUT

HIRING THAT EFFICIENCY EXPERT MAY NOT HAVE BEEN SUCH A HOT IDEA, AFTER ALL.

easily produce the kind of profits obtainable from the fur trade. As time went on, however, the high risks also became obvious. The fur market depended on Paris fashions, and although fashions changed less suddenly in those days than they do now, the demand for furs could go down as well as up.

Besides, getting the furs to market became harder after a while. As the beaver became scarce near the settlements, new areas had to be opened up in the interior. This meant rising costs, including the building of trading posts, and a longer wait for profits. Furthermore, as more traders competed for furs, profits were even harder to obtain.

Competition seemed to be the greatest threat to a solid fur trade and, in turn, to the establishment of a firm French foothold in North America. The answer, the French government decided, was to grant a *monopoly*. Thus a group of merchants would receive a charter from the king granting them control of the fur trade in New France and the exclusive right to market furs in France. In return, the merchants had to agree to organize settlements in New France. The granting of a monopoly seemed to be a way of spreading the French empire to the New World at little expense to the King—and of improving the stability of the economy.

EUROPEANS FIRST TRADE WITH INDIANS

In this document about one of the first times Europeans traded with Indians, Cartier describes his experiences:

... we set out on Monday the sixth (of July), after hearing mass, in one of our long-boats, to examine a cape and point of land, that lay seven or eight leagues to the west of us, and to see in which direction the coast ran. And when we were half a league from this point, we caught sight of two fleets of Indian canoes that were crossing from one side (of Chaleur bay) to the other, which numbered in all some forty or fifty canoes. Upon one of the fleets reaching this point, there sprang out and landed a large number of Indians, who set up a great clamour and made frequent signs to us to come on shore, holding up to us some furs on sticks. But as we were only one boat we did not care to go, so we rowed towards the other fleet which was on the water. And they (on shore), seeing we were rowing away, made ready two of their largest canoes in order to follow us. These were joined by five more of those that were coming in from the sea, and all came after our long-boat, dancing and showing many signs of joy, and of their desire to be friends, saying to us ... words, we did not understand. But for the reason already stated, that we had only one of our long-boats, we did not care to trust to their signs and waved to them to go back, which they would not do but paddled so hard that they soon surrounded our long-boat with their seven canoes. And seeing that no matter how much we signed to them, they would not go back, we shot off over their heads two small cannon. On this they began to return towards the point, and set up a marvellously loud shout, after which they proceeded to come on again as before. And when they had come alongside our long-boat, we shot off two fire-lances which scattered among them and frightened them so much that they began to paddle off in very great haste, and did not follow us any more.

Cartier spent from July 16th until July 25th in Gaspé Harbour because of poor weather conditions:

During that time there arrived a large number of savages, who had come to the river [Gaspé basin] to fish for mackerel, of which there is great abundance. They [the savages] numbered, as well men, women as children, more than 300 persons, with some forty can-

Cartier's ships on the St. Lawrence

oes. When they had mixed with us a little on shore, they came freely in their canoes to the sides of our vessels. We gave them knives, glass beads, combs and other trinkets of small value, at which they showed many signs of joy, lifting up their hands to heaven and singing and dancing in their canoes. This people may well be called savage; for they are the sorriest folk there can be in the world, and the whole lot of them had not anything above the value of five sous, their canoes and fishing nets excepted. They go quite naked, except for a small skin, with which they cover their privy parts, and for a few old furs which they throw over their shoulders. . . . [4]

A LIGHTER LOOK AT THE FUR TRADE

W. A. McKay, a biologist employed by the modern Hudson Bay Company presents the story of the fur trade authentically, but in a style somewhat different from that of the historian.

Cartier reported that the Indians he met were very happy to trade, and were leaping and dancing in their canoes when he left. He also reported, somewhat unnecessarily, that they were a small tribe. Any tribe that practises dancing in canoes is bound to be small.

The fact that the Indians were holding up their furs on sticks is of some significance in assessing the motives of early trade. These early furs were not beaver pelts as we know them today, but beaver robes, which the Indians were wearing as clothing, fur side in. They consisted of five to eight pelts trimmed into rectangular shape and sewn together with bone needles and moose sinews. Under constant wear, the guard hairs wore off, and Cartier describes them as being 'well greased, pliable, yellow in colour and downy'. Under further constant wear, they probably also became smelly. If the Indians were

68

holding their furs out on sticks, Cartier must have arrived just in time.[5]

1. McKay's facts are basically true, but his method of reporting them is unusual. Does his presentation help you to see history in another light, or do you feel that he is treating a serious subject too lightly?

Phases of the fur trade and exploration

The first fur trade, at least as early as the 1500s, was carried on as a sideline by European fishermen. Boats from France, England, Spain and Portugal made regular visits to the Grand Banks, the name given to the fishing region off the east coast of Newfoundland. From time to time they made contact with coastal Indians, as the French did at Tadoussac on the Gulf of St. Lawrence, and exchanged trinkets and utensils for furs.

For the half century or so after Cartier's visits, the fur trade continued in this way. Around 1600, however, Frenchmen interested in organizing the fur trade on a permanent basis were able to get the backing of their government to try to establish a **colony** in the New World.

a territory which a country brings under its control

Fur trade and exploration: St. Lawrence & Great Lakes area

Champlain's founding of Quebec in 1608, the first permanent settlement in New France, marked the beginning of a new phase in fur trading and exploration. Though the "Founder of New France" died in 1635, this period of monopolist enterprise lasted until 1663, when the French government took over direct control (Royal Government). For more than a half century, the French competed with the Iroquois, originally allies of the Dutch*, for control of the St. Lawrence-Ottawa River route, which had become the great trade route into the interior.

*The Dutch were replaced as the main competitor of the French by the English in the 1660s.

To sustain his settlement at Quebec, Champlain depended on the Indians—the Algonquins—of the area to bring furs down the rivers of the Shield. The Algonquin tribes, such as the Montagnais and the Abenakis, were hunters and trappers. As the territory around Quebec was exhausted by intensive trapping, the fur trade was obliged to move into the hinterland and thus into contact with more remote tribes.

In this situation, the Hurons of the St. Lawrence Valley and the Algonquins were ideally located to act as *middlemen*. Champlain realized this and decided that an alliance with these tribes was worth the

Samuel de Champlain

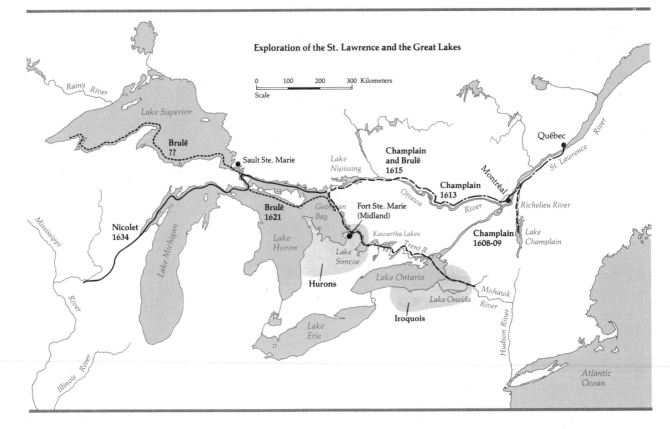

Exploration of the St. Lawrence and the Great Lakes

risk of trouble with the Iroquois. The Iroquois were the traditional enemies of the Huron and Algonquin.

In 1609 Champlain was persuaded to join an expedition against the Iroquois, whose territory was south of the St. Lawrence River, in what is now upstate New York. Near the lake which now bears his name, Champlain and his men frightened the Iroquois with French guns in a brief encounter. Champlain thus cemented his alliance with the Algonquins and explored the Richelieu River-Lake Champlain region, which was to become one of the main avenues for raids and counter-raids between New France and New England. He also aroused Iroquois bitterness against New France and set the stage for future attacks that would endanger the life of the colony.

Rumours of a "salt sea" in the north, possibly Hudson Bay,* inspired Champlain to undertake an expedition along the Ottawa River in 1613. His search for this sea was unsuccessful. The party turned back after two weeks of hard canoeing, having reached Lake Allumette, upriver from the location of present-day Ottawa. However, Champlain put this exploration to good use two years later. The Iroquois were trying to control this route over which furs flowed from Huron country around Georgian Bay to Quebec. Champlain and his small band set out by way of the St. Lawrence and

*Word had been received of Henry Hudson's discovery of 1610.

70

Champlain's protegés

ETIENNE BRULE

One of the men sent by Champlain to live among the Hurons, Brulé is believed to be the first European to reach Lake Huron. He accompanied Champlain as interpreter on the expedition of 1615, and was then sent as an emissary to the Andastes and Susquehanna Indians, in present-day Pennsylvania, to seek their aid against the Iroquois. He was not heard of until 1618 when he returned to the St. Lawrence with a group of Indian fur traders. Apparently, during the intervening three years, he had followed the Susquehanna River to Chesapeake Bay and then returned westward. After a thrilling escape from his Iroquois captors, he finally reached Huron territory and then traveled along the north shore of Lake Huron. He may also have reached Lake Superior. The strange and adventurous life of Etienne Brulé came to a mysterious end in 1632 when he was killed by the Hurons, among whom he had lived since he had been a teenager.

JEAN NICOLET

Nicolet's incredible journey took him to Green Bay, in the present state of Wisconsin. It was a long way, in every respect, from China, which Nicolet hoped to reach when he was sent out by Champlain in 1634. He had even taken along Chinese robes to wear in case he should be presented in the court of the Sovereign of China.

Nicolet did not reach the Orient, but did start an active trade with such western tribes as the Winnebagoes, Illinois and Assiniboians. He also charted the route for fur flotillas to the French trading posts on the St. Lawrence. Furthermore, he had opened a route to the Mississippi, which in succeeding years carried fur traders, explorers and missionaries to the Gulf of Mexico.

Ottawa and over waters connecting to Georgian Bay in order to join the Huron war party. Proceeding along the chain of waterways that connected with the "Thousand Lakes" portion of the upper St. Lawrence and Lake Ontario, they did battle once more with the Iroquois. This time, near Lake Oneida, the Iroquois were equipped with Dutch weapons and they drove the French-Huron force into retreat.

Though the results were ominous for the French fur trade, Champlain and his companions, including Etienne Brulé, had traveled the Ottawa River route to the Great Lakes. This alternative was soon to become the principal artery to the west and the north. It would be followed by several young protegés of Champlain—Brulé and Nicolet—who would push French influence far into the continental interior.

Montreal was founded as a mission centre and trading post in 1642. From the beginning it was threatened with extinction by the Iroquois. Their objective of complete control of the Ottawa route involved an all-out effort to eliminate the Hurons and the French. Through the 1640s the sparsely populated colony of New France was too weak to prevent Iroquois war parties from swarming up the Richelieu and into the upper St. Lawrence and Ottawa Valley. As a result, in 1648 and 1649, the Huron villages and the Jesuit missions were wiped out and the Hurons ceased to exist as a separate people. New France was more vulnerable than ever.

Dollard des Ormeaux: willing martyr or accidental hero?

Why is it that Adam Dollard des Ormeaux is treated in detail in some histories, yet scarcely mentioned—or even ignored—in others? Was he a gallant soldier whose selfless death in battle saved a colony, or one of many who accidentally lost their lives in the early struggles between European and aborigine?

Facts upon which historians seem able to agree are that Dollard was a twenty-five-year-old soldier who commanded the garrison at Montreal in 1660, at a time when the Iroquois harassment of the colony was at a peak. Characteristically the Iroquois had harassed settlements in New France with small war parties that struck quickly, claimed a few victims, and vanished into the wilderness. Having destroyed Huronia, the Iroquois had perhaps decided on a knock-out blow for Montreal, the western outpost of the French colony. Dollard and sixteen companions, most of them in their twenties, went up the Ottawa River to the Long Sault Rapids. With a small band of Hurons and Algonquins, they fought an Iroquois force of more than 700 for seven days before perishing.

The traditional account credits Dollard with selfless heroism in having gone out to meet the enemy and so impressing the Iroquois with the valour of the French that Montreal—and perhaps New France itself—was spared an all-out attack. Since the 1920s, however, some historians have questioned this interpretation, and the resulting debate seems to have lowered Dollard from "hero-saint" to "hero by accident."

It is claimed that Dollard was expecting to carry out an ambush ("petite guerre") on a small band of Iroquois, who often came fearlessly down the Ottawa in the spring bearing canoeloads of beaver pelts. He may have been intending to provide safe journey for the returning Radisson-Groseilliers expedition. An army of Iroquois surprised and trapped the seventeen French and their Indian allies, numbering less than fifty, in a crude fort. It was a matter of time before the defenders, caught with little food and less water, were overwhelmed. The Iroquois did not continue with an attack on Montreal. However, the reason is more likely to be their custom of returning to their villages after a battle carrying news of the results and displaying prisoners, than fear of an encounter with the French.

If the traditional version of Dollard at the Long Sault is partly myth, and his exploits were really less dramatic than once believed, is Dollard any less deserving of admiration?[7]

The colony struggled on through the 1650s, almost as if waiting for the Iroquois to launch an all-out attack. In 1660 the French fears might have come true, had it not been for the fierce battle at Long Sault. Adam Dollard and a small band of Frenchmen and Indian allies were killed after a long siege, but the Iroquois decided against an attack on Montreal.

Exploration and fur trade soon entered a new phase. With the establishment of Royal Government (1663), New France was under the direct control of the French government. This meant more support from overseas, including soldiers, whose presence made the colony more secure. Explorers carried the influence of the colony as far west as Lake Superior, and began the pattern of building outposts for even further expansion.

1669: Louis Jolliet—journeyed to the north shore of Lake Superior.

1671: Saint Lusson—travelled to Sault Ste. Marie, made a formal French claim to the western lands.

1679-80: Sieur de Lhut (after whom the city of Duluth, Minnesota is named)—travelled the area around Thunder Bay and built trading posts.

The English challenge to French control in North America

The English were coming. Not only had the French lost the Hurons, their most important middlemen in the fur trade, but they were now faced with competition from a new and powerful foe. In 1664, the year after Royal Government came to New France, the English supplanted the Dutch in New Netherlands (present-day New York). Allied with the Iroquois, the English proceeded to siphon off furs from the Indians around the Great Lakes; the Mohawk River—Hudson River route loomed more seriously than ever as a threat to commerce on the St. Lawrence. Furthermore, in less than a decade, the English challenged from the north, with the formation of the Hudson's Bay Company in 1670.

Ironically two Frenchmen were instrumental in establishing the English challenge from the North. Pierre Radisson and Medard Groseilliers, whose daring in the face of the growing Iroquois power was already well-established, left Three Rivers for the Lake Superior country in 1661. Defying the Governor's refusal to grant them a fur trading permit, they traded over a wide area of the Canadian Shield. They may even have reached Hudson Bay, before they returned to Montreal in 1663 with large quantities of furs, the only furs to reach the St. Lawrence by the Ottawa route that year. Their reward? Heavy fines and confiscation of their cargo. After fruitless appeals to the authorities in New France and in France, the embittered *coureurs-de-bois* ("runners of the woods") went to England, where they convinced investors, and ultimately the English government, of the profits to be made from the all-water route to Hudson Bay.

The chartering of companies had been used many times in the previous century. By granting charters to the East India Company, the British Crown had extended its influence into Asia, and the Virginia Company had already established a strong British presence in North America. In other words, a monarch could advance his power by authorizing merchants to engage in trade—in return for obligations to the crown.

The Hudson's Bay Company was formed when King Charles II of England granted a charter to his cousin, Prince Rupert, and a number of prominent English merchants. Dated May 2, 1670, the charter granted the "Company of Adventurers" nearly a million-

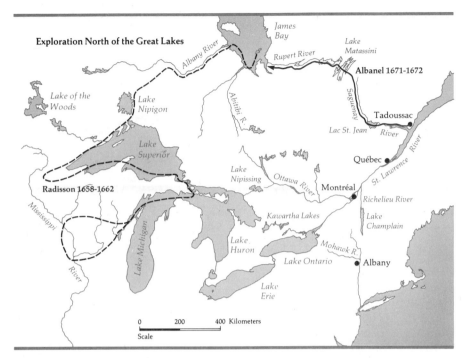

Exploration North of the Great Lakes

James Bay

Lake Matassini

Rupert River

Albany River

Albanel 1671-1672

Lake of the Woods

Lake Nipigon

Abitibi R.

Saguenay River

Tadoussac

Lac St. Jean

River

Lake Superior

Québec

St. Lawrence River

Lake Nipissing

Ottawa River

Montréal

Radisson 1658-1662

Richelieu River

Mississippi

Lake Michigan

Kawartha Lakes

Lake Champlain

Lake Huron

Mohawk R.

River

Lake Ontario

Albany

Lake Erie

0   200   400 Kilometers

Scale

and-a-half square miles of land—more than one-third of present day Canada! In addition, the charter gave to the Hudson's Bay Company the rights to all resources in the region, and the power to establish government and laws. The Company responded by establishing posts at the mouths of the major rivers flowing into the Bay—the Hayes, Albany, Moose, Nelson and Severn Rivers. From these posts English traders went out to try to reap profits from the fur trade—and, if necessary, to take trade away from the French.

The French did not falter in the face of the English challenge. They responded in several ways. The expedition of Father Albanel in 1671 by way of the Saguenay and Rupert Rivers to James Bay established links between the St. Lawrence and the Bay. Pierre le Moyne Sieur d'Iberville successfully attacked English posts in the Bay area. As a result, the English, by the Treaty of Ryswick (1697), conceded temporary French supremacy over Hudson Bay.

Meanwhile, French traders, or *coureurs-de-bois*, took the initiative in the fur trade. Rather than relying on Indian "middlemen" to deliver furs to the trading posts on the St. Lawrence, they went into the interior. There they secured furs directly from Indians and transported the pelts to Quebec. Meanwhile, the English were applying pressure from the south. Fur traders were partly responsible, and they had an advantage. English tools and rum were cheaper to obtain than French tools and brandy. The English colonies along the Atlantic coast were expanding, and the population would soon begin to penetrate the Appalachians in search for land.

The French tried to keep the English from moving toward the

The *coureur-de-bois* was a remarkable character. Not content with a settled life in the colony, unwilling to conform to the many restrictions imposed by government and church, he took to the wilderness. He not only traded with the Indians, he often chose to live among them. Radisson and Groseilliers are the best known to history, but thousands of men were attracted to the freedom and danger that went with being a *coureur-de-bois*.

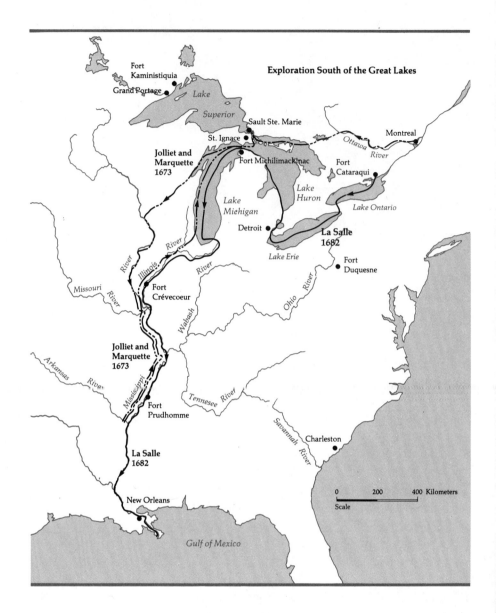

Exploration South of the Great Lakes

vast interior of North America. Following the lead of explorers like Jolliet, Marquette, La Salle and d'Iberville, the French built a string of posts and forts all the way from Cataraqui (where Kingston, Ontario now stands) to New Orleans. By the early 1700s, the English colonies were being encircled, as trade and exploration thrust the lines of French empire through the heartland of North America.

CANADA'S FORGOTTEN HEROES

In the period of canoe culture the ideal incentive was the conversion of the Indians to Christianity, but the real economic incentive to exploration was the fur trade. The French missionaries and *coureurs-de-bois* remained heroic figures in Canadian culture until the end of the nineteenth century. Then, under the impact of American mass media, at first restricted to books and the press, but later including films, radio, television and advertising, the Daniel Boones and the cowboys closed in on the Canadians for one of the greatest cultural kills of history. The image of the French explorers, missionaries, and fur traders was replaced in our collective unconscious by the 'Western.' Even the noble effort, several years ago, of the CBC to rehabilitate Pierre Radisson in a series of television programmes, lost out to Davy Crockett![8]

1. In your mind, do the *coureurs-de-bois* compare with Davy Crockett or Daniel Boone as heroes? When you think of modern heroes, are any of them Canadian?

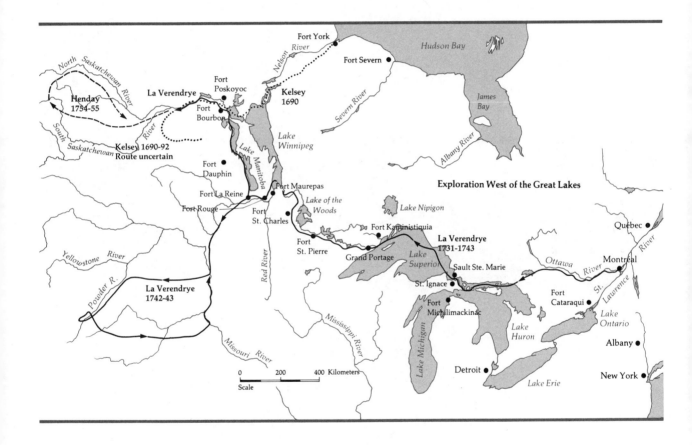

Exploration West of the Great Lakes

The saga of La Verendrye

The case of Pierre La Verendrye illustrates the mixture of motives which underlay French expansion in North America by the mid-1700s. Trading north and west of Lake Superior in the 1720s, he saw the challenge posed by the English forts on the Bay. France had acknowledged English sovereignty there in the Treaty of Utrecht

Voyageurs

(1713). The Hudson's Bay Company was evidently now secure in its monopoly.

La Verendrye, however, obtained a French monopoly to trade in the west. Between 1731 and 1742, La Verendrye, with the help of his sons and his nephew, explored an area stretching from the Saskatchewan River in the north to the Black Hills and Missouri River in the south. Between Lake Superior and the Saskatchewan, he built a number of strategically located posts which formed the backbone of a potential western French empire.

Yet La Verendrye had many troubles to contend with, besides those involved in exploring and trading with the Indians. His financial backers in Montreal demanded a return on their investment and pressured him to deliver large quantities of furs. The French government, on the other hand, insisted that his monopoly obliged him to

La Verendrye: self-seeker? or servant of France?

La Verendrye was a controversial figure in his own time and has remained so among historians, who have debated his motives.

Was he primarily a man bent on amassing a personal fortune, or was he a man with a sense of French destiny and power in North America?

FRENCH GOVERNMENT'S VIEW

Comments by the Minister in charge of French colonies:
1731: "the stopping of this officer at Kaministiquia would appear susceptible of the suspicion of self-interest."
1738: The Minister wrote to the Governor of New France that information about La Verendrye's activities "confirms the suspicion I have always entertained, and which I have not concealed from you, that the beaver trade had more to do THAN ANYTHING ELSE with the Sieur de la Verendrye's Western Sea expedition."

A MODERN EXPERT ON THE HISTORY OF THE FUR TRADE

It seems quite clear from their own reports of their own speeches and actions that the Verendryes were primarily fur traders exploiting a new and very rich monopoly in an elaborate and expensive way, who also knew that they could earn approval at Quebec and Versailles by finding one of the rivers which flowed into the Western Sea.[9]

LA VERENDRYE'S OWN WORDS

Believing he had done nothing wrong, La Verendrye writes these words after arriving in Montreal to come to his own defence:
People do not know me: money has never been my object; I have sacrificed myself and my sons for the service of His Majesty and the good of the colony; what advantages shall result from my toils the future may tell.

Besides, should no account be taken of the great number of persons to whom this enterprise means a living ... and the furs of which formerly the English got the benefit?

In all my misfortunes I have the consolation of seeing that the General enters into my views, recognizes the uprightness of my intentions, and continues to do me justice in spite of the opposition of certain parties.[10]

concentrate on exploration in search of a "Western Sea". Caught between the two, he satisfied neither. A large part of the five years before his death in 1749 was spent trying to secure financial and political support for a project that never materialized.

Settlement in New France

The history of French settlement in North America is a story of slow beginnings followed by gradual and frequently interrupted progress. But New France, because it failed to attract immigrants, did not enjoy the spectacular increase in population that the English colonies did. Why not? One can point to several reasons. The fur trade—the lifeblood of the colony—did not foster a large increase in population. Moreover, conditions in France never encouraged large-scale migration to the New World. The climate and economic opportunity of New France rarely attracted large numbers of Frenchmen during the 150 years leading up to the British conquest. Nevertheless, from its beginnings in Acadia and Quebec in the early 1600s, New France had grown by the 1750s to a population of more than 60 000. These settlers formed a distinctive society with firmly rooted traditions.

Settlement in Acadia

The expedition of Marquis de la Roche shows how difficult it was to find willing settlers. In order to fulfill his charter, de la Roche had to resort to transporting a group of sixty convicts. He landed them on Sable Island, off the coast of Nova Scotia. When a storm blew up, he returned to France, leaving them behind. Five years later, an expedition found fewer than a dozen survivors.

From its early years, Acadia, roughly the area of the present-day Maritime provinces, offered little inducement to settlers. Its climate was less hospitable than that of areas to the south; it lacked readily exploitable resources. Acadia was, however, strategically valuable to both the French and the British empires. Thus it was a major area of conflict, open to attack from New France and to British expeditions sailing out of ports like Boston.

The French were the first white men to permanently settle in Acadia. In 1605 a small group, including Samuel de Champlain, founded Port Royal on the Bay of Fundy, near the place where the town of Annapolis Royal now stands. Champlain soon moved on to the St. Lawrence, but others stayed, in spite of challenges from the first English attacks and the first attempted colonization by English in the area they called Nova Scotia (New Scotland). In fact, for a century after Champlain's arrival, strife between rival French groups and harassment from New England kept the future of the area in doubt. Nevertheless a French-speaking population slowly grew, even after France, by the Treaty of Utrecht (1713)*, ceded control to England. France more or less abandoned the Acadian settlers, even before officially turning their lands over to the English in 1713 (Treaty of Utrecht). Yet a French-speaking population continued to grow and struggle to keep its way of life intact under foreign rule.

*See chapter 5, p. 118.

In establishing a North American empire, the French government stressed the development of the St. Lawrence valley. Even though the fur trade did not require large numbers of people, the creation of a stable economy was bound to depend on a growing population.

The early years of attempted settlement at Quebec were hardly more promising than they were in Acadia. From 1608, the year he chose Quebec ("the place where the river narrows") as his new location, Samuel de Champlain struggled against impossible odds. As the man in charge of the colony, he had the authority to arrange for grants of land. There were few takers, however. Most people who came to Quebec were traders, and even they were small in number. Almost in spite of the French government and an assortment of profit-seekers, Champlain kept the colony alive.

In 1627, the situation seemed about to improve. The Company of One Hundred Associates was granted all French claims in North America from "Florida to the Arctic circle." The Company agreed to some heavy demands. Included in these was the responsibility to bring out some 300 settlers in the first year, and to raise the population to 4 000 after fifteen years.

The enterprise started badly when the first ships sent to the colony were captured by English **privateers**, who then occupied Quebec for three years. Thereafter the Company did actually give out some sixty land grants, but most of these were made to friends. Few of them took the grants seriously, so that the population of the colony was still only a few hundred by the 1640s, the decade when the devastating Iroquois attacks on New France began.

When Royal Government was introduced (1663), the French Government of Louis XIV had much more ambitious aims for its colonies. He was not content to follow the practice of former rulers. They had entrusted the spread of French influence to businessmen, in the hope that political prestige and even military advantage might develop as a by-product. The king's chief economic advisor, Jean Colbert, believed that colonies could be developed as units giving strength to the mother country within an expanding empire.

THE BRIDES OF NEW FRANCE

During Talon's term, the female population of New France increased substantially in a short time. Until then, women had arrived in small groups:

... the immigration of girls and widows was begun, at first on a voluntary basis and then encouraged by the religious and civil authorities. The immigrants were assured that when they arrived they would find husbands suited to their own station in life. Almost 1 000 came to Canada in this way between 1636 and 1673.

The framework for encouraging settlement was the *seigneurial system*. All land was, in a sense, the property of the Crown (king or queen). The Crown assigned a block of land to a person fairly high on the social ladder in exchange for traditional obligations. That person, in turn, assigned parcels of land to settlers. In other words, settlement was in the hands of the government, and was seen as one of the ways of carrying out the government's plans in New France. (See Chapter 4 for an account of the seigneurial system.)

Privateers were commanders of privately-owned ships authorized by their government to attack the ships of another country.

Mercantilism:
how colonies serve the
mother country

Colbert, Louis XIV's chief minister, was an advocate of the seventeenth century idea of mercantilism as the basis of empire. In other words, a country gained strength and greatness to the extent that it achieved self-sufficiency. To accomplish this, a country must be surrounded with colonies which serve the mother country as sources of raw materials and markets for finished products. Not only would this trading system, closed to other nations, stimulate trade between the mother country and its colonies, it would also free the mother country from dependence on other nations.

Those who were out for scandal were bound to look askance upon the reputations of these maidens who threw themselves blindly into marriage.

In fact only girls, orphans mostly and some widows, hand-picked and of spotless reputation, were sent to New France. Those chroniclers of the time who are most to be trusted, Marie de l'Incarnation, the Intendant Talon, Pierre Boucher, and all the Jesuits who had helped to compile *Relations* are agreed on this. . . . Orphans from every walk of life, young widows with no security, working women and farm workers, devoid of a future in their own country, they all hoped to find one in this uncharted land. . . .

The emigration:

This emigration of women was accomplished in two stages. From 1634 to 1662 and from 1662 to 1673. All through the first period young women and widows from fifteen to twenty-five years of age sailed either alone or in family groups of three or four. Most of these came from the west of France, and accompanied relatives from their province or family friends. Others, currently servants in the households of middle-class families, agreed to follow their employers, who in turn would be repaid either in money or by work should the girls marry or prefer to return to France. These girls were all orphans. Often they were children of poor families who would not or could not emigrate themselves. Some of those who came from the Ile de France, and particularly those from Paris, had been educated in the workhouse. . . .

The girls arrive:

. . . 'The arrival of the girls who come here to get married is quite an event . . . lofty officials and Jesuits, middle-class people, artisans and colonists hasten smilingly to welcome them, these daughters of France who bring sunshine to a new country while they wait for a morrow which will bring them new homes in which they will later become the mothers of many children.'

A case study:

Here is a typical example of the way in which undreamed-of wealth could be acquired by emigration: Madeleine Couteau of Saint Jean-d'Angely, widow of Etienne de Saint-Père, had two daughters, Jeanne and Catherine. She was in a state of near-poverty when she heard that certain acquaintances, among them members of the Guillet family, had embarked at La Rochelle on their way to New France, which they found so much to their liking that they made up their minds to settle there. She followed their example and took her two daughters with her. Jeanne was twenty and Catherine thirteen. The widow married first on October 12, 1647, to her second husband. He, like her, was a Saintongeois as one Emery Caltaut. He brought her to Cape La Madeleine where he owned land and where two

TOP: *Potential brides depart from France.*
BOTTOM: *The Brides of New France arrive.*

brothers Pierre and Mathurin Guillet also lived. Caltaut was killed in 1653 by Iroquois. Some months later his widow married Claude Houssant, a native of Plessis-Grimoire in Anjou. She had no children by her Canadian husbands, but her two daughters simultaneously married the two Guillet brothers. Catherine de Saint Pierre's husband, Mathurin, was killed by Iroquois in 1653. She then married Nicolas Rivard, who came from Tourouvre in the Perche. The latter's brother, Robert Rivard, was to marry in his turn in the year 1664, Madeleine, daughter of Pierre Guillet and Jeanne Saint-Père, and thus became Madeleine Couteau's granddaughter. In short, when Madeleine Couteau died on September 9, 1691, aged eighty-five and after forty-four years of life in Canada, she had given to New France through her two daughters twenty-one grandchildren and sixty-five great grandchildren. As was customary at this time these families subdivided and changed their original names, and from them descended the families of Lavigne, Laglanderie, Lacoursière, Lanouette, Préville, Beaucour, Dufresne, Loranger, Feuilleverte, Montendre, Bellefeuille, Maisonville, Saint-Marc, Cinq-Mars, Lajeunesse and others, not to mention the stock of the Rivards and the Guillets and the colonists who married the daughters of Nicolas Rivard and Pierre Guillet; the families of Rouillard, Moreau, Macé, Baril, Deshaies, Champoux, Dutaut, Lafond and Marchand. This then was the heritage which a young widow of La Saintonge, who one fine day had decided to emigrate to New France with her two daughters, bequeathed to her adopted country.

Thanks to official records and family histories, it is possible to follow the destinies of most of these immigrants. . . . [11]

Important responsibility for putting Colbert's plan into effect was given to Jean Talon. He was appointed in 1665 to the position of intendant, to act as a kind of business manager of New France. Approaching his task in a systematic manner, Talon arranged for Canada's first census. Finding that the population of just over 3 000 included a minority of female persons, he urged the government to send marriageable women to the colony. In addition, he encouraged early marriages, offered bonuses to parents of large families, and fined reluctant bachelors. Talon also arranged for land grants to soldiers, disbanded after a campaign against the Iroquois, along the Richelieu River—thus strengthening the colony's defence along a major route used by the Iroquois. When Talon left New France in 1672, after a mere seven-year stay, the population of the colony had doubled, to more than 7 000. The "Talon era" was the last period of large-scale migration from France to New France. The majority of French-Canadians today are descended from people who arrived 300 years ago, and formed the basis of a **Canadien** society.

By the 1760s, approximately a century later, New France had a population estimated at 60 000-70 000. The fur trade, which had first

At the time (1760s) the British took over New France, the inhabitants were referred to as Canadians, or *Canadiens*.

84

Symbols of Canada: the beaver

Known as busy, hard-working and industrious, the beaver has long been thought of as one of our national symbols. Ever since the days of the fur trade, Canadians have put pictures of beavers on stamps, coins and banners and have associated themselves with the favourable qualities of this animal.

It came as a surprise to Canadians, therefore, when they learned that they were not alone in the use of the beaver as a symbol. In the United States, two states—Oregon and New York—adopted the beaver as state emblem in 1975. In the light of these developments, Canada's unofficial symbol, the beaver, was made officially a sign of Canada in March, 1975.

1. You are a Canadian representative at meetings in the United States. Prepare a statement in which you explain why the beaver should be exclusively a Canadian symbol.
2. You are a Canadian journalist who thinks that some symbol other than the beaver should be chosen for Canada. Write an editorial explaining your choice.

given life to the colony, was still the dominant industry. In pursuit of trade, New France had extended itself by way of a network of posts throughout the Great Lakes area and the river systems of the Ohio and Mississippi. The effect was an intense imperial rivalry with the English colonies, from which people pushed westward in search of needed land. At some point in time, an all-out conflict seemed inevitable between the colonies of the two nations that so frequently clashed in Europe.

4

Institutions of New France

"All human societies, without exception, develop their own institutions. The institutions vary from group to group, from place to place, and from time to time. . . . Some institutions are simple while some are complex. Some are very important in one society and less important in another. The basic institutions found among African Bushmen will be very different from ours. However, both societies have established or customary ways of doing things. Both have institutions that may be thought of as the invisible structures—the invisible castles—by which a society organizes its actions."[1]

You may have heard a hockey broadcaster say something like, "You know, Slapshot Jones is a real *institution* on this team." What did he mean? Probably that Slapshot Jones had been with the team for a long time and was an established player. People were accustomed to seeing him whenever the team skated onto the ice. At other times, you may hear a business or a school referred to as a "fine institution".

These uses of the term *institution* are part of everyday language. Their meanings are not quite the same, however, as the one given to the term by historians and other social scientists. When they use the word "institution", they are referring to the established laws, customs, practices or systems of a society. Examples of institutions include government, the economic system*, religion, education and

*Matters of economics were introduced in Chapter 3.

the family. Institutions develop in a society to meet basic human needs.

Government

ORIGINS OF ROYAL GOVERNMENT

The system under which New France was governed for most of its existence was known as **Royal Government**. This phrase distinguishes the governmental system from the initial, unsuccessful attempts by the French Government to secure a colony without costs to itself. Originally, the government gave governing power to the persons to whom the fur trade monopoly was awarded. These people were responsible for settling New France as partial payment for the monopoly. Thus, Samuel de Champlain from the time he founded Quebec in 1608, struggled for more than twenty years with many facets of government. He was the fund-raiser, military head, explorer, administrator of business and laws, settler and religious leader, in fact, a one-man government. He was a kind of *institution* himself.

Unfortunately, in the three decades following Champlain's death in 1635, the Company of One Hundred Associates—a group of businessmen—were preoccupied with profits from the fur trade for which they held the monopoly. Thus the Company failed to take its responsibilities for colonization and government seriously, with the result that even the fur trade was unsuccessful. By 1663, the colony was in danger of being destroyed by the Iroquois. Its population was small and dependent on support—even food supplies—from France to survive.

France meanwhile had a new youthful king, Louis XIV. He was ably supported by advisors like Jean Colbert. They were determined to complete the job that had been going on for some years; namely, to centralize political power in France in the hands of the king. In bringing about an absolute monarchy within the country, they did not intend to ignore the colonies, like New France. They saw colonies as an important source of strength* in France's rivalry with other countries. England, one of her chief rivals, had a foothold in North America with growing colonies to the south of New France, along the Atlantic coast.

New France, then, was not to remain a feeble, loosely-managed colony. If the colony were defended by French troops and provided with settlers, farming could provide it with the needed food. The business life and industry of New France could grow, reducing the colony's dependence on the fur trade. Instead of clinging to existence as a series of outposts, New France could become a strong

In a system of Royal Government, the political power was centred in the hands of the king.

The "Great Man" theory, popular among historians in the nineteenth century, is a tempting manner of explaining history whenever leaders such as Champlain, Napoleon, Bismarck or Churchill are on the scene. Viewing historical developments as the result of a "Great Man's" genius is much simpler than analyzing economic and other types of causes.

Few periods in Canadian history lend themselves to a "Great Man" interpretation so well as the years 1604-1635. Samuel de Champlain was the man in charge—first at Port Royal, then, from 1608, at Quebec.

*See the note, page 81 on *mercantilism*, or the economic benefit of a colony to its mother country.

France was on the threshold of a great era when Louis XIV arrived on the throne. In the previous reign, Cardinal Richelieu had done much to break the power of the nobles, and thus strengthen the monarchy. The country was prosperous. Foreign enemies, like Spain, were declining in power and Germany was badly divided as a result of the Thirty Years' War (1618-1648). During Louis XIV's long reign, which lasted until 1715, France would become the political, military and cultural leader of Europe.

The code of laws used in Paris

*Criminal law concerns cases where persons break the laws of a country; civil law covers disputes between persons, where one may sue another.

community on the banks of the St. Lawrence—potentially a vital unit in a global empire.

New France was thus placed directly under Jean Colbert and the ministry of the marine, which answered directly to Louis XIV. The form of government was modeled on that of a French province. The governor, who reported to Colbert, was the head of the Sovereign Council. This appointed Council was responsible for carrying out all the functions of government in the colony.

THE SOVEREIGN COUNCIL

The Sovereign Council was an appointed body consisting of governor, bishop and intendant, as well as a small number of lesser officials. The Council put into effect the policies and laws decided upon in France. When necessary, it passed laws for the colony, subject to the approval of the king. In general, it was responsible for the day-to-day affairs of the colony, including the maintenance of law and order. Since the **Custom of Paris** was introduced to the colony in 1664, New France had an organized code of law from the beginning of Royal Government.

In its capacity as the highest court in New France, the Sovereign Council dealt with all serious cases, both criminal and civil.* Lower courts were set up in Quebec, Trois-Rivières and Montreal. These were like municipal courts, with authority over things like traffic and fire regulations. On some of the larger seigneuries, there was even another level of courts, where seigneurs dealt with local disputes.

Of the leading officials in the colony, the governor had the most

The Intendant's Palace at Québec

prestige. Unlike governors of provinces in France, whose power had been stripped away, the governor in the colony still had a fair amount of authority. Because of his distance from France, he often had the opportunity—and responsibility—for making important decisions. In particular, he was called upon to provide for the defence of the colony and to handle relations with the Indians and the English colonies.

The Bishop of Quebec was another important official. He was expected to give religious leadership to the colony and to organize missionary work among the Indians. As the church provided schools and hospital care and help for the needy, the Bishop had a variety of concerns. Furthermore, he often wielded political power, and influenced the decisions of the governor and the intendant.

The best known governor of New France was Frontenac, who held office for two terms (1672-82 and 1689-98). A member of the old French nobility, he was a man who gloried in the role of colonial leader and military commander. His famous campaigns against the Iroquois and defiance of the English in their efforts to conquer Quebec earned him a prominent place in Canadian historical writing. More recently, however, historians like W. J. Eccles, in his book *Frontenac: The Courtier Governor*, have exploded some of the myths that gave Frontenac a larger-than-life reputation.

A JUST REWARD?

The coureur-de-bois, Nicolas Vignau, was the accused in one of Canada's earliest criminal trials. He had been travelling among the Algonquins:

Nicolas returned from his adventure with an extraordinary tale of a trip northward to the shores of Hudson Bay. There, he said, he had seen the wreck of an English vessel. Champlain reported the news in Paris. High authority was alarmed at the menace of an English intrusion from the north. Champlain was ordered to make the journey to Hudson Bay and verify the report. Nothing could please an explorer more. In 1613 he took Nicolas for guide, and pushed up the Ottawa. On the way Nicolas made a weak endeavor to get his chief and benefactor drowned in the rapids. When they arrived at Ile Allumette, the Indians protested that Nicolas had never left their village during his sojourn, that there was not a word of truth in his story. 'Kill the liar!' they cried.

Champlain questioned Nicolas closely, and finally made him admit that he had invented the whole adventure tale. Champlain was transported with anger, he says, for all his project of exploration was confounded, and a Frenchman was convicted of falsehood and treason before the Indians, and the delicate prestige of the French was threatened. And especially, he was, in his own eyes, convicted of bad judgment, of misplaced confidence. He had let himself be fooled and betrayed by a stupid rascal. It is not surprising that he was transported with anger. It would have been very natural if he had let the traitor meet his just punishment.

'Shortly afterwards,' he says, 'and very sorrowfully, I went and informed the Indians of the deceit of this liar, telling them that he had confessed the truth to me. At this they were very much pleased, but reproached me with having had so little confidence in them, who were chiefs, my friends, and who always spoke the truth. "This very wicked liar must die," said they. "Do you not see that he wanted to kill you? Give him to us, and we promise you he will tell no more lies." And because they were all howling to get at him, and their children still more loudly, I forbade them to do any harm, and made them also keep their children from doing so.'

Champlain brought Nicolas back to the Great Rapids. There, in 1613, took place the first formal trial in Montreal's history. The French condemned and rejected Nicolas; the Indians, despite Champlain's prayers, refused to receive him. 'We left him in God's keeping,' says Champlain. I suppose this means that he was turned into the woods, to fend for himself. We never hear of him again. I doubt if he survived long.[3]

1. Did Vignau receive "a just reward"?
2. Do you think he should have been treated differently? If so, how?

The office of intendant was generally held by someone of lesser social rank than either that of governor or bishop, but in practice it was the most influential.

*See page 114.

With the *captains of militia** acting as liaison between him and the habitants, the intendant was in charge of law and order, public works, trade, and the distribution of land.

1. What are some examples of "customary," or "established," ways of doing things that were carried on in New France by the *institution* of government?
2. Imagine a situation in which the governor, the bishop and the intendant are having a discussion. The problem is whether or not to encourage the building of a road through a district bordering on an Iroquois trading route. What would be the main concerns of each? On what points could they disagree? What things could influence the decision they make?

Characteristics of Royal Government

Royal Government was set up during the "age of absolutism," as historians have called that period in European history. In France, as in most European countries, the theory of government was clear: the monarch (king, queen, emperor or whatever the title) had final authority in all matters. Louis XIV claimed to rule by "divine right," answerable only to God. There was no such thing as *democracy* as we understand it today, no notion that the people had any basic rights or any say in how the government was run.

Jean Talon set a high standard during his term (1665-1672). As "business manager" of the colony, he encouraged settlement, improved agriculture, started a number of industries, and generally affected life in the colony.

In New France, the governor's job was to carry out instructions from Paris. "The king knew what was best" for his subjects, whether they lived 48 km or 4800 km away. Similarly, the intendant was an agent of the king. His function seemed to be at least partly to

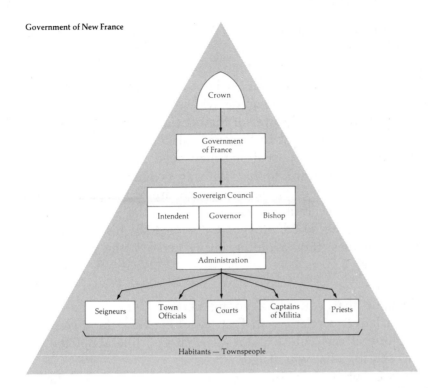

Government of New France

Crown

↓

Government of France

↓

Sovereign Council

| Intendent | Governor | Bishop |

↓

Administration

Seigneurs | Town Officials | Courts | Captains of Militia | Priests

Habitants — Townspeople

stand in the way of any governor's desire to set himself up as a "miniature king." The bishop may have represented the interests of the Pope* in religious matters. As a political figure, however, he was part of the system that governed "from the top down," part of the chain of command between the king and his subjects.

Government based on the idea of absolute rule required the continuous flow of decisions from the top of the system to the king's subjects. In theory, at least, the king made a decision, which was then put into writing by his advisor. The resulting instructions were sent, usually in the spring of the year, to New France. The governor or intendant then put them into effect through whatever regulations were necessary.

The system of government in New France may be described as one in which power was centralized, not shared by the leaders. The king was a kind of "father" to his subjects. They responded as respectful children to his direction. Many rules and regulations kept the population mindful of its place in an orderly society.

The theory behind an institution is one thing; however, the actual operation may be somewhat different. Consider the following facts:

—the capital of New France was more than 4800 km away from the king;

   —orders from the king could only be sent by ship, and then only during the time the St. Lawrence was open to navigation. Decisions

*The Pope was, and is, the official head of the Roman Catholic Church. See, however, p. 98 for information about the conflict between the interests of the Church and the French Government.

In 1647, the habitants were allowed to elect members known as *syndics*, to the Council of Quebec. Although the elected members had no vote, the people of the colony had representatives speaking on their behalf directly to the governor and the other officials. The circumstances that permitted this interlude did not last, of course. Once Louis XIV had come to power and Royal Government was in effect, the Council of Quebec was changed into the Sovereign Council, and the "experiment" whereby government consulted the citizens was ended.

often had to be made in the colony without the chance to ask for approval beforehand;

—the main officials in New France were frequently in conflict; for example, the intendant and bishop might disagree on whether brandy should be used in trade with the Indians. The effect was often to neutralize the power of the officials over the people;

—settlers were important to the survival of the colony. The authorities were interested in satisfying their needs; oppression of settlers was likely to be harmful to the colony as a whole;

—if a settler rejected the way in which life was regulated, he had the choice of becoming a *coureur-de-bois*. If he went into the fur trade, in fact, he could prosper by smuggling his product to the English colonies, thus avoiding heavy taxes to the government of New France.

1. Imagine that you are a young person living in Trois-Rivières. Write a letter to relatives in France, telling how the government in the colony affects you. Explain (a) what you like about the government, and (b) what you dislike.

2. In a country where the government closely regulates the lives of the people, what advantages may there be for (a) the individual (b) society as a whole? What disadvantages?

3. What do you think are the basic *rights* of an individual living in society? What do you think are the basic *responsibilities* of the individual toward the society in which he lives?

The Church

When people talk about the changes that have swept through our society in the 1960s and 1970s, one they often mention is the decline of the churches. Although religion is still very important to people, and religious topics can be very controversial, the decline in regular church attendance and financial support is a fact of our time. The church even has a diminished role in providing for people's spiritual needs—its primary function, and the one among its traditional functions that it still maintains to any extent.* Many of its other functions have been taken over by such institutions as the public school system, social security, the media and government.

In the society of New France, things were very different from what they are today. The Roman Catholic Church was really several *institutions* in one. It assumed responsibility for the religious life of the colony, both for people in the settlements and for the Indian people among whom the missionaries worked. The church looked after education, hospitals, and charity. Furthermore, it was influen-

*Exceptions to this general statement readily come to mind. Many churches, such as the Salvation Army, continue to provide social services. Others maintain schools, and serve in health care and similar capacities that are not strictly religious.

What is government?

When you hear the word "government," do you think of
—the traffic policeman who gives out tickets for speeding?
—taxes?
—politicians (in general? an individual or group in particular?)
—a certain building?
—the armed forces?
—welfare?
—unemployment insurance?
—grants of money to theatres and symphonies?

It may be that government means something negative to you, or something vague and far removed. If you think about it, however, you may realize that what governments decide can affect you greatly. Like other institutions, government is supposed to serve certain needs of people in a society.

Wherever people live in groups, governments exist in some form. The functions of government, such as leadership, decision-making and protection develop out of the needs of a group. In stories about people being shipwrecked on a desert island and marooned by a plane crash in the Arctic, we hear about a certain person taking charge, about rules being made to ration food and water, and so on. When a group lives together over a period of time, the procedures become formalized, laws are recorded and organized, the roles of leaders and followers are more clearly defined.

In all societies, even the simplest, there is likely to be a governing person or group to organize certain parts of the community's life. Depending upon the size and nature of the community and its circumstances—for example, location and climate—there will be tasks which can be carried out more effectively by "government" than by individuals. For example, if a group needs to protect itself against enemies, the strongest may become the leaders, with the others giving up some of their freedom in return for security. The leaders may assume a number of powers over the others, and these powers may increase over a period of time.

If the danger passes, and the need for government is not directly related to immediate survival, the people being governed may want to recover some of their freedom. They may wish to have more say in the making of decisions. If the number of people is small, agreement may be possible through face-to-face discussion. The people may make decisions by reaching common agreement, or *consensus*.

If hundreds or thousands are involved, reaching a consensus is often too time-consuming and inefficient. More formal procedures

93

are required to take the needs and interests of all people into account. If *conflict* occurs between persons or groups, and that conflict cannot be settled by the people involved, government in some form becomes necessary. *Law and order*, then, is an important function of government. In performing this function, government may acquire a great deal of *power*. A few people may hold this power, which may threaten the *rights* of the general population.

In all societies, there are jobs to do which make it possible for people to live together. Some of those jobs are mainly of a *political* type, and the institution which handles them is *government* in some form. The form of government depends on many factors, including beliefs, traditions and historical experiences. Whatever the form, all societies need ways of making decisions and controlling conflict. At the same time, they face such problems as how to limit the power of government and provide certain rights for the citizens.

In the case of New France, the form of government was transferred from the mother country, where government had been developing over many centuries, to the colony. The problem was not one of inventing a system that suited the needs of colonial society, but of adapting a ready-made system to a new and changing situation. Although France imposed its system, which eventually took the form of Royal Government, the circumstances of the New World altered it in many ways.

1. What kind of "government" on the simplest level would emerge if an elevator in a department store were to be lodged between floors?
2. What problems—other than food, shelter and clothing—could arise for a group of people stranded on an island? How do you think they might be solved?
3. Why is it necessary for any society which intends to endure over time to have an institution of government?
4. What needs of the people of New France did its government fulfill?
5. What might have happened to the colony if the government had changed every week?
6. Explain how it was possible that the people of New France had many rights and freedoms, even though they lived under a system of "absolute monarchy."

---

tial in government; the Bishop was one of the principal members of the Sovereign Council. The Church was also the single biggest land-holder in the colony.

The Priest's Farm, Montréal. What can you tell about the power of the Church in New France from this picture?

Origins of Church activity in New France

The early exploration and settlement of New France coincided with the Counter Reformation in Europe. This movement was the response of the Roman Catholic Church to the challenge of Protestantism. For decades the continued spread of Protestantism had kept the Catholic Church on the defensive. Taking the signal from the determined king of Spain, Philip II (1556-1598), Catholic leaders had become much more aggressive. Besides the regular clergy, the Catholic Church was served by religious orders like the Jesuits.

France was involved in religious civil war between Catholics and Protestants (Huguenots) throughout the last half of the 16th century. After a brief period of Protestant success, the power of Catholicism was established. As Samuel de Champlain struggled to attract settlers to New France, the shrewd and ruthless Cardinal Richelieu was the "power behind the throne." Because of him, only Catholics were allowed to migrate to New France, to preserve the religious unity of the colony.

In the early 1500s, Martin Luther, a German priest, had organized a "protest" against the Catholic Church. He and other critics attacked what they regarded as unreligious practices that had grown up in the Catholic Church. As a result, he and other "Protestants" formed separate churches: for example, the Lutheran Church in Germany and Scandinavia; the Calvinist Church (Huguenot in France and Switzerland, and the Presbyterian Church in Scotland); the Church of England (Anglican).

Men like Champlain and Maisonneuve, the founder of Montreal, believed they had a responsibility to advance the cause of Catholic Christianity. Thus they encouraged the power of the Church in the settlements and the efforts of missionaries among Indian peoples.

Missions among the Indians

*See map, p. 70.

In the early years of New France, considerable effort went into attempts to convert Indians to Catholicism. By the 1640s, Jesuit priests had started a number of missions among the Hurons, who were important allies of the French. The area of *Huronia** was the original location of French missionary work after Samuel de Champlain invited the Jesuits to New France. In the 1630s, such dedicated Jesuits as Brébeuf and Lalemant worked out of Fort Ste. Marie (near present-day Midland, Ontario), which was the headquarters for missions scattered through the region.*

*The first mission was established at Port Royal, in Acadia, in 1611, but missionary work there was on a smaller scale and received less support from overseas.

INDIANS' CONCEPT OF CHRISTIANITY

When the priests first came 'most all the Indians were witches. Some were willing to be christened, some were unwilling. They asked the priest. "What is Christening for?'... "If you are not christened, you are lost for good.'... 'Lost, in the woods?'... 'No, in hell.'...'Where is hell?'...'Black place, fire there burns the soul.'... 'How do you go there, by road?'... 'No, your soul goes there.'... 'Where is my soul?'... 'You might sicken and die. After you die you might see your soul.'... 'How can a soul go out from the birch-bark cover around the dead body, tightly bound?'... 'You should dig a hole and put the dead in it.'... 'That would be even harder to get out of, couldn't go anywhere then.'... 'Yes, you could go to Heaven.'...'Heaven? What is Heaven?'...Nice band (of music) in Heaven, nice berries there.'... 'How go there?'... 'If you do not fight, do not talk bad, you can go there. If you murder, steal, you will go to Hell, for your sin.'...'Sin? What is sin?' They knew nothing.[4]

1. Do you suppose the priests' training would have prepared them for such questions from the Indians? Why do you think as you do?

martyr: one who sacrifices himself or herself for a cause

French hopes of success in converting the Indians were set back by the brutal fur trade wars of the 1640s. A concerted offensive by the enemy Iroquois led to the destruction of Huronia. Fathers Brébeuf, Lalemant and other Jesuits are remembered as **martyrs** for the courageous efforts which ended in their deaths at the hands of Iroquois warriors. In later years, priests like Father Albanel did explore and work among the Indians. After 1650, however, the

Ignatius Loyola and the Jesuit Order

The Jesuit Order, an organization of Roman Catholic priests, was founded by Ignatius Loyola in the 16th century. Loyola was a young man and a soldier in the army of a Spanish overlord when, through an accident, his leg was injured and he was lamed for life. During his convalescence, he began to read books about the lives of the saints and the life of Christ. Giving up the thought of returning to military life, Loyola decided to become a "soldier of Christ." When he was well enough to travel, he went to a monastery where he declared himself a pilgrim of God and exchanged his clothing and weapons for the rags of a beggar. He made a detailed confession of his sins and for three days he endured self-inflicted penances and fasting to make peace with God. Some time after this he is reported to have had a spiritual vision which lasted eight days in which the entire program for the Society of Jesus (Jesuit Order) was revealed to him.

For the remainder of his life, Loyola went on pilgrimages recruiting followers for the Society of Jesus.

Known as one of the most strict and rigorous of the orders, the Jesuits based their lives on a series of Spiritual Exercises which included self-examination and self-control, repenting of sins and cleansing of the soul, fasting, meditation and above all, spiritual discipline.

In 1540, when the Pope recognized the Jesuit Order, it was organized like a spiritual army and ready to undertake any mission which the Pope assigned. It was priests from the Jesuit Order who were among the first missionaries in New France.

The Jesuits developed a tradition for excellence in education. Many schools and colleges have been operated by them over the years, in Canada and many other countries.

Catholic Church turned much of its attention to the needs of the French people in the settlement.

HARDSHIPS OF THE MISSIONARIES

Gabriel Sagard, who came to New France with the Recollet priests in 1623, describes life among the Indians:

In order to practice patience in good earnest and to endure hardships beyond the limit of human strength, it is only necessary to make journeys with the savages, and long ones especially, such as we did; because besides the danger of death on the way, one must

Before the Jesuits arrived, missionaries from the Recollet order came to Quebec. They travelled and lived among the Algonquins and Father Le Caron compiled the first dictionary of the Algonquin language. The Recollets were a small order, however, and were eventually unable to carry on.

A missionary in New France

make up one's mind to endure and suffer more than could be imagined, from hunger, from sleeping always on the bare ground in the open country, from walking with great labour in water and bogs, and in some places over rocks, and through dark thick woods, from rain on one's back and all the evils that the season and weather can inflict, and from being bitten by a countless swarm of mosquitos and midges, together with difficulties of language in explaining clearly and showing them one's needs, and having no Christian beside one for communication and consolation in the midst of one's toil.

Yet for that matter the savages are quite kind (at least mine were), indeed more so than are many people more civilized and less savage; for when they saw me for several days almost unable to eat their *sagamité*, so dirtily and badly cooked, they had some compassion for me and encouraged and helped me as well as they could, and what they could was not much.[5]

The Church in the settlement

Once Royal Government was established and the settled population of New France grew quickly, the demands on the Church increased accordingly. The influential role of the Church was clearly established by Laval, the first Bishop, who served as a leading member of the Sovereign Council. In fact, François Laval was often in conflict with other officials over matters in which the jurisdiction of church and state overlapped. He took the position that the Church was answerable to the Pope, not the king.

STATE V. CHURCH

In France, those who believed in the power of the king over that of the Pope were known as *Gallicans*. Their opponents were called *ultramontanists*, because they were loyal to the Pope, who was "over the mountains" (Alps) from France.

Gallicans believed:	Ultramontanists believed:
The Church is subject to the will and pleasure of the Crown since the monarch rules by Divine Right.	The Pope reigns supreme in the affairs of the Church.
The Church is to be used as an instrument in carrying out government policy.	The Church is not subject to control by the Crown.
If necessary, the interests of the Church are to be subordinated to the needs of the Crown.	This position favoured by the Jesuits and Bishop Laval.

1. Can you summarize in your own words the basic difference between ultramontanism and gallicanism?
2. Are there any modern examples of the problems of separation of "church and state"?

The many functions of the Church

The need for priests in New France led to the establishment of seminaries, where *Canadien*-born men could be trained. In Laval's time priests lived in the seminary and under the Bishop's direct control. Later they lived in the parish (church district). The priest, or *curé*, was close to the people, and the church was often a social as well as a religious centre. People looked to the priest for spiritual guidance, advice on everyday problems, and education for the children.

The church was indeed the only provider of education in the colony. Even before Royal Government, the Jesuits established a college in Quebec (1635). Shortly after their arrival (1639), the Ursuline nuns started a school for girls. Eventually, schools were operating in all the main centres, and the *petites écoles* provided an elementary education in the parishes. The curriculum of religious exercises, reading, writing and arithmetic was suited to the needs of the time. Pupils were often absent from school and spent most of their childhood helping with the many chores necessary for family survival.

Types of Schools

Those students who did go on to secondary school studied what is known as a "classical curriculum", including grammar, Latin, philosophy and rhetoric (public speaking). The main purpose was preparation for the Jesuit college.

Crafts and trades schools, on the other hand, provided training in wood-carving, carpentry, shoe-making and other trades. The schools at Quebec and St. Joachim, a few miles downstream from Quebec, were known for their religious artwork.

L'Hôtel Dieu

Bishop Laval

Bishop Laval was already in office when Royal Government was set up. During its first decade, he was successful in establishing the church as an important arm of government.

HIS BACKGROUND AND CHARACTER:

... Laval's family of Laval-Montmorency was one of the oldest and noblest in France and always he was the aristocrat with the air of command. Members of his family had married into royal houses....

... His family sacrificed everything for church and state. Two brothers died on the field of battle, another became a Benedictine monk, the only sister became a nun....

... In his later years at Quebec he slept in a bed where he was tortured by fleas; to avoid indulgence of the flesh he kept meat until it rotted; and he lived a life of poverty in order to have the means to give to the poor. No one could charge Laval with seeking personal gain. In times of pestilence [plague] he nursed the sick night and day, made their beds with his own hands, and shrank from no humble or disgusting service....

... It was not long before, in the depth of winter and in peril from the Iroquois, Laval was going out on snowshoes to discharge his duties and, in summer, was kneeling in a frail canoe and, during long days, taking his part in the paddling.... [6]

HIS INFLUENCE:

Laval guided the destinies of the Church in New France for thirty-four years, ruling in a more authoritarian and absolute fashion than any representative of the all-powerful Sun King. He left more of a mark upon the colony than any governor except the great Frontenac, with whom he had quarreled violently, as might have been expected when two autocrats were thrown together in a small settlement. There was no doubt to whom Frontenac was referring when he wrote to Colbert: 'Nearly all the disorders existing in New France have their origin in the ambition of the ecclesiastics, who wish to add to their spiritual authority an absolute power over temporal matters.'[46] The tradition of Bishop Laval has been a major force in the history of French Canada: his desire to subordinate state to Church, his authoritarianism, ... his ultramontanism, have cropped up again and again in his spiritual heirs who have benefited from the prestige and ascendency which the first Bishop of Quebec won by his domineering will, his zeal, and his ceaseless effort.[7]

The burden of health care in modern Canada has been taken over to a large extent by various levels of government. Traditionally, however, the churches have established and maintained hospitals. Canada's first hospital, the Hôtel-Dieu, was founded in Quebec in 1639 by three nuns of the Hospitalières order. Twenty years later, the same order also set up the first hospital in Montreal. In a colony where doctors were always scarce, the nursing sisters of religious orders like the Ursulines had a very important role. Besides the sick, people who were unable to take care of themselves, including the disabled, the orphans and the old, were often dependent on the church for support.

The church occupied an important place in the life of New France. It was active not just in religious matters but throughout the affairs of the colony, where it exercised day-to-day influence and power. New France was a Roman Catholic as well as a French colony, and the spiritual authority of the Roman Catholic Church was unquestioned. Its role in education gave it further influence on the way people thought. Even in the political and economic life of the colony, the church was one of the major institutions.

Social organization

Before looking at society in New France imagine the following modern situation:

Scene: a town in province "A"

Time: Autumn, 1978

Situation: The local citizens have been called to a town hall meeting to discuss an urgent issue involving taxes. Among the people who attend are the following:

—the mayor
—the president of a local company
—a plant foreman and his wife
—two residents of a low-cost housing development
—a teacher
—a policeman
—a clergyman
—a political science professor

In the meeting, the people tend to sit with others in the same social class—upper, middle, or lower class.

1. Which of the people at the meeting would you think would feel they were lower class? Middle class? Upper class? (Compare your answers with those of other members in your classroom.)

Marie de L'Incarnation (1599-1672), first superior of the Ursuline convent at Quebec, was born at Tours, France, on October 28, 1599, and was the daughter of Florent Guyard, a dealer in silk. At the age of seventeen, she was married to Claude Martin, a silk manufacturer of Tours; but her husband died in 1619, leaving her with an infant son, to whose education she devoted herself for twelve years. In 1632 she entered the Ursuline convent at Tours; and in 1639 she accompanied Madame de la Peltrie to Canada to found an Ursuline convent at Quebec. Of this convent she became the first superior, and she retained the position until her death on April 30, 1672. Her *Lettres spirituelles et historiques*, written to her son Claude, were collected and published by him in 1681 (2nd ed., 2 vols., Paris, 1876; 3rd ed., by Dom Albert Jamet, 3 vols., Paris, 1929-36), and form a valuable source for the history of the period. She also composed a catechism in Huron, three catechisms in Algonkian, and a dictionary of French and Algonkian. She received beatification by papal decree in 1877.[8]

There are few people who would label themselves "lower class." In answering the questions about classes, did you find that the three categories—lower, middle, and upper class—were too restrictive? Did you want to write that some people would see themselves as "upper-middle class," or "lower-middle class"? Even though "lower" may be intended just to *describe* the situation of a person who has less—money, influence, property—people commonly use "lower class" as a pejorative term (a "put down").

One of the trends of the present-day, not just in Canada but around the world, is the movement toward *egalitarianism*—more equal opportunity, a fairer share of resources, and so on. For many, this is still an ideal. However, changes of the last twenty-five to thirty years point in the direction of less distinction between peoples. In Canada, for example, the division between 'upper class' and 'middle class' is generally unclear. The same is true of the many new countries that have come into being, since World War II, in Asia and Africa.

2. What things would they consider in "classifying" themselves? Have you considered family background, contribution to the community, social connections, habits, leisure time activities, place of residence, ethnic background, sex?

3. How might one's social class affect his or her behaviour in the town hall meeting?

4. The term "upward mobility" refers to the rise from one class to another. Do you think most Canadians wish to be "upwardly mobile"? What incentives are there for Canadians to move to a higher class? What circumstances favour "upward mobility"? What are some of the obstacles? Do all Canadians have equal opportunity to improve their position in society? What might be some examples?

Even today we may think of some people as "upper class" and others as "lower class". Though the basis for class distinctions may have shifted over the years (from family name to wealth, for example), distinctions still do exist. The dividing lines between "classes", however, are not easy to see.

In any society, past or present, that you study, you will find that there are different groups, and that some groups are more influential than others. A certain group may derive its influences from tradition, wealth, talent, or a combination of these. As you look at the situation in New France, keep in mind that you are studying a society that is both similar to and different from the one in which you live.

In older societies, such as those in Europe, the differences between classes were more easily identified than they are in modern democratic societies. Simply stated, societies were once divided into upper (lords or nobles) and lower (peasants) classes. This was the case in the feudal system, or feudalism, which reached its peak in Europe in the twelfth century. The class system was based on mutual protection and dependence: the nobles provided leadership and protection, the peasants or serfs provided loyalty and service. A wide social and economic gap existed between a noble and the peasants who farmed his land.

Gradually a middle class of craftsmen and businessmen emerged, especially with the growth of towns and cities and the rise of trade between different regions of the globe. Because of these and other changes, feudalism in Europe had broken down to a considerable extent by the time New France was settled. But the seigneurial system introduced to the colony had features of the feudal class system, and seemed to have some of the relationships between classes.

The impression that New France had a feudal-like class system stems from the procedure for *land-holding* in the seigneurial system.

Rights and duties

Carefully spelled out rights and duties governed the relations between the classes in the seigneuries of New France. The following are some of the more common examples:

THE CROWN

RIGHTS	OBLIGATIONS
The Crown provided the seigneur with: —grant of land —possibility of prestige, higher status (place in society)	The Crown required the seigneur to: —keep detailed records —show map and descriptions of property assigned to habitants, land under cultivation, names of habitants, payments collected —reserve oakwood (for ship-building) and minerals for the Crown —pay heavy tax if he decided to sell his rights to the seigneurie

THE SEIGNEUR

RIGHTS	OBLIGATIONS
The seigneur received from the habitants: —honour (very important); special recognition in social events, church, etc. —annual rents —fees for use of facilities e.g. flour mill —corvée, i.e. three or four work days yearly on the seigneur's land	The seigneur was required to provide the habitants with: —assigned farm lots —a manor house as the administrative centre of the seigneurie —the building and operating of a mill —a local court (in some cases) —certain social activities

THE HABITANT

RIGHTS	OBLIGATIONS
The habitant received from the seigneur: —grant of land —facilities e.g. flour mill —local courts (in the larger seigneuries) —other services, varying from seigneurie to seigneurie	The habitant was required to provide the seigneur with: —annual payment of rent —fees for using facilities —corvée —other services, varying from seigneurie to seigneurie

NOTE: Military obligations were not part of the seigneurial contracts, but all persons, seigneur and habitant alike, were dependent on one another for security. This was especially true during the times of Indian attacks. During wars (for example, with the English) all persons, regardless of position in society, could be expected to serve in the militia.

1. It seems as though there was a great deal of "red tape" involved in having land in New France. If you bought a farm in Canada today, would you be completely free to do whatever you wanted with it?
2. Is there more or less freedom for a property owner in the city?

"... in 1663 more than half the seigneurial land was held by women (54.5%), in comparison with 2.7% in 1645. The importance of women in this respect was due not so much to the women's religious communities as to the twelve widows, remarried or not, who had control of land inherited from their former husbands or in tutorship for a son of minor age. This was not brought about by any concerted effort on the part of women, but by a series of chance circumstances."[9]

"Since systematic settlement only began in 1633, the population was young. The average age, calculated from 84.2% of the male and 96.1% of the female population was only 20.6 years, 22.2 for men and 18.2 for women; it was lowest in the Trois Rivières region, where the average man was 21.7 years old and the average woman a mere adolescent of 16.8 years. Half the population was under twenty!"[10]

In contrast to the British "freehold" system, in which land was bought and sold outright, all land in New France in a sense belonged to the Crown. The king, theoretically the supreme landlord, granted large tracts of land to persons of influence, who became known as *seigneurs*. Each seigneur parcelled out farms to habitants, in return for a number of rights and obligations. On the surface, a seigneur appeared to occupy a very special place in the society of New France, and the habitants owed him a variety of services.

The system was closely supervised, however, by the government. French kings had no intention of allowing the rise of a noble class in a colony; the nobility in France had been one of the main threats to the power of the monarch. Thus, seigneurs generally had a good share of social privileges, but their power was checked by a host of obligations, both to the Crown and to the habitants. Through the intendant, the Crown was able to keep a watchful eye on the seigneurs, in order to restrain them from taking advantage of their tenants.

The seigneurial system was, in part, a means of encouraging settlement in New France. The habitants were thus very important to the success of the scheme. Their rights were well protected, and their obligations were not burdensome in most cases. In the event that life on the seigneurie was unacceptable, the habitant could always choose the life of the *coureur-de-bois*. The seigneur seldom achieved the position of privileged lord. Similarly, the habitant, unlike the person at the bottom of the ladder in the "old country", was not a peasant, subject to a master's whim.

The society of New France

New France was mainly an agricultural community, although nearly one-quarter of the *Canadiens* lived in the towns of Quebec, Montreal

The pattern of settlement

Seigneuries varied in size according to location, type of land and the importance of the seigneur. Some could be compared to a small Canadian farm of today; others covered areas larger than modern-day cities like Montreal and Toronto. In either case, the pattern of land grants was largely determined by the rivers, especially the St. Lawrence. The people of New France preferred farms that fronted on water, because of the convenience for transportation. With the passage of time, farms became narrower and narrower, and houses were often no more than a few yards apart.

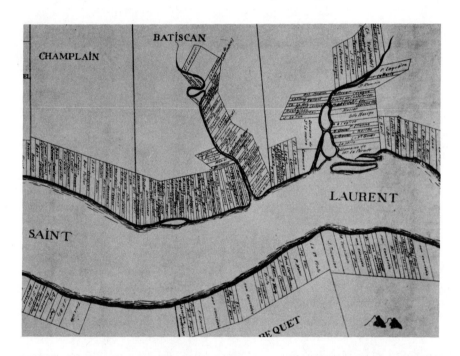

and Trois-Rivières. The following readings illustrate aspects of life and relationships between classes. What do they say about the variety of life in the colony? About the people's attitudes toward authority? About the values of the population?

THE INTENDANT: FATHER OF THE KING'S FAMILY

In 1686, when Jean Bochart de Champigny was appointed intendant of New France, he was given very detailed instructions governing all aspects of his responsibilities:

His Majesty wishes him to know that his entire conduct must lead to two principal ends; the one to ensure that the French inhabitants established in that country enjoy complete tranquillity among themselves, and are maintained in the just possession of all that belongs to them, and the other to conserve the said inhabitants and to increase their numbers by all means. . . .

His Majesty wishes him to visit once a year all the habitations that are situated between the ocean and the island of Montreal, to inform himself of all that goes on, pay heed to all the inhabitants' complaints and their needs, and attend to them as much as he possibly can, and so arrange it that they live together in peace, that they aid each other in their necessities and that they be not diverted from their work.

In other words, the intendant, as the King's representative, was to act as the father of the King's large family of loyal subjects living on the banks of the St. Lawrence River.[11]

FAMILY LIFE

Winter was an important factor in the determining of the social entity into which the settler of Canada evolved. Little by little he became civilized, more shrewd, and more conscious of his worth. His existence was composed of his family life, his leisure, the sensible manner in which he performed his everyday domestic duties. Even the animals became tamer, since they were visited, cared for and fed three times a day in their stalls, where they were likewise confined until the coming of the summer days. When these tasks had been attended to, and when he was not obliged, as he was on stormy days, to clear the snow in order to avoid being cut off from his neighbours, the settler lived in the bosom of his family. He sat before his hearth, busying himself with little tasks which required a degree of skill, intelligence and thought. Sometimes he would develop his natural artistic talents in the making of furniture for his house; winter saw the fashioning of tables, chests, chairs, beds, cradles and toys for the children. In this sort of household where the settler was all the time developing a new outlook, his wife had an important part to play. If she were educated she would teach not only her children but her husband as well to read and write, for a colonist who was able at least to sign his own name had climbed a rung of a social ladder in the parish hierarchy. The woman of the house was also in charge of the daily devotions. She set an example for hard work by weaving, sewing and cutting out all the clothes and dresses for her family as well as the bedcovers and the carpets. She showed great ingenuity in cooking meals which had to be at once varied, substantial and appetizing, since a good table was one of the most important assets in these months of apparent inactivity.[12]

TOP LEFT: *Country dance of les Canadiens;* TOP RIGHT: *Habitant family at home;* BOT-TOM LEFT: *Habitant family at prayer;* BOTTOM RIGHT: *Intendant Talon visiting settlers. What can you learn about daily life in New France from these illustrations?*

SEIGNEURIAL STATUS

The following excerpt from the novel TWO SOLITUDES *(1945), by Hugh MacLennan, describes Athanase Tallard, a former seigneur in rural Quebec. Although the setting of the novel is World War I, the role of the seigneur was much the same as it had always been:*

Athanase Tallard was the only limit, under God and the law, to the priest's authority in Saint-Marc. Since the days of the early French colonization, the Tallards had been seigneurs. For more than two hundred years social opinion in Saint-Marc had depended not only on the parish priest, but also on whoever happened to be the head of the Tallard family. Most of their seigniory had been broken up during the latter half of the nineteenth century and they collected no more rents. But the family still seemed enormously rich to the rest of the parishioners. Athanase owned by inheritance three times more land than anyone else in Saint-Marc, and he hired men to work it. He also owned a tollbridge over a small tributary river at the lower end of the parish, and this brought him far more money than came from his crops. In many respects his surface authority was a great as that of the priest himself, and his manner of a great gentleman increased it.[13]

1. What statement from the document best suggests the power and importance of the seigneur?

2. Why do you suppose the seigneurs remained important in Canada long after the seigneurial system had changed?

3. What kinds of ceremonial gestures or customs are shown toward important, powerful people in our society? What kinds of ceremonial privileges do you suppose were afforded the seigneur in New France? Why might these have been very important to the seigneur?

Manor house of the Seigneur of Beauport, Robert Gifart

THE HABITANT'S PLEASURES: LEISURE IN NEW FRANCE

The *habitant* did not let his work interfere unduly with his pleasures. It was estimated that what with festivals and various religious observances he did not have more than ninety days available for labour between spring thaw and autumn freeze-up. (Some nineteen saints' days eventually were stricken from the calendar in order to provide him with more working time.) Between Christmas and Ash Wednesday everyone stoked up in anticipation of Lent; each family made the rounds of the neighbourhood; they danced and sang and listened to professional storytellers, who would appear to have arrived in the colony at an early date. Hospitality was the law of every hearth; it was said that a traveller could make his way over the 175 miles from Quebec to Montreal without spending a sou for food, carriage or lodging. No matter how tardy his rentals the seigneur felt obliged to entertain his tenants on May Day and St. Martin's Day. Then the board groaned with rich foods set out for an all-day feast; the host groaned afterwards as he surveyed his depleted larder. The priests were frequent and welcome house guests; they carried not only the keys of heaven but also the gossip of the neighbourhood.[14]

SOCIAL CLASSES IN NEW FRANCE

...No real bourgeoisie arose; commerce was too firmly monopolized by the mother country for many Canadian merchants to grow prosperous, while most of the chief administrative posts were held by transient Frenchmen. Lawyers were excluded from the colony in order that justice might be more speedy, less expensive, and less sought after. Doctors came out from France, as did artists and architects. There were really only two classes in New France: the ruling elite of administrators, clergy, and noble seigneurs; and the mass of the people. The elite was either French or French by assimilation; the people called themselves Canadians and were jealous of Frenchmen. This social division was to survive tenaciously in French Canada, and to set it apart from the rest of North America, whose greatest strength lies in a dominant middle class which plays no part in the traditional French-Canadian scheme of things.[15]

INDUSTRY IN NEW FRANCE

Several basic industries were founded in New France, but they were all characterized by a difficult birth and a sickly childhood. These included coal mining, the manufacture of pitch resins and potash, tanneries and glue factories, brewing and distilling, and, most important, iron-making. Although these industries were started during the French régime, it was not until after the Conquest that there could really be said to be a viable manufacturing industry in Canada.

The best-known manufacturing establishment of New France was Les Forges St. Maurice at Trois Rivières. Les Forges St. Maurice were not, as is often claimed, the first iron works in America.

Boucher, Pierre

(1622-1717), governor of Three Rivers, was born in France in 1622, and came to Canada with his father in 1635. He spent four years in the country of the Hurons learning several Indian languages, and on his return to Quebec became interpreter in the garrison, and took part in various expeditions against the Iroquois. In 1645 he settled at Three Rivers, where he became chief interpreter, and for nearly a quarter of a century he served there in various capacities, civil and military. In 1652 he became governor of Three Rivers, and he filled this office, with short intervals, until 1667. In 1661 he was sent to France to obtain reinforcements, was received by Louis XIV, and given a patent of nobility, and returned to Quebec with a number of colonists. Although he was not an educated man, he wrote at this period a work entitled *Historie véritable et naturelle des moeurs et des productions de la Nouvelle-France*, which has remained an authority, and which has been four times reprinted since its first publication in Paris, in 1664. In 1667, as a reward for saving Three Rivers from an attack of the Iroquois, he was granted the seigniory of Boucherville, whither he retired to spend the rest of his life. He died there on April 19, 1717. He married first, in 1649, Marie Chrestienne, a Huron girl, and second, on July 9, 1652, Jeanne Crevier, by whom he had fifteen children.[16]

Successful enterprises in Virginia and Massachusetts had preceded it by a hundred years, but the Canadian venture is remarkable for its long life. Most of the early iron works of North America went out of business within twenty years of their founding, and none survived to celebrate a centennial. But the St. Maurice iron works, which produced its first iron in 1733, was still going strong a hundred years later....

... The iron works ... played an important part in the development of Canadian industry by supplying a basic raw material over two centuries. Most of the pots and pans and stoves and bells found throughout New France were made of St. Maurice iron.[17]

CONDITIONS OF WORKERS IN NEW FRANCE

Professor Guy Frégault explains about the limited evidence historians have been able to uncover about the conditions of workers:

In the light of present information, it is harder to describe the living conditions of the workers than it is to describe those of the peasants. It is known that, owing to the shortage of skilled craftsmen, workers had high wages. A carpenter was better paid than a member of the Superior Council. Being well paid, they had to do as they were told. One day when the naval dockyard workers in Quebec decided to go on strike, Hocquart [the Intendant] threw them all into prison, the proper way, in his opinion, to deal with a strike.[18]

RULES AND REGULATIONS

The Government of New France was constantly introducing rules to guide the daily living of citizens. For example, people were expected to marry young—girls by the age of fifteen and boys by nineteen; otherwise they were liable to fines. This document explains liquor regulations:

A ... problem in Montreal, Quebec and Trois Rivières was the excessive number of taverns. Any house became a tavern merely by hanging an evergreen branch over the door. In 1726 the intendant Dupuy, limited the number of licenses and issued stringent regulations which are quite revealing:

> It is hereby forbidden for tavern keepers, hotel keepers, and inn keepers to sell soldiers anything to drink in the morning except a little brandy or wine, nor to sell any liquor to lackeys or domestic servants, in or out of livery, at any hour of the day, without the written permission of their masters, on pain of fifty livres fine, and the closing of the establishment for a second offence ...

> It is forbidden for tavern keepers, hotel keepers and inn keepers to accept from any youth, valet or soldier, in payment for wine

A little-known fact about Canadian history is that slavery existed in Canada as early as 1632. Colonists as well as Indians took other Indians as slaves, and Blacks from Africa were imported to be sold as slaves. King Louis XIV of France legalized the importation of slavery in 1689. There were jobs to be done and a shortage of unskilled labourers such as mill workers, harvesters, household help, miners and fishermen in the colony to do them.

Although the church did not speak out against the practice of slavery, it did try to make conditions for slaves more humane through education and religion. Slavery never became an issue or an institution in New France—rather it appears to have been one answer to labour problems which plagued the colony—, and it eventually declined considerably.[20]

or other drinks, any table ware, cutlery or other utensils, on pain of being named accepters of stolen goods and of being punished as such.[19]

RULES FOR EVERYDAY LIVING

The main ordinances concerned the prevention of fire, public health and the public market. Every house must contain 'latrines and privies'; the owners must clean the front of their houses each day; no person must keep fodder within the house or in any place where it could catch fire; no straw or manure must be thrown into the streets; each house to have exits by way of the attic to allow access to the chimneys or alternatively to have ladders fixed to the roofs, chimneys to be swept every two months. To guard even more completely against the constant danger of fire a tax of thirty *sous* was imposed upon every chimney, half the tax to be paid by the tenant and half by the owner of each house. This sum served to purchase 100 leather buckets. The authorities even succeeded in forbidding people to smoke in the streets of the town. Other rules were directed towards tradespeople: no one was to go round offering fowl, game, eggs, butter or wood for house to house sale without first putting their goods on display until eleven o'clock in the morning on market days. Publicans, butchers, and hucksters must not purchase goods in the market before eight o'clock in the morning in summer and before nine o'clock in the morning in winter, since past experience had proved that the poorer artisans had been exploited by these people who made a clean sweep of all the goods and offered them for resale at exorbitant prices.[21]

CRIME AND PUBLIC PUNISHMENT

This population, so small but at the same time so carefree and lighthearted, . . . felt at times the need for entertainment. . . .

The carrying out of sentences produced some extraordinary sights. After an enquiry had been held into dealings in alcohol which were being conducted with neighbouring Indians, some of the best-known citizens were found guilty and condemned to thirty days in prison. For the last fortnight of this sentence they were to be 'daily exposed to public spectacle on the back of a wooden horse with placards round their necks bearing the words: "For having dealt in firewater with the Savages".' An exciting scene which idle people would not have missed for anything; the great sitting in pillory! An even more diverting spectacle was staged in 1673. Four men broke into the house of Ameau, the notary, and from it stole wine and brandy. They were immediately arrested, put on trial and condemned 'to be exposed at the doors of the parish Church on a feast-day or on Sunday, after the termination of High Mass'. The lock-smith who have provided forged keys, one Louis Martin, was to ap-

That Run-Down Feeling

Unlikely as it may seem, New France did have traffic problems. The following comment notes that pedestrians had their problems long before the coming of the automobile:

In Montreal traffic was a continual source of annoyance. Most of the streets were only eighteen feet wide, and pedestrians were frequently run down by wagons or sleighs. The intendant Raudot complained that those on horseback or driving vehicles paid no heed to pedestrians and expected them always to get out of the way. Present-day pedestrians in Montreal might well be inclined to remark: "Plus ça change, plus c'est la même chose."[2]

111

pear bareheaded, his hands bound together, and bearing round his neck keys and bottles, with the following inscription hung about his breast and back: 'Wine-stealer, stealer of brandy and eels, and forger of keys'. Around the necks of the other offenders hung only empty bottles. When these ridiculous rites had been carried out the accused men took their respected places once more among their fellows. Honour was restored to them.[22]

During the 150 years of its existence as a French colony, New France (Quebec) developed a deeply rooted way of life. From the small beginnings at the time of Champlain's settlements, through generations of uncertain growth and in spite of limited support from France, a French-Canadian culture had been formed. Its unity would be tested time and time again. But the unity was there, maintained by culture, language and institutions—government, church, seig-neurial system, family—that gave the people a distinctive lifestyle and the basis for a sense of identity.

Selling Canadian homespun cloth

Ideas from the social sciences: sociology—role and status

Among all the social sciences, the discipline of sociology is the one most concerned with the study of man in society. To understand how and why man behaves the way he does in interactions with other people and groups is the business of the sociologist. One of the key areas of study in sociology is the area of social roles. A role is a set of expectations which a society applies to a person. A person's role is also characterized by certain obligations and privileges. People who live within the same society and culture have come to expect that people who play certain roles will act in certain ways.

For example, the role of student in our North American culture has particular expectations and obligations attached to it. Duties of a student could include attending and participating in classes, completing assignments and perhaps taking part in extra-curricular activities. The rights or privileges a student receives in return could include praise for a job well done, good grades, respect and education.

However, everyone plays many roles. A student is also a son or daughter, and could also be a sister or brother, friend to others, niece or nephew, star field hockey player or swimmer, and part-time employee. In each situation the person would be playing one or more roles with obligations and privileges attached to each role.

Problems occur, however, when one or more roles are in conflict. That is, the expectations exacted of a person playing one role might be in conflict with the expectations of one of his other roles. Consider the case of a girl swimmer. In her role as athlete, she may learn to be keenly competitive in order to win races. In her role as friend or sister, she may find competitive actions offend or hurt other people. In other words, what may be acceptable behaviour in one role may not be in another. Even if the person realizes this conflict, she may not be able to resolve it completely.

Closely related to role is the concept of *status*.* A person's *status* is his position, or rank, in a group or in society generally. According to the way other people view the roles he plays, a person may have higher or lower status. In addition to the importance of his role, a person's status depends on certain other factors, such as age, sex and income. A doctor may have a high status because she cures illness, earns a large income and represents the improving status of women in general.

*This explanation may be detailed enough for your present study. However, both concepts, role and status, may be defined more precisely. For example, a sociologist may speak of a status which is *achieved* by an individual, as differentiated from one that is *ascribed* or assigned to an individual by society.

SOCIAL ROLES IN NEW FRANCE

Society in New France was one in which status was quite clearly defined by law and custom. The seigneur, the priest, the artisan and the habitant each had a place which was understood and generally accepted. There was little opportunity, and thus little incentive, for a person to change his status. Of course, each person had more than one *role*, in that a seigneur could also be a father, a brother, a friend —but in public the seigneur nevertheless had certain rights and obligations, a certain level of importance.

One kind of person who enjoyed high status and whose position involved several roles was the *captain of militia,* as the following document explains:

THE CAPTAINS OF MILITIA

The long period during which the captains of militia in Canada retained their position and influence is a proof of the usefulness of the system they embodied, and of the happiness of their choice for the functions they discharged. Every one of them was an *habitant—* the foremost in his locality for intelligence, activity, and good character. He was a true representative of the people, and at the same time he was an agent of the central power, an *homme de confiance,* a factotum in every sense of the word. He dealt direct with the governor-general, with the lieutenant-governor, the judges, the curé, the seignior, and with every family. He served without pay, but the honour was great.

It is a strange oversight on the part of the historians that they have not, as a rule, seen the extraordinary significance of the captain of militia in Canadian history. They must have been deceived by the military aspect of the title. As a matter of fact, the captain of militia was not only a military personage; he was five or six other personages, all in the same man. He was recorder, and he was superintendent of roads. No government case before a tribunal was examined without his being present, notwithstanding that the official attorney was there also. Any dealings between the seignior or the curé and the civil authorities passed through him. If an accident happened somewhere, it was the captain of the place who wrote the report, and any action taken subsequently was under his management. If a farmer wished to approach the government or the judge, the captain took the affair into his hand. When a seignior trespassed on the land of a farmer, the captain came between the two, and his report was considered first of all. When the high functionaries, such as the governor, the intendant, or the judge, travelled, they were invariably the guests of the captain. He had even an eye on the mail bags and the transport of packages. He was of more importance in the community than is one of our members of parliament to-day.[23]

1. What are the different roles the captains of militia played?
2. What personality traits might the people expect a captain of militia to have? What attitudes and behaviour toward him might a habi-

tant who was a captain of militia expect *from* the people of his community?

3. Because the captain of militia was both a representative of the people and an agent of the central power, he could experience role conflict. For example, what kinds of conflict might the captain of militia feel if a farmer wanted him to approach the judge on a matter of the farmer's inability to do all the tasks the seigneur asked of him?

4. What roles do you play? What are some of the expectations and duties attached to these roles? Have you experienced role conflict in carrying out any of these roles?

5. How might it be easier for one to change his or her status in Canadian society today than it was in the 1700s? What limitations are there on one's ability to change one's status?

The French fort of Louisbourg, one of the battle sites in the Seven Years' War

5

Canada becomes British

How did New France pass from French to British control? The story is one of struggle between rival empires. The struggle went on for more than seventy-five years, starting among the fur traders and ending with professional soldiers. The end came when the British army took over New France in 1760.

During the early 1600s, both France and England started colonies in North America. About the time New France started with Champlain's settlements at Port Royal and Quebec, the English were settling along the Atlantic coast of what is now the United States. From the early beginnings at Jamestown, Virginia (1607) and Plymouth Rock, Massachusetts (1620), the Thirteen Colonies grew. Eventually they extended from Maine to Georgia. New France, meanwhile, expanded by way of the St. Lawrence and Great Lakes into the Ohio Valley and the Mississippi.

The main Anglo-French wars affecting North America occurred between 1689 and 1760. Actually the rivalry went back much further. England and France had fought each other in Europe for centuries. They began to acquire colonies to add to their power. Whenever war broke out between the parent countries, it usually involved their colonies as well.

Earlier conflicts had given little advantage to either side, but the war ending with the Treaty of Utrecht (1713) was an important

The goals of British leaders were not always the same as those of British settlers in a particular colony. The person living in Massachusetts or Virginia thought of his own safety and that of the region in which he lived. The politician in London, England, was concerned with the fortunes of a world-wide empire. Thus he was willing to trade off losses in one region for gains in another.

turning point. The French officially gave up claims to Acadia (the part approximately equivalent to mainland Nova Scotia), Newfoundland and the Hudson Bay area. Although the French kept Isle St. Jean (Prince Edward Island) and Isle Royale (Cape Breton), the English had improved their position in the St. Lawrence area. The resumption of English trade on Hudson Bay was a challenge to the fur trade of New France.

The position of the French was still far from hopeless. The area of present-day New Brunswick remained in their hands, as did Cape Breton. On this strategic island, they constructed Louisbourg, one of the biggest and most elaborate forts in North America. Not only did Louisbourg attract new settlement and protect French shipping, but it was intended to serve as a base from which the French could attack the English colonies.

CHRONOLOGY OF ANGLO-FRENCH RIVALRY

1605—1608:	Port Royal and Quebec founded; beginnings of French presence in North America
1607:	Virginia founded; beginnings of British presence in North America
1629, 1654, 1690:	Successful English attacks on Acadia
1689—1697:	King William's War (War of the League of Augsburg); French gains in the Hudson Bay area
1702—1713:	Queen Anne's War (War of Spanish Succession); Treaty of Utrecht
1740—1748:	King George's War (War of Austrian Succession); Louisbourg, captured by Anglo-Americans during the war, was returned to the French.
1756—1763:	Seven Years' War; Treaty of Paris, English conquest of New France.

The War of Austrian Succession (1740-1748), as did most European wars then, involved—on opposite sides—France and Britain and their respective empires.

The English colonists were understandably alarmed. During the War of Austrian Succession,* an expedition from Massachusetts did manage to capture Fort Louisbourg. However, it was handed back at the peace conference concluding the war. It seemed that Britain was prepared to sacrifice the interests of her North American colonists in exchange for gains in other parts of the world.

Britain, however, acted quickly to counteract the French advantage and to reassure the English colonists. Halifax, founded in 1749, was to become one of the most important naval bases in the British Empire. Should war break out with France, Britain would have Halifax, manned by British **regular troops**, as a military base. Furthermore, Fort Lawrence was constructed in 1750 on the isthmus of Chignecto (the connection between present-day Nova Scotia and New Brunswick), a few miles from the French-built Fort Beausejour.

Regular troops were professional soldiers, rather than settlers doing militia duty as an obligation.

The Acadian expulsion

Part A

THE SITUATION

By the 1750s the Acadian population of fewer than 15 000 lived mainly by farming marshlands around the Bay of Fundy. The largest concentration of settlement, besides Port Royal, was located at the head of the Bay. These French-speaking people posed a special problem for the English governor at Halifax, Charles Lawrence. As another war between England and France seemed imminent, the British authorities saw them as a security risk. The British thus decided to take steps to ensure the Acadians' loyalty—or else.

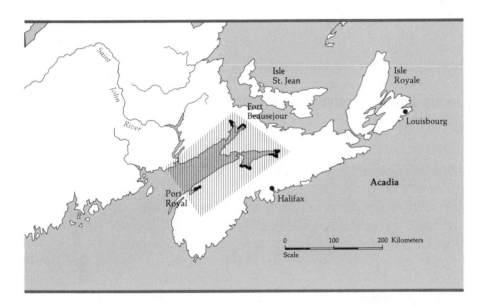

With Britain and France again moving toward war, the increased French activity among the Acadians was seen by the British as a direct challenge to their position in Nova Scotia. A generation of Acadians had refused to take an unqualified oath of allegiance to the British Crown. More than once a proposal was made to expel them and settle New Englanders in their place. Allowed to remain, it was argued, the Acadians could be a decisive advantage for the French in a fight for one of the most strategic areas of Anglo-French conflict. Then in June, 1755 an Anglo-American force laid siege to Fort Beausejour, captured it, and found some 300 Acadians in the service of France. Governor Lawrence and his Council decided to expel a number of Acadians known to be pro-French and to order the others to take the unqualified oath. When representatives of the Acadian

One problem that worried the British government was the lack of British settlement in Acadia. New Englanders had shown little interest in moving north from thriving colonies like Massachusetts or Connecticut. Although a number of immigrants from Britain settled in the Halifax area, the British arranged for German and Swiss Protestants (non-Catholic Christians) to settle at Lunenberg. The hope was that the newcomers, loyal to the British , would offset the Acadians and Micmac Indians.

119

population refused, as expected, Governor Lawrence effected a plan for deportation. More than 6 000 Acadians were forced from their homes and shipped to the English colonies from Massachusetts to the Carolinas; some even ended up in England and France.

1. Do you think Lawrence was right in expelling the Acadians?
2. If you think Lawrence was wrong, what actions do you think he might have taken instead?

Part B

BACKGROUND: THE ACADIANS' DILEMMA

The Acadians' situation was very complicated. For more than a century, Acadians had lived under French rule on the Bay of Fundy side of what is now Nova Scotia. In 1713 Acadia (Nova Scotia), by the Treaty of Utrecht, became British territory. The treaty provided that Acadians had a year in which they were free to leave, and several hundred did move to Isle St. Jean (Prince Edward Island) and Isle Royale (Cape Breton Island). The majority remained on their farms, however, in spite of the possibility of having to conform to changes that British rule might bring.

As the years passed, the Acadians lived pretty much as they had under French rule—without having to take on British citizenship. In 1728, they agreed to a qualified oath of loyalty, which permitted them to keep their properties and the practice of the Catholic religion, but did not require them to undertake military service. The British were prepared to let the Acadians stay rather than have the land unoccupied or see Louisbourg strengthened by Acadian settlers.

At the conclusion of the War of Austrian Succession (1740-1748), the long-standing rivalry of France and Britain was more serious than ever before, and the effects were felt in North America. The British began to put pressure on the Acadians to take an unqualified oath of allegiance, in case another war broke out and the British wanted their support in defending the region. The French meanwhile, were pressuring the Acadians to resist the British. Such agents of France as the priest, Abbé le Loutre, based at Fort Beausejour, used persuasion and threats, including that of attacks from Micmac Indians.

Still, the Acadians tried to remain neutral, avoiding open support to the French, and refusing to take an unqualified oath of allegiance to Britain which could obligate them to fight French armies.

A DESCRIPTION OF THE ACADIANS

This unhappy people were in fact between two fires. France claimed them on one side, and England on the other, and each demanded their adhesion, without regard to their feelings or their welfare. . . . By the Treaty of Utrecht France had transferred Acadia to Great Britain, and the inhabitants had afterwards taken an oath of fidelity to King George. Thus they were British subjects; but as their oath had been accompanied by a promise, or at least a clear understanding, that they should not be required to take up arms against Frenchmen or Indians, they had become known as the 'Neutral French.' This name tended to perplex them, and in their ignorance and simplicity they hardly knew to which side they owed allegiance. Their illiteracy was extreme. Few of them could sign their names, and a contemporary well acquainted with them declares that he knew but a single Acadian who could read and write. . . . Their pleasures were those of the humblest and simplest peasants; they were contented with their lot, and asked only to be let alone. . . . [1]

1. Because of the additional information in this section, have you changed your mind about whether the expulsion of the Acadians was right or wrong? Why or why not?

Part C

THE BRITISH COMMANDER EXPLAINS

Governor Lawrence, in a letter to the governors of the Thirteen Colonies (British), gives his reasons for expelling the Acadians:

. . . These Inhabitants were permitted to remain in quiet possession of their lands upon condition they should take the Oath of allegiance to the King within one year after the Treaty of Utrecht by which this province was ceded to Great Britain; with this condition they have ever refused to comply, without having at the same time from the Governor an assurance in writing that they should not be called upon to bear arms in the defence of the province; and with this General Philipps did comply, of which step his Majesty disapproved and the inhabitants pretending therefrom to be in a state of Neutrality between his Majesty and his enemies have continually furnished the French & Indians with Intelligence, quarters, provisions and assistance in annoying the Government; and while one part have abetted the French Encroachments by their treachery, the other have countenanced them by open Rebellion, and three hundred of them were actually found in arms in the French Fort at Beauséjour when it surrendered.

. . . I offered such of them as had not been openly in arms against us, a continuance of the Possession of their lands, if they would take the Oath of Allegiance, unqualified with any Reservation whatsoever; but this they have most audaciously as well as unanimously refused.

As by this behaviour the inhabitants have forfeited all title to their lands and any further favor from the Government, . . . it was now from their refusal to the Oath absolutely incumbent upon us to remove [the Acadians].

As their numbers amount to near 7000 persons the driving them off with leave to go whither they pleased would have doubtless strengthened Canada with so considerable a number of inhabitants; and as they have no cleared land to give them at present, such as are able to bear arms must have been immediately employed in annoying this and neighbouring Colonies. To prevent such an inconvenience it was judged a necessary and the only practicable measure to divide them among the Colonies where they may be of some use, as most of them are healthy strong people; and as they cannot easily collect themselves together again it will be out of their power to do any mischief and they may become profitable and it is possible, in time, faithful subjects.[2]

1. Can you find three reasons in Governor Lawrence's letter for the explusion of the Acadians? Does Lawrence's explanation strengthen or weaken your original opinion about the rightness or wrongness of his decision?
2. Do you need more information to help you decide? What kinds of information?
3. Does the issue seem as clearcut to you as it did after Part A? Parts A and B?

Part D

THE EVACUATION: THE PERSONAL SIDE
These excerpts give further information about the dilemma of the Acadians:

THE NEUTRAL FRENCH
Why did the Acadians try so hard to stay neutral?

The explanation must lie in their primary concern with a love for their ancestral lands, however clouded their legal title, and for their distinctive way of life. Their folk memories reached back over a century of repeated attack and counterattack, with alternating success and control by the two competing powers, and they seemed to have had an almost intuitive wariness of deep involvement on either side that might give an excuse to the eventual victor to deprive them of their rich but hard-won grainfields and pastures behind the dykes.[3]

AN ACADIAN REMEMBERS
. . . we were made Prisoners, and our Estates, both real and personal, forfeited for the King's Use; and Vessels being provided, we

were some time after sent off, with most of our Families, and dispersed amongst the English Colonies. The Hurry and Confusion in which we were embarked was an aggravating Circumstance attending our Misfortunes; for thereby many, who had lived in Affluence, found themselves deprived of every Necessary, and many Families were separated, Parents from Children, and Children from Parents.[4]

CAUGHT IN THE MIDDLE

In truth, these simple folk who chose to style themselves 'neutrals,' whose only desire was to live in obscurity, isolated from the trends of the age, were fated to be used by both England and France as pawns in the tremendous game of empire-building in North America, a game that continued to be played from the early part of the seventeenth century for over a hundred and fifty years.[5]

1. Has your initial reaction to the Acadian expulsion been influenced any further by the additional information?
2. Do you still see the issue as whether the expulsion was right or wrong? Or do you think another issue (or issues) related to the expulsion was more important?
3. Do you feel the need for still more information?
4. Could it be that more information, by itself, will not enable you to reach a "final" conclusion?
5. What else, besides the "facts," influences your view on the rightness or wrongness of the expulsion?

Part E

HISTORICAL INTERPRETATION

How many people in your class concluded that the expulsion of the Acadians was right? How many disagreed? Why?

In studying the issue of the Acadian expulsion, you have just been though an experience common to historians. You started with a limited amount of information—or "facts"—and probably formed an opinion. Then you worked through several stages of new information, which either supported your initial opinion or changed it. Even if your basic view has remained the same, you are now probably aware of more sides to the issue.

Furthermore, you are likely to have observed—from the varied opinions of your classmates—that "facts," by themselves, do not determine people's opinions. Our past experiences, personalities, and values all colour our points of view.

Yet "facts" are important, and even though students or historians may not agree on all of them, there are many facts about which agreement can be reached. The same is true about the analysis and interpretation of facts. If people explore an issue in depth, they are more likely to find points on which they agree.

Consider the following statements by modern Canadian historians:

> [The expulsion] was an act that exceeded any deliberate intention of the British government and which left a tragic legend as part of Canada's racial heritage. Yet while the methods may have been needlessly brutal, the step itself was the outgrowth of the situation. Not Britain, but France by ruthless and aggressive policy, which used the Acadians with complete disregard of the risk that it drew upon them, was the real author of the expulsion. Possibly Nova Scotia would have been safe without it, but the authorities can be excused for their reluctance to take such a chance in the face of the war that was already looming and the certainty that the most extreme efforts would be made to stir up the Acadians to armed revolt. . . . [6]

> It was necessary that she [Nova Scotia] should become a truly English colony and, in view of the circumstances, that she become one rapidly. However, no colony without colonisation. The English colonial policy struck an obstacle: the old French people of Acadia. At first she attempted to absorb them. The terrain and also the time were lacking to bring this task to a satisfactory conclusion. There was nothing else to do but to overcome Acadia. . . .
>
> Nova Scotia was at war and she was part of an intensive movement for colonisation. The expulsion of the Acadians was an episode in this war and in this movement. . . .
>
> . . . Acadia could only die, either through being exterminated by the conqueror or by continuing to decay slowly, in the sunlight of the British world, and this would, by definition, come to very much the same thing. [7]

> . . . Colonel Charles Lawrence, had previously decided to expel all the Acadians from the province. He made this decision for military reasons. Despite the absence of an official declaration of war, hostilities had begun and he had no desire to fight the French with some ten thousand Acadians in his midst who might very well support an invading French army. This decision—but hardly the manner in which it was carried out—might be justified on the grounds of military expediency, but if so, the actions of Abbé Le Loutre and of the Acadians who resisted the British must also be condoned. Regardless of the way it was done and the moral and legal issues involved, the fact remains that the Anglo-American forces successfully removed the French and Acadian threat to the Nova Scotian frontier. [8]

1. All three historians seem to be saying that the expulsion was inevitable. What reason or reasons does each give? Are they the same?*

*For a contemporary example of a similar situation, see Volume 2, Chapter 9, which deals with the case of the Japanese Canadians in World War II.

The Seven Years' War

If the European struggle for North America is represented by . . . a trial of strength between an expert swordsman who could not swim and an expert swimmer who could not fence, the overall strategy of both is obvious. The swimmer (Britain) wants to swim first and fence later (in America) as surely as the swordsman (France) wants to fence first (in Europe) and swim later.[9]

The above image serves as a reminder that the "final struggle" between France and Britain for control in North America was part of a conflict that embraced Europe and, in fact, the colonies of the two imperial rivals around the globe. Basic strategy for this world-wide conflict shaped the course of the war in North America. France, with her much larger armies and many European allies, hoped to secure victories in continental Europe while New France was fighting a defensive war. France then could expect to win colonial advantages at the conference table, as she had done rather successfully in the past. Britain, on the other hand, planned to use her powerful navy to cut France off from her overseas possessions and hope for a stalemate in Europe, where Britain's ally was Prussia, a rising military power led by Frederick the Great. In North America, Britain could possibly have New France at its mercy.

COMPARISON OF THE RIVALS

Until the 1750s New France managed to claim vast territories in the North American interior, even though French settlement was relatively small and concentrated in the St. Lawrence Valley. Long lines of strategic forts stretched out to the Great Lakes and beyond to the Ohio and Mississippi, to the far west and the north. Wars with the English took the form of bloody but small-scale raids on one another's outposts. The French, with their many Indian allies, more than held their own in such a style of combat. The English colonies, notwithstanding their greater numbers and resources, were notoriously unable to cooperate, even against a common enemy, and for the most part they were indifferent to the issue of French expansion.

In an all-out war, however, New France stood little chance. Her total population of some 60 000, almost matched by that of the New York colony, contrasted sharply with an English colonial population twenty-five times greater. New France was also handicapped by dependence on the mother country for supplies and reinforcements.

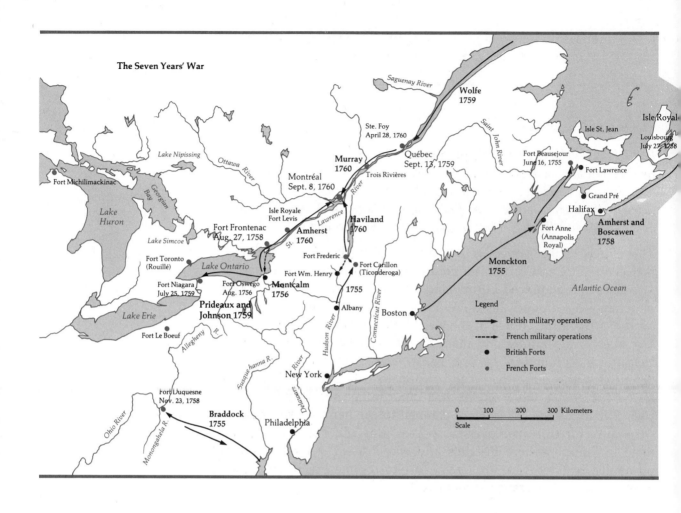

The Seven Years' War

Saguenay River

Wolfe
1759

Ste. Foy
April 28, 1760

Isle St. Jean

Isle Royal

Louisbourg
July 27, 1758

Murray
1760

Québec
Sept. 13, 1759

Fort Beausejour
June 16, 1755

Fort Lawrence

Montréal
Sept. 8, 1760

Trois Rivières

Saint John River

Grand Pré

Fort Michilimackinac

Lake Nipissing

Ottawa River

Lake
Huron

Georgian
Bay

Isle Royale
Fort Levis

Amherst
1760

Haviland
1760

Halifax

Amherst and
Boscawen
1758

Fort Frontenac
Aug. 27, 1758

St. Lawrence River

Fort Frederic

Fort Anne
(Annapolis
Royal)

Lake Simcoe

Fort Toronto
(Rouillé)

Lake Ontario

Fort Wm. Henry

Fort Carillon
(Ticonderoga)

Monckton
1755

Atlantic Ocean

Fort Niagara
July 25, 1759

Fort Oswego
Aug. 1756

Montcalm
1756

1755

Prideaux and
Johnson 1759

Lake Erie

Albany

Boston

Legend

Fort Le Boeuf

Allegheny R.

Connecticut River

→ British military operations

┄┄ French military operations

● British Forts

● French Forts

Susquehanna R.

Hudson River

Delaware River

New York

Fort Duquesne
Nov. 23, 1758

0 100 200 300 Kilometers

Braddock
1755

Philadelphia

Scale

Ohio River

Monongahela R.

Manufacturing hardly existed in New France; her farms produced little more than sufficient food for home consumption in time of peace. The Thirteen Colonies, on the other hand, boasted a diversified and expanding economy, with shipping and maritime trade, an agricultural industry that ranged from wheat to cotton, and many forms of manufacturing.

The Thirteen Colonies were anything but united. New France could probably have survived a short, hit-and-run war. It had done so in the past. If the war lasted a long time, the much greater British resources—including the navy—would likely mean the conquest of New France.

1. How much of this comparison of the rivals might have been known to anyone in New France in 1755? In New England?
2. Assuming you could have been a Canadian editor of a Montreal newspaper in 1755, write an editorial explaining what you think will happen if France and Britain go to war.
3. What different predictions might you make if you assume the role of editor of a newspaper in Boston? The role of a visiting editor from a neutral country?
4. What things might a historian, looking at the same kind of dilemma, take into account that the editors might not?

THE FIRST ENCOUNTER—THE OHIO VALLEY

During the century and a half since Britain and France had first laid claims to North America, areas of conflict had included Hudson Bay, the St. Lawrence, the Richelieu River—Lake Champlain region, and Acadia. The latter so often had been the area where hostilities broke out, where battles were fought. However, the all-out war that formed part of the global Seven Years' War began in the Ohio Valley and culminated on the banks of the St. Lawrence.

French expansion to the southwest was becoming a concern to English colonists. New France had not only claimed the Ohio Valley, but had built a number of forts to keep the English out. But the English interest in land was shown by George Washington,* who had organized a company to make claims in the area. The twenty-one-year-old Washington led an expedition against the French, but he was defeated in skirmishes near Fort Duquesne (present-day Pittsburgh, Pennsylvania).

*Later the first president of the United States of America.

THE CONFLICT SPREADS

The next year, 1755, Britain decided to help the colonists turn back the French expansion into the Ohio. Again, the result was failure, as

Studying the future?

Futuristics, or the study of alternative futures, has emerged in the 1970s as a way of thinking about problems and possible solutions and how they may affect the future. Futurists like Alvin Toffler, Arthur C. Clarke, John McHale or Herman Kahn, whether they be scientists, social scientists or writers, often think of three types of future—*probable*, *possible*, and *preferable*.

Take the problem of non-renewable natural resources. Studies may show that present rates of consumption will mean the exhaustion of petroleum, for example, within the lifetime of the present generation of teenagers. This kind of study reveals something of the *probable* future. An investigation of the *possible* future may show that there are alternative futures, depending on how people—either individually or collectively—choose to use their resources, techniques, etc. It may be decided, for example, either to put great efforts into developing new sources of energy or educating people to consume less and live simpler lives. At this point, one is faced with deciding which future is *preferable*. Such a choice depends on several things, including the study of the likely consequences of each choice, but, in the final analysis, the decision rests on the values people hold. If people persist in valuing "progress" in terms of wealth and material goods, such as large cars and complicated appliances, they will prefer the discovery and use of solar energy, nuclear power and so on. On the other hand, people may believe that such efforts are not going to succeed without serious damage to the environment. They may decide that it makes more sense to work at creating new attitudes about what is important in life. In other words, they are *preferring* an alternative future, based on a different set of values.

Futuristics, then, is not a way of *predicting* the future, in the fashion of a mystic peering into a crystal ball or cup of tea leaves. It is a kind of inquiry into the alternative forms the future may take—for the individual and/or for society as a whole. Futuristics is, in some respects, a uniquely 20th century way of thinking. Never before have individuals had such a bewildering array of personal choices, for example about how they will make a living, where they will live, what kinds of friends they will have, what values will be important to them.

Alternative futures and the Seven Years' War

See pages 132 and 134 for a prediction about the Seven Years' War.

1. What things might a futurist, looking at conditions before the Seven Years' War, have taken into account that editors and historians might not?

2. Voltaire (1694—1778), the French writer, philosopher and historian was an early futurist. What methods and tools of analysis are available to the modern futurist that were not available to Voltaire?

3. Why do you think the study of alternative futures is more urgent in the 20th century than it was in the 18th century?

Louisbourg today

This "great grey ghost" as the brochures distributed to tourists sometimes call Louisbourg has risen again on the fog-bound southeast coast of Cape Breton Island. Funds from the Canadian Government and the efforts of thousands working for well over a decade have contributed to the reconstruction of the once fabled fortress. Captured by the British in the summer of 1758 and subsequently demolished, Louisbourg was reduced to a stone quarry until the Canadian Government set the area aside as a national historic site in 1928. No longer could residents of the area haul away stone from the rubble to build foundations for their houses, and digging was now carried out by archaeologists and others interested in what could be learned from the remains. Small-scale reconstruction began as early as the 1930s, when a museum was built, but in 1961 the Canadian Government started a program to rebuild Louisbourg as it appeared when it was a French stronghold in the 1740s. Historians and archaeologists began the enormous task of research necessary to construct an authentic recreation of the fortress that had been

The fortress of Louisbourg in the early stages of reconstruction

destroyed 200 years before. They spent countless hours in the archives (public records) of Canada, the United States, Britain and France. At the site itself, weapons, tools, cookware and other relics were excavated and put on display, either in the museum or in the rooms of the more than forty buildings being restored. From the research, the teams of designers, engineers, draftsmen and tradesmen, many of the latter being retrained Cape Breton coal miners, have constructed the main buildings, and great efforts have been made to furnish the interiors as they were. The work goes on, as crowds of tourists pass through. Louis XV would be amazed.

1. Have you ever been to the public archives in your province? In your town? What does an archivist do?
2. Why do you think the Canadian Government would put so many resources into rebuilding an historic place? Do you think this is a waste of public money and effort? Why?

General Braddock's British army was routed. Expeditions against French forts in other areas were also unsuccessful, except for the capture of Fort Beausejour in Acadia.

The final struggle was underway in North America, even while France and England were still officially at peace. In 1756, when the expected European war began, New France undertook a vigourous defence. The new military commander, General Montcalm, prepared his French and Canadien forces for a series of assaults against key English forts. The capture of Fort Oswego on Lake Ontario and the victory at Ticonderoga on Lake Champlain secured two important approaches to New France.

THE TIDE TURNS: 1758–1759

The early trend toward French victories was reversed a short time after William Pitt, the new British Prime Minister, took charge of the British war effort. Recognizing the power of a combined land-and-sea operation against New France, Pitt encouraged a concerted attack in the main areas of French-English conflict. One by one the French forts fell in 1758. The capture of Fort Frontenac and Fort Duquesne gave the British control of the Ohio and upper St. Lawrence. Louisbourg, the key to French defence of the St. Lawrence, was blockaded by the British fleet and captured by the army under General Amherst.

Montcalm still held Ticonderoga, but he had no choice but to concentrate on a defence of the St. Lawrence Valley. In 1759, rear-

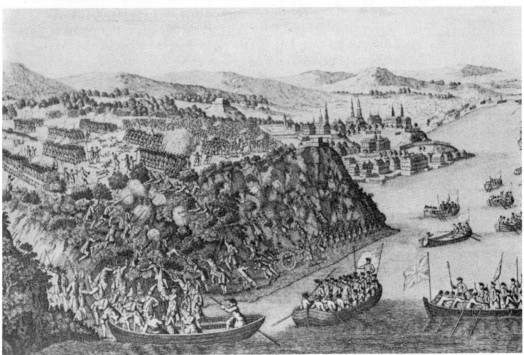

TOP: *General Wolfe directing his troops at the Battle of Quebec in 1759.* BOTTOM: *The Battle of Quebec. Why do you think this cove was left unprotected by the French forces?*

Even the fall of Quebec left the French with one last chance. They still held Montreal. In the spring of 1760, a French force moved down the St. Lawrence to attack Quebec. West of the town, at Ste. Foy, they defeated the English and prepared to lay siege to Quebec itself. Then the British navy came to the rescue once more. Further French resistance was hopeless, and at Montreal on September 8, 1760, Governor Vaudreuil surrendered New France.

guard actions delayed the British advances overland, but the British fleet proceeded up the St. Lawrence. On board was the army of General James Wolfe.

In the late summer of 1759, British guns bombarded Quebec atop the cliffs, but a landing seemed impossible. It appeared that the French could hold out until winter came and forced the British to withdraw. Then General Wolfe's army discovered the poorly defended cliff upstream from the French position. In September, Wolfe managed to slip past the French defences and land his troops for a surprise attack. Montcalm went forward at the head of his forces to meet the British on the open fields of the Plains of Abraham. The battle lasted less than an hour, and both Wolfe and Montcalm were killed. But the French had been defeated, and Quebec, the heart of New France, was in the hands of the British.

1. What reasons can you give for the defeat of New France?

MONTCALM'S PREDICTION OF FRENCH DEFEAT

Sir Richard Cartwright, a prominent Canadian politician, wrote in the 1880s:

The other day I came across a strange letter from the distinguished French General Montcalm, who fell in the great battle which finally decided the fate of North America. I find that Montcalm, who was not only a great general but a very able statesman, put on record a prediction of his own fall, declaring he would be defeated, and that he would not survive the loss of North America. He predicted also that ten years after Canada was conquered, the other colonies would assert their independence. As you know, who have paid attention to history, that was fulfilled almost to the hour and day. Canada was ceded to Great Britain in 1763, and within twelve years thereafter the first blood was drawn in the struggle which resulted in the independence of the United States of America. The letter first predicts that if General Wolfe understands his trade that Montcalm must be defeated; and declares that as this defeat means the total loss of North America, he will not survive.

"I console myself, nevertheless, for the prospect of my own defeat, and of the loss of the colony, by my firm conviction that this defeat will prove in the long run better than a victory for France, and that the conqueror, England, will find a tomb in her own conquest. This may appear a paradox, but a little reflection and a glance at the political situation in North America will prove the correctness of my opinion. A large portion of the English colonists are the children of men who left England during the period of the civil war, and betook themselves to America to find a country where they might live and die in freedom and independence. I know them thoroughly, not by hear-say, but by means of sure information and correspondence which I have arranged

Problems of writing history: "Just the facts" or "Facts plus..."?

History, to **romantic** historians like Francis Parkman, was more than maps in schoolbooks, constitutions, and generals making proclamations. History was made by people, and the people and their lives were as much a part of the history as were events, dates and places. When writing about a historical event, romantic historians tried to include as much of the drama and flavour of real life as they could. Sometimes, they were accused of inventing excitement or manufacturing suspense. Their reply, however, was that any historical event was more than a mere incident. The purely objective or scientific treatment of an event was not enough. The people who made history, they maintained, were fascinating individuals whose characters brought colour and life to events in which they played a part.

meaning dramatic, personalized history, not stories about love and passion

Thus it is that Francis Parkman writes the following of the great generals of the Seven Years' War, Wolfe and Montcalm:

> ...Wolfe himself led the charge, at the head of the Louisbourg grenadiers. A shot shattered his wrist. He wrapped his handkerchief about it and kept on. Another shot struck him, and he still advanced, when a third lodged in his breast. He staggered, and sat on the ground. Lieutenant Brown, of the grenadiers, one Henderson, a volunteer in the same company, and a private soldier, aided by an officer of artillery who ran to join them, carried him in their arms to the rear. He begged them to lay him down. They did so, and asked if he would have a surgeon. 'There's no need,' he answered; 'it's all over with me.' A moment after, one of them cried out: 'They run; see how they run!' 'Who run?' Wolfe demanded, like a man roused from sleep. 'The enemy, sir. Egad, they give way everywhere!' 'Go, one of you, to Colonel Burton,' returned the dying man; 'tell him to march Webb's regiment down to Charles River, to cut off their retreat from the bridge.' Then, turning on his side, he murmured, 'Now, God be praised, I will die in peace!' and in a few moments his gallant soul had fled.
>
> In the night of humiliation.... Surgeon Arnoux... whose younger brother [was] also a surgeon, examined the wound and pronounced it mortal. 'I am glad of it,' Montcalm said quietly; and then asked how long he had to live. 'Twelve hours, more or less,' was the reply. 'So much the better,' he returned. 'I am happy that I shall not live to see the surrender of Quebec.' He is reported to have said that since he had lost the battle it consoled him to have been defeated by so brave an enemy.... [11]

1. What are the "facts" in these statements?
2. What are the interpretations or judgments in these statements?

3. What are the benefits and limitations of romantic history? Of objective or scientific history?

---

myself, and which if my life had been prolonged, I had meant to turn to the advantage of France. In fact all the English colonists would have shaken off the yoke long ago, and every one of them would have become a little independent republic had it not been for the fear of France at their doors. As between two masters they preferred their own fellow countrymen to foreigners, taking care, meanwhile, to render no more obedience than they could help; but if Canada is conquered, and if the Canadians and the English Colonies become one people the very first occasion on which England will appear and interfere with their interests, do you suppose the Colonists will obey her? What have they to fear if they do revolt? I am so perfectly certain of the truth of what I have written that I will only allow ten years after the conquest of Canada to see my predictions accomplished. Now you see the reason which consoles me as a Frenchman for the imminent danger France is incurring of seeing Canada lost forever."[10]

1. In what ways did Montcalm seem to qualify as a futurist? (See pp. 128-129). What events does he accurately predict?
2. What reasons does he give for his prediction that France would lose the Seven Years' War in North America?

Military rule—a temporary state of affairs

The North American part of the Seven Years' War ended early with the Articles of Capitulation (terms of surrender). They were signed by the governor of New France and the British commander-in-chief for North America, General Geoffrey Amherst. Under the terms of surrender, Canadien militia were allowed to return to their homes, and, like other Canadiens, were assured that their property would not be taken away. Passage to France was provided for senior officials of the former colonial government. Others were free to leave, and some businessmen did so.

Most Canadiens chose to remain; in fact, hundreds of French soldiers, many of whom had married Canadien women, decided to stay. The Jesuits were not allowed to stay, but the orders of nuns, whose maintenance of hospitals was appreciated by the British, continued their work undisturbed. The "free exercise" of the Roman Catholic religion was not disturbed, and the Bishop and other church officials remained in the colony.

Meanwhile, the global war between Britain and France was still

The effects of the conquest

What were the effects of the Conquest, the British takeover of Canada? About the immediate effects, there is a large measure of agreement. The Canadiens were a conquered population, drained by a long war and faced with rule by foreigners. The future of their way of life was in danger. Historian Mason Wade explains:

> The position of the French Canadians was indeed desperate, and few contemporary observers would have risked much on their survival. The New France which had been so utterly dependent upon the mother country throughout its existence was now separated and isolated from the France which had supplied its rulers, its educators, and its apostles. If the French Canadians were to remain French, they had to do so on the strength of their own resources, under . . . a foreign power whose religion, language, laws, and customs were very different from their own. This foreign power had been the traditional enemy of the conquered people ever since the first seeds of French settlement had been sown in the New World.
>
> The French Canadians had lost much of their boldest and bravest blood in the wars which had occupied half their history, and they were exhausted by the long battle against overpowering odds. Their economic position was equally sorry: France had left them a legacy of 41,000,000 *livres* ($8,200,000) of inflated paper money, on which payment had been suspended and which was only partially redeemed years after the conquest. Merchant and farmer alike were ruined; Quebec stood shattered after two months' bombardment, and the lower St. Lawrence countryside had been systematically devastated by the conquerors as they advanced up the river.[12]

Interpreting the long-term significance of the Conquest is more difficult. For example, some claim that it caused the *decapitation* of a "nation in the making". Left without political and business leaders, French Canada fell to a lowly position under the domination of "les Anglais".

According to this view, the Conquest prepared the way for some two hundred years of less-than-equal status for French Canada. A change seemed possible only with the growth of confidence that accompanied the "Quiet Revolution" in Quebec.* For some, only the separation of Quebec from Canada would finally eliminate the unhappy heritage of the Conquest.

*See Volume 2, Chapter 10.

One of the best-known exponents of the "decapitation" theory is Michel Brunet. According to Brunet, French-Canadien leaders were denied "either the opportunity or the means to win prestige in public life." He notes that "the administration, the army, the navy and external trade were all preserves of the British."[13] Thus the French Canadiens, handicapped by the system that followed the Conquest, developed a sense of inferiority.

Critics of the "decapitation" theory claim that it is unsupported by factual information. The evidence, they say, suggests that New France was *not* a flourishing society at the time of the Conquest. Rather, it was an underdeveloped colony that was very dependent on France. Under French rule, conditions in the colony did not give rise to a business class or a diversified and stable economy. Thus New France was economically weak at the time of the Conquest.

Fernand Ouellet, specialist in social and economic history, writes:

> "The Conquest did not engender any essential change in the life of the inhabitant of the Laurentian [St. Lawrence] valley. It even, by eliminating the profiteers of the old system, clarified many situations and benefitted a number of merchants.... Immediately after 1760, the citizen of New France is not a being whose psychological buoyancy has been shattered and whose single destination is bondage. Fruitful perspectives open before him, multiple choices are evident in the challenges that bring themselves to his attention. His fate thus is related to the quality of his responses."[14]

British troops were appreciated by the inhabitants in one very important respect: the soldiers paid for goods in coin. Inflation—the decline in the purchasing power of money—had been severe in the last years of New France. At the time of the British takeover, paper money in circulation was almost worthless. Times were also hard because many businesses —including the fur trade—had been shattered by the war. Farms, especially in the area around the town of Quebec, had also been hard-hit. Income in the form of metal coins was particularly valuable.

being fought elsewhere, including Europe. Until the main war ended, the future of New France was undecided. There were two possible futures: (1) it would be permanently transferred to the British Empire; or (2) it would be exchanged by Britain for territories elsewhere, and returned to French control.

In the meantime, the British army holding New France had to set up a temporary government. The French districts were retained and military governors were put in charge of each: General Murray at Quebec, General Burton at Trois Rivières and General Gage at Montreal. All were answerable to the commander-in-chief, General Amherst, in New York.

While many questions about the future were unanswered, the British at least tried to remove fears of an "Acadian-type" solution. They were anxious to prevent any unrest that might lead to further trouble in a colony already disrupted by war. The affairs of the colony were carried on in French, with the governors assisted by French-speaking aides. The captains of militia acted as justices of the peace, to look after matters of law in the local areas. The seigneurial system was left untouched. British troops were well disciplined and generally an attitude of mutual respect existed between them and the Canadiens.

The Canadiens generally accepted the presence of the British during the period of military rule. No doubt there were many who clung to the hope that New France would be restored to French control some day. Yet there was a widespread feeling that France had neglected, even abandoned the colony. Thus the Canadiens had already begun to face the reality of being conquered and the likelihood of a future under foreign rule.

In 1763, the Treaty of Paris finally ended the Seven Years' War. Although there was some discussion that Britain might exchange the colony at the conference table for other territories, the Treaty finalized the status of Canada as a part of the British Empire. France gave up all claims to Canada, Acadia and Cape Breton. Of its once far-flung North American domain, France kept only the islands of St. Pierre and Miquelon.

Whether the period of military rule was mild or harsh is an old Canadian question. The French-Canadian historian, François Garneau, started a century of debate in the 1850s when his *History of Canada* depicted the "Reign of the Soldiery" as unnecessarily rigid and prolonged. Later writers, especially English-speaking ones, argued that the British were unusually considerate in their treatment of a conquered population. It is now apparent that the British were mainly practical. They had little, if anything, to gain from disturbing the Canadien population with sudden changes while the army was in charge. Military rule was the only alternative after the fall of New France and until a civilian government could be instituted following the Treaty of Paris (1763).

1. How important to the morale of a people engaged in war are the following:
(a) fear of losing
(b) national pride
(c) expectation of victory
(d) military supplies
(e) economic resources?

2. A people conquered in any struggle often fear that the worst is about to happen to them. What kinds of things do you suppose a Canadien journalist might have written in an editorial about the prospect of military rule in 1760?

3. What, in fact, happened under military rule was not nearly as calamitous as the Canadiens feared. Why not?

4. The Conquest is an important period in Canadian history and, like other important periods, is highly controversial. How do the following "problems of writing history" make it difficult to arrive at a single explanation of the Conquest: (a) availability of facts (b) new ways of examining the facts, e.g. applying ideas and methods from the social sciences (c) the values of the writers (d) the political situation at the time of writing?

6

Experiments in government: the early days of Canadian biculturalism

The scene is Governor James Murray's headquarters in the town of Quebec. The date is late 1763. Seated around a huge table strewn with maps and many official-looking papers are eleven men. They look very troubled, and seem to be debating a difficult problem.

Characters:
General James Murray, governor of the colony
General Haldimand, lieutenant-governor, Trois-Rivières
General Thomas Gage, lieutenant-governor, Montreal
Eight councillors,* just appointed, from among the residents of the colony.

*Including army officers, an engineer, a doctor, and an English-speaking, Protestant businessmen.

The forerunner of the Colonial Office; in charge of deciding, in general terms, how a colony was to be run.

Remember that *Canadien* meant French inhabitants of the colony.

Murray: As you all know, I am expecting further instructions from the **Board of Trade** any time now. Members of the Board have been trying to work out an overall government plan for British colonies in North America. Since Quebec is so different from all the others, any plan is bound to be unsuited to it in some ways. We can expect problems—especially if we impose an English system on the **Canadiens**.

Gage: One thing is certain. The situation is going to get more complicated now that the colony is going to have civil government instead of keeping the army in charge.

1st Councillor: The army did manage fairly well. The Canadiens were able to live, by and large, as they had before we took over. But we were just marking time, in a way. Sooner or later the army was going to hand government over.

2nd Councillor: That's right. But the fact remains that the problems are huge. Most of the people here are French-speaking and Catholic. What are the figures? 70 000? 80 000? They are used to French laws. Their ways are different. . . .

3rd Councillor: But I would remind you that the Canadiens must expect a government in which they don't have a voice. Under the French system, they expected their political leaders to make the decisions. It would take a while before Canadiens could take part in **representative government**, if it was set up like the ones in the Thirteen Colonies.

Gage: What is your point?

3rd Councillor: I'm really saying two things. One, Englishmen are moving into Quebec—mainly from our colonies to the south. A merchant who comes here from Massachusetts is bound to want the rights of Englishmen here. Quebec is a British colony now. Second, the Canadien is going to have to learn English ways—for his own survival.

2nd Councillor: But the first problem is what to do about the Canadiens in the near future. Right now, and probably for some time to come, they are a huge majority. They aren't going to become Englishmen overnight.

Murray: The councillor makes sense. The Canadiens are the first concern. What alternatives could the Board of Trade be thinking about?

> Any system of government in which the people are able to elect representatives to speak on their behalf.

This scene is purely imaginary. However, it does suggest a conversation that *could* have taken place among British officials after the Treaty of Paris (1763) completed the transfer of New France to the British Empire. The British were the victors; the Canadiens— French-speaking and, for the most part, born and raised in the St. Lawrence Valley—were a conquered people. The conversation ends with Murray thinking aloud about alternatives. What, in fact, were the choices available to the British?

Expulsion, like the Acadians?

Anglicization, so the Canadiens would think, talk and act like Englishmen?

Continuation of a system that the Canadiens are used to, in the hope that they would be loyal to Britain—even if they kept their French culture?

Separate territories, with separate systems of government and laws, for the Canadiens and the English?

1. In the above conversation, what attitudes are expressed by (a) Governor Murray (b) Gage (c) each of the councillors?
2. What were the "pros" and "cons" of each of the four alternatives?

	"PROS"	"CONS"
Expulsion Anglicization "French" system Separate territories		

3. Which alternative would you expect the British to try first? Why?

> In studying the "experiments" in government, one must keep in mind that the *big decisions* were made in England. The British Parliament, on recommendations from the Board of Trade, decided that a certain form of colonial government was best. The governor in the colony then received written instructions on how to put the policies of Britain into action. But this arrangement still left the governor and his council much leeway—and therefore power—in interpreting how acts of Parliament and instructions from England could be best applied in the colony.

The first experiment: Royal Proclamation, 1763—Anglicization

UNDERLYING IDEA

The Royal Proclamation, 1763, was Britain's first "experiment" in governing Quebec. Britain hoped that its new colony could be governed in much the same way as its other North American colonies. To make this possible, the Royal Proclamation introduced a program of *Anglicization*. The Canadiens would be expected, in as short a time as possible, to adjust to the English language, English government and English laws. The key to *Anglicization* was the hope that it would attract, from the Thirteen Colonies mainly, an influx of English-speaking settlers. They would help to give the colony an English character and rebuild the shattered economy.

Britain had more to worry about than setting up a new government in Quebec. Its North American territories stretched from Hudson Bay to Florida and from the Atlantic Ocean to the Mississippi. The cost of maintaining the colonies had risen sharply as a result of the Seven Years' War. Besides the French, many new groups of

Pontiac's uprising

In the spring of 1763, before news of the Treaty of Paris reached the interior, Pontiac, a chief of the Ottawas, launched an attack in the area of Detroit that touched off an Indian uprising. South of the Great Lakes, from Fort Niagara to Michilimackinac, the warfare spread. Several posts were overcome and hundreds of settlers killed. It took several expeditions of British troops to end the bloody fighting which raged through the summer.

What had caused the sudden, and apparently spontaneous attacks by the "western" tribes—the Senecas, Ottawas, Shawnees, Chippewas, to name a few? Most of these Indians had a long history of trading with the French. French traders still operating on the Mississippi encouraged the Indians to think that a return of French power to North America was still possible. Most of the former French forts were now held by the English, however, and the absence of competition enabled them to pay much lower prices for furs. Perhaps even more serious was the influx of English settlers, who took up land near the posts and seemed intent on occupying Indian territory.

> The conquest was seen by the Indians as an attempt at their eventual extermination. Thus the Ottawa chief Pontiac gave this message to his people:
> "Why do you suffer the white men to dwell among you?... Why do you not clothe yourselves in skins, as your ancestors did, and use the bows and arrows, and the stone-pointed lances, which they used?... You have bought guns, knives, kettles, and blankets, from the white men, until you can no longer do without them; and, what is worse, you have drunk the poison firewater, which turns you into fools. Fling all these things away... And as for these English .... you must lift the hatchet against them ... "[1]

1. In this passage, what two actions is Pontiac urging his followers to take?
2. Could one be accomplished without the other? Why or why not?
3. In what way does Pontiac blame the Indians for part of their own predicament?

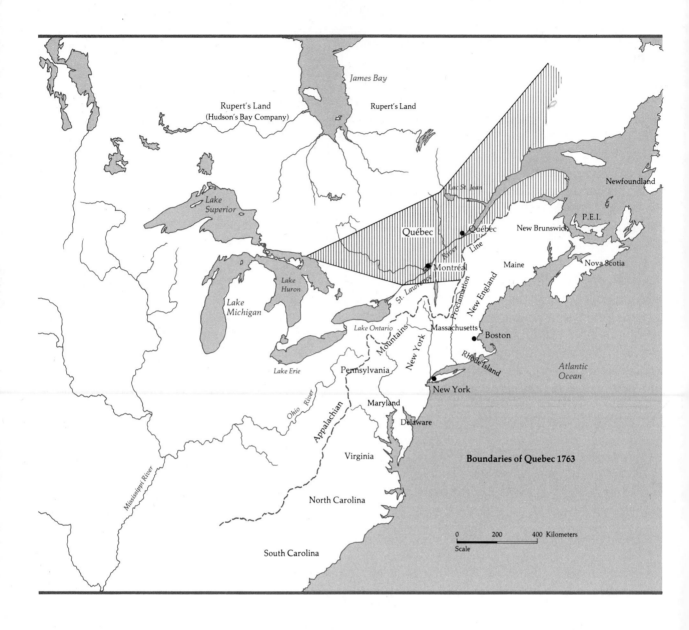

Rupert's Land
(Hudson's Bay Company)

James Bay

Rupert's Land

Newfoundland

Lake
Superior

Lac St. Jean

P.E.I.

Québec

Québec
Line

New Brunswick

Maine

Nova Scotia

Lake
Huron

Montréal

New England

Lake
Michigan

St. Lawrence River

Proclamation

Lake Ontario

Massachusetts

Boston

Lake Erie

Mountains

New York

Rhode Island

Atlantic
Ocean

Pennsylvania

Ohio River

New York

Maryland

Delaware

Boundaries of Quebec 1763

Appalachian

Virginia

North Carolina

Mississippi River

0   200   400 Kilometers

Scale

South Carolina

Indians had come under British rule. For such reasons as these, Britain decided upon an overhaul of its entire colonial system in North America.

GOVERNMENT
—capital: the town of Quebec
—structure of government:
(1) governor, appointed
(2) council appointed, including the lieutenant-governors of Trois-Rivières and Montreal, and residents or property owners in the colony
—an elected assembly *promised for later*, as soon as circumstances would permit
—Roman Catholics *not allowed* to hold public office

LAWS
—English law was to replace Canadien law (i.e. law based on that of France); this was not to happen overnight, since drastic changes were involved. The two sets of laws were very different. Furthermore, Governor Murray had no legal training himself, and there were very few English lawyers in the colony.
—Canadien law had to be continued, for the time being, in civil cases. Most of these involved disputes between persons over property, and therefore concerned the seigneurial system, with the laws, duties and customs left over from New France.

RELIGION
—Freedom of worship continued; permission was granted for a Roman Catholic bishop* to be appointed by the Pope.
—The Church of England (Anglican) was to be promoted as the Protestant (non-Catholic) church; it was hoped that the Canadiens would eventually switch from Catholicism to Protestantism.
—Protestant schools were to be set up and given financial aid.

*Bishop Briand, a personal friend of Governor Murray's, was appointed in 1766.

MURRAY'S INSTRUCTIONS
Among instructions sent to him by his superiors in England, Murray was advised that:

And whereas We have stipulated, by the late Definitive Treaty of Peace concluded at Paris the 10th day of February 1763, to grant the Liberty of the Catholick Religion to the Inhabitants of Canada, and that We will consequently give the most precise and most effectual Orders, that Our new Roman Catholick Subjects in that Province may profess the Worship of their Religion, according to

The first "experimental" British government in Quebec produced much confusion. Other than the disastrous example of Acadia, Britain had no past examples to learn from; the British had no choice but to try to invent a new system. They had a general idea in Anglicization, but it was such a sweeping plan for changing Quebec that it was going to take time. Changes had to be made in bits and pieces; some parts of the old system continued, while parts of a new system were being tried. Therefore, there could be nothing clear-cut about government, laws or religion.

the Rites of the Romish Church, as far as the Laws of Great Britain permit. . . .

And to that End that the Church of England may be established both in Principles and Practice, and that the said Inhabitants may by Degrees be induced to embrace the Protestant Religion, and their Children be brought up in the Principles of it; We do hereby declare it to be Our Intention, when the said Province shall have been accurately surveyed, and divided into Townships, Districts, Precincts or Parishes, in such manner as shall be hereinafter directed, all possible Encouragement shall be given to the erecting Protestant Schools in the said Districts, Townships and Precincts, by settling, appointing and allotting proper Quantities of Land for that Purpose, and also for . . . Maintenance of a Protestant Minister and Protestant School-Masters; and you are to consider and report to Us, by Our Commissioners for Trade and Plantations, by what other Means the Protestant Religion may be promoted, established and encouraged in Our Province under your Government.[2]

1. What do Murray's instructions say about
   a) the Canadiens and their Catholic religion,
   b) the Protestant religion?

REACTIONS

From the beginning, the Royal Proclamation seemed doomed to failure. The boundary was unrealistic. The restrictions on the fur trade in the newly-created Indian reserve inhibited the industry which remained the prime hope of Quebec's economic growth. Other businesses—agriculture, fishing and the iron industry at St. Maurice—grew but slowly. Moreover, the hoped for influx of English-speaking settlers did not occur.

The French-speaking population, meanwhile, grew quickly through natural increase, and assured the continuation of the social structure as it was in the days of New France. Yet the dominant groups, the clergy and the seigneurs, were uneasy with the Proclamation. Because the French Catholic citizens no longer had to pay the tithe, or church tax, the financial basis of the Catholic Church in Quebec was in doubt. And because English law was being gradually introduced, the future of the seigneurial system, under which the Church was a major landholder, was also insecure. The promise of an elected assembly was alarming. Such an assembly might pass restrictive laws and levy taxes. Such obligations had rarely been imposed on the Canadiens during French rule.

The British merchants had mixed feelings about the Proclamation at first. They welcomed the promise of an elected assembly and other changes that heralded an "anglicized"* colony. An assembly,

*Remember that "anglicized" means converted to English ways and institutions.

which by English law would not admit Catholics, would give the British minority the political power to dominate the colony. However, the merchants soon found that Governor Murray did not intend to hand over lawmaking powers to less than 500 in a population of 80 000. Such a move would certainly have undermined whatever goodwill had been created by the lenient treatment of the Canadiens in the first years of British rule.

James Murray

Murray found himself in an impossible position as the governor responsible for trying to make the Proclamation Act work. The army, which he had previously commanded, was removed from his control. He frequently disagreed with the new officer in charge. Tension between the army and the English merchants led to a number of incidents. The English merchants were impatient about Murray's lack of enthusiasm for pushing ahead with the "anglicization" of the colony. And Murray was concerned about the fears of the Canadiens. He believed it would be unwise and unfair to impose an English system on them. Furthermore, he was a soldier. Without competent legal advice he would have been hard-pressed, without all the other problems, to organize a new system of government and laws.

Under the circumstances, Murray devoted considerable energy to meeting the needs of the Canadiens. He admired the peaceful, law-abiding people who, it seemed, knew their place, and kept it. Eventually he saw the ambitious and aggressive merchants as "Licentious Fanaticks," who favoured democracy which Murray thought was not suited to Quebec and which was a definite threat to orderly government there.

CANADIEN CONFUSION ABOUT ENGLISH LAWS

Most writers have given their sympathy to the Canadians, and understandably. They had been accustomed to . . . simple and cheap justice. . . . French law, both civil and criminal, was expressed in general maxims, interpreted and applied by the judge to the particular case. Courts sat weekly or oftener under the eye of the intendant who was prepared to intervene at any stage if he disapproved of the proceedings.

In contrast to this method and approach the English system must have appeared extraordinarily cold, heavy, and brutal, with its rigid substantial and procedural laws, its elaborate machinery, and above all its terrifying impersonality, its apparent dedication to method and form with complete indifference to the results. . . . It was difficult for them to understand the stubborn tradition which associated the sacredness of the written law, of clearly defined customary procedure, and above all of trial by jury, with the liberty of the individual; it might have been still more difficult for them to understand why this abstract liberty was more precious than speed, economy, simplicity, and a reasonable chance of an equitable decision. It was equally impossible for the English to understand how anyone could prefer the former Canadian system.[3]

The merchants saw Murray as an obstacle, and made their protests against him known to the British government. Since the merchants had strong influence in Britain, they were able to force Murray's recall in 1766.

MURRAY AND THE MERCHANTS

English merchants in Quebec petitioned the King for the recall of Murray and the granting of an elected assembly:

The Governor instead of acting agreeable to that confidence reposed in him by your Majesty, in giving a favorable Reception to those of your Majesty's Subjects, who petition and apply to him on such important Occasions as require it, doth frequently treat them with a Rage and Rudeness of Language and Demeanour, as dishonorable to the Trust he holds of your Majesty as painful to those who suffer from it.

We could enumerate many more Sufferings which render the Lives of your Majesty's Subjects, especially your Majesty's loyal British Subjects, in the Province so very unhappy that we must be under the Necessity of removing from it, unless timely prevented by a Removal of the present Governor.

Your Petitioners therefore most humbly pray your Majesty . . . to appoint a Governor over us, acquainted with other maxims of Government than Military only; . . . to order a House of Representatives to be chosen in this as in other your [sic] Majesty's Provinces; there being a number more than Sufficient of Loyal and well affected Protestants, exclusive of military Officers, to form a competent and respectable House of Assembly. . . . [4]

Governor Murray gave the British government his view of the English merchants:

Little, very little will content the New Subjects but nothing will satisfy the Licentious Fanaticks Trading here, but the expulsion of the Canadians who are perhaps the bravest and the best race upon the Globe, a Race, who cou'd they be indulged with a few priveledges w^{ch} [sic] the Laws of England deny to Roman Catholicks at home, wou'd soon get the better of every National Antipathy to their Conquerors and become the most faithful and most useful set of Men in this American Empire.

P.S. I have been informed that Messrs Willm Mackenzie, Alex^r Mckenzie and Willm Grant have been solliciting their Friends in London to prevail upon your Lordships to get them admitted into his Majesty's Council of this Province. I think it my Duty to acquaint your Lordships that the first of these Men is a notorious smugler and a Turbulent Man, the second a weak Man of little character and the third a conceited Boy. In short it will be impossible to do Business with any of them.[5]

Historian A. L. Burt describes Murray's dilemma as first governor of Quebec:

The history of Murray's civil administration of the province of Quebec is the story of a man overwhelmed by a sea of troubles. Probably no British governor has ever been thrust into a more impossible position than that in which he found himself. Being forced to oppress a people whom he admired and pitied was only one part of his embarrassment. He was involved in a most confused and exasperating three-cornered quarrel with the garrison of the colony and with the little community of English-speaking merchants who had come to seek their fortunes on the shores of the St. Lawrence. He had also to face a task which under any circumstances would have been far from easy—that of inaugurating the civil regime; and for this he was given means that were utterly inadequate. The upshot was that the home government recalled him in disgrace before he was able to accomplish much for his beloved Canadians.[6]

During his brief term, Murray had introduced a only partial system of English law. Much of the Canadien law, as well as the seigneurial system, remained. The Catholic Church had been permitted to appoint a bishop. Murray had taken no action to set up an elected assembly, nor to grant many other demands of the English minority. In other words, very little start had been made on **assimilating** the Canadiens.

Sir Guy Carleton succeeded Murray in Quebec. The influence of Murray's enemies had given him a negative view of Murray and his policies. Soon after his arrival in the colony, Carleton dismissed some of Murray's associates from the Council and showed signs of being willing to work with the English merchants.

It was only a matter of time before Carleton began to see the situation in Quebec in much the same way that Murray had. Firmly establishing the authority of Britain in the colony was the primary duty of the governor. Essential to that goal, Carleton believed, was winning the support of the Canadiens, who were by far the majority of the population.

the idea of anglicization underlying the Proclamation Act meant assimilating the Canadiens into an English way of life.

Guy Carleton

Carleton, the soldier-aristocrat, admired Canadien society, and felt a kinship with its leaders, the seigneurs and the clergy. By the same token, he found the English merchants hard to get along with. He found them to be aggressive and believed them to be misguided in their desire for an assembly.

CARLETON'S VIEWS ON THE SITUATION IN QUEBEC

Carleton had come to the conclusion that the Proclamation Act was unsuited to the situation in Quebec:

(A) ...barring Catastrophe shocking to think of, this Country must, to the end of Time, be peopled by the Canadian Race, who already have taken such firm Root, and got to so great a Height, that any new Stock transplanted will be totally hid, and imperceptible amongst them, except in the Towns of Quebec and Montreal.[7]

(B) ...the better Sort of Canadians fear nothing more than popular Assemblies, which, they conceive, tend only to render the People refractory and insolent [hard to handle]; Enquiring what they thought of them, they said, they understood some of our Colonies had fallen under the King's Displeasure, owing to the Misconduct of their Assemblies, and that they should think themselves unhappy, if a like Misfortune befell them. It may not be improper here to observe, that the British Form of Government, transplanted into this Continent, never will produce the same Fruits as at Home, chiefly, because it is impossible for the Dignity of the Throne, or Peerage to be represented in the American Forests....[8]

The following imaginary conversation might have taken place between Governor Carleton and his adviser, Francis Maseres, perhaps in 1770:

Maseres: I agree that the Proclamation Act is not suited to this colony.

Carleton: As we have discussed many times, the Proclamation Act is not realistic. The promise of an elected assembly disturbs me, since it only encourages the unruly streak in our English businessmen. Along with the idea of English laws and the promotion of the Protestant religion, the assembly offends our Canadien friends. Even if we give them the chance to hold public office, they prefer a more orderly system.

Maseres: No doubt you are right about the attitudes of Bishop Briand, and the more important seigneurs. Yet I can see the benefits to the Empire of a Canadien population that is separated from its dependency on the Pope and his agents.

Carleton: That is not practical, nor wise. The church leaders are anxious to be our allies; through them we can influence the whole population.

Maseres: The seigneurs have also expressed their wish to be of service to His Majesty.

Carleton: I agree wholeheartedly that the seigneurs should be important. They are essential to a stable society, in which a man knows his place. A class of seigneurs with a tradition of military and political service to the government would be a valuable kind of support.

Maseres: And the habitants?

Carleton: Surely, they will follow their leaders, and act in a spirit of loyalty.

Maseres: It is urgent that we have the support of the Canadiens.

Carleton: Absolutely urgent. The agitation in the colonies to the south of us could lead to revolution. If it does, we can expect trouble from France, and meddling among the Canadiens by agents of Louis XVI. We must assure ourselves of a loyal Canadien population.

In this imaginary conversation, Carleton states certain facts. He also makes some important assumptions (things taken for granted). What are these assumptions? What if Carleton is wrong? Which ones prove to be wrong? You will find out the answers to these questions when we look at the Quebec Act and the American Revolution.

1. For what reasons was the Proclamation of 1763 proving to be unsuitable as the basis for governing Quebec?
2. What groups did Carleton believe must be encouraged to support British rule in Quebec?
3. What changes in the constitution of Quebec did Carleton seem to have in mind?

The second experiment: the Quebec Act—Anglicization reversed

THE UNDERLYING IDEA

The Quebec Act of 1774, was, in many ways, a reversal of the policy of "anglicization" attempted by the Proclamation Act. In the opinion of Carleton and his close advisers, Quebec was likely to remain **Canadian** in character far into the future. The trickle of English settlers into the colony was not changing the make-up of the population to any extent. "Anglicization" of the Canadians, if it ever was to succeed, would take many years. And then it might lead to the kind of unrest that had become evident in the Thirteen Colonies,

"Canadian" means "French Canadian"

where the colonial assemblies were challenging Britain's authority.

The continuation of Quebec within the British Empire seemed to require the active loyalty of the Canadians. To win this loyalty, Carleton advised the British government to cooperate with their leaders, the seigneurs and clergy. They, in turn, could be expected to persuade the habitants to appreciate and support the British.

There was little time to lose. Conditions in the Thirteen Colonies were getting worse, and the danger of revolt against Britain was growing. The possibility that France would take advantage of Britain's difficulties was even more disturbing. Steps had to be taken to make Quebec secure against appeals from Britain's enemies, and to strengthen it as a base from which to launch military operations if the need arose.

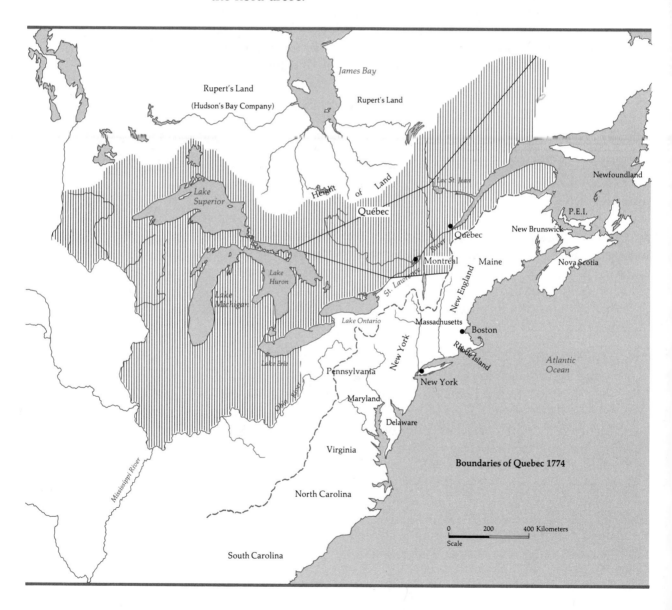

BOUNDARIES

The Quebec Act of 1774 enlarged the colony considerably. There was a growing need for a system of law and order in the region between the Mississippi and Ohio Rivers. The fur trade, dominated by St. Lawrence merchants and traders, was expanding. Relations with Indians of the area were becoming more complicated. Thus a vast territory immediately west of the Thirteen Colonies was brought under the laws of Quebec.

GOVERNMENT

—capital: the town of Quebec
—structure of government:
(a) governor, appointed
(b) council appointed, enlarged to include between 17 and 23 members
—elected assembly *denied*
—Roman Catholics *allowed* to hold public office; i.e. able to be members of the council, judges, and so on.
—Government income to be provided by customs duties (taxes on imported rum and molasses)*.

*According to Quebec Revenue Act, also passed in 1774.

LAWS

—English *criminal* law was to continue.
—Canadian civil law was to remain fully intact; the attempt to introduce English law as an instrument for assimilating the Canadian to the "English way of life" was dropped.
—The governor was given authority to grant lands according to the British **freehold** system.

Whereby a person bought land outright, without any dues to a seigneur.

RELIGION

—The right to practice the Catholic religion was guaranteed.
—Rather than being merely tolerated, the Roman Catholic Church was officially restored to its "property and civil rights." Among other things, this meant that the Church now had the legal right to enforce payment of tithes (church taxes) by Catholics.
—A special oath, acceptable to Catholics, was provided, so that Catholics would not be barred from holding public office.
—Government support of "the Protestant religion" was to continue.

REACTIONS

The Quebec Act evoked immediate, and quite different reactions. Within a year, the American Revolution* tested the intended purpose of the Act, with some results that surprised the British.

The English minority had mixed feelings. The fur traders approved of the extended boundary, which strengthened their hold

*See pages 165-173. The reaction to the American Revolution is inseparable from the immediate reactions to the Quebec Act.

on the trade of the vast region south of the Great Lakes. Nevertheless, they resented the provisions of the Quebec Act concerning government and laws.

AN EXTREME REACTION

On the morning when the detested act came into force, the citizens of the town awoke to find that during the night some unknown hands had taken insulting liberties with the king's bust on the Place d'Armes. The face was blackened, and around the neck hung a rosary of potatoes bearing a wooden cross with [an insulting inscription] . . . * The guilty were never discovered, though a reward of fifty guineas was promised by the officers or the Twenty-sixth Regiment, then in Montreal, and another of two hundred dollars by the governor.[9]

*Voila le Pape du Canada ou le sot Anglais."

Needless to say the insult to His Majesty raised many tempers to the boiling point. One of the new councilors . . . who was present . . . when the officers' reward was published, cried out that he would like to see "the detestable wretches whipped by the hands of the hangman and then turned out of the province," and he added that this penalty "would be too lenient, for they deserved to be hanged." His words were caught up by a young man named Franks. He was the son of a Quebec merchant and had just completed his education in Philadelphia. To his retort, "Hanged! What, for such a trifle!" . . . [The councillor] burst out, "What! Do you look upon the transaction as a trifle? You are a giddy-headed insolent spark." . . . [The councillor] seized him by the nose, and the young fellow "returned the compliment by a blow with his fist over the right eye which deprived the old gentleman of his senses for some time and was the occasion of the loss of some blood."[10]

PETITIONS FOR THE REPEAL OF THE QUEBEC ACT.
TO THE KING'S MOST EXCELLENT MAJESTY.
THE PETITION
(Of Your Majesty's most Loyal and Dutiful
Your Ancient Subjects settled in the Province of
Quebec)

MOST HUMBLY SHEWETH

THAT We upon the Faith of your Sacred Majesty's Royal Proclamation bearing Date the Seventh Day of October which was in the Year of Our Lord One thousand seven Hundred and Sixty three Did come and Settle ourselves in the said Province purchasing Houses and Lands and carrying on extensive Trade Commerce and Agriculture whereby the Value of the Land and Wealth of it's Inhabitants are more than doubled during all which Time, We humbly crave leave to say that we have paid a ready and dutiful Obedience to Government and have lived in Peace and Amity with your Majesty's new Subjects. Nevertheless we find and with unutterable Grief presume to say that by a late Act of Parliament intitled "An Act for the making more effectual Provision for the Government of the Province of QUEBEC in North America" We are deprived of the Franchises granted by Your Majesty's Royal Predecessors and by us inherited from our Forefathers THAT We have lost the Protection of the English Laws so universally admired for their Wisdom and Lenity and which we have ever held in the highest Veneration and in their Stead the Laws of CANADA are to be introduced to which we are utter Strangers disgraceful to us as Britons and in their Consequences ruinous to our Properties as we thereby lose the invaluable Privilege of TRIAL by JURIES. THAT in Matters of a Criminal Nature the HABEUS CORPUS Act is dissolved and we are Subjected to arbitrary Fines and Imprisonment at the Will of the Governor and Council who may at Pleasure render the Certainty of the Criminal Laws of no Effect by the great

Power that is granted to them of making Alterations in the same.

WE therefore MOST HUMBLY IMPLORE your Majesty to take our unhappy state into your Royal Consideration and grant us such Relief as your Majesty in your Royal Wisdom shall think meet.
And your Petitioners as in Duty bound
Will ever Pray.[11]

The church leaders responded most favourably. The Roman Catholic Church had been restored almost to the position of strength it had enjoyed in the days of New France.

The seigneurs as a class reacted in a similar way. The Act retained the social structure which gave them a special role in the colony. Ther position of the seigneur had been seriously threatened by the Proclamation of 1763, but the Quebec Act had apparently restored them to a leading position. The war-time conditions caused by the American Revolution increased the hopes of many siegneurs for a military and political status even more prominent than that they had held under the French.

The general Canadian population was less enthusiastic about the Quebec Act than the British expected. The habitants did not automatically follow their leaders. During the American Revolution, large numbers rejected the appeals from clergy and seigneurs to join the British efforts against the Americans.

The habitants were, at best, indifferent. The Quebec Act did encourage the continuation of the "Canadian way of life"; however, it also re-established the tithe (church tax) and seigneurial dues.

"THE SILENT MAJORITY"

Historian Hilda Neatby explains the difficulty of finding out the reactions of the Canadians:

It is difficult to determine what were the general views and wishes of the Canadian people in 1774. As most critics would agree that justice and humanity demanded at least some attention to the wishes of the Canadians, this gap in historical evidence is a serious one. Formal petitions by Canadians have survived. Some other evidence exists. Unfortunately, the majority of Canadians at that time could not write and it may be assumed that many things written have not survived or have not been found. Among the clergy, especially, many whose views would have been interesting may have thought it wiser not to express them in writing. It is difficult even today with the aid of scientific polls to say what, at a given moment, a given group of people 'want.' On the wants of Canadians in 1774, it is inevitable that the fragmentary evidence surviving should be interpreted in different ways.[12]

*See Chapter 7, p. 165.

In the Thirteen Colonies, the British Americans viewed the Quebec Act as one of Britain's "intolerable acts."* The extended boundary, which attached the Ohio Valley to Quebec, was seen as proof that Britain meant to prevent the westward expansion of American settlement. The terms dealing with government, laws and religion increased suspicions that Britain was "trying to turn back the clock" to a time when colonies were more tightly controlled.

The immediate value of the Quebec Act has been questioned, since it did not unite the population of the colony against a foreign threat. It further provoked already hostile American leaders; some would consider the Quebec Act to be one of the causes of the American Revolution. The Quebec Act did perpetuate Canadian culture in terms of the French language, laws and customs of French origin, and the Roman Catholic Church. These conditions were preserved in Lower Canada when the Quebec Act was replaced by the Constitutional Act in 1791.

1. What new developments had made the Quebec Act unsuitable as the basis for administering Quebec?

2. What new features of government, laws and so on seemed to be necessary to handle the new situation?

The third experiment:
separate territories—the Constitutional Act, 1791

THE UNDERLYING IDEA

The American Revolution may not have been Carleton's "catastrophe too shocking to think of", but it made the Quebec Act obsolete within a decade of its passage. After the Revolution, thousands of Loyalists poured into the area of Quebec west of the Ottawa—St. Lawrence junction, making it an English-speaking non-Catholic region. Promised the rights and liberties of Englishmen, the Loyalists would not be satisfied with the Quebec Act, designed as it was to ensure the loyalty of French Canadians.

Once more Britain was obliged to devise a new scheme for ruling her North American colonies—the third time in about twenty-five years. Again, the system needed to be adjusted to the major population groups. A new concern was to prevent the remaining colonies from drifting away from the British Empire. It was widely believed in Britain that the assemblies in the Thirteen Colonies had had too much power. They had gained so much control over government spending that they were able to challenge the authority of their governors, and eventually felt strong enough to defy the British Empire itself.

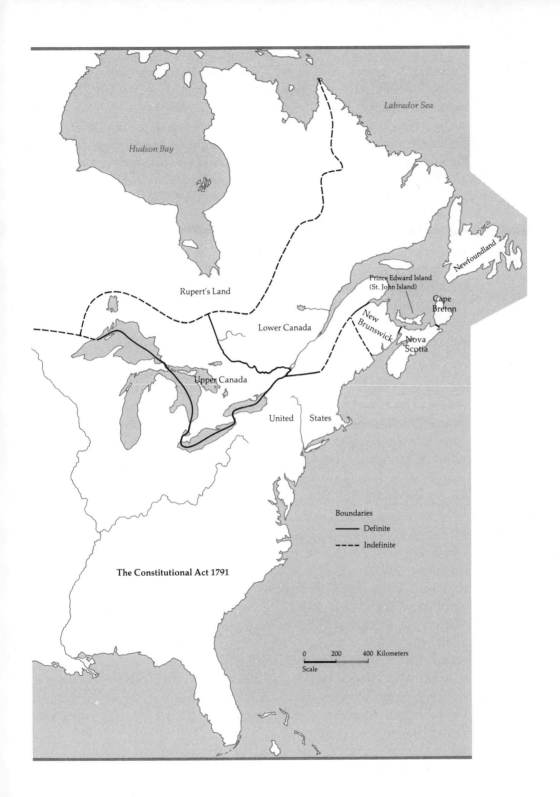

Hudson Bay

Labrador Sea

Rupert's Land

Lower Canada

Prince Edward Island
(St. John Island)

New
Brunswick

Cape
Breton

Nova
Scotia

Newfoundland

Upper Canada

United   States

The Constitutional Act 1791

Boundaries
——— Definite
- - - - Indefinite

0   200   400 Kilometers
Scale

A form of representative government was to be granted in the Canadian colonies. An elected assembly had been established in Nova Scotia in 1758. Therefore, the Loyalists expected the same rights in Quebec. Furthermore, introducing an elected assembly could save the British government some of the costs of administering and defending the colony. Taxes could be levied through the people's elected representatives. Thus Britain would not be accused of "taxation without representation."

However, the power of the assemblies was to be kept in check. They were not to become the instruments of "mob rule" as many British thought they had been in the rebellious American colonies. Real authority was to remain in the hands of the top officials, appointed by the British government. Further guarantees of orderly government and society would be provided by the creation of a colonial upper class and an established Protestant church.

BOUNDARIES

The international boundary between *British* North America and the new United States had been established by the Treaty of Versailles (1783). The Constitutional Act then assumed the division of the colony of Quebec into two parts: Lower Canada (east) and Upper Canada (west). In an attempt to simplify the governing of French Canadians and English Canadians, Britain decided that two separate territories might be the answer—even though a minority of English remained in Lower Canada.

GOVERNMENT
—capitals:
(a) Lower Canada—the town of Quebec
(b) Upper Canada—Newark (now Niagara-on-the-lake), transferred to York (now Toronto) in 1793.
—structure of government (the same in both Upper and Lower Canada):
(a) governor,* appointed by Britain
(b) executive council, appointed by the governor; advised the governor; very influential in the *execution* (carrying out) of decisions. Answerable to the governor, and through him, to the British government, rather than to the general public.
(c) legislative council, appointed by the governor; concerned with making the laws about matters of local concern—land, public works, education. Had the power to block bills proposed by the assembly.
(d) assembly, elected at least every four years by qualified voters; also concerned with legislative, or law-making, activity. Had a voice in the levying of taxes within the colony. Bills proposed by the

*Actually each colony had a lieutenant-governor. The lieutenant-governor of Lower Canada played two roles, since he was also the governor of all British North America.

assembly could be blocked (vetoed) by the councils and/or the governor.

—government income:

So as not to be dependent on local taxes, which had to be raised through the assembly, the governor was given a separate source of revenue. This money would come from the sale of Crown reserves, land grants equivalent to one-seventh of all public lands.

LAWS

—Lower Canada: continuation of the system under the Quebec Act; that is, English criminal law and Canadian (based on French) civil law.

—Upper Canada: English laws, both criminal and civil, were in force. Land would be sold according to the British freehold system.

RELIGION

—Lower Canada: continuation of the system under the Quebec Act; that is, the continued security of the Roman Catholic Church.

The Franchise of Upper Canada was similar to that of Lower Canada, both being determined by the Constitutional Act. All residents* of the province who were twenty-one years, natural-born British subjects, subjects naturalized by act of the Imperial Parliament, or subjects by the conquest and cession of Canada, and who had not been convicted of treason or felony nor disqualified by provincial statute, were eligible to enjoy the franchise. These residents could exercise the franchise if as residents in a rural riding they possessed for their own use property to the yearly value of 40s. sterling above all charges, or as residents in an urban riding they possessed for their own use a dwelling house and lot of ground of the yearly value of £5 sterling or having been residents within a town for twelve months had paid a year's rent for a dwelling house to the amount of £10 sterling.[13]

*Actually women did not get the right to vote in Canada until World War I.

The Evolution of Government

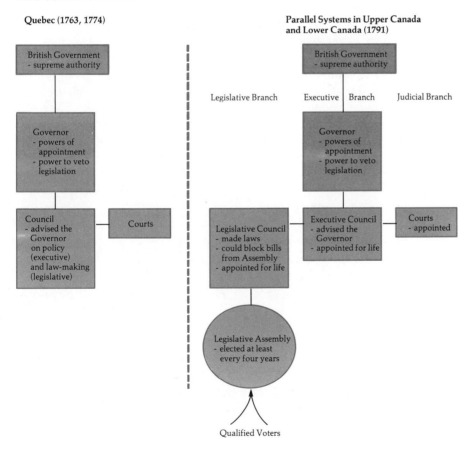

Quebec (1763, 1774)

British Government
- supreme authority

Governor
- powers of appointment
- power to veto legislation

Council
- advised the Governor on policy (executive) and law-making (legislative)

Courts

Parallel Systems in Upper Canada and Lower Canada (1791)

British Government
- supreme authority

Legislative Branch   Executive | Branch   Judicial Branch

Governor
- powers of appointment
- power to veto legislation

Legislative Council
- made laws
- could block bills from Assembly
- appointed for life

Executive Council
- advised the Governor
- appointed for life

Courts
- appointed

Legislative Assembly
- elected at least every four years

Qualified Voters

—Upper Canada: clergy reserves, equivalent to one-seventh of all public lands, were to be set aside for the support of a "Protestant clergy."*

The Constitutional Act: the path to Canadian unity?

Three earlier "experiments" at integrating the Canadian colonies within the British Empire had, one after the other, proved to be inadequate.† In the Constitutional Act, which provided separate territories for the French-speaking majority and for the English settlements to the west, the British thought they had found a solution:

> The division of the province was intended to put an end to the competition between the French-Canadians and the British. The idea was distinctly stated by Pitt [the British Prime Minister]: the creation of two separate colonies which should be left to work out their own destinies. The guiding force, however, was the reproduction as far as possible in each province of the eighteenth-century British constitution, with a local aristocracy and an established church. This reproduction was to act as a kind of charm. It was to prevent the repetition of the first great colonial tragedy; and Pitt actually believed that Lower Canada, seeing the beneficent workings of this venerable constitution in the neighbouring province, would sigh for the gift and embrace the whole system from conviction. . . . The future unity was to come, because the French-Canadians, initially satisfied by being separated from the British, would actually become dissatisfied because of the separation. They would finally sink race, religion, and traditions and rush to accept the British constitution out of sheer jealousy, lest Upper Canada should enjoy a monopoly in such a life-giving, wonder-working scheme.[14]

Such hopes could only have been based on optimism. Unlike the earlier "experiments," the Constitutional Act would have to be fully effected. Leadership would need to be of a consistently high quality. The future would have to be free from sudden changes.

What was likely to happen if any, or all of a number of developments occurred?

What if—

1. The British appointed governors who were unfamiliar with the colonies, who had pre-set attitudes, and/or who lacked good judgment about the people and their situation?

2. The appointed councils made it a practice to block bills proposed by the elected assemblies?

*The meaning of the term "Protestant" was soon to be the cause of quarrels. In the early years of British rule, "Protestant clergy" meant those of the Church of England (Anglican). However, there was also the Presbyterian Church, the official church of Scotland. Other Protestants, such as the Methodists and Baptists, also entered the dispute as their numbers increased. Creating an "established church" as an arm of government would not be an easy accomplishment in Canada.

†Expulsion of the Acadians, Proclamation Act, Quebec Act

The first Parliament in Lower Canada, 1791

3. The assemblies refused, year after year, to grant supply—the spending by government of money raised through taxes?

4. The land grants to the government and a "Protestant" church —crown and clergy reserves—were left as wilderness in the midst of pioneer farms?

5. An elite developed, with a stranglehold on the power of government and other institutions?

6. A large influx of settlers had problems obtaining land grants?

7. A large part of the population of either Upper or Lower Canada developed the feeling that it was being exploited?

8. Popular leaders, hostile to the system of government, emerged?

The next three chapters tell of events and circumstances in British North America. You can find out how many of the British assumptions proved to be true, and how many of the "what ifs" occurred.

Canadian literature

Perhaps you are startled to find a section in a history book entitled "Canadian Literature." Does it seem that the two subjects, history and literature, are distinct and always have been (and should be) kept separate? Some people have said that literature is a mirror for mankind—a way we have of seeing ourselves as others see us. If this is true, then literature can mirror not only our present lives, but our past and even what may be our future. Not all of the people you read about in this book were historians. But many of them recorded glimpses of life as they lived it. Many others wrote stories of other people who lived in this country. Sometimes, too, the way a layman views an event is different from how the historian views it. For example, a novelist writing about her life in northern Quebec may describe it quite differently than would a historian. Because of these similarities and distinct differences, Canadian literature is a complement to Canadian history.

At several points in the book, you will find sections on Canadian Literature. They cannot provide you with a comprehensive view of our literature, but they can give you a hint of what developments were occurring at the time. You may then want to explore some of these on your own time.

Development of a Canadian literature: 18th Century

BACKGROUND

The 18th century in British North America was not a time for novelists, poets and playwrights. The harsh realities of settlement and life in a new land left little time for the luxury of describing events. Everyone had to work to survive, and it is only from time to time that someone recorded what life was like in the new colony. Many of those who did write returned to their homeland and made little mark on our literature, but their works give us an insight into what effect the new culture had on new settlers.

Literary Time Line
1736 John Gyles, *Memoirs of Old Adventures*
1751 First printing press in British North America established by Bartholomew Green at Halifax
1752 *Halifax Gazette* established
Joseph Robson, *An Account of Six Years Residence on Hudson's Bay*
1764 *Quebec Gazette* established
1766 *Nova Scotia Gazette* published

1769	Frances Brooke, *The History of Emily Montague* (first novel from anywhere in North America)
1780	John Howe founds the *Halifax Journal*
1789-92	*The Nova Scotia Magazine*
1792-4	*The Quebec Magazine*
1793	Lady Simcoe's *Journal*
1795	Samuel Hearne, *Journey . . . to the Northern Ocean*

Highlight:

Frances Brooke

Frances Brooke was the first Canadian novelist and, in fact, the first novelist in all of North America. Emigrating to British North America following the British victory on the Plains of Abraham in 1759, Mrs. Brooke used a Canadian setting and gave a firsthand view of the times. Her aim was to give a realistic view of everyday life in the colony.

In her novel, *The History of Emily Montague*, we find comments on the relationship between the cold climate and the arts (or lack of them):

> "I must venture to Quebec tomorrow, or have company at home: amusements are here necessary to life; we must be jovial, or the blood will freeze in our veins.
>
> "I no longer wonder the elegant arts are unknown here; the rigor of the climate suspends the very powers of the understanding; what then must become of those of the imagination? Those who expect to see
>
> > "A new Athens rising near the pole,"
>
> will find themselves extremely disappointed. Genius will never mount high, where the faculties of the mind are benumbed half the year."[15]

7

British North America divided: The early days of Canadian-American relations

In the late 1960s and 1970s, Canadians across the country debated the dangers of "American domination." The issue was not whether American influence was increasing—everyone agreed that it was. The issue was: to what extent was increasing American influence harmful or beneficial?

Few Canadians would deny the value of American influence in at least some areas of their lives. They acknowledge the role of American "know-how" in improving their lives: American technology in its many forms, scientific research, medical discoveries, methods of organizing and managing business, innovations in education—the list seems endless. Canadians enjoy entertainment—music, comedy, sports and so on—by way of American television, radio, recording, books, magazines and personal appearances of American performers in the larger urban centres. Canada benefits from the ideas and writings of American scholars. Investment from the United States is important in many parts of the Canadian economy, and is seen by many Canadians as essential to the maintenance of Canada's "good life."

A sizeable number of Canadians, however, have been expressing alarm about the growth of American influence, particularly cultural and economic. A "Canadian identity" seems harder to define and maintain in the face of the "cultural invasion" from south of the border. Companies with headquarters in the United States have come to dominate parts of the Canadian economy, notably the petroleum industry, automobile manufacturing, mining, appliances and publishing. Other American influences drawing attention include the purchase of recreation land and the number of American professors in the faculties of Canadian universities.

Some Canadians think that present-day American influence is unusual, that Canada faces dangers from the United States as never before.* Yet history shows that American threats to Canada's existence are not new, nor is Canadian concern about its powerful neighbour. In fact, it may be said that Canada's first conflicts with the United States occurred even before that country was formed. And they continue to occur from one generation to the next.

*For a more detailed look at American influence in Canada, see Volume 2, Chapter 12.

In the fall of 1775, the year the American Revolutionary War broke out, an American army under General Montgomery captured Montreal. It joined another army led by Benedict Arnold in an unsuccessful attack on Quebec. During the next eight years, the fate of Canada hung in the balance, as the American colonies fought to break away from British control.

The Americans succeeded in winning their independence, acknowledged by Britain in the Treaty of Versailles (1783). By that time, Canada was no longer in danger of invasion. The new United States concentrated on the challenge of uniting under a new form of government. But the American Revolution had a profound effect on Canada in the form of the migration of some 40 000 Loyalists.

The Loyalists, refugees from the United States, gave Upper Canada and New Brunswick in particular a "British foundation". Their distaste for American ways strengthened their attachment to British institutions, ideas, attitudes and values. Because the Loyalists and their descendants were so prominent in government, church and education, their attitudes carried great weight in Upper Canada, and throughout British North America.

The War of 1812 reinforced the Loyalist position. While the war was really a struggle between Britain and the United States, Canada was again invaded by American armies. The combined effort of Canadian militiamen and British forces successfully repelled the invasion. The experience, however, was to remain in the memories of Canadians for many years to come.

1. Do you agree that the survival of an independent Canada is one of the most important issues facing Canada today?
2. The possibility of military invasion from the United States has not worried Canadians for more than a century. Other than military,

what forms can an "invasion" take? If one takes place, are others sure to follow?

3. How could Canada defend herself against "peaceful invasions"? Would a strong "Canadian identity" be important? What does "Canadian identity" involve?

4. Can you think of any limits on the extent of Canada's independence from the United States? From the world community? Is there such a thing as total independence? Why or why not?

5. What is the difference between "independence" and "interdependence"?

6. When, historically, do you think Canada was most independent? What are some of the problems in trying to decide whether the trend today is toward greater or lesser independence?

let's keep it Canadian

The survival of Canada as an independent nation is one of the most important issues facing Canadians today.

The time for mere talk is past; action is very urgently needed.

Let us join together in urging our elected representatives to commit themselves honestly and enthusiastically to Canadian independence.

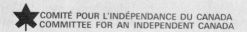
COMITÉ POUR L'INDÉPENDANCE DU CANADA
COMMITTEE FOR AN INDEPENDENT CANADA

SUITE 1105, 67 YONGE STREET, TORONTO 1 / TEL. (416) 863-0173 / SUITE 1105, 67 RUE YONGE, TORONTO 1

The American Revolution

The British victory over the French in the Seven Years' War confirming Canada as a British possession, was a dramatic event in the political history of North America. The relations between Britain and the thirteen American colonies suddenly changed. As Britain saw the situation, the main issues were: reorganizing its North American empire, contending with Indian unrest, and deciding what to do about the huge war debt and possible future costs of defence. In the eyes of the British, the colonies should share some of the financial burden which had built up, partly on their behalf. The solution seemed to be an enforcement of trade regulations within the Empire, since the collection of tariffs and other fees would put money into the imperial treasury. The British believed that a further step was necessary for the first time—direct taxation of the colonies.

Most American colonists saw the situation quite differently. For some years, the feeling had been growing that American interests were often very different from those of Britain. The elimination of the French threat from the north removed much of the colonies' feeling of dependence on Britain. The Thirteen Colonies had developed a strong and varied economy and the beginnings of a sense of identity apart from Britain. There were leaders able to speak out about the need to preserve the "rights of Englishmen" in the colonies as well as in Britain itself.

Following the Treaty of Paris (1763), the British navy began to enforce regulations on trade, and colonial authorities began to punish American "smugglers." The Stamp Act (1765) was the first of a series of direct taxes on the colonies. The next ten years was a time of confrontation, as Americans organized resistance against what they saw as British oppression.

The British Empire, like that of France and other European countries which had established colonies, was still based on *mercantilism.** The purpose of colonies was to increase a nation's self-sufficiency by providing raw materials, and a market for the products of the parent country. Through regulations on colonial trade and tariffs on imports from other countries, the parent country tried to keep the benefits of trade within the empire. The arrangement was not one-sided by any means, since colonial producers had a protected market. In the British Empire, however, regulations had not been very well enforced for many years. Many merchants in the Thirteen Colonies had grown accustomed to this "salutory neglect," which enabled them to trade with other countries, especially France and its colonies in the West Indies. A large number of "American" traders were bound to be displeased if Britain suddenly tightened up the system.

*See page 81.

1. Why did Britain feel it had the right to tax the Thirteen Colonies?
2. Why did the Thirteen Colonies feel differently?

By 1775, the tension in the colonies had reached the danger point. Citizen armies were gathering weapons and secretly preparing to fight. A Congress of delegates from the various American colonies was meeting in Philadelphia. Though efforts were made on both sides to find a peaceful solution, an incident at Lexington in Massachusetts proved to be the first event in the American Revolution. Following the bloodshed between British troops and colonial militiamen, the Congress authorized the recruitment of an army and appointed George Washington as commander-in-chief.

Canada and the American Revolution

Under the Stamp Act of 1765, taxes were levied on a variety of items, such as newspapers, legal documents and licenses. A stamp on the item was proof that the tax had been paid. This *direct* tax was the kind that Americans had come to expect would be levied only by their own assemblies. Many different groups were affected by the Stamp Act, but editors, lawyers and businessmen— some of the more influential people in the colony—were the hardest hit. They were also the people most able to organize effective opposition.

At the time of the American Revolution, Canada was known as British North America and the parts that were likely to be affected by the Revolution were Quebec and Nova Scotia. Quebec was the vast area defined by the Quebec Act; Nova Scotia included present-day New Brunswick. Both regions were potential participants in the American revolution. All but 2 000 of Quebec's population of 80 000 were French Canadians and might be expected to support a revolt against Britain, the country that had so recently conquered them. And Quebec had a long border with the Thirteen Colonies. Nova Scotia was more geographically removed, but the majority of its population had come from the Thirteen Colonies.

The Americans saw Quebec as an important territory in their struggle with Britain. The cooperation—or capture—of Quebec would provide a much needed source of weapons and ammunition. It would also eliminate a base from which the British could launch an attack on the rebellious colonies. Months before the Revolution began, the inhabitants of Quebec were invited to send delegates to a "continental congress."

The "Boston Tea Party" in 1773 was one of the most dramatic incidents leading up to the Revolution. The trouble started when the British imposed a tax on imported tea that gave the British East India Company a competitive advantage over American companies. To protest the tea tax, a group of Boston citizens, some disguised as Indians, boarded British ships and dumped their cargo of tea into Boston harbour. Provoked by this action, the British government sent additional troops to Boston and Parliament passed a series of laws which were intended to make an example of the city. Sympathy for Massachusetts—and hostility to Britain—rose sharply in other colonies.

1. For what reasons might the Americans have expected that a) Quebec and b) Nova Scotia would be an ally in the American Revolution?

ADDRESS OF THE GENERAL CONGRESS TO THE INHABITANTS OF THE PROVINCE OF QUEBEC

October 26th, 1774

Friends and Fellow-Subjects,

We, the delegates of the colonies . . . have accordingly assembled, and taken into our most serious consideration the state of public affairs on this continent, have thought proper to address your province, as a member therein deeply interested.

These are the invaluable rights [e.g., representative government, trial by jury, freedom from arbitrary arrest] that form a considerable part of our mild system of government; that sending its equitable energy through all ranks and classes of men, defends the poor from the rich, the weak from the powerful, the industrious from the rapacious, the peaceable from the violent, the tenants from the lords, and all from their superiors.

These are the rights, without which a people cannot be free and happy. . . .

These are the rights you are entitled to, and ought at this moment in perfection to exercise. . . .

. . . . You are a small people, compared to those who with open arms invite you into fellowship. A moment's reflection should convince you which will be most for your interest and happiness, to have all the rest of North America your unalterable friends, or your inveterate enemies. . . .

We do not ask you, by this address, to commence hostilities against the government of our common sovereign. We only invite you to consult your own glory and welfare, and not to suffer yourselves to be inveigled or intimidated by infamous ministers so far as to become the instruments of their cruelty and despotism, but to unite with us in one social compact, formed on the generous principles of equal liberty. . . . In order to complete this highly desirable union, we submit it to your consideration, whether it may not be expedient for you to meet together in your several towns and districts, and elect deputies who after meeting in a provincial congress, may chuse [sic] delegates, to represent your province in the continental congress, to be held at Philadelphia, on the tenth day of May, 1775.[1]

1. What rights does this address say would be granted to the people of Quebec if they joined the Thirteen Colonies?
2. The purpose of this address is *not* to ask Quebec to join in a revolution. What *is* the purpose of the address?

The British found that they could depend on the loyalty of both the clergy and the seigneurs. The Quebec Act had consolidated their appreciation of British policy toward the colony. Bishop Briand placed the influence of the Catholic Church squarely against any cooperation with the Americans:

May 22, 1775

A troop of subjects in revolt against their lawful Sovereign, who is at the same time ours, have just made an irruption into this province, less in the hope of maintaining themselves here than with a view of dragging you into their revolt or at least preventing you from opposing their pernicious design. The remarkable goodness and gentleness with which we have been governed by his very gracious Majesty, King George the Third, since the fortune of war subjected us to his rule; the recent favours with which he has loaded us, in restoring to us the use of our laws and the free exercise of our religion; and in letting us participate in all the privileges and advantages of British subjects, would no doubt be enough to excite your gratitude and zeal in support of the interests of the British Crown. But motives even more urgent must speak to your heart at the present moment. Your oaths, your religion, lay upon you the unavoidable duty of defending your country and your King with all the strength you possess.[2]

1. For what reasons does the bishop urge French Canadians to oppose the Revolution?

The death of General Montgomery

Appeals to the people of Quebec did not arouse any revolutionary spirit; nor did a military operation succeed in involving the colony in American plans. In November, 1775, General Montgomery's army captured Montreal, and Governor Carleton was forced to retreat to Quebec. There the armies of Montgomery and Benedict Arnold, who had trekked overland from Maine, were unable to overcome the defences of the capital. Montgomery was killed and Benedict Arnold, himself wounded in the siege, commanded the American forces who remained on the scene.

However, the British fleet arrived in May, 1776, with reinforcements, and the Americans abandoned their invasion of Canada. For the rest of the revolutionary war, they concentrated on driving the British out of the American colonies.

WHY DID QUEBEC NOT JOIN THE REVOLUTION?

The American hope that Quebec might join the Revolution did not materialize. What explanation can be inferred from the attitudes of the different population groups in Quebec?

THE ENGLISH MINORITY

Among the English minority in Quebec, some 2 000 strong, were recent immigrants from the American colonies. Yet they were mainly merchants who had strong financial connections with England. In some ways they now saw themselves as competitors, at least in matters of trade, with their "cousins" to the south. They were unhappy about the Quebec Act, but the great commerical opportunities in Quebec helped forestall any opinion favourable to revolution.

FRENCH CANADIAN LEADERS

"In 1774, everything united the clergy and seigneurs to the government. The belief in absolute monarchy and divine right took on an even greater significance since the bourgeoisie [English merchants in Quebec] was now demanding parliamentary government and proposing its own system of values. Loyalty to the king, being based on the religious convictions of these two social groups, remained the strongest sentiment. Therefore, simply because of the basic adhesions of this elite, there could be no question of its rising up against England. . . . Were the values proposed by the rebels acceptable? Condemnable in principle, the Revolution aimed moreover at breaking the traditional political relationships. The rebels invoked the theme of liberty, whereas, the French-Canadian elite believed in authority, in obedience, and in aristocratic values."[3]

THE FRENCH CANADIANS

The French Canadians remained neutral, for the most part, in the struggle between the British and the Americans. Aside from the clergy and the seigneurs, they had little reason for being enthusiastic about either side. On the one hand, the Quebec Act had benefited the **elite** much more than it benefited the habitants, who generally resisted the appeals of their leaders to volunteer for fighting against the Americans. The latter, on the other hand, had little to offer except vague promises.

the upper class, the favoured few

NOVA SCOTIA: WHY DID IT NOT JOIN THE REVOLUTION?

The majority of Nova Scotia's 20 000 people were former New Englanders, and no doubt there was a great deal of sympathy among them for the American Revolution. But Nova Scotia was geographically isolated from the Thirteen Colonies, and its population was widely scattered. The main concentration of settlement was Halifax, established in 1749 as a British military base. The British navy was a powerful reminder of the colony's ties with the mother country. The business community in Halifax was heavily dependent on connections with Britain.

The following documents illustrate the reasons for Nova Scotia's preference for neutrality.

Perhaps, then, the principal clue to Nova Scotian behavior . . . lies in her insulation from the rest of North America. . . . Nova Scotia has always had to contemplate the possiblity that she may be in North America but not of it. . . . In 1710 New England and Old found it imperative to conquer her, but . . . their support was an intermittent and barely adequate counter to the efforts of France and New France. Her people of that day, the Acadians, had made the land support and increase them, but they were mere pawns in international politics. Small wonder, then, that their one persistent aim from 1710 to 1755, when it sealed their fates, was to be, and to be generally accepted as, neutrals—'the neutral French.' Small wonder, too, that after a brief flurry of conflicting aims in 1775, Nova Scotians a bare fifteen years out of New England naturally and almost inevitably, when confronted by the Revolution, made the same plea.[4]

ANCHORED IN THE EMPIRE

There is a simple explanation for the failure of Newfoundland and Nova Scotia to participate in the movement of the 1760's that led to the American Revolution. Both were dependent on Great Britain to an infinitely greater degree than any of those colonies that finally accepted the leadership of the Congress at Philadelphia. Officially Newfoundland was not a colony at all. Nova Scotia was not financially self-supporting and her trade was chiefly in British hands. Newfoundland had no experience of democratic action and Nova Scotia had just begun to acquire it. In both, public opinion was largely inarticulate [unclear] because the interest of those who made it compelled them to shelter beneath the wing of Britain. This simple explanation acquired complexity with the march of events. Had Britain proved lamentably weak, the two communities would have been but as straws in the wind. But since sea power converted this entire region of the North Atlantic into something like a fortress for the Crown, their status as British colonies was to remain unchanged. . . . after the initial impact of the Revolution, there was little doubt that these colonies would continue within the imperial fold.[5]

1. What does the phrase "neutral Yankees" reveal about the reasons that Nova Scotia did not join the Revolution?

The American Revolution had many effects on Canada. The economy benefited as Britain spent large sums in the colonies for supplies, especially farm products to feed the troops. In Quebec, the Revolution widened the gap between population groups. Among French Canadians, for example, the clergy and seigneurs supported the British, while the habitants refused to follow their leaders and tried to remain neutral. The most obvious effects were the creation of the international border, which divided North America into the territories that would become Canada and the United States, and the Loyalist migration which gave Canada a new, and distinctive, population.

1. Suppose the American Revolution had never occurred. How might Canada today be different?

Britain recognizes United States' independence, 1783

In 1783, by the Treaty of Versailles, Great Britain recognized the success of the American Revolution and agreed to the independence of the new **republic**, the United States of America. The terms were very generous to the Americans, as the location of the international boundary showed; they received a vast region south of the Great Lakes even though much of the territory remained under British control at the end of the war. Furthermore, the United States was granted the right to fish in Canadian waters off the coasts of Newfoundland and Nova Scotia and in the Gulf of St. Lawrence.

Britain had several reasons for being so agreeable in negotiating with the Americans. One was the danger that France, whose support had helped the Americans succeed, would be in a position to regain territories in North America if Britain took a hard line. Another was that a friendly United States would be beneficial to the security of the remaining British North American colonies (Canada). Furthermore, the chance for trade and other economic benefits was more likely if relations between the United States and Great Britain got off to a good start.

a country in which the head of government is an elected or nominated president, not a monarch; supreme power is vested in the people who, in theory at least, can choose and remove their leaders. Republics were not common at the time the United States was formed; in the present day, most countries have some form of republican government.

The Treaty of Versailles did not settle the entire boundary between Canada and the United States. Part of the boundary could be defined according to waterways and land features. In several places, notably between Maine and New Brunswick and in the far west, the boundary's lack of exactness would be the cause of friction several times in later years.

The British fleet prepares to leave New York harbour, 1783

"The shot heard 'round the world"

As the old expression, "the shot heard 'round the world," suggests, the effects of the American Revolution were not confined to Canada, or even to North America. The example of a people rising up against their rulers in the name of liberty has influenced many countries.

France was the first European nation to be affected. Many Frenchmen had actually served in America during the Revolution, and they carried revolutionary ideas home at the conclusion of the war. A famous example was Lafayette, a veteran of the American Revolution. He was a prominent figure in the early stages of the French Revolution (which started in 1789, only six years after the Treaty of Versailles).

Other nations, too, have been inspired by the example of the United States and the ideas expressed in the Declaration of Independence. Freedom-seeking people all over the world have been influenced by the "spirit of '76."

The Declaration of Independence, signed on July 4, 1776, proclaimed war against Britain and independence for the United States. The signers took an irreversible step. Because they could be tried for treason if the revolution failed, signing their names meant pledging everything to the cause.

Of course, the ideas in the Declaration of Independence were not solely the work of Thomas Jefferson, its author. Jefferson and others were highly influenced by the writings of earlier British scholars like John Locke. According to Locke, government is a necessary evil, required to maintain the "social contract"—the limitations on their freedoms which people accept in order to live in harmony with others, and thereby to enjoy their "natural rights." Government, Locke believed, should be an agent of the people, which they control at all times.

Thus Jefferson adapted and applied the theory of "social contract" in the Declaration of Independence:

> "We hold these truths to be self-evident: that all men are created equal, that they are endowed by their Creator with certain unalienable rights, that among these are life, liberty, and the pursuit of happiness.
>
> "That, to secure these rights, governments are instituted among men, deriving their just powers from the consent of the governed;
>
> "That whenever any form of government becomes destructive of these ends, it is the right of the people to alter or to abolish it, and to institute new government, laying its foundation on such princi-

ples, and organizing its powers in such form, as to them shall seem most likely to effect their safety and happiness. Prudence, indeed, will dictate that governments long established should not be changed for light and transient causes; and accordingly all experience hath shown that mankind are more disposed to suffer while evils are sufferable, than to right themselves by abolishing the forms to which they are accustomed. But when a long train of abuses and usurpations, pursuing invariably the same object, evinces a design to reduce them under absolute despotism, it is their right, it is their duty, to throw off such government, and to provide new guards for their future security."

Two hundred years later in 1976, the United States celebrated its Bicentennial. Amidst the Bicentennial festivities, many Americans thought seriously about the ideals on which the United States was founded. Wide gaps remained between the *principles* and actual *practices* of American society. The "American dream" has too often turned to nightmares like racial violence, assassinations, Vietnam and Watergate. Yet most Americans are mindful of a heritage in which the United States stands for liberty, justice, and opportunity for all. Many believe that the United States can restore its image, in the eyes of its own citizens as well as in the world, by striving to fulfill its early ideals.

1. What qualities do Americans possess which you admire and which you think Canadians could benefit by adapting to their own situation?
2. How do you think most Canadians view the United States on the following: (a) international relations, especially with Canada regarding such things as border problems, (b) continental resource sharing and (c) media?
3. If you could have given the Americans a Bicentennial "gift" on behalf of Canada, what would it have been?

173

The Loyalist migration

"You Canadians should be proud of the founders of your country. The United Empire Loyalists were a grand type of loyal, law-abiding, God-fearing men. No country ever had such founders, no country in the world."[6]

Lady Tennyson

... whatever has been said, thought or written in Canada about the Loyalists is part of the Loyalist Myth—"grist for the mill", so to speak. The Loyalist have been described and analyzed by historians. They have been commented upon by intellectuals. They have been hymned in patriotic verse. They have been romanticized by historical novelists. They have been laughed at by Canadians of non-Loyalists descent. ... [7]

The American Revolution led to the creation of not one, but two nations in North America. The United States was formed directly by a war of independence from Great Britain. Canada did not become a nation in its own right for many decades, but part of its character was formed by the events of the 1770s. For example, Canada was confined to a northern existence, and important aspects of its culture originated with the Loyalist population which migrated from the United States.

The fallacy of exclusively upper-class origins of the Loyalists has been thoroughly exposed by historians in this [20th] century. Class distribution among the Loyalists seems to have been quite similar to that in the society they left behind.[19] The only variation between the Loyalists and American Society in class structure was that urban dwellers seem to have been over-represented in the Loyalists. It is this latter point that probably explains much of the ineptness of the Loyalists as pioneers.[8]

Who were the Loyalists? They were those people in the Thirteen Colonies who opposed the revolt against Great Britain. It was estimated that no more than one third of the population actively supported the revolutionary cause, with one third remaining neutral and the remainder supporting Great Britain. That is, many British Americans, from a variety of motives, chose to remain loyal to Britain. Loyalty to the British monarchy was a deep-rooted tradition, not confined to any particular social class or occupation, and among the Loyalists were professional people, office holders, merchants with British connections and farmers and craftsmen of modest means. Many of the Loyalists either aided the British forces or fought in Loyalist units alongside British regular troops.

During the revolution, Loyalists and suspected Loyalists were on the receiving end of rough treatment in the name of revolutionary ideals. Merely labeling a man a Loyalist was equivalent to denouncing him as a traitor to the revolution and marking him for action by vigilante groups, who took the law into their own hands. Suspected Loyalists suffered indignities, persecution, loss of livelihood and even personal harm. Persons in office, who disagreed with the revolution, were subjected to political persecution and driven from their positions. Those who fought on the side of Britain or who were suspected of aiding Britain were often deprived of their property and possessions. Unruly mobs looted the homes of Loyalists, who had no protection from the law. Many were condemned without judge or jury; some were imprisoned or banished. In areas where the forces of revolution suffered setbacks, feelings ran high and mobs vented their anger against suspected British sympathizers. Nor did the feeling of hostility against the Loyalists abate with the success of the revolution. Victory only increased the hatred against those who had failed to display enthusiasm for the revolutionary cause.

At the peace conference following the war, Britain spoke for the Loyalists, requesting that the newly formed United States consider their claims for damage suffered during the revolution, return property seized from them and pay debts owed by Americans to Loyalists. The American delegates promised to use the good offices of the Congress and recommend to the individual states involved that the Loyalist claims be considered justly. But since Congress at that time had no jurisdiction over individual states, it could do nothing to enforce its recommendations and very little compensation was made.

Given the hostile environment, many Loyalists found life in the United States unbearable, and approximately 50 000 departed to start life anew within the British Empire. Those with the means and connections in England went there, and some found their way to the West Indies. The majority went to British North America, either overland to what was left of the area known as Quebec or by sea to Nova Scotia, the name that applied to most of what we know today as the Maritimes.

1. How are the following facts contradictory?
(a) The American Revolution was based on the idea that people had "inalienable rights" such as life, liberty and the pursuit of happiness.
(b) Loyalists who did not want to break away from Britain but who wanted to remain part of the Empire were rejected, sometimes persecuted and forced to leave their homeland.
Can you suggest any way in which this contradiction might be explained or justified?

Loyalists in the Maritimes

New York, which remained in British hands until the close of the Revolutionary War, became the gathering place for Loyalists, especially for those from settlements on the Atlantic coast. The former governor of Quebec, Guy Carleton, was the British officer in charge of the evacuation of the thousands who had decided to leave the

"A Tory [Loyalist] is a thing whose head is in England, and its body in America, and its neck ought to be stretched."— as defined by an American in a New York newspaper in 1775.[9]

175

United States. By the spring of 1784, at least 20 000 people—including Acadians and some 2 000 former Negro slaves—had made their way to Nova Scotia, doubling the population there.

Historians disagree about exact numbers, but several hundred Loyalists settled in Prince Edward Island and Cape Breton. Up to 10 000 attempted a settlement at Shelburne, an unsuccessful effort on the southeastern coast. The largest number to establish themselves were the 10 000 who settled on the Saint John River and founded both Saint John and Fredericton.

MEMORIES

Recollections of a Loyalist who was an eleven-year-old girl at the time of the migration:

... (Father) said we were to go to Nova Scotia, that a ship was ready to take us there, so we made all haste to get ready, killed the cow, sold the beef and a neighbour took home the tallow and made us a good parcel of candles and put plenty of beeswax in them to make them hard and good. Uncle came down and threshed our wheat, twenty bushels, and grandmother came and made bags for the wheat, and we packed up a tub of butter, a tub of pickles, and a good store of potatoes.

Then on Tuesday, suddenly the house was surrounded by rebels and father was taken prisoner and carried away. Uncle went forward and promised those who had taken him that if he might come home he would answer for his being forthcoming the next morning. But no, and I cried and cried that night. When morning came, they said he was free to go.

We had five wagon loads carried down the Hudson in a sloop and then we went on board the transport that was to bring us to Saint John. I was just eleven years old when we left our farm to come here. . . .

There were no deaths on board, but several babies were born. It was a sad sick time after we landed in Saint John. We had to live in tents. The government gave them to us and rations too. It was just at the first snow then and the melting snow and the rain would soak up into our beds as we lay. Mother got so chilled and developed rheumatism and was never well afterwards . . .

We lived in a tent at St. Annes [Fredericton] until father got a house ready. He went up through our lot till he found a nice fresh spring of water. He stooped down and pulled away the fallen leaves that were thick over it and tasted it. It was very good so there he built his house. We all had rations given us by the government, flour, butter, and pork. Tools were given to the men also.

One morning when we awoke we found the snow lying deep on the ground all round us and them father came wading through it and told us the house was ready. . . .

There was no floor laid, no windows, no chimney, no door, but we had a roof at least. A good fire was blazing and mother had a big loaf of bread and she boiled a kettle of water and put a good piece of butter in a pewter bowl. We toasted the bread and all sat around the bowl and ate our breakfast that morning and mother said: 'Thank God we are no longer in dread of having shots fired through our house. This is the sweetest meal I ever tasted for many a day.'[10]

1. How might the following justify his choice of a course of action:
(a) the Loyalist who puts his home and family before his beliefs and remains "undercover" while the revolution occurs so that he may retain his stable home life,

OR

(b) the Loyalist who decides to pack his belongings and his family to emigrate to a new land to be able to hold to his beliefs?

The Loyalists who came to the Maritimes relied on British promises of land and supplies as reward for their remaining loyal to the Empire. The British government did instruct Governor Parr of Nova Scotia to provide land grants, tools and provisions to the new arrivals. Yet the authorities were overwhelmed by the large numbers. They arrived before land could be surveyed; some Loyalists, who had served with British forces during the war, accused others of having avoided the fighting and having taken refuge behind British lines—yet claiming equal compensation. The majority of the Loyalists had been town-dwellers, and pioneer life caused widespread hardship. Some groups, especially the blacks, experienced special difficulties.

BLACKS IN THE MARITIMES

The Loyalist migration to the faithful British lands in North America brought the first really major influx of Negroes to the maritime areas. . . . Some of the Loyalists had owned large plantations in the rebellious colonies, with household slaves and field hands. . . . Many took slavery for granted, and those who owned slaves found important work for them to do in the new land—clearing fields, chopping wood against the long winters, and building ships.

. . . . The number of slaves increased rapidly. . . . Since a number of the Negroes were freedmen, slave and free Negroes now lived side by side.

But in time the effect of the Loyalist and Negro immigration was the reverse of the initial trend. The slaves, given the example of free Negro agricultural settlers nearby, cannot have continued to assume that black skins automatically decreed servitude. Many of the Loyalists found that they could not afford to maintain gangs of fifty or more field hands, and that once the land was cleared it was not sufficiently productive to require an extensive labor force.... a number of the Loyalists already had been moving toward antislavery positions; and once they resettled, they tended to look upon slavery as too closely associated with the new Republic which they had cause to hate. Although the Loyalists temporarily gave new members and new strength to slavery in Canada, within two decades those same Loyalists had all but ended the practice.[11]

A serious problem was the hostility between the Loyalists and the earlier settlers. The Loyalists were frustrated by delays in the distribution of land, and believed they were not rewarded adequately for their years of sacrifice. They resented the "neutral Yankees" for their failure to rally to Britain's cause during the Revolution.

Loyalists who settled on the Halifax side of Nova Scotia had to contend with the established influence of the military and the merchants. The large number of settlers located on the Saint John River believed that they were too isolated to participate in government centred in Halifax. They petitioned Britain for the creation of a separate colony.

In Prince Edward Island (the name given later, in 1798, to St. John's Island), the Loyalists found they had been tricked; the lands they settled and developed, as it turned out, actually were owned by absentee landlords.* Cape Breton, a separate colony from the time the Loyalists arrived until it was rejoined to Nova Scotia in 1821, suffered a long period of neglect.

*The problem of absentee landlords lasted until after P.E.I. joined Confederation, nearly a century later. See page 303.

The first twenty years after the coming of the Loyalists was a time of difficult adjustment for the newcomers and for the colonies of which they became a part. Though each of the Maritime colonies was very different from the others, all were affected significantly by the arrival of the Loyalists.

Loyalists in Quebec

Even before the war was over, Loyalists were making their way overland—mainly from New York and Pennsylvania—into Quebec. With the tide of battle going in favour of the Americans, there was little chance of returning to their former homes. Hundreds of Loyalists drifted northward. At Sorel, at the junction of the Richelieu River and the St. Lawrence, Governor Haldimand set up a kind of reception centre to deal with the immediate needs of the arrivals. Other Loyalists, carrying what possessions they could, fled to border points near the upper St. Lawrence or Niagara.

The uninhabited regions west of Montreal were recognized as promising areas for Loyalist settlement. As fast as surveys could be carried out, free lands were assigned to Loyalists and their families. The main areas of settlement were the upper St. Lawrence, where towns like Cornwall now stand; the lands around the Bay of Quinte; the Niagara Peninsula, where disbanded members of Butler's Rangers had previously indicated they wished to settle; and the lands on either side of the Grand River, granted to the Six Nations Indians led by Chief Joseph Brant.

A great many settlers had been members of Loyalist militia units which served with the British army, and thus they had become more accustomed to muskets than to axes and ploughs. However, most had been farmers before the war, and they were accustomed to physical labour. They had to be, since starting settlements in the wilderness was a back-breaking task, even though the British provided supplies and tools and grants of land. The following documents illustrate the early hardships:

Sir John Johnson and Colonel John Butler were the best known of the Loyalists who organized attacks against the Americans. It has been said that the battles in which Johnson's and Butler's Rangers fought were some of the most brutal and bloody of the war where neighbours and relatives often were on opposite sides. The Rangers sometimes allied themselves with Indian bands and Indian warfare was employed throughout the battles. Troops of British regulars also came to their aid.

As the fighting went poorly for the British, however, many of Johnson's and Butler's Rangers were forced to retreat to refuge in Quebec where they were able to secure land grants and to take up farming.

HAPPINESS AMID HARDSHIPS

The Country at that time was a complete wilderness but by energy and perseverance and a long time we got on very happily....

Mother used to help to chop down the Trees, attended the household duties, and, as the children grew up, they were trained to Industrious habits. We were very useful to her, attended the cattle, churned the butter, making cheese, dressing the flax, spinning, (in those days the spinning-wheel looked cheerful), made our own cloth and stockings.... We had no neighbours but an old Englishman who lived at some distance off who was an occasional visitor. Before our crops came round, having brought seed with us, supplied by Government, we had rations from the Military posts; also, when these were nearly exhausted, father collected our Butter, Cheese, and spinning, taking them in a Batteaux to Kingston, which he traded off for salt, Tea, and flour. We had no Grist Mill at that time nearer than Kingston. The first Mill was put up at Napanee afterwards.

The Bay of Quinte was covered with Ducks of which we could obtain any quantity from the Indians. As to fish, they could be had by fishing with a scoup. I have often speared large Salmon with a pitchfork. Now and then provisions ran very scant, but there being plenty of Bull frogs we fared sumptuously. This was the time of the famine, I think in 1788; we were obliged (to) dig up our potatoes after planting them to eat.

We never thought of these privations but were always happy and cheerful. No unsettled minds, no political strife....

We had no Doctors, no Lawyers, No stated Clergy. We had

prayers at home and put our trust in Providence. An old woman in the next clearing was the Chief Phys(i)cian to the surrounding Country as it gradually settled.

THE "HUNGRY WINTER" OF 1787–1788

No one can tell the privations we all underwent on our first moving into the Bush.

The whole country was a forrest [sic], a wilderness which had to be subdued by the axe and toil.

For a time we led a regular Robinson Cruso(e) life and with a few poles and brushwood, formed our tents on the Indian plan.

———————————

The most trying period of our lives, was the year 1788 called the year of scarcity—everything at that period seemed to conspire against the hardy and industrious settlers.

All the crops failed, as the earth had temporarily ceased to yield its increase, either for man or beast—for several days we were without food, except the various roots that we procured and boiled down to nourish us. We noticed what roots the pigs eat; and by that means avoided anything that had any poisonous qualities. The officers in command at the military stations did all in their power to mitigate the general distress, but the supplies were very limited, consequently only a small pittance was dealt out to each petitioner.

We obtained something and were on allowance until affairs assumed a more favorable aspect. Our poor dog was killed to allay the pangs of hunger, the very idea brought on sickness to some, but others devoured the flesh quite ravenous. . . . We next killed a horse which lasted us a long time and proved very profitable eating; those poor animals were a serious loss to our farming appendages, but there was no help for it.[12]

*See pages 149–154.

The struggle for survival occupied the time and energy of most Loyalists in the early years. The immediate political issue, as we have seen, was the Quebec Act*, which, until 1791 kept the Loyalists under a system of government and laws to which they were not accustomed. The feelings of bitterness against the United States began to decline, and, in the 1790s the Loyalists were soon outnumbered by American settlers. Thousands immigrated to Upper Canada in response to the offer of free land advertised in the United States by the first governor, John Graves Simcoe.

Even though they soon became a minority, the Loyalists had established a "British foundation" in the area which would eventually become Ontario. They stood for the value of ties with Britain and of British institutions. They were suspicious of American ideas—which were branded with the negative catch-all expression "republicanism." Loyalists wanted no part of changes that might lead to the kind of political and social disorder that had caused the "Loyalist migration."

1. Are Canadians still more conservative in their ways than Americans? For example, how are they different in their approach to:
(a) clothing styles?
(b) political leaders?
(c) improvements in education?
(d) saving their money?

Effects of the Loyalist migration

The coming of the Loyalists to British North America brought many benefits but also caused many problems. Some of the Loyalists migrated because they cherished their British heritage and links to the mother country. They valued the British empire, its laws and their rights as Englishmen. They both despised and feared what they thought was the "radical republicanism" of the United States. Since there were so many Loyalists who came to British North America, it was inevitable that these attitudes would be transferred to other colonists, and that the tone of British loyalty would be set for years to come.

The migration to British North America brought the first substantial increase in population to the colony since the early days of French settlement. The frontier extended westward and the people brought a demand for more goods and services. Because they had been fairly well-established in trades and professions in the Thirteen Colonies, the Loyalists brought these skills with them. Because of the doctors, lawyers, shopkeepers, farmers and tradesmen among the Loyalists, the colony soon benefited from more schools, newspapers, and other small business enterprises. In addition, the coming of the Loyalists enabled British North America to expand its fishing, lumbering and shipbuilding activities. All of this new economic growth coupled with the already established fur trade, stimulated the economic life of the colony.

Politically, the emigration of the Loyalists had far-reaching effects on British North America as well. In the Maritimes, the province of New Brunswick was created (1784) within months of the Loyalists' arrival in the Saint John River valley. Since New Brunswick was to have representative government, it did not present a political problem for the Loyalists. Protestant Loyalists coming to Quebec, however, were another story. Here the Quebec Act of 1774 was alien to the British supporters, and the French law would be replaced by the Constitutional Act of 1791.

" . . . [The first parliament of Upper Canada] provided for the gradual abolition of slavery in the province. . . . this measure was strongly pressed by Simcoe and accepted with some reluctance by several members of the legislature. Many of the Loyalist settlers had brought Negro slaves with them, and expected to go on using them. The high cost and scarcity of labour were stressed by those defending the use of slaves. After Simcoe's measure was moderated, however, the members agreed to pass it. Slaves already in the province would continue in that state to the end of their lives, but no new slaves would be admitted. Children born to female slaves in the province were to become free upon reaching the age of twenty-five years."[13]

When the Loyalists arrived in Nova Scotia, the colony included what are now the provinces of Nova Scotia and New Brunswick. The majority settled on the Saint John River, far removed from Halifax, the colonial capital and centre of activity for the province. This distance isolated them from the mainstream of life in the province. As the result of petitions to the British government, New Brunswick was created, with Fredericton named as the capital. Today, New Brunswick is still known as "the Loyalist province."

Alienation: square pegs and round holes—a conflict in values

What do the following people have in common:

the teenage boy who wears the long hair and beads of the hippie generation of the 1960s;

the senior citizen who feels he no longer contributes to society;

the young woman who feels that society has no standards or rules by which she can judge what is right and what is wrong;

the policeman who refuses to take bribes even though his senior officers encourage him to do so;

all the people who feel they are powerless to change their lives?

Each of these people is exhibiting one of the characteristics of a phenomenon known as *alienation*. During the 1960s, the term "alienation" was usually associated with "hippies," "drop-outs" and drugs. Young people, unable to understand the world around them, especially with its seeming hypocrisies, rejected the lifestyles being presented to them and became aliented from the larger culture. The phenomenon of the "alienated youth" was common.

It would be wrong, however, to associate alienation only with the 1960s. The alienation which people felt then was very similar to the way people have felt at varying times throughout history. Only the reaction to it was different.

Just what is this phenomenon of alienation? "Feeling out of it" is a cliché which sums up the feelings of the alienated. They may feel that they do not belong, that they do not fit in, that they have no power to change their situation, and that nothing they do could ever matter.

Social scientists may investigate this phenomenon according to the following characteristics :

social isolation—feeling separated from others;
meaninglessness—feeling that one's life is futile;
normlessness—feeling there are no standards or rules by which a person can judge things;
estrangement—feeling out of step with society's accepted standards;
powerlessness—feeling that the person has no power to change anything.

Many groups throughout history have exhibited some or all of the characteristics of alienation. One of the most important ideas to understand, however, is that what matters is the *degree* of alienation a person feels and what he does about those feelings. Everyone, at one time or another, has felt some of these feelings, but it is when one is overcome by these feelings that alienation becomes of more concern. Then, too, the alienated individuals throughout history have often been those who have effectively changed society. Without the alienation felt by Christ or Ghandi, our world would be a vastly different place.

Alienation and the United Empire Loyalists

Since the American colonies were striving for independence from Great Britain during the 1770s they were eager to gather total support from the colonists and were not going to look favourably upon dissenters. When talk of revolution came into the open, lines were drawn and people had serious personal decisions to make. Many decided to support a war of independence, but many others wished to remain loyal to the king and to work for a better situation between England and the colonies. As the fever of revolution increased, however, those who maintained their positions of loyalty found themselves in difficult positions. Members of the civil service, the Anglican church, people associated with British businesses and thousands of craftsmen, farmers and artisans were in conflict with those who supported the revolution. As their differences grew, the Loyalists became increasingly alienated from American society.

The Loyalists exhibited many of the characteristics of alienation. From the start they were *socially isolated* from the revolutionaries. Even suspected Loyalists were shunned or harassed in the towns. In the later stages of the Revolutionary war, those who chose not to flee northward were without protection from the law. Mobs looted and pillaged their homes, and those Loyalists who were captured by revolutionaries were badly mistreated.

Since the legal authorities did not act to protect them, the Loyalists had *no power to change things.* As the war went on the American revolutionary armies, with French military and naval support, scored victory after victory.

Perhaps the most pervasive characteristic of alienation which the Loyalists exhibited was *estrangement.* Part of the reason the Loyalists chose to remain loyal to Great Britain was out of rejection of the growing American value system. The revolutionaries placed emphasis on a republican system of government, egalitarian and achievement-oriented society, admiration for wealth and success, and individual rights. The Loyalists, on the other hand, were more conservative, elitist and monarchical. In other words, they distrusted acquisition of great wealth and decentralized government; they respected the

What an individual values is sometimes difficult to pin down. In theory, a person would value something and act accordingly. In real life, we know this is not always the case. For example, one may say she values human life, but will she always act upon that value? What if she is confronted by a knife-wielding attacker? What if the wife of a policeman is asked to sign a petition to abolish capital punishment?

To know what value a person holds about the sanctity of human life or honesty, for example, you need to observe the person's actions as well as words. However, the way a person acts on a value may vary—depending not only on the strength of the value but also on whether the situation involves another value which conflicts with the first.

Another problem is that two people may hold the same value but express or act on it in different ways. For example:

1. What values with regard to the well-being of his family might (a) a Loyalist who migrates to Canada; and (b) a patriot during the Revolution who joins a mob to drive away a British tax collector have in common?

A Loyalist camp on the banks of the St. Lawrence

rule of law and, in general, wished to maintain strong ties with the mother country. Each of these values has had great implications for the development of the American and Canadian nations.

The way in which many of the Loyalists coped with their feelings of alienation was to leave in order to begin a new life in British North America. In rejecting the American revolution and way of life, the Loyalists had a powerful commitment to the values for which they had suffered. Given the opportunity to promote their values, the Loyalists were likely to have a profound impact on the colonies where they settled—Quebec and Nova Scotia.

1. Which of the characteristics—social isolation, powerlessness, or estrangement—do you think had the most effect on Loyalists?

2. John Donne, the English poet, wrote, "No man is an island, entire of itself; every man is a piece of the continent, a part of the main. . . . " What do you think Donne meant and how could his statement apply to a man who decided *not* to join the American Revolution?

3. Each of the Loyalists had to decide whether to remain in the Thirteen Colonies or emigrate to Canada. These people made their decisions based on a system of values.

List as many things as possible that these people valued:

A Patriot or Revolutionary	A Loyalist Who Remained	A Loyalist Who Emigrated

4. Are there groups in present-day Canadian or American society who have rejected the value system of the majority and found themselves with choices similar to those facing the Loyalists?

The War of 1812

"The annexation of Canada this year as far as the neighbourhood of Quebec, will only be a mere matter of marching, and this will give us experience for the attack on Halifax next, and the final expulsion of England from the American continent."[14]

The War of 1812 was the only time in history that Canada and the United States went to war against each other. Yet it was Britain and the United States which declared war. Canada was mainly a bystander, caught between the two giants because it was a British colony that bordered on the United States.

Circumstances in both Europe and North America had been building toward armed conflict for many years. As part of its struggle with France, Britain used its navy to intercept neutral ships trading with the French. Ships from the United States were no exception. Moreover, British sailors boarded American vessels to search for deserters, who frequently escaped the harsh life of the British navy for better conditions in the American "merchant marine." Even American sailors were sometimes forcibly removed and put into service aboard British ships. This high-handed use of the "right of search" roused widespread resentment, especially in the coastal regions of the United States.

Meanwhile, in North America, many sources of bad feeling between Britain and the United States remained. The Treaty of Versailles, which recognized the independence of the United States, left many potential problems. One was the American accusation that Canadians were behind the growing number of Indian attacks. Many Indians still occupied lands south of the Great Lakes, lands which Britain had turned over to the United States without consulting the Indians. At the same time, Britain hung onto its trading posts in this region because of the fur trade, until Jay's Treaty in 1794 provided for Britain's offical withdrawal. The American frontier pushed steadily westward, until the Indians, led by the Shawnee chief, Tecumseh, were driven to organized warfare.

Tecumseh's coalition was destroyed by the United States' victory at Tippecanoe*, but sections of American public opinion were aroused by charges that Canadians had supplied the Indians with weapons and encouraged them to fight. The *War Hawks*, the nickname for members of Congress from states like Kentucky and Tennessee, took advantage of the situation. They demanded war with Britain and an invasion of Canada.

"The War of 1812 was caused by the land-hungry Americans, who looked west and saw the savage Indians, looked north and saw the peaceful Canadians, and agreed that Canada was ripe for emancipation."[15]

Britain had been engaged in almost continuous warfare with France for nearly twenty years. The struggle became more intense as Napoleon Bonaparte pushed his ambitions to dominate Europe and extend the size and power of the French Empire. Following Admiral Nelson's victory at Trafalgar, the British navy tried to cut France off from outside help. Any ships that tried to run the blockade were likely to be intercepted and seized.

*Tippecanoe is located in what is now Indiana.

185

In June, 1812, when President James Madison of the United States advised his government to declare war on Britain, the majority of Americans seemed as reluctant to fight as the Canadians and the British. Officials of both British and American governments tried, right up to the start of the war, to maintain peace. In New England, opposition to war with Britain and Canada was particularly strong. Yet by June 18, 1812, political efforts had failed; the U.S. declared war and plans for invasion went forward.

The Hartford Convention

The Americans were far from united in their feelings about the War of 1812. A group of prominent politicians from New England states met in secret session in Hartford, Connecticut. Because of their opposition to the war, they proposed that states be given the right to ignore decisions of the United States' government which they disagreed with. Their action came very late in the war and did not affect the outcome, but the Hartford Convention reflected the division in American attitudes.

What reasons do these documents give to explain the Americans' belief that an invasion of Canada would be easy?

John Harper of New Hampshire declared:

"North of the Great Lakes a population of four millions [sic] may easily be supported. And this great outlet of the northern world [the St. Lawrence] should be at our command for our convenience and future security. To me, sir, it appears that the Author of Nature has marked out limits in the south by the Gulf of Mexico, and on the north, by the regions of eternal frost."[16]

General Hull, whose army was the first to invade Canada—and retreat—issued a proclamation to Canadians:

"Inhabitants of Canada! . . .

"The army under my command has invaded your country, and the standard of Union now waves over the territory of Canada. To the peaceable, unoffending inhabitant it brings neither danger nor difficulty. I come to *find* enemies, not to *make* them. I come to protect, not to injure you.

_____

"In the name of my country, and by the authority of my Government, I promise protection to your persons, property and rights. Remain at your homes, pursue your peaceful and customary avocations, raise not your hands against your brethren. . . . the arrival of an army of friends must be hailed by you with a cordial welcome.

"You will be emancipated from tyranny and oppression and restored to the dignified station of freemen. Had I any doubt of eventual success I might ask your assistance, but I do not. I come prepared for every contingency. I have a force which will look down all opposition, and that force is but the vanguard of a much greater. If . . . you should take part in the approaching contest, you will be considered and treated as enemies, and the horrors and calamities of war will stalk before you.

"The United States offer you peace, liberty and security. Your choice lies between these and war, slavery and destruction."[17]

Henry Clay, outspoken "war hawk" from Kentucky, spoke to Congress:

"It is absurd to suppose that we will not succeed. We have the Canadians as much under our command as Great Britain has the ocean, and the way to conquer her on the ocean is to drive her from the land. I am not for stopping at Quebec or anywhere else: but I could take the whole Continent from her and ask her no favours. I wish never to see peace till we do. God has given us the power and the means. We are to blame if we do not use them. . . . The conquest of Canada is within your power. I trust I shall not be deemed presumptuous when I state, what I verily believe, that the militia of Kentucky are alone competent to place Montreal and Upper Canada at your feet. Is it nothing to the British nation—is it nothing to the pride of her monarch to have the last of the immense North American possessions held by him in the commencement of his reign, wrested from his dominion? Is it nothing to us to extinguish the torch that lights up savage warfare? Is it nothing to acquire the entire fur trade connected with that country, and to destroy the temptation and opportunity of violating your revenue and other laws?"[18]

If Americans had known how nervous General Brock was about Canadian lack of readiness, they would have been even more confident. In a letter to the governor in Lower Canada, Brock explains about the "cool calculators":

The Militia which assembled here immediately on the account being received of war being declared by the United States have been improving daily in discipline, but the men evince a degree of impatience under their present restraint that is far from inspiring confidence—So great was the clamour to return and attend to their farms, that I found myself, in some measure, compelled to sanction the departure of a large proportion, and I am not without my apprehensions that the remainder will, in defiance of the law, which can only impose a fine of twenty pounds, leave the service the moment the harvest commences—There can be no doubt that a large portion of the population in this neighbourhood are sincere in their professions to defend the country, but it appears likewise evident to me that the greater part are either indifferent to what is passing, or so completely American as to rejoice in the prospects of a change of Governments—Many who now consider our means inadequate would readily take an active part were the regular troops encreased—these cool calculators are numerous in all societies.[19]

The War Hawks claimed that Canada would be easy to conquer, and they seemed to have good reason. The long, thinly defended border appeared to be no obstacle to an American army. The population of Canada, only a fraction of the population of the United States, included many people of recent American origin. Surely they would welcome American forces as liberators. And Britain was tied up in Europe, able to offer only a token defence of her North American colonies.

Aside from the appeal of an apparently easy victory, the United States had the opportunity to "teach Britain a lesson," even drive it from the American continent. A victory could boost the prestige of the young United States, and put an end to the economic depression which the British blockade on trade had helped to cause. Americans could occupy the fertile land of Upper Canada and control the St. Lawrence trade route.

Brock, Sir Isaac (1769-1812), soldier, was born in the island of Guernsey, on October 6, 1769, the eighth son of John Brock and Elizabeth de Lisle. In 1785 he obtained a commission, by purchase, in the 8th Regiment; and by 1797, at the early age of twenty-eight years, he was lieut.-colonel of the 49th Regiment. In 1799-1801 he saw service in Holland and at Copenhagen; and in 1802 he was sent with his regiment to Canada. Here he was stationed, either at Quebec, at Niagara, or at York, until the outbreak of the war of 1812. He was promoted colonel in 1805, and major-general in 1811; and, just before the outbreak of hostilities, in 1812, he was appointed president and administrator of Upper Canada. In the early months of the war, he was the heart and soul of the defence of Upper Canada. With brilliant audacity, he captured Detroit on August 15; and on October 13 his troops defeated the American invaders at Queenston Heights on the Niagara frontier. During the engagement, however, Brock fell, mortally wounded, and died the same day. For his services in connection with the capture of Detroit, he had been gazetted, three days before his death, a K.C.B. He was not married.[20]

Cows, chocolates and beaver dams

A popular image of Laura Secord is the one where she herds her cows through enemy lines, carrying a message that changed the outcome of a battle. In 1913, a chocolate manufacturer decided her image was well enough known that it would sell his product. Who was this lady and what was the reason for her fame?

Laura Secord and her husband James lived in what is now southern Ontario at the time of the War of 1812. While some American officers were visiting her home, Laura overheard their plans for a surprise attack on the British forces at Beaver Dam. She felt compelled to act. Laura decided to walk twenty miles through the woods to warn the British Lieutenant James FitzGibbon of the planned attack. Thus the British were able to win the Battle of Beaver Dam, and Laura Secord became known as the heroine of the War of 1812. The legend of Laura Secord inspired poets and other admirers to pay tribute to her in the form of writings, paintings and even monuments.

Later historical research, however, was skeptical. Although it was true that Laura Secord walked the twenty miles to warn FitzGibbon, he had already been informed by the Indians of the upcoming attack. In fact, some went so far as to say that Laura Secord walked in vain, and that the incident is not of historical significance.

1. If FitzGibbon already knew of the impending attack, is Laura Secord's walk any less significant?
2. What are the qualities you associate with heroines and heroes?
3. What should be Laura Secord's place in history?
4. Laura Secord is one of those Canadians who has been a legend — in a way, a myth. In what ways might myths be important to a country?

What war was like

The war began, following the United States' declaration, with the invasion from Detroit by General Hull's army. In reply the British commander in charge of Upper Canada's defence, General Isaac Brock, launched two actions which took the advantage away from the Americans. He managed to bolster the morale of Canadians at the same time as he strengthened the loyalty of his Indian allies. The United States responded with an attempted invasion through the Niagara Peninsula. At the decisive Battle of Queenston Heights, the combined forces of British regulars, Indians and Canadian militia held firm, in spite of the death of General Brock.

Many Americans were shocked. Canada was not to be an easy conquest after all! American invaders were regarded not as liberators but as enemies. The Loyalist spirit had spread throughout the population. Even within the United States, particularly in New England and New York, people spoke mockingly of "Mr. Madison's War."

CHRONOLOGY

1812:	June	United States declaration of war
	July	U.S. invasion from Detroit British capture of Michilimackinac
	August	British victory at Detroit
	October	British defence of Queenston Heights Death of Sir Isaac Brock
1813:	April	Burning of York (now Toronto)
	May	British blockade of U.S. ports extended and strengthened
	June	Indian allies of British defeated Americans at Beaver Dam
	September	American naval victory at Put-in-Bay gave the United States supremacy on Lake Erie
	October	5th—U.S. victory at Moraviantown, on the Thames River Death of Tecumseh 26th—British troops, supported by French-Canadian militia, turned back Americans at Chateauguay, south of Montreal
	November	Americans defeated at Chrysler's Farm, up river from Montreal
1814:	July	5th—U.S. victory at Chippewa Large but inconclusive battle at Lundy's Lane
	August	British burning of Washington
	September	U.S. victory at Plattsburg, New York
	December	Armistice (Treaty of Ghent)
1817:	April	Rush-Bagot agreement officially ended the war.

Two of the more shocking episodes of the war were the result of naval attacks. In April, 1813, the Americans landed at York (Toronto) and burned the colony's parliament buildings. In retaliation, the British bombarded Washington and set fire to the capitol buildings. As part of that same offensive, British guns shelled Fort McHenry (Baltimore). It was this battle which inspired Francis Scott Keyes to write "The Star Spangled Banner," the United States' national anthem.

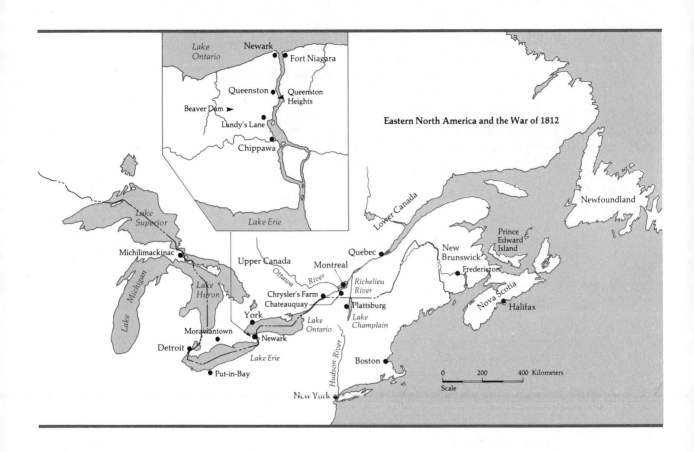

Eastern North America and the War of 1812

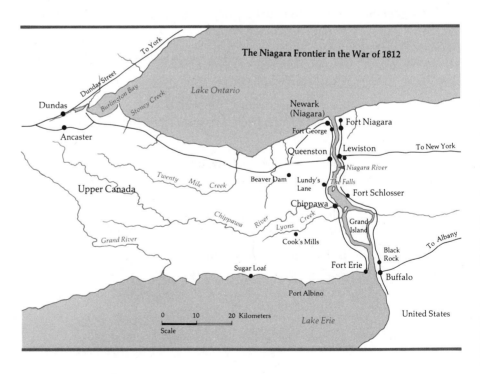

The Niagara Frontier in the War of 1812

The war, nevertheless, dragged on for more than two years. As the chronology on page 189 shows, most of the fighting was on land. Naval warfare was confined mainly to Lake Ontario and Lake Erie, where the American navy, though small, held the advantage. In the Maritime region, although privateers carried out raids on coastal villages, the British navy provided protection against major attacks.

New Brunswick and Lower Canada were vulnerable, but American strategy failed to take advantage of the thinly defended borders. Instead of concentrating on larger strategic centres like Montreal, Americans struck at Upper Canada, through the Niagara district and further west, where Canada seemed to be more vulnerable. The fighting took the form of Canadian defensive stands against American raids, which failed to gain any territory.

1. How was Canada "caught in the middle" between British and American interests during the War of 1812?

The attempt to find a lasting peace

By the summer of 1814, after the defeat and capture of Napoleon, Britain was able to divert forces to North America and take the offensive. The result was a military stalemate, and with both sides tired of the war, the governments of the United States and Britain agreed to a truce. The Treaty of Ghent, signed on Christmas Eve, 1814, was the beginning of negotiations on important issues in the relations between Canada and the United States.

One important result of the lengthy bargaining was the Rush-Bagot Agreement (1817) which not only made the peace agreement official but provided for naval disarmament that remained effective for more than a hundred years*. The United States and Britain agreed to prevent an arms race, limiting armed ships to one each on Lake Champlain and Lake Ontario and two on the other Great Lakes.

*In the 1920s, vessels were armed to intercept "rum runners" carrying liquor illegally into the United States during "Prohibition." In 1940 the Rush-Bagot Agreement was altered, but the reason was military cooperation, not hostility, between Canada and the United States during World War II.

The following year, agreement was reached on the troublesome boundary issue. At the close of the war, Britain held territory in Maine and south of the Great Lakes. Canada could have expected to gain land lost at the conclusion of the American Revolution; the fur-trade, in particular, would have benefited. Yet the United States seemed to be prepared to continue fighting, rather than to give up any territory. Consequently, although the New Brunswick-Maine boundary remained vague, Britain agreed to a clarification of the border in the west. Beyond the Lake of the Woods, the 49th parallel was to be the dividing line all the way to the Oregon territory, which was to be shared indefinitely.

The human side of war

Many statements have been made about war, and the War of 1812 is no exception. Wars may be the tools of governments or the necessary outcome of nations in conflict, but too often we think only of the countries involved. Wars are fought by people, and these people do not leave their humanity behind when they march to the front lines of battle.

Here are several examples of the human side of the War of 1812.

AN EYE FOR AN EYE...?

"The war revealed the emptiness of retaliation, which nonetheless remains the code of combat. Retaliation is an insatiable appetite, a pitcher that will not stay filled. When used against noncombatants it only adds to war's inhumanity and tends to make victory more difficult—the United States lost Canadian sympathy when Americans burned the border towns. When used against declared enemies it only incites stronger opposition—after the enemy devastated Washington, Madison at last commanded a virtually united nation."[21]

THE MORALITY OF WAR: THE ART OF SMUGGLING

"At Ogdensburg, New York, there was an immediate rush to get imports into Canada before the customs' officials clamped down restrictions. After shipments were stopped a large supply of potash remained in storage in the United States and the price rose sharply on the Canadian side of the river. Owners of the American potash resorted to a ruse. They loaded a wagon and when it was about six miles from town had the customs authorities notified of the smuggling attempt and of the general location of the wagon. Summoning his deputies, the collector rushed to the country and three hours later returned in triumph with the lumbering captive wagon. Meanwhile the warehouses had been cleaned bare of all remaining potash and six bateau loads were on the other side of the river, already sold to the Canadians."[22]

WAR AS DESTROYER OF MAN'S LIFE

"There is hardly on the face of the earth a less enviable situation than that of an Army Surgeon after a battle—worn out and fatigued in body and mind, surrounded by suffering, pain and misery, much of which he knows it is not in his power to heal or even to assuage. While the battle lasts these all pass unnoticed, but they come before the medical man afterwards in all their sorrow and horror, stripped of all the excitement of the 'heady fight.'

"It would be a useful lesson to cold-blooded politicians, who calculate on a war costing so many lives and so many limbs as they would calculate on a horse costing so many pounds... to witness such a scene, if only for one hour. This simple and obvious truth was suggested to my mind by the exclamation of a poor woman. I had two hundred and twenty wounded turned in upon me that morning, and among others an American farmer, who had been on the field either as a militia man or a camp follower. He was nearly sixty years of age, but of a most Herculean frame. One ball had shattered his thigh bone, and another lodged in his body, the last obviously mortal. His wife, a respectable elderly looking woman, came over under a flag of truce, and immediately repaired to the hospital, where she found her husband lying on a truss of straw, writhing in agony, for his sufferings were dreadful. Such an accumulation of misery seemed to have stunned her, for she ceased wailing, sat down on the ground, and taking her husband's head on her lap, continued long, moaning and sobbing, while the tears flowed fast down her face; she seemed for a considerable time in a state of stupor, till awakened by a groan from her unfortunate husband, she clasped her hands, and looking wildly around, exclaimed, 'O that the King and the President were both here this moment to see the misery their quarrels lead to—they surely would never go to war without a cause that they could give as a reason to God at the last day, for thus destroying the creatures that He hath made in his own image.' In half an hour the poor fellow ceased to suffer."[23]

HUMANITY VS. VICTORY AT ANY COST

"After the action was over, and it was drawing towards dusk, I rapidly traversed the ground with a strong party to look out for wounded, and finding only a few of the enemy, I ordered them to be carried to the hospital, but I preceded them to make preparations for their reception. When nearing the Camp, I found a party of the band of our Regiment carrying in a blanket an American officer mortally wounded, who was greedily drinking water from one of the soldiers' canteens. I ordered them to lay him down, and set myself to dress his wound. He calmly said, 'Doctor, it's all in vain —my wound is mortal, and no human skill can help me—leave me here with a canteen of water near me, and save yourself—you are surrounded, and your only chance of escape is to take to the woods in a northerly direction, and then make your way east for Queenston,—there is not a man of your army who can escape by any other means—I am not at liberty to tell you more.' I, however, ordered the men to carry him to a hut belonging to an officer of my own Regiment, who undertook to sit by him till my return. After he had been put to bed I left him, and when I returned during the night from my hospital, he was dead. He proved to be Colonel Wood of the American Engineers—a man equally admired for his talents and revered for his virtues. His calmness and courage in the hour of death, with his benevolence and kindness to myself and others; who were doing any little they could to render his last moments easy, convinced me that he deserved the high character which all his brother officers that I afterwards met with uniformly gave him."[24]

1. "The Human Side of War" tries to bring out the effects of war on the people involved. The woman tending her dying husband says: "O that the King and the President were both here this moment to see the misery their quarrels lead to—they surely would never go to war without a cause that they could give as a reason to God at the last day...." Do you think she is right? Would her statement be right about all wars?

Fishing rights were another difficult issue. Britain finally agreed to allow Americans to continue fishing in the coastal waters of British North America. A further important concession was the right of American fishermen to dry their fish on the shores of Newfoundland and Nova Scotia.

How was the War of 1812 regarded by the three main participants? In British history, the war takes a back seat to the struggle against Napoleon and France. Americans regarded the War of 1812 as a defence of "national honour," which they believed had been insulted by Britain. For Canadians, the war was the second time in two generations that they had to withstand an American invasion.

Why was the outcome of the War of 1812 so significant to Canada? Why has the event been given a more important place in Canadian history than in the history of either the United States or Britain? The following statements should help you decide:

ABOUT UPPER CANADA:

Suspicion of American republicanism increased generally throughout the province, but it was at its highest among those in or close to the government.... Men such as John Strachan and his former pupil John Beverley Robinson, who were to provide the conservative leadership of the coming generation, emerged from the conflict convinced that they had narrowly escaped absorption by the United States. Their still-infant province was fated to go on living beside "a powerful and still treacherous enemy" who would seize the first opportunity to repeat the attack. The war had shown how essential it was to hold fast to the British tie as the only sure means of protection.... [26]

The Battle of Queenston Heights

ABOUT THE MARITIMES:

The War of 1812 with the United States had the effect of lifting the Atlantic colonies to a new feeling of self-confidence and self-importance. The redoubled movements of fleets and armies everywhere provided a martial glamour, swelling provincial revenues and increasing commerical prosperity. The five colonies become [sic] more conscious of a British kinship of their own and looked with sympathy to the hard-pressed Canadians as New Brunswick's 104th Regiment, gathered together from distant garrisons, made its celebrated winter march to their assistance.[27]

ABOUT LOWER CANADA:

...the French Canadians demonstrated much greater loyalty than they had shown in 1775. A new Canadian loyalty was beginning to spring up among both groups, [French and English in Quebec] who had fought together to repel invasion and whose doubts about the other had been dispelled by common effort. This new Canadianism was to be demonstrated in the years to come by a collaboration of members of both ethnic groups in favor of Canadian self-government and against British misrule.[28]

Ethnocentrism: my country, right or wrong

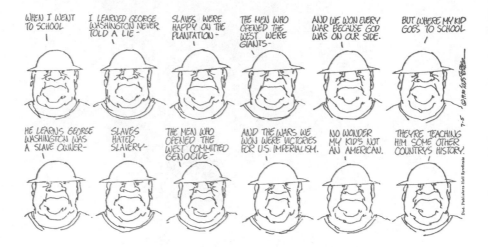

WHEN I WENT TO SCHOOL

I LEARNED GEORGE WASHINGTON NEVER TOLD A LIE –

SLAVES WERE HAPPY ON THE PLANTATION –

THE MEN WHO OPENED THE WEST WERE GIANTS –

AND WE WON EVERY WAR BECAUSE GOD WAS ON OUR SIDE.

BUT WHERE MY KID GOES TO SCHOOL

HE LEARNS GEORGE WASHINGTON WAS A SLAVE OWNER –

SLAVES HATED SLAVERY –

THE MEN WHO OPENED THE WEST COMMITTED GENOCIDE –

AND THE WARS WE WON WERE VICTORIES FOR U.S. IMPERIALISM.

NO WONDER MY KID'S NOT AN AMERICAN.

THEY'RE TEACHING HIM SOME OTHER COUNTRY'S HISTORY.

The man in the cartoon says that "his country's history" talks about honesty, heroes and truth, and that "another country's history" portrays the same events differently. How is it that this fellow could see winning wars as good and someone else could see it as bad?

The idea he is expressing is called *ethnocentrism* by the sociologist. A dictionary would define this term as someone's belief that his own group or culture is superior. That person would also measure everything else by his own culture. In other words, the man in the cartoon was taught that whatever happened in his country was good and he saw only the good side of any event. The history he was taught was *ethnocentric*. When his child studies a different interpretation of those events, or even both sides of an issue, the man says it is "some other country's history." If it is not positive, then it is not *his* country's history.

Of course, the Feiffer cartoon is exaggerated, but to some extent all history is ethnocentric, even nationalistic. A country's history written by its own historians will tend to interpret events from the perspective of a citizen of that country. In other words, Canadian historians are historians, trained to strive for objectivity in describing, analyzing and interpreting events, but they are also Canadians. They share feelings, attitudes and values with other Canadians. The stronger they feel toward a particular event, or the closer they are linked to it emotionally, the more difficult it is to avoid bias in the historical account.

It is said by some that historians should be nationalistic, that they should convey to people a love for their country and a national identity. These people believe that the more Canadian historians reveal to us about our country, the more we will know and appreciate, and the stronger will be our feelings of Canadian identity.

The danger, though, lies in a country's blind devotion to nationalism.* If people have an unthinking faith in their country and its ways, they could easily become uncritical of problems and inequalities which exist. If they feel their country can do no wrong, this puts a great deal of power in the hands of the country's leaders, and this power could be abused. History shows that nationalism can lead to tyranny, or the unrestrained use of power.

*Extreme nationalism is known as *chauvinism*, meaning belligerent patriotism.

Nicholas Chauvin was the French soldier in Napoleon's army, after whom the term "chauvinism" was coined because of his loud-mouthed patriotism. He might be surprised to learn the way the term is used in our culture— *male chauvinism* or the belief in the natural superiority of males over females.

1. What is Canada's national anthem? Do you know the words? Do you ever sing it in public places? What purpose could a national anthem or other songs about Canada serve?
2. When travelling in the United States, have you ever looked for car license plates of Canadian provinces? Why do you think people might do this? What is there that is unique about "a Canadian"— that separates us from Americans, for example?
3. Are Americans or Canadians more ethnocentric? More nationalistic? What examples can you give?
4. (a) Write a brief campaign statement for a political candidate who is appealing to nationalism to get elected when the main issue is a continental energy-sharing plan. (b) Write your reply to his position.

The theme of Canadian-American relations is one of the oldest in the history of both Canada and the United States. That Canadians have generally been more conscious of its importance is easily explained, since the United States has always had the greater potential for dominating the relationship. In the early years, much of the "Canadian-American" relationship was between the United States and Britain, since Canada was a British colony.

Nevertheless, the modern situation, in which Canada and the United States continue to work at sharing a continent, is part of a long experience. The War of 1812 was a low point in that experience; conflicts grew less violent with the passage of time. In the twentieth century, the two nations with the world's longest "undefended border" have become close military allies and developed procedures for resolving political differences through discussion and negotiation.*

*See Volume 2, Chapter 12.

Thus the issues of the present-day in Canadian-American relations, certainly from the Canadian point of view, are primarily economic and cultural. On these issues, the government of Canada* is often involved with the United States through its citizens rather than on a government-to-government level. American companies and

*Provincial governments are increasingly involved in relations with other countries, especially in matters of trade.

The War of 1812 and the Canadian Indian

Tecumseh

Conditions as they were before the war.

Giving up rights to land.

It is well known that an Indian chief named Tecumseh was a hero in the War of 1812. A chief of the Shawnee tribe, Tecumseh was a true statesman who was widely admired among the Indian peoples of the Ohio region. He had organized a coalition of tribes in an unsuccessful effort to protect Indian lands against the advance of American settlers. When the War of 1812 began, he allied himself and his followers with the British, and was prominent in the fighting on the Detroit frontier. He was killed in action at Moraviantown, on the Thames River, on October 6, 1813.

What is less well known is the fate of the Indian people after the War of 1812. The following gives some explanation:

Whether the Indian had in any way improved his own situation is doubtful. The terms of the treaty were a rejection of an Indian state and a return to the **status quo ante bellum**. For the Indian this meant continued pressure and encroachment by the white settlers. The initiative was out of his hands, but he continued to manoeuvre where he could, bending when desirable or necessary, but always resilient.

In view of the military role into which Indians were cast, it is not surprising to find that in historical writing, when Indians are not discussed in military or fur trading terms, in both cases as adjuncts of European activities, they tend to drop out of the story of Canada altogether. When the Indians no longer engaged in military action, however, they were not removed from the considerations of the white society around them. By more peaceful means (perhaps), they were under an unremitting pressure of which they, or at least their leaders, were conscious. The process now became one of **land alienation** and treaties, settlement on reserves, and the three-fold efforts of administrators, missionaries, and teachers to change their culture.[25]

individuals are present in Canada through investment, ownership and other endeavours that raise Canadian concern about American influence. True to the Canadian identity and the Canadian-American style of handling mutual difficulties, the method of dealing is negotiation and compromise.

THE WAR OF 1812 AS A TRADITION:

The war itself became a valued tradition and to the close of the century, at least, the texts used in the schools of the province reflected the deeply Loyalist point of view of the war. Indeed, the history texts, commonly in use in this period, presented but two facts of contact between the United States and Canada—the coming of the Loyalists at the close of the Revolution and the fighting of the War of 1812, both being utilized to strengthen the sense of British allegiance. The losses and sufferings of the Loyalists at the hands of the Americans received special emphasis. The story of the war dwelt particularly upon the victories. Moreover, the Canadian song best known to all school-children, 'The Maple Leaf,' echoed this sentiment:

> At Queenston Heights and Lundy's Lane,
> Our brave fathers, side by side,
> For freedom, homes, and loved ones dear,
> Firmly stood and nobly died;
> And those dear rights which they maintained,
> We swear to yield them never.
> Our watchword ever more shall be,
> The Maple Leaf forever.

A sentiment of hostility to the United States, based upon the traditions of the Loyalists and of the events of the War of 1812, was thus nurtured long beyond the pioneer society in which it first originated.[29]

In an earlier time, Canadian history textbooks highlighted certain events to promote loyalty to Britain. Should they do the same thing *now* to promote a sense of "Canadian identity"?

Tearing down the statue of George III in New York.

8

New people,
new technology,
new frontiers

"On Sturgeon Lake you will find six settlers. Certainly this is not many, but then four of them have been at an University, one at the Military College at Woolwich, and the sixth, though boasting no such honours, has half a dozen silver spoons and a wife who plays the guitar."[1]

In 1833, thousands of people emigrated from Great Britain to British North America. Those who settled here were anxious to have friends and relatives from their homelands join them. Thus, their letters home would often glorify their new-found land. Apparently, judging from this letter written by John Langton in August of 1833, what Sturgeon Lake lacked in *numbers* of settlers, it made up for by unique "qualities"!

THE COLONIES OF BRITISH NORTH AMERICA ENTER A NEW CENTURY

Between the American Revolution and the War of 1812, the British North American colonies enjoyed a period of growth and increasing prosperity. The Maritimes benefited from new opportunities for trade, which resulted from British preference* for colonial products and from the extra markets created by war. The same was true of Upper and Lower Canada, which also experienced population booms. In the west, the confrontation between the Hudson's Bay Company and the Montreal traders opened up routes all the way to

*Remember that Britain charged duties on imports, which increased their prices compared to colonial goods.

200

the Pacific. Each of the colonies was developing in its own way within Britain's reorganized North American empire.

In all of the colonies, most people made their living from primary products or staples—fish, timber, wheat, fur—and closely related industries, such as ship-building and flour mills. In towns like Montreal and Halifax, there were small numbers of wealthy businessmen who had financial connections in London and carried on a far-flung trade with the West Indies or Britain. However, most Canadians lived simple, hard lives in rural areas, struggling to clear a farm or scrape together a living from the sale of products which they "harvested" from the soil, the forests or the sea.

THE WAY IT REALLY WAS

A visitor in the 1820s comments on what settlers' letters did not reveal:

They who invite their friends extol the *absence of taxes*, the salubrity [healthfulness] of the climate, the pleasures, amusements, pastimes, &c. They must not say a word about the *difficulty of clearing the woods*, the toils of the hatchet, the heavy lifts, rheumatic complaints, &c.; they must not say that only a mere speck of the country is yet cleared, and that they may get *land almost for nothing*; for what is its value, remote from towns and places, where it may be brought to some account? Not one of the *logs* that are seen landed on our shores is cut on the farm of any settler; there is no cleared land within 300 miles of where they are obtained. There are no taxes of any extent, because there are very few who could pay them were they imposed. Where there is little taxation in a country, there is often little wealth.[2]

THE BRIGHT SIDE OF THINGS

Conditions were difficult, but some things made settlement worthwhile:

(a) the Town of Newark is situate [sic] in lat. 43 north, on the west bank of the river, extending along the Lake about a mile, enjoying in the summer, the fresh breezes from this little sea, in almost every direction, plentifully supplied with fish at all seasons of the year. In the winter here are caught by seines, quantities of white fish, which seem to be peculiar to that river, they are generally from two to six pounds weight, and are considered the best fish in the lakes; besides, there are sturgeon, bass, and many other excellent fish, in great plenty; salmon are taken in all the creeks round the Lake; these varieties of fish are not only esteemed a luxury, but a great assistance to the new beginners in supporting their families, many laying in a half a dozen barrels or more for their winters' use.[3]

(b) . . . There is still plenty of vacant lands of the best kind, and such as shew a disposition to settle and improve them, meet from

What does this picture reveal about the problems of settlement?

the Governor every encouragement they merit, who makes liberal grants to all such as do actually bring on settlers, and prove themselves desirous of promoting the interest of the country, the whole of which is well adapted for raising wheat, Indian corn, and other summer grain; flax (where the land has borne a few other crops) succeeds remarkably well, and the face of the country yields grass in abundance; hopes of a good quality blackberry, strawberry, raspberry, and grapes.—Orchards are in great forwardness, for the age of the settlement, some of which already bear fruit.—Peaches, cherries, and currants are plenty among all the first settlers.—The farmers raise a great quantity of pork, without any other expense than a little Indian corn, for a few weeks previous to killing, and often kill their hogs out of the woods, well fatted on nuts. In many places salt springs have been discovered, and some of them are already worked to such advantage that in all probability that article, which generally comes heavy in the interior part of the country, may in a short time be afforded here as low as in many of the old settled places in the United States.—Many valuable streams for water works, run in every direction through this country; and upon some of them are mills built, which prove very lucrative to the owners, particularly saw-mills, from the quantity of good timber and great demand of boards, as more buildings are going on than carpenters and masons can be found to finish: Stones being scarce, bricks are generally used in mason work.[4]

A TYPICAL PIONEER HOME?

Susanna Moodie, one of Canada's first authors, describes life in this new land:

The prospect was indeed dreary. Without, pouring rain; within, a fireless hearth; a room with but one window, and that containing only one whole pane of glass; not an article of furniture to be seen, save an old painted pine-wood cradle, which had been left there by some freak of fortune. This, turned upon its side, served us for a seat. . . .

When things come to the worst, they generally mend. The males of our party no sooner arrived than they set about making things more comfortable. James, our servant, pulled up some of the decayed stumps, with which the small clearing that surrounded the shanty was thickly covered, and made a fire, and Hannah roused herself from the stupor of despair, and seized the cornbroom from the top of the loaded waggon [sic], and began to sweep the house, raising such an intolerable cloud of dust that I was glad to throw my cloak over my head, and run out of doors, to avoid suffocation. . . .

The rain poured in at the open door, beat in at the shattered window, and dropped upon our heads from the holes in the roof. The wind blew keenly through a thousand apertures in the log walls; and nothing could exceed the uncomfortableness of our situation. For a long time the box which contained a hammer and nails was not to be found. At length Hannah discovered it, tied up with some bedding which she was opening out in order to dry. I fortunately spied the door lying among some old boards at the back of the house, and Moodie immediately commenced fitting it to its place. This, once accomplished, was a great addition to our comfort. We then nailed a piece of white cloth entirely over the broken window, which, without diminishing the light, kept out the rain.[5]

THE CUSTOM OF COURTING

In the summer of 1800, my mother had a very nice help as nurse. . . . My mother soon discovered that Jenny had a wo[o]er. On Sunday afternoon young Daniel McCall made his appearance with that peculiar happy awkward look that young lads have when they are keeping company, as it is called. At that time when a young man wanted a wife He looked out for some young Girl whom he thought would be a good helpmate and, watching the opportunity, with an awkward Bow and blush, He would ask her to give him her company the ensuing Sunday evening. Her refusal was called 'giving the mitten', and great was the laugh against any young man if it was known that He had 'got the mitten'. All hopes of success in that quarter would be at an end, but young McCall had not 'got the mitten', and it was customary on those occasions when the family retired to bed for the young wo[o]er to get up and quietly put out the candles and cover the fire if any, then take a seat by the side of his lady love and talk as other lovers do, I suppose, until 12 or 1 o'clock, when He would either take his leave and a walk of miles to his home that He might be early at work, or lie down with some of the Boys for an hour or two and then be away before daylight. . . . [6]

A. The Western fur trade: overland to the Pacific

The conquest of New France did not eliminate competition from the fur trade for the Hudson's Bay Company. A rugged assortment of English traders from the Thirteen Colonies and Britain were attracted to Montreal. Their ambition was to take over the old French trade, and, in the early years after 1763, they made their profits from the territory south of the Great Lakes. However, the American Revolution changed the picture. When the International

Canoe manned by voyageurs

Much of what you have read in this book so far would be called history. What is history?

History is the story of great men and women.

History is the study of politicians and governments, generals and war.

History is the record of everything that actually happened in the past.

History is bunk.

History is the long struggle of man, by the exercise of his reason, to understand his environment and to act upon it.

History is a fable agreed upon.

History is the memory of mankind.

History is an account written by winners.

History is like a novel with the good parts removed.

History is a story of man's progress.

History is tricks we play on the dead.

History is a way of thinking about human behaviour in order to analyze personal and social problems of the present.

People often think they know the meaning of this word, until they try to define it. This is not surprising, since even historians have debated about the term, ever since the Greek writer, Herodotus, used the word "history" 2 500 years ago to mean "to inquire". At different times through the centuries and in different parts of the world, historians have concerned themselves with so many sides of human behaviour that nothing man has done seems beyond the interest of the historian.

At different points in this book you have been introduced to history as a kind of record of human activity, a method of analyzing the past, a discipline practised by trained professionals, and a way of trying to understand the present and anticipate the future. We have also looked at many different kinds of "problems of writing history."

The following are comments about history by some noted historians:

THE HISTORIAN AS DETECTIVE

Canadian-born Robin Winks, a historian at Yale, tells of the "Sherlock Holmes" aspect of his work:

Much of the historian's work, . . . like that of the insurance investigator, the fingerprint man, or the coroner, may to the outsider seem to consist of deadening routine. Many miles of intellectual shoe leather will be used, for . . . uninformative diaries, blank checkbooks, old telephone directories, and other trivia will stand between the researcher and his answer. Yet the routine must be pursued, or the clue may be missed; the apparently false trail must be followed in order to be certain that it is false; the mute witnesses must be asked the reasons for their silence, for the piece of evidence that is missing from where one might reasonably expect to find it is, after all, a form of evidence in itself.[7]

DIFFERENT KINDS OF HISTORY

A business historian notes the increase in importance of economic history:

In a nation that has slowly divested itself of the mantle of the motherland, naturally there has been a concentration of interest on constitutional and political issues. Further, in a nation that was a colony for so long, and continues to live under the shadow of a much larger neighbour, there has naturally been a search for a separate identity. These questions have turned many historians' eyes to such problems as biculturalism, northern approaches, and fortunately for business history, the search for an economic framework into which an individual Canadian identity can be fitted. Thus, although political considerations continue to dominate Canadian historiography, economic theories have gradually assumed a more respected place. . . . [8]

IS HISTORY UNSCIENTIFIC?

British historian G. M. Trevelyan, comments on the difference between history and science:

The study of mankind does not resemble the study of the physical properties of atoms, or the life history of animals. If you find out about one atom, you have found out about all atoms, and what is true of the habits of one robin is roughly true of the habits of all robins. But the life history of one man, or even of many individual men, will not tell you the life history of other men. . . . Men are too complicated, too spiritual, too various, for a scientific analysis.[9]

HISTORY AND OTHER DISCIPLINES

In his book What Is History? *British historian E. H. Carr states:*

Scientists, social scientists, and historians are all engaged in different branches of the same study: the study of man and his environment, of the effects of man on his environment and of his environment on man. The object of the study is the same: to increase man's understanding of and mastery over, his environment.[10]

EVERY MAN HIS OWN HISTORIAN

An authority on historical method once wrote:

Every normal adult knows, has read, and has written enough history to find pat illustrations ... of the problems [of historical research] ....The normal adult has a memory that embraces several years of experience. In the course of that experience he has read and heard many historical documents—among them newspapers, letters, public and legal papers, radio announcements, political speeches, official statistics, advertisements, and ordinary conversations. He has also written many potential historical documents— school exercises, tax reports, personal and business letters, speeches, notes in notebooks or on scraps of paper, comments in the margins of books he has read, expense accounts, household budgets, journal and ledger entries, bills and orders at the stores, minutes of his club, score cards, datebook and diary entries, and so on. Any one of these, if it should fall into the hands of a historian interested in him, or the place in which he lived, or his times, or the activities in which he engaged, might become a source of some knowledge, no matter how meager and unreliable. The people who threw away old household and business accounts in ancient Egypt thousands of years ago probably had no thought of today's historian.[11]

You can see that people have many different views of history. This does not mean that history is strictly a personal matter, that anybody can write history according to his or her individual tastes. In fact, the methods of history have been refined over the years, and those who practise historical research and writing agree on many basic procedures.

The best way for you to understand the basic procedures of the historian is to try some of them. One way to do so is to investigate the history of your family.

1. *The historian poses a question.*

   You may ask: What was my great-grandfather's name? Where did he live? What did he do for a living?

2. *The historian may form a hypothesis.*

   You may make an "intelligent guess." My great-grandfather emigrated to Canada to seek a better life for himself and his family.

3. *The historian gathers evidence.*

You may collect information by asking your parents and/or other relatives. This may give you evidence in the form of *oral reports*. You may be able to obtain family records in the form of old photos, a Bible or other special possession, or even letters that have been handed down. Such *written evidence* could be a real discovery. To supplement information available within your own family, you can go to such places as the *public archives*. Records there may not include data about your family, but they may reveal interesting facts about other people who lived at the same time and had similar experiences.

4. *The historian tests the evidence.*

You may ask: Is my evidence *valid*? Are my sources, such as a grandparent, likely to have forgotten some of the facts? Are the recollections clear or hazy? Could nostalgia have influenced memories of "the good old days"? Are family photos labelled, to include names and dates? Can written items be shown to be authentic? Would any ancestor have had a reason to "invent" a letter, a page in a diary or other record?

Once you can establish the validity of a source, can you be reasonably sure that the evidence contained is *reliable*? Do facts check out with other information which may be available, for example, from records in a municipal office or in the appropriate government department? Are references to major events, such as an election, accurately related to accounts given in commonly-used history books?

5. *The historian uses his evidence.*

You may ask: How shall I present my findings? Have I discovered enough information to answer the questions with which I began? Am I able to confirm or disprove my hypothesis? Are my findings of interest to anyone but myself—my family, friends, people at school, the local historical society? Should I present my history in the form of an oral report, a written article, a photo essay with written commentary?

Learning about your family's history can be rewarding. You may discover a famous relative or learn that great-uncle Harry really *was* a horse thief. Even if you find out very little, the practice of *inquiry* can help you become more systematic in analyzing problems. The methods of the historian are much like those of any other investigator. The training in questioning, analysis and critical thinking can be put to many uses.

German critic Gotthold Ephraim Lessing said: "Without history . . . we shall be in hourly danger of being deceived by ignorant braggarts, who not infrequently hail as a new discovery what men knew and believed many thousands of years ago."[12]

---

boundary was drawn through the Great Lakes and Britain eventually vacated its posts in what had become United States' territory, the Montreal traders were forced in the direction of the Northwest.

The Hudson's Bay Company, which for a century had fought with French companies for the fur trade, now faced renewed competition, this time from English-speaking rivals. The aggressive Montrealers pushed westward to do business directly with Indian tribes, who normally hauled their furs along the rivers to the posts on the Bay.

Increasing competition and rising costs eventually became too burdensome for the small partnerships that centred in Montreal. While vying with the Hudson's Bay Company, the Montreal traders were also competing among themselves. As their numbers increased, as they had to travel further and further into the Northwest, their costs rose sharply: the need to construct inland trading posts, for more supplies and more employees—all pushed up the investment required and decreased profits. The sheer distance between Montreal and the richest fur-bearing areas, such as the Athabasca country, imposed the need for a large-scale organization.

The North West Company, formed in the 1780s, was the result. The Montreal traders were obliged to cooperate in order to compete successfully with the Hudson's Bay Company. They also had to work toward efficiency in organization and aggressiveness in trading practices. To overcome the problem of distance, the North West Company set up a system that operated over the "trans-Canada canoeway"—a network of waterways, portages and strategically placed trading posts.

Anthony Henday, an employee-explorer of the Hudson's Bay Company, travelled in 1754 from Fort York on Hudson Bay to the foothills of the Rockies in order to convince the Indians to bring their furs to "the Bay."

A few years later (1771-1774), Samuel Hearne explored the West, discovered the Coppermine River and Great Slave Lake.

TYPICALLY CANADIAN?

Can you find examples of later Canadian enterprises that exhibited the traits attributed to the North West Company?

[The North West Company] was the prototype of the great Canadian business organizations; it was the first of that long line of co-partnerships, companies and public enterprises which began with continental objectives or developed them in course of time. But the North West Company came in the first flush of Northern maturity . . . . it was an organization dependent ultimately upon individual heroism and endurance. . . .

These intensely individualistic traders were taught to combine only with great difficulty and after failures, quarrels and violence.[13]

Alexander Mackenzie

a person of mixed parentage, Indian and non-Indian, e.g. Indian mother/French father.

Traders and explorers like Alexander Mackenzie, Simon Fraser and David Thompson had spearheaded the creation of Canada's first transcontinental business operation. However, their very achievement signalled difficult days for the fur trade. They had reached the western limits of the continent. The next stage was "head to head" competition with the Hudson's Bay Company.

The possibility of a showdown suddenly increased when Lord Selkirk, a wealthy and determined Scottish nobleman appeared on the scene. He managed to purchase a controlling interest in the Hudson's Bay Company, and, in the spring of 1811, obtained a land grant of 290 324 square kilometres in what is now Manitoba, Minnesota and North Dakota. Selkirk's objective: to give poverty-stricken British farmers a new chance by creating a settlement in the Red River Valley—a settlement which would cut across the main routes of the North West Company. The Nor'westers realized that settlement—especially one backed by the Hudson's Bay Company—would be a threat to their business. Not long after the first Selkirk settlers arrived, in the spring of 1812, the Nor'westers began to apply the pressure. Then, in 1814, the Governor of Assiniboia, the name given to the Selkirk land grant, issued the "pemmican proclamation." By forbidding the export of pemmican from the colony, he was trying to protect the food supply of the settlers. However, the Nor'westers viewed the proclamation as a hostile act against them and their **Métis** allies who profited from the sale of pemmican. Two years of conflict ensued, reaching a climax with the Battle of Seven Oaks, in which twenty settlers were killed by a band of Métis and Indians.

SIMPLE FOOD BUT HEALTHFUL

Pemmican was an Indian food which the Nor'westers bought from the Métis. In the days before canned goods, it was valuable for long-distance travel since it did not spoil easily and was very nourishing. Trader Daniel Williams Harmon describes this food:

This is the first Day [August 3, 1800] I ever past (since my infancy) without eating either Bread or Biscuit, but as a substitute for them we now have what the Natives call *Pimican* (pemmican), which is a compound of lean Meat dried and pounded fine & then mixed with melted Fat, and then put into Bags (made of the Skins of Buffaloe [sic] &c.) and when cold becomes a solid body and if kept in a dry place will preserve good for years, but if in a damp place it soon becomes musty. Our people like it much better than Milled

Nor'westers vs. Hudson's Bay

WINTERERS: also known as "wintering partners" because they spent most of their time in the West, trading for furs with the Indians. In the summer they transported their furs to Fort William.

PORKEATERS: a term for the Montreal partners who collected the furs from the "winterers" and transported the furs back to Montreal for export.

ATHABASCA COUNTRY: the region of Lake Athabasca and many other rivers and lakes; one of the richest fur-bearing areas exploited by the North West Company.

VOYAGEURS: French-Canadian canoemen whose strength and skill was so important to the Scottish traders who dominated the North West Company.

Alexander Mackenzie, who began as a teen-age explorer for the North West Company, was the first European to reach the Arctic Ocean (1789) and the Pacific Ocean (1793). Looking for a navigable water route to the Pacific for a less expensive transportation route for North West Company furs, Mackenzie travelled along what he named Disappointment River (today the mightly Mackenzie River) to the Arctic Ocean. Undaunted, he set out again, this time travelling down the treacherous Fraser River, eventually reaching the Pacific. He won world recognition when a journal of his exploits (*Voyages*) was published and widely read, and in 1801 he was knighted by King George III of Britain.

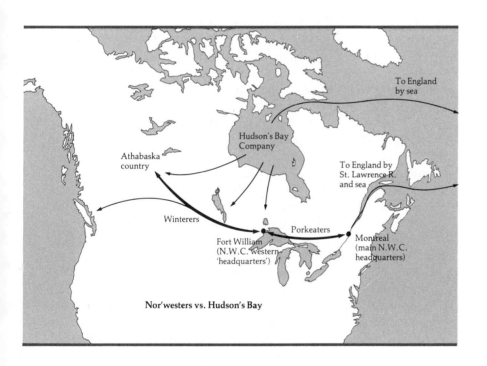

Nor'westers vs. Hudson's Bay

Indian Corn & then boiled as it is cooked in this Country & I although not accustomed to it, find it very palatable and it is said to be very nourishing & healthy Food.[14]

Selkirk, meanwhile, was returning to Red River from Upper Canada when he heard the news. He reacted by contacting approximately 100 **mercenaries**, disbanded Swiss soldiers of the Des Meurons regiment who had been hired by the British during the War of 1812. They travelled with him to Fort William, seized the North West Company fort, and arrested the leader, William McGillivray. Selkirk proceeded to Red River, where he restored the colony.

The long struggle had left both sides exhausted and near financial ruin. His company badly divided, William McGillivray began negotiations with the Hudson's Bay Company and in 1821—the year after Selkirk's death—the old rivals joined under the name of the Hudson's Bay Company.

professional soldiers who hire themselves out, usually to a government

In the next three years, the little farming community enjoyed a peaceful existence. More than twenty land grants were made to settlers and land was set aside for schools and churches. In 1818, Father Provencher arrived and opened a Catholic school at St. Boniface for the French-speaking settlers. Reverend John West, the first Anglican clergyman to arrive, started a school for Protestant children.

A BANQUET FOR THE HUDSON'S BAY COMPANY MEN AND OLD NOR'WESTERS, 1821

Partners from both sides found the union very difficult to accept:

....At length the bell summoned us to dinner, when forthwith in walked the heterogenous mass of human beings, but in perfect silence and with the most solemn gravity...though joined together [they] would not amalgamate, for the Nor'westers in one compact body kept together....But that crafty fox...George Simpson, coming hastily to the rescue with his usual tact and dexterity on such occasions, succeeded....Their previously stiffened features began to relax a little; they gradually but slowly mingled together, and a few of the better disposed, throwing themselves unreservedly in the midst of the opposite party, mutually shook each other by the hand. Then, and not till then were they politely beckoned to their appointed places at the mess-table. [Some, however, found themselves misplaced.] For instance, he whom they called blind McDonnel...found himself directly in front of his mortal foe of Swan River, the vivacious Chief Factor Kennedy....[They] had hacked and slashed at each other with naked swords only a few months before....One of them still bore the marks of a cut on his face, the other, it was said, on some less conspicuous part of his body. I shall never forget the look of utter scorn and utter defiance with which they regarded each other the moment their eyes met. The highlander's nostrils actually seemed to expand; he snorted, squirted, and spat...between his legs, and was as restless on his chair as if he had been seated on a hillock of ants....I thought it fortunate that they were without arms....[15]

212

Lord Selkirk

Lord Thomas Douglas Selkirk undertook to settle poor people of the British Isles in British North America. At his own expense in 1803, he arranged the transportation and settlement of some 800 people from Scotland to Prince Edward Island. There, along the shore of the eastern peninsula, farms and villages were started.

Lord Selkirk

After a second venture, not far from Lake St. Clair in Upper Canada, proved to be a failure, Selkirk launched his incredible project in the Canadian West. Because of the bitter struggle between the Hudson's Bay Company and the Nor'westers, the early years of the Red River colony were "touch and go", marked by hardship and tragedy. But the colony survived both the immediate troubles and the decades of isolation between Selkirk's departure (1819) and the birth of Manitoba (1870).

Selkirk's personal story ended in tragedy. Following the Battle of Seven Oaks and Selkirk's retaliatory capture of the Nor'westers' post at Fort William, he was embroiled in costly lawsuits with the North West Company. His fortune diminished and his health destroyed, Lord Selkirk died in 1820, unaware that he would one day be regarded as one of the builders of the Canadian West.

The effect of the union was to leave the west isolated for a generation. Furs were now transported exclusively by sea from the posts on the Bay; the "trans-Canada canoeway" was abandoned. Times were changing, and furs were no longer "king staple." Timber and wheat had already begun to replace them as the main commodities of trade in British North America.

THE BORING FUR TRADE?

Thus ... the fur trade has been the subject of the most detailed examination in all its phases, and new material is constantly coming out. Certainly it provides a romantic topic which has attracted many amateur historians as well as taking up a disproportionate part of the available time of the few Canadian business historians. It has also, unfortunately, spilled over into the public school textbooks. As a result, generations of Canadian students have had their interest in Canadian history killed by the stories of innumerable traders, whose names could be neither spelled nor pronounced, paddling in all directions on a vast number of rivers with equally unintelligible names.[16]

1. Do you agree with the sentiments expressed? Has over-exposure to the story of the fur trade killed *your* interest in Canadian history? Does this explain why you know of no Canadian "Daniel Boones"? Is the statement about the names of traders and rivers accurate?

B. Immigration

Major migrations to Canada before Confederation

1660s, 1670s: French settlers brought in under Royal Government in New France

1760s: New Englanders migrated to Nova Scotia after the expulsion of the Acadians

1780s: Loyalists

1790s, early 1800s: Americans (primarily to Upper and Lower Canada)

1815-1850: "great migration" from Great Britain

Most of Canada's population today, including the native peoples, is descended from immigrants, people who came into the country from elsewhere. Therefore, most Canadians would not be here but for ancestors who endured the hardships of leaving a homeland, travelling great distances and struggling to make a living in a strange land. From a national point of view, immigration was important historically in opening up new areas, in providing manpower for industries, and supplying much needed human resources. Efforts have frequently been made to attract new settlers; at other times, large movements of population to Canada were the result of sudden changes or harsh conditions elsewhere—war, revolution, famine.

Between the coming of the Loyalists (1780s) and Confederation (1867), Canada experienced two important periods of immigration. The first influx of settlers came from the United States. Following the War of 1812, the pattern changed and British citizens were the ones who came.

BEFORE **1812**

There were two notable facts about the immigration to British North America in the 1790s and early 1800s: most of the immigrants came from the United States; and, they settled mainly in Upper Canada (now Ontario). The extended war between Britain and France in Europe and on the high seas was not conducive to overseas travel. Americans, however, were moving westward overland, and many of them learned from relatives or from news circulated in the United States that land was plentiful and cheap in Upper Canada.

The lieutenant-governor of the colony in the 1790s, John Graves Simcoe, had been the leader of a Loyalist fighting unit during the American Revolution, but he welcomed American settlers in Upper Canada. He believed most of them were simply misguided, not really anti-British. Simcoe was convinced of the value and good influence of the British form of government introduced by the Constitutional Act (1791). He expected American settlers would discover their loyalty to the mother country once they had settled in Upper Canada.

Thanks to the generous attitude of Simcoe and his successors, the population of Upper Canada jumped from some 12 000 in 1791

Simcoe was realistic enough to fear the intentions of the United States. Consequently, he started to build roads which would be important to the movement of troops in defending Upper Canada against invasion. The capital of the province was moved from Newark (Niagara) to York (Toronto), which became the starting point for roads, such as Yonge Street and Dundas Street.

214

The nature of immigration

Read the following documents illustrating the story of immigration.
What kind of picture do they give you?

ADVICE TO EMIGRANTS

People interested in migrating had plenty of advice in the form of pamphlets telling them what to do and what not to do:

... every young farmer or labourer going out (who can pay for the passage of two) to take an active young wife with him. ...

Unmarried Women, who have no fortunes, and are *active*, and *industrious, without much pride or vanity*, and who relish a *quiet* and *retired* life ... have an opportunity of being well married. ...

... as the settlers must scramble about in all weathers ... stout flannels and coarse cloths ... must not mind fashion; the best coat and breeches are those that can come farthest through the brush with fewest holes in them ... there is not a better article for the purpose than Scotch blanket ... called plaiding.

... religious and loyal prints—coloured Scriptural subjects with texts attached, home scenery of school and village churches. Portraits of Her Majesty, Prince Albert and the royal children, Wellington and Nelson, views of Windsor Castle, the House of Parliament, our cathedrals. ...

Above all things do not take your decanters or your corkscrew. ... You are going to a country where you may literally swim in whiskey or gin, and pretty nearly in brandy or rum. But resolve never to taste either. Drinking is the great vice of the country.[17]

1. Whom might this "advice" deter from emigrating? Whom might it encourage?

SOME IMMIGRANTS NO BETTER OFF THAN SLAVES

Most immigrants were poor. Some were lucky enough to receive help from private individuals or charity organizations; local governments helped others. Yet others had to find someone to "sponsor" their travel:

A despicable trade was carried on by some of the more unscrupulous captains and their confederates on the American side. Very poor people frequently mortgaged themselves to captain or shipowner for the amount of their passage and that of their families, and then worked off their indebtedness in America, and possibly on board ship as well. An early guidebook, in referring to this iniquitous system of slavery, states that "immense numbers (from

215

Ireland particularly) emigrate on these conditions. When the ship in which he sails arrives at her destined port, the captain turns him over to someone who requires his services, who redeems him, paying the captain his demand, and paying himself out of the labour of the poor emigrant who is bound to work for the man who redeemed him until he cancels the debt." While a superficial glance at this system might suggest that it facilitated the emigration of the poverty-stricken, deeper consideration shows its abuses, thousands of men being virtually slaves for a period often five times as long as it would have taken to earn the passage money anywhere else in the labor market. One of them compared himself to "Joseph the Israelite; for he had been entrapped, and indented to work several years for his passage; and he considered himself little better than a slave till his term was expired."[18]

LIFE ABOARD THE SHIPS

Although conditions eventually improved, many immigrants crossed the ocean in ships that reached England with a cargo of timber, and returned to ports like Halifax or Quebec with a "cargo" of people. Cramped conditions, inadequate facilities and diseases such as cholera and dysentery all made the crossing a nightmare for such passengers:

"It was scarcely possible to induce the passengers to sweep the decks after their meals or to be decent in respect to the common wants of nature: in many cases, in bad weather, they would not go on deck; their health suffered so much that their strength was gone, and they had not the power to help themselves. Hence the between-decks were like a loathsome dungeon. When the hatchways were opened under which the people were stowed, the steam rose and the stench was like that from a pen of pigs. The few beds they had were in a dreadful state, for the straw, once wet with sea water, soon rotted, besides which they used the between-decks for all sorts of filthy purposes."

"Our water for some time past has been very bad. When it was drawn out of the casks it was no clearer than that of a dirty kennel after a heavy shower of rain; so that its appearance alone was sufficient to sicken one. But its dirty appearance was not its worst quality. It had such a rancid smell that to be in the same neighborhood was enough to turn one's stomach; judge then what its taste must have been. . . . The stink it emitted was intolerable."

"A little child who was playing with his companions suddenly fell down, and for some time was sunk in a death-life torpor, from which, when she awoke, she commenced to scream violently and writhed in convulsive agony. A poor woman who was warming a drink at the fire for her husband, also dropped down quite sense-

Cholera

The ignorance about the disease was complete, and most of the remedies prescribed came out of the memories of the middle ages. Quebec newspapers warned their readers against putting bare feet on a cold floor, or sleeping with windows open, or drinking on an empty stomach. They suggested camphor fumigations, tinctures of lavender, opium, or rhubarb, and recommended liberal use of warm, spiced drinks, or brandy and water, or maple syrup and ginger . . . everyone watched himself and those near him for the failing appetite, the white, furred tongue, the nausea and sinking of the stomach or rumbling of wind in the bowels that might be the first warning, to be followed by the spasms and cramps, the numbness and apathy, the cold, bluish pallor, and the shrinking and wasting of the face.[20]

less and was borne to her berth. . . . The first symptom was generally a reeling in the head, followed by a swelling pain, as if the head were going to burst. Next came excruciating pains in the bones, and then a swelling of the limbs, commencing with the feet, in some cases ascending the body and again descending before it reaches the head, stopping at the throat. The period of each stage varied in different patients; some of whom were covered with yellow, watery pimples, and others with red and purple spots, that turned into putrid sores. . . . The moaning and raving of the patients kept me awake nearly all night; and I could hear the mistress stirring about until a late hour. It made my heart bleed to listen to the cries of 'Water, for God's sake some water!'"[19]

ARRIVING IN THE NEW WORLD

Some met success:

"I really do bless God every day I rise, that he was ever pleased, in the course of his providence, to send me and my family to this place [Lanark County, Upper Canada]. Were you here and seeing the improvements that are going on among us, you would not believe that we were once Glasgow weavers!

Urge my brothers to come out if ever they wish to free themselves from bondage . . . this is the land of independence to the industrious—the soil that will repay the labourer for the sweat of his brow."[21]

Others met untold hardships:

[The immigrant often found himself] in a foreign land, far distant from his relations and friends, fixed in a desolate wilderness, shut up in a miserable hut called a shanty, the cold winter winds penetrating through its crevices and piercing his benumbed limbs with their chilly blasts; he will wildly look around the place he has chosen for a habitation for his beloved wife and family, whom he has, perhaps, dragged from home almost against their will; he views them with cheerless glances, and their returning looks of despair must wound his very soul,—all this he will have to endure with the prospect of spinning out a miserable existence.[22]

1. Compare and contrast the two letters from new settlers. Which excerpt seems most realistic? Which seems most idealistic? Which would you rather read if you were a relative hoping to emigrate? Why?

to approximately 75 000, mostly former residents of the United States, by the outbreak of the War of 1812. And for whatever reasons, this population did not welcome the American invaders, as the British feared and the United States expected, when hostilities broke out in the summer of 1812.

AFTER 1812

The War of 1812 ended the migration of Americans to British North America for a long time. The bitterness of the struggle made the international boundary a real dividing line between the loyal British colonies and the wayward republic to the south. The Loyalist spirit was supreme, and anti-American attitudes were reinforced by discriminatory laws.* Canada was no longer an attractive destination for Americans; but for various reasons, a flood of British immigrants crossed the ocean in search of opportunity.

*An American immigrant was denied the right to own property, and thus the right to vote or hold public office, for a period of seven years after his arrival.

In the decades after 1815, people risked the difficult ocean voyage only because they found conditions in Britain unbearable and believed North America would be different. The end of the Napoleonic wars brought severe depression to Britain; the slowdown in production contributed to the rise in unemployment, just when thousands of men had been released from military service. As the years passed, and the Industrial Revolution gained momentum, the factory system eliminated many traditional jobs and created new ones at which people worked long, tedious hours in depressing conditions for low wages.

British North America offered new hope. Cheap rates were available on the immigrant ships. If a traveller survived the trip across the ocean, he or she had the prospect of cheap land, or the chance to practise a trade—either in British North America, or south of the border.

*See page 210.

A combination of developments in Great Britain created a "surplus population" anxious to try their luck elsewhere. Besides the effects of the Industrial Revolution, which spread even to Scotland, as the story of the Selkirk settlement* illustrates, natural disasters like the Irish potato famine of the 1840s left people at the point of starvation. Many were ready to emigrate in the simple hope that British North America would offer a better future for themselves and their families.

Immigration policy: everybody, the select few, or none?

SITUATION #1

An earthquake has devastated a large part of continent X. Thousands of people have died; thousands more have been left homeless. Relief pouring into the continent can only provide for immediate needs of food and medical supplies. Some of the homeless learn about Canada being a vast land with a relatively small population. Though they speak no English or French, they feel that somehow they would probably be better off in Canada, "the land of opportunity."

You are an immigration officer who is assigned to handle such cases.

1. If you allow these people to immigrate, what might be the consequences of this decision for
   (a) the earthquake victims?
   (b) the citizens of the town or city in which they settle?
2. If you do not allow these people to immigrate, what might be the consequences of this decision for
   (a) the earthquake victims?
   (b) the citizens of the town or city in which they would have settled?
3. Are there other alternatives available to you?
4. What things would you consider in making your decision?
5. What would your decision be and why?

SITUATION #2

Several families of a religious minority who feel persecuted in the country of their birth are now able to leave that country after many years of waiting. Although their government previously refused to allow these people (many of whom are scientists, authors, doctors and philosophers) to leave, the pressure of world opinion has led to a change of policy. As a result, many people of this religious minority are seeking landed immigrant status in Canada.

You are an immigration officer who is assigned to handle such cases.

1. If you allow these people to immigrate, what might be the consequences of this decision for
   (a) the families who wish to immigrate?
   (b) the town or city in which they settle?
2. If you do not allow these people to immigrate, what might be the consequences of this decision for
   (a) the families who wish to immigrate?
   (b) the town or city in which they would have settled?
3. Are there other alternatives available to you?
4. What things would you consider in making your decision?
5. In your opinion, how does the situation here differ from the situation involving the earthquake victims? Do the differences affect your decision? If so, how? What would your final decision be, and why?

The Industrial Revolution

The Industrial Revolution, a term commonly used for the mechanization of industry and its effects, developed earlier in Britain than elsewhere. In the textile industry, for example, wool, cotton and other basic materials were available— either in Britain or in its colonies. Capital, shipping and other transportation facilities, and manpower in the fast-growing towns and cities were other necessary ingredients for the rapid growth of an industrial economy.

Significantly, this was a capitalist economy,* based on supply and demand, profit-seeking and private ownership of the means of production. In the pursuit of profit, the businessman could be taking considerable risk; the worker also had to sell his "product"—his labour—on the competitive market. If business was good, the worker had a job at the lowest wage the employer was willing to pay. If business was poor, the worker could be laid off with no compensation.

*See pages 64-66.

A "landed immigrant" is a person who has been given permission to enter and live in Canada with all the same privileges that a citizen enjoys except the right to vote and to hold public office. Landed immigrant status is the first step to becoming a *naturalized citizen* or one who becomes a citizen through a legal ceremony rather than by birth.

SITUATION #3

Most of the immigrants to Canada arrive at Montreal, Toronto or Vancouver. Since they are unfamiliar with the country and need to save some money before moving on, they stay at least for awhile in these cities. Population is already becoming a problem in Canada's largest cities, and many urban planners are studying ways of encouraging people to move out of these heavily-populated urban areas.

Of the 30 families who applied for landed immigrant status today, only two expressed an interest to settle in places other than Montreal, Toronto and Vancouver. All the rest have relatives in these three cities and plan to begin their life in Canada in one of these places.

You are an immigration officer who is handling these 30 cases.

1. If you allow the families to immigrate to Canada's three largest cities, what might be the consequences of this decision for
   (a) the families?
   (b) the cities of Toronto, Vancouver and Montreal?
2. If you do not allow the families to immigrate to Canada's three largest cities, what might be the consequences of this decision for
   (a) the families?
   (b) the cities of Toronto, Vancouver and Montreal?
3. Are there other alternatives available to you?
4. What things would you consider in making your decision?
5. In your opinion, how does this situation differ from situations one and two? Do the differences affect your decision? If so, how? What would your final decision be, and why?

As the dilemmas reveal, Canada's position on immigration is a perplexing one. On the other hand, a person favouring large-scale immigration into Canada can point out that we have a great deal of sparsely inhabited territory—much more than other large countries such as China or even the United States. As of the 1970s, Canada for the most part is not suffering the effects of over-population. Food, too, is plentiful, and although unemployment and inflation are problems, it seems that economic planning may have at least provided temporary improvements here. By and large, Canada could accept large numbers of immigrants, at least for the next decade or so.

Others question how many people Canada *could* or *should* accommodate in the years to come. If she has an "open door" policy, Canada could eventually be faced with overcrowding, a more severe pollution problem, and higher levels of unemployment. There may be problems in providing social services such as medical care, recreational facilities and education for all people. Social assistance or welfare and unemployment funds may also be taxed to the limit. All in all, a policy of unrestricted immigration would present numerous problems.

In playing the role of immigration officer, you had to consider different cases. Each case had to be judged on its distinctive characteristics, but there are general considerations which must also be taken into account. Later, in Volume 2, you will have the opportunity to look at particular instances of immigration to Canada and their unique problems*. At this point, though, answer yes or no to the following statements, giving your reasons why or why not:

*The theme of immigration appears in Chapter 4.

1. Canada should not have an "open door" policy on immigration.
2. There should be no "special considerations" for potential immigrants. All those who wish to come to Canada should be judged on the same criteria as every other person.
3. It would be wrong to insist that a criterion for landed immigrant status be that immigrants *must* settle in less densely populated areas.
4. If Canada has a shortage of workers in particular trades or professions, she should advertise in foreign newspapers to encourage suitable people to immigrate, (e.g. doctors for rural and northern areas, geophysicists, university professors).
5. Canada has an obligation to accept immigrants from any

You may be interested in contacting your local office of the federal Department of Manpower and Immigration to find out the exact criteria used to award people landed immigrant status.

What does this picture say about immigrating to North America by ship?

nation which has been devastated by disasters such as wars and earthquakes (e.g. Vietnamese refugees, victims of the Irish troubles, South African blacks).

C. The land problem

The hope of many immigrants was land of their own, where they could make a fresh start as "their own boss." Yet they were faced with many problems. Their lands were likely to be remote from the main towns, and since roads were poor or non-existent, they were isolated from supplies and markets. Clearing their land, building a house and barn, providing for the educational and religious needs of themselves and their families, even finding some form of social and recreational life—all these were difficult challenges.

Yet one of the most serious problems was to obtain land in the first place. Since Upper Canada was the destination of the largest number of immigrants, the situation in that colony was one that needs to be examined. Most of the good land was assigned to influential persons—loyalists, ex-army officers and others with connections. Two-sevenths of every township had been retained by the government in the form of crown reserves and clergy reserves.

Speculation is the term for obtaining land or other resources and holding them back from the market until higher prices can be charged.

Generally speaking, **speculation** is a way of realizing the greatest profits from land ownership. If the available land is plentiful and public services, such as roads, are poor, prices are likely to be low. Therefore, a landowner is inclined to keep the land until circumstances increase the market value. In the case of Upper Canada, the British government retained ownership of the crown reserves until the middle 1820s; an immigrant could rent a farm on government property, but could not buy it. The same was true of clergy reserves.

By 1826, John Galt, an enterprising Scottish novelist, had become the key person in the business affairs of the Canada Land Company. This was the largest of the land companies. It was successful in obtaining from the government more than 808 000 ha at bargain prices, between the present city of Cambridge, Ontario, and Lake Huron. In the next decade, as the number of immigrants sharply increased, settlers poured into the "Huron Tract". In spite of the "red tape" involved and because of the rising prices, many immigrants went heavily into debt to obtain title to a farm.

The profits from the land companies went into the pockets of leading businessmen, whose connections with the government and with each other led to their being nicknamed the "Family Compact." The pattern was repeated in Lower Canada, where the British American Land Company was the creature of John Galt and his son, Alexander Tilloch Galt —later a prominent "father of Confedera-

Colonel Thomas Talbot: a one-man land company

In 1803, when he was thirty-one, Colonel Thomas Talbot, an ex-army officer, received a grant of 2020 hectares in what is now the London-St. Thomas area of Ontario. During the next three decades, he accumulated upwards of 26 260 hectares for himself, and personally supervised the settlement of a large part of Upper Canada north of Lake Erie.

Port Talbot, 1801. Site of the Talbot settlement

Far removed from York, the provincial capital, the "Talbot settlement" was like a feudal estate. Although Talbot was officially acting on behalf of the government, he set many of his own rules for granting—and repossessing—properties. The following excerpts tell something of the man and his methods:

INTIMIDATING THE CUSTOMER

To protect himself as much as possible from intrusion he had a window adjusted on the . . . post-office . . . ,the pane arranged so that it would open and shut from within. During the audiences Geoffrey [Talbot's "man-Friday"] stood behind him to hand down the maps, and the intending purchaser was left on the path outside. The inevitable query was, 'Well, what do you want?' The trembling applicant made an answer, the land was given or refused as the case might be, and to speed the parting guest the equally inevitable concluding remark, 'Geoffrey, turn on the dogs' . . . [23]

---

tion." In the Maritimes, the New Brunswick and Nova Scotia Land Company was a similar operation.

Defenders can claim that the land companies served a useful purpose in opening up vast areas of territory, and that no other method was available for providing farms for the flood of poor immigrants who arrived in the 1820s and 1830s. Governments of the day, so much smaller and with much less responsibility for the well-being of citizens than governments of the present, lacked the resources to set up a well-organized and supervised system of land-granting.

Yet even if the immigrants were aware of these realities, it was little consolation. Such settlers were likely to see the abuses, to suspect the politicking and the profiteering by those with power and influence. Thus the land problem, especially in Upper Canada, was one of the main reasons for unrest among new settlers, and helped to cause the Rebellions of 1837 and later social conflict in British North America.

LAND DEVELOPMENT: PARKING VS. PLAYGROUNDS

City Council meetings in Elm River are generally concerned with the usual local issues—parking by-laws, dog licenses, street repairs and so on. Most of the citizens are apathetic about the work of the Council, and don't even know when the meetings are held.

Tonight is different, however. At eight o'clock, council will hear briefs from various groups interested in the development of a prime piece of land in the heart of the city. The land was purchased some years ago, when the price was much lower than it is now, by the Crossroads Development Corporation.

Ever since Crossroads demolished the old buildings on the property, residents of the area have wondered about its use. It is the only possible location for playground space and recreational facilities in that part of the inner city.

Recently, however, the newspaper reported that Crossroads was applying to City Council for a permit to build a seventeen-story office building and parking lot. Representatives of Crossroads had the support of businessmen in the area in emphasizing the service, commercial opportunities and tax revenue for the city, that an office building-parkade could offer. Neighbourhood citizens groups reacted angrily stating that the needs of inner city families were being dismissed in the interests of profits.

City Council is caught between the two groups. Before granting Crossroads its permit to build, council has decided to hold public hearings.

CITIZENS' ACTION GROUP

The Citizens' Action Group represents 150 families from a six-square block area of Elm River. For years the city has promised playgrounds and recreational area for the children. Up until now there has been no available land. With residential construction projects almost at a standstill, many of the people are forced to live in these inner city apartment buildings. The children must go eleven blocks to the nearest park, and parents cannot always go with them so they lack proper supervision. It is common knowledge that playing in the streets and back lanes is unsafe. Newspaper editorials have hinted that much of the juvenile delinquency in the area could be traced to youngsters with "nothing to do".

Now that Crossroads has announced its plans, the C.A.G. thinks the city should rezone the area to prohibit high-rise buildings and should save the land for the long-promised recreational facilities.

Representatives of the C.A.G. are leary of going to the council meeting, however, because they don't think 150 families can be as influential as a large development corporation.

CROSSROADS DEVELOPMENT CORPORATION

Crossroads Development Corporation is aware of the Citizens' Action Group and its demands. It sympathizes with their problems, but sees the office building-parkade as the best solution all around.

In the first place, it may look like Crossroads is only out to make money. On the contrary, as C.D.C. sees it, the city needs more office space, and it can always use parking. Most small businesses are complaining of the inadequate downtown parking now. Instead of taking up space for several blocks, a high-rise building could give more office and parking space than regular structures would.

In the second place, if City Council allows C.D.C. to develop that land its own way, the city can use the revenue it will gain to develop land for recreational use in another area of Elm River. This would satisfy everyone.

Assume you are a voting member of the Elm River City Council who has not taken a side on this issue. After hearing the two briefs, answer these questions:

1. Which seems more important to Elm River—parks and recreational facilities or an office building-parkade? Why?
2. Which of the two groups is most able to influence the council? Why?
3. Does there seem to be any compromise solution here?
4. Which group do you think would win out in an actual city council meeting? Why?
5. If a council member votes in favour of Crossroads Development Corporation, which of his values seem to get high priority? If he votes in favour of the Citizens' Action Group?
6. Which group would you favour? Why?
7. How does the "land problem" in a modern inner city differ from the land problem facing frontier settlers more than 100 years ago? How is it similar?

D. The rise of towns

One of the principal effects of the Great Migration, particularly in Upper Canada, was the growth of towns. The efforts of the land companies led to the creation of such new towns as Galt, Stratford, Goderich and Peterborough. These were born as service centres to the neighbouring farming areas. Typically the population consisted of merchants, tavernkeepers, shoemakers, blacksmiths, millers, carpenters, a few professionals and a transient population of unskilled labourers.*

Such older towns as York [Toronto after 1834], Kingston, Montreal, Halifax or Saint John had their populations dramatically increased. Toronto, for example, had a population of 2 500 in 1815; the census of 1850-51 showed an increase to 30 775. Overwhelmingly British, the total was more than one-third Irish, with that large group divided between Protestants and Catholics.

The economic life of the colonies was affected more and more by the rise of metropolitan centres. In Upper Canada, Toronto was the location where ambitious men launched banking ventures, canal

*See David Gagan and Herbert Mays, "Historical Demography and Canadian Social History", *Canadian Historical Review* , (March 1973).

Maitland's Wharf, Toronto

projects, importing businesses and other money-making enterprises. Similarly in Lower Canada, Montreal was the economic hub. The successors to the North West fur trade, following the demise of the North West Company, included the Bank of Montreal, the Molson undertakings in steamships and breweries, and a host of other businesses controlled by the predominantly Scottish merchant class.[26] Halifax and Saint John occupied similarly prominant positions in their respective Maritime colonies.

THE BANK OF UPPER CANADA

One of the earliest of Canada's banks, chartered in York [Toronto] in 1821, the Bank of Upper Canada opened its doors in the midst of controversy. From the beginning it was regarded as an attempt by the Family Compact to secure a monopoly in the banking field. A look at some of its prominent personnel confirms the Bank's close association with the ruling clique of Upper Canada. One of the first presidents was William Allen, who was a member of the Legislative Council and one of the first directors of the Welland Canal Company. Twelve of the original directors of the Bank of Upper Canada were appointed high officials of the Government. At the same time, the Government appointees among the directors were also private owners of large numbers of shares. Not surprisingly, the Reform Party, whose most aggressive members led the Rebellion of 1837, found "the Bank" to be a ready target.[26]

SOCIAL CLASS DIVISIONS IN HAMILTON 1851–52

The group that controlled economic, political, and social power within Hamilton contained at most 10 per cent of the household heads. People within elite positions formed slightly more than 8 per cent of men aged twenty and older. This figure is quite close to the 10 per cent estimated elsewhere as wealthy. It is close, in fact, to the approximately 75 per cent of elected city officials who we know to have been within the top ten income percentiles. Hence we can conclude that about 8 or 10 per cent of the adult men, at the very maximum, controlled virtually all the resources necessary to the health, well-being, and prosperity of the rest.

In Hamilton the rulers, the owners, and the rich were by and large the same people. They clearly headed the stratification system. At the bottom the grouping was likewise clear: poor, propertyless, powerless men made up about 40 per cent of the workforce or between a fifth and a quarter of the household heads. In between fell the rest. About 40 per cent were marginal; they owned no property, they possessed no power, but they were prosperous enough to differentiate themselves from the poorest families. Their margin seems so slim and the consequences of falling so appalling, however, that these people must have lived always with great tension and great fear. Between them and the wealthy, comprising about a fifth of the families, was a qualitatively more affluent group. Most of them employed a servant and lived in a brick house, which they owned. They were likely to vote but still not very likely to hold political office.[27]

CITY PLANNING IN THE FUTURE: TWO SCENARIOS

In a mere ten years from now, you could be in the market for a home of your own. You may be married with one or more children, and you are likely to be employed on a full-time basis, unless unemployment is such that you can't even find a job. If these predictions are true, consider the following possible **scenarios**:

The Murray Family

You, Robert Murray, have been married to your wife Joan for two years this month. Your daughter Sarah is 11 months old, and your wife has decided to stay at home to be a full-time wife and mother. You own an apartment in a condominium on the east side of a city whose population will reach 3½ million this year. In order to get to your job as a computer programmer, you must travel to the far west side of the city. Since gasoline is so expensive and automobile traffic too heavy, you do not drive your car to work. You must take a commuter train and then two buses which means travelling time of 1½ hours—when all systems are on time. You work from 9 a.m. to 5 p.m., but you are away from Joan and Sarah from 7:30 a.m. until 6:30 p.m.

During your lunch hour at work, you like to take your lunch to

A scenario is a short passage which tells a story or paints a scene. Futurists (those people who study the possible, probable and preferable alternative futures available to us) use scenarios to describe future situations in order to evaluate what might be possible and to choose what would be preferable. They feel that only if we begin to plan for the future will we be able to have any control over it.

228

Problems of writing history: interpretation

TOWN AND COUNTRY—AND BEYOND

The relationship between urban centres and the rural—especially the *frontier*—areas has been the basis of several approaches to the writing of Canadian history.[28]

One view, reflected in the writings of such historians as Frank Underhill, A. S. Morton and Arthur Lower, is sometimes called "frontierism" or "environmentalism." Earlier writers saw the transfer of British ways and/or the growth of Canadian political institutions according to British examples as having over-riding importance. Beginning in the 1930s, however, historians influenced by some American forerunners began to apply the idea of a dynamic frontier. That is, the expansion of the frontier across the continent set up a process of adaptation to the environment that created a North American lifestyle, distinctive from any in the Old World (Europe). "Grass roots democracy," for example, it was argued, was formed on the frontier and filtered back into the general society which had begun as a transplant from overseas.

A second and related view, advanced by H. A. Innis and Donald Creighton, is known as that of the "Laurentian School." According to this approach, the central theme in Canadian history is the evolution of the "commercial empire of the St. Lawrence." As the great river developed as a system of transportation and trade, it drew on an ever-expanding part of the interior and thus became the economic and social basis of a transcontinental Canadian nation. Montreal is seen as the principal centre, first as the headquarters of a far-flung fur trade (North West Company), then as financial capital and terminal for canals, railways, agriculture and industry—linking the New World and the Old.

Related to both the idea of the "frontier" and the potent influence of the St. Lawrence River is a third approach—"metropolitanism". When a big city, a "metropolis", emerges, it may dominate not only the area around it, but other smaller cities and their countrysides. The domination extends through economic, social, cultural and even political life. A city like Winnipeg may be the metropolis for much of central Canada, west of Lake Superior. In turn, Winnipeg is subordinate to Toronto and Montreal, which themselves are bound in many ways to London, England and New York.

None of the three approaches summarized in such simple fashion here is distinct from the others, nor could any be held up as "the" way to interpret Canadian history. Indeed, a particular historian may exhibit tendencies of all three. Nevertheless, separately or together, these views may help give some perspective on the relationships—either local ones or national ones—that exist among parts of Canada.

1. Can you explain the idea that the frontier (hinterland) and the metropolis are like "two sides of the same coin"?
2. Which of the three approaches do you find most helpful in understanding the relationship between Toronto and the newly settled regions of Upper Canada in 1830s? In understanding the unique position of Montreal in the society of Lower Canada in the 1830s?

---

the park, but you must walk (the buses are too crowded, and you feel you need the exercise) and when you arrive, the park is usually so crowded that there is hardly any green space, let alone privacy.

Your family's dream is to own its own home out of the city, but this seems improbable during your life time. The prices of houses which are for sale begin at $100 000, and there are precious few of them. In the meantime, Joan and Sarah are always restless about being cooped up in the apartment. For relaxation, you are trying to rent a garden plot in the south end of the city. The city has some land where slum dwellings used to be located which it has reserved for residents to plant flower and vegetable gardens. There are two problems here for you, however. First, you are number 300 on the waiting list, and secondly, the cost of seeds, tools and travel to the land might be more than your limited budget could bear.

You content yourself with frequent family picnics to the city park, but so do millions of other city dwellers.

The Anderson Family

You, Marie Anderson, and your husband Tim live in a comfortable duplex in Riverview Manor, a satellite city several miles from the heart of a large metropolitan centre. Your house is adequate for the needs of your husband, yourself and your six-year-old son, Tommy. Through federal home buyer's plans you were able to get a mortgage for this house, but you would someday like to own a larger, single-family unit. Right now, this house suits your family, and the neighbourhood is a nice one. City planners have provided for green space and recreational areas so that nearby is a sizeable play area complete with playground, baseball diamond, hockey rink and swimming pool. Surrounding this area is a large park with plenty of grass, trees and flowers. Nearby also are golf courses, a zoo, a library and tennis courts—many services to occupy your leisure time, and all of them within walking distance of your home.

Speaking of leisure time, you have more of it since you and your husband each work only a three-day week and have the other four days to spend with your son. Since you save money on leisure-time activities year 'round, you are able to afford a holiday once a year when you "get away from it all." This year your family is planning to take a holiday on a ranch in southern Alberta where you will live for two weeks with a family who owns a cattle ranch.

Although there is a fine system of rapid transit which is inexpensive and takes you to the centre of the city in little time, you find there is no pressing need to go there. The art galleries, museums, and larger theatres are located in the core city, and you do go there for occasional entertainment; but most of the time you find what you need close to home. Shopping centres and specialty shops have moved from the core area to the satellite cities, so it is just as convenient for you to drive your car, walk or bicycle to any stores you wish to visit.

On the whole, although you are worried about ever present problems such as pollution, inflation and unemployment, you are generally satisfied with your lifestyle and your accommodations in Riverview Manor.

1. Which alternative scenario do you think is closest to what life will actually be like in ten years?

2. Consider the following projections* about the growth of cities in Canada:

POPULATION (thousands)

	1981	1986	1991	1996	2001	change
CANADA	24041	25383	26591	27570	28370	+ 18%
Atlantic	2164	2221	2266	2286	2287	+ 6%
Nfld.	578	610	641	665	683	+ 18%
P.E.I.	116	119	122	123	123	+ 6%
N.S.	807	817	821	816	804	− 0.4%
N.B.	663	675	682	682	677	+ 2%
Quebec	6269	6398	6472	6462	6383	+ 2%
Ontario	9028	9747	10433	11055	11629	+ 29%
Prairies	3782	3919	3988	4037	4051	+ 7%
Man.	1000	1006	1005	993	972	− 3%
Sask.	827	776	714	636	547	− 34%
Alta.	1907	2060	2205	2334	2450	+ 28%
N.W.T.	48	56	64	74	83	+ 73%
West Coast	2799	3119	3432	3731	4020	+ 44%
B.C.	2775	3092	3403	3698	3984	+ 44%
Yukon	24	27	30	33	36	+ 50%

*The tables are taken from *Hindsight on the Future*, prepared by John Kettle, a consultant on studies of the future, and published in 1976 for the Ministry of State for Urban Affairs. The figures are "educated guesses" about the future based on mathematical manipulation of statistics about present conditions and trends.

The Canadian Government has undertaken several studies on future forecasts, since present policies will have consequences in the years ahead. Many other organizations, both public and private, are involved in future forecasting.

(a) Which province will have the most people by 2001? The fewest? Which will have the most dramatic increase or decrease in population?

(b) Which Canadian region will have the highest increase in population from 1981-2001? Which region will have the lowest increase in population from 1981-2001?

*In order to be labeled as a "Census Metropolitan Area" (CMA), a city must have at least 100 000 people.

CENSUS METROPOLITAN AREAS (CMAS)* (thousands) '71 BOUNDARIES

	1981	1986	1991	1996	2001
Atlantic	2163.8	2220.9	2265.9	2286.0	2286.8
N.S.	807.0	816.7	820.9	815.8	803.8
Halifax	229.5	231.5	230.7	226.0	218.4
Other 3	1356.8	1404.2	1445.0	1470.2	1483.0
St. John's	151.7	163.8	175.4	185.2	193.5
Saint John	111.4	113.3	114.1	113.3	111.4
Total Atl CMAs	492.7	508.7	520.2	524.5	523.3
as % of region	22.8%	22.9%	23.9%	22.9%	22.9%
Quebec	6096.0	6215.1	6281.1	6265.6	6184.7
Chicoutimi	134.2	134.2	133.4	131.2	127.9
Montreal	2999.3	3099.3	3167.1	3189.6	3174.2
Quebec City	532.9	554.6	570.1	577.0	576.5
Total Que CMAs	3666.4	3788.1	3870.6	3897.8	3878.6
as % of Que	60.1%	60.9%	61.6%	62.2%	62.7%
Ontario	8507.9	9197.4	9859.4	10466.2	11032.6
Hamilton	584.2	632.0	680.5	727.5	773.9
Kitchener	284.3	315.5	346.6	376.7	406.2
London	335.9	364.7	393.8	422.1	450.0
St. Catherines	342.7	366.6	391.1	415.0	438.6
Sudbury	185.1	206.5	230.4	256.0	283.8
Thunder Bay	121.6	128.1	135.0	141.8	148.5
Toronto	3190.7	3505.4	3821.1	4126.6	4427.0
Windsor	295.4	317.4	339.8	361.6	383.2
Total Ont CMAs	5339.8	5836.2	6338.3	6827.3	7311.2
as % of Ont	62.8%	63.5%	64.3%	65.2%	66.3%
Ottawa-Hull	693.3	733.1	764.5	784.6	794.8
Prairies	3781.6	3897.8	3988.3	4036.6	4051.1
Calgary	542.5	617.8	690.8	758.6	820.2
Edmonton	611.8	665.3	709.7	743.3	766.6
Regina	147.4	140.5	130.3	116.4	99.8
Saskatoon	133.7	128.3	119.6	107.3	92.4
Winnipeg	608.6	653.9	704.3	758.5	818.9
Total Pra CMAs	2044.0	2205.8	2354.7	2484.1	2597.9
as % of region	54.1%	56.6%	59.0%	61.5%	64.1%
West Coast	2798.7	3118.5	3432.2	3730.9	4019.6
Vancouver	1301.1	1413.9	1519.7	1616.5	1708.6
Victoria	222.2	232.1	238.1	240.0	238.5
Total WC CMAs	1523.3	1646.0	1757.8	1856.5	1947.1
as % of region	54.4%	52.8%	51.2%	49.8%	48.4%
Canada	24041.4	25382.9	26591.4	27569.7	28369.7
total CMAs	13759.5	14717.9	15606.1	16374.8	17052.9
as % of Cda	57.2%	58.0%	58.7%	59.4%	60.1%

The proportions of CMA populations to total populations in Quebec and Ontario are based on the population of the province without Ottawa-Hull.

(c) How much of an increase in population will there be in your city or region over the next 35 years?

DWELLINGS (thousands)

	Atlantic		Quebec		Ontario		Prairies		West Coast		Canada		Total
	houses	"apts"	houses	"apts"	houses	"apts"	houses	"apts"	houses	"apts"	houses	"apts"	
1981	498	140	869	1231	2028	1073	944	349	647	353	4986	3146	8132
											61.3%	38.7%	
1986	531	168	880	1449	2202	1350	966	447	694	478	5273	3892	9165
											57.5%	42.5%	
1991	558	198	864	1668	2350	1654	961	560	726	618	5459	4698	10157
											53.7%	46.3%	
1996	587	233	826	1916	2509	2011	941	698	756	783	5619	5641	11260
											49.9%	50.1%	
2001	622	274	770	2198	2701	2450	907	871	789	982	5789	6775	12564
											46.1%	53.9%	
'81—'01	+124	+134	−99	+967	+673	+1377	−37	+522	+142	+629	+803	+3629	+4432
% change	+24.9	+95.7	11.4	+78.6	+33.2	+128.3	−3.9	+149.6	+21.9	+178.2	+16.1	+115.4	+54.5

(d) Will there be more houses or apartments in your region by the year 2001? Will the number of houses increase or decrease in your region over the years? Number of apartments? What might these projections mean for your own personal future plans?

OCCUPATIONAL GROUPS (thousands)

	Managerial	Prof. & Tech.	Clerical	Sales	Tpt., Comm.[1]	Farm, Fish, Log, Mine	Cftsmn.	Labourers	Total
1981	1153	2002	1995	684	1667	468	2466	214	10649
	10.8%	18.8%	18.7%	6.4%	15.7%	4.4%	23.2%	2.0%	100.0%
1986	1311	2448	2380	714	1657	400	2565	126	11601
	11.3%	21.1%	20.5%	6.2%	14.3%	3.4%	22.1%	1.1%	100.0%
1991	1448	2874	2768	724	1602	333	2587	26	12362
	11.7%	23.3%	22.4%	5.9%	13.0%	2.7%	20.9%	0.2%	100.0%
1996	1585	3320	3204	728	1538	275	2588	—	13238
	12.0%	25.1%	24.2%	5.5%	11.6%	2.1%	19.5%	—	100.0%
2001	1725	3788	3700	727	1471	226	2570	—	14207
	12.1%	26.7%	26.0%	5.1%	10.4%	1.6%	18.1%	—	100.0%

[1] transport and communications

(e) By 2001 which occupational group will employ most Canadians? If there will be no labourers by 1996, what jobs that now exist might be eliminated? How would these tasks be handled?

AUTOMOBILES

	No.	Per 100 pple.	Per 100 adults (20 +)
1981	10 340 000	43.0	63.2
1986	11 380 000	44.8	63.4
1991	12 030 000	45.6	63.2
1996	12 220 000	44.3	61.4
2001	12 190 000	43.0	58.6

(f) What changes between now and 2001 could affect the prediction about automobiles? Are automobiles of 2001 likely to resemble the ones of today? If not, how might they be different?

3. What effect will the growth of cities have on such things as

(a) pollution?

(b) non-renewable natural resources such as electricity, natural gas, oil?

(c) municipal or provincial services such as police protection, medical care, education, recreation?

(d) violence?

4. What can be done now to make our cities more liveable in the future?

5. (a) Should city planners or government officials control urbanization by limiting the number of people who can live in any city? (b) If so, how might this be done?

E. New products and new technology

The economy of British North America, like that of New France before, was highly dependent on *staple* products. But the beaver pelt was no longer the product that the St. Lawrence valley, the main settled region, relied on for income. The fur trade was still important, but it drew on the resources of remote areas. *Timber* was now the principal staple, and the "square timber" rafts floating down the Ottawa River, or along the St. Lawrence to Quebec, became a familiar sight.

The new emphasis on timber and lumber products brought many changes to the St. Lawrence region. In the 1820s, the timber ships brought immigrants on their return voyage to the colonies from England. In contrast to the fur trade, the lumber industry required large numbers of workers and created a market for farm products.

Wheat and flour, in other words, were also becoming major products in central Canada. Larger and larger surpluses were becom-

The square timber trade was extremely wasteful by modern standards. In preparing the trees for the timber rafts, lumbermen cut away not only the bark but large quantities of wood. In those days, however, the forest reserves seemed endless, and people could not imagine a shortage. Settlers, in fact, saw the forests as an obstacle to be overcome in clearing the land for farming and opening roads into the frontier.

Timber rafts in cove at Quebec

ing available for export, and the colonies had the advantage of "protected" markets in Britain: that is, British duties raised the cost of foreign imports and gave a price advantage to colonial products.

The change from furs to timber and wheat created serious problems for transportation on the St. Lawrence—Great Lakes system. The rapids above Montreal, and especially Niagara Falls, were critical obstacles for the newer, larger ships required.

The invention of steam power and its application to shipping increased the need to improve upon the natural qualities of the St. Lawrence, the "avenue to the heart of the continent". Travel by road was almost as primitive as it was when Canada was discovered. Waterways, altered by the technological efforts of man, were still the best hopes for the commercial progress of the Canadas.

THE EXCITEMENT OF CORDUROY ROADS

The roads were throughout so execrably bad that no words can give you an idea of them. We often sank in mudholes above the axle-tree; then over trunks of trees laid across swamps, called corduroy roads, where my poor bones dislocated. A wheel here and there, or a broken shaft lying by the roadside, told of former wrecks and disasters. In some places they had, in desperation, flung huge boughs of oak into the mud abyss, the rich green foliage projecting on either side. This sort of illusive contrivance would sometimes give way, and we were nearly precipitated into the midst. When I arrived at Blandford my hands were swelled and

Roads remained primitive until many years later. Except for military roads, originally planned by Simcoe, the available land routes were likely to be toll roads. If a traveller was headed for a pioneer town, he would probably have to travel over a *corduroy road*—one made of logs laid side by side. In 1837 one-way fare by stagecoach from Montreal to Toronto cost approximately $24.00.

TOP: *Corduroy Road;* BOTTOM: *Steamship wharf, Montreal. What can you learn about transportation in Canada from these two pictures?*

blistered by continually grasping with all my strength an iron bar in the front of my vehicle to prevent myself from being flung out.[29]

Canals, therefore, took on particular value. With the backing of Montreal merchants, the governments of Upper and Lower Canada initiated a series of canal systems. The Lachine Canal, which opened in 1824, went around the treacherous Lachine Rapids. The Welland Canal, completed in 1829, by-passed Niagara Falls. In 1832, the Rideau Canal, connecting Lake Ontario with the Ottawa River, was financed by the British government as an alternate water route in the event of an American seizure of the St. Lawrence.

The canal systems created a seaway which contributed to the expansion of the carrying trade. Steel vessels, powered by steam, gradually replaced the wooden sailing ships. The "Royal William", built by Samuel Cunard, a Nova Scotian, was the first to cross the Atlantic under steam power (1833). More rapid travel by steamships not only expanded immigration and commercial development but also strengthened the Canadian connection with the mother country, now that it took only twenty-five days to cross the Atlantic.

By 1850 only 66 miles of railway had been constructed in British North America, compared to the thousands of miles in Europe and the United States. The few small railways in the Provinces of Canada were built to supplement transportation by river and canal. However, in the 1850s railways were to become a major concern in the transportation system of the colonies.

THE MANY USES OF STEAM POWER

I have a great regard for the town of Dundas, because more than any other place in Upper Canada, it appears to depend upon its factories; its situation in the midst of a fertile and beautiful country; its ever working stream, turning wheel after wheel, and keeping in movement factory after factory; the neat cottages of the artizans, and the snug, comfortable, and unpretending appearance of the whole place, are highly interesting to the stranger. Its growing wealth and importance is of particular interest to the farming community. As capital, created by industry, gathers there, you will find the fabrication of article after article now imported from abroad introduced; you will find, that successful enterprise in manufactures, reproduces itself, more naturally than any other kind of enterprise. The horse power in a country brewery, induces the steam engine; the steam engine requires, in its construction, the founder, the turner, the machine maker; he brings the boiler maker; and so on by degrees, until every article belonging to the trade is made upon the spot. All this leads to the enquiry, in how

Technology and human values

The technological marvel of 125 years ago was the steam engine. In the "generation of steam", steam power was the energy source for ships, flour mills, sawmills and furnaces in iron works. Critics of this new technology were few; bigger and better machines were seen as essential to material progress in a pioneer land, especially one so vast and rugged as Canada. Since land, forests, water and other resources were so plentiful, people in those days would have found it hard to imagine a time when the environment would be threatened by technology.

Imagine their surprise if they could see headlines like the modern ones below.

ADVANCES IN TECHNOLOGY AID SCIENTIFIC RESEARCH
SCIENTIST WARNS BALANCE OF NATURE UPSET BY CHEMICAL
 POLLUTANTS
"SAVE THE TREES" CAMPAIGN GAINS MOMENTUM
TECHNOLOGY CAN MAKE LIFE EASIER—IF WE WANT IT
NUCLEAR ENERGY CAUSES CONCERN TO U.N.
ELECTRIC LAWNMOWER GOES WILD—NEIGHBOUR SUES FOR
 DAMAGES

Technology, the rate of technological change, and the effects on people and their surroundings cause much more concern in our lives than they did in the lifetimes of your great-great-great-great grandparents. When you think of changes in technology, do you think of the benefits it can bring you—for example, safer automobiles, permanent press clothing, quadraphonic sound, or perhaps some day, climate control? Or do you think of the negative effects of technology, such as air pollution, traffic congestion, oil spills or impure lakes and streams?

The fact is that technological changes have always brought both positive and negative "payoffs". For the many benefits technology brings, there are drawbacks too. For example, in the early 1950s, a new technological age, the age of electronics, was underway. Homemakers were awed by thoughts of fully automated, even robot-controlled, kitchens which were supposed to be "right around the corner."

Robot servants have not become a household fixture, but we have seen the development of microwave ovens, no-frost refrigerators and all kinds of labour-saving appliances. At the same time, we have more frequent power shortages, or "brown-outs", and the trouble and expense of increased maintenance and repair of complicated equipment.

New technology has created a need for new manufacturing plants. These plants can supply us with a variety of products or can refine our natural resources, but, we have found, not without harm to people and the environment. Where rivers and streams were once providing a living for some and recreation for others, many of them are now so polluted with factory waste that fish are contaminated and shores reek with an unbearable stench.

Technology often provides a solution to a problem, then creates new problems in the bargain. During severe infestations of insects, we may use chemical sprays to protect plant growth. The sprays, on the other hand, may be unpleasant and even dangerous to the health of people, especially those with respiratory problems.

There seems to be no end to "life and death" issues arising from our ingenuity in various fields of technology. Cryogenics, for example, is the science of keeping a seriously-ill person alive indefinitely by lowering body temperature, until some time in the future when a cure may be found. Theoretically, it may soon be possible to maintain people in a healthy state indefinitely or create people in test tubes. Meanwhile, one of the problems already facing the world is overpopulation. Who will decide the uses for such technology?

Every technological advance brings with it new problems, both technological and social, or human, problems. For example, harnessing the power of the atom presented problems of use or abuse. Nuclear power can be used to propel submarines and rockets, but it can also be part of weapons capable of unspeakable destruction. Technological advances necessitate choices—value choices—and we must decide how, and for what purposes, we are going to use technology.

1. When you think of technology, what do you think of? What are the negative and positive aspects of these examples?

2. Who has the power to control the use of technology? What responsibility lies with the individual?

3. If doing without as many "machines" as you now have in your home would mean conserving energy or resources for future generations, what, if anything, would you be willing to give up?

4. How can we take steps toward changing the attitude of people who feel "bigger is better"—that is, the more technology can provide us with, the more we want? Should we try to change this attitude in people? Why or why not?

many ways steam can be employed. The blacksmith who commences by shoeing horses, and tiring waggon wheels, finds that he can repair, and finally that he can make axes; from this he proceeds to the manufacture of other tools. Those who use the tools find that the home-manufactured articles are better than the imported; they learn that some of the cheapness of the latter is owing to their want of goodness, and they discover that there is no worse economy than the use of inferior implements however cheap.[30]

ISSUES IN TECHNOLOGY

Where investors imagined profits, British engineers saw significant differences in technology. John Mactaggart perceived the Rideau Canal's masonry dams and lock chambers, built by Royal Engineers, as an example of 'British substantiality'. The widespread use of wood in building the Welland Canal seemed to him simply another instance of North American shoddiness. Railway construction also involved serious differences of technical opinion. The question of a proper gauge for Canadian rails, for instance, pitted British tradition against North American experience. And because English capital was a critical source of funding, the gauge question became a political as well as a technical issue, not finally settled until the whole country shifted to the four foot, eight-and-one-half inch standard.[31]

TRAVEL BY STEAMSHIP

The first steamship on Lake Erie was christened *Walk-in-the-Water*. She was built at Black Rock, near Buffalo, and was launched on May 28, 1818. The *Walk-in-the-Water* was named in honour of a well-known Indian Chief. She was 135 feet long. . . . The 290-mile trip from Buffalo to Detroit was completed in 44 hours, 10 minutes. . . . . The fare from Buffalo to Detroit was $18 for first class, and $7 for steerage. Steam whistles were not in common use at that time, for there was no steam to waste in making a noise; so in place of a whistle a four-pound cannon was securely lashed on the forward deck, and when the steamer was nearing a town the cannon came into action to announce to all and sundry that they might expect her approach.[32]

A NEW INDUSTRIAL TOWN

And now some of the "city folks" come out and take up a water privilege, or erect steam power, and commence manufacturing. Iron is bought, cut into nails, screws and hinges. Cotton is spun and wove, and all the variety of manufactures introduced, because here motive power, rents and foods are cheaper, and labour more easily controlled, than in the cities, while transportation and distance have by the Railroad been reduced to a minimum. A town has

"By the middle fifties [1850s], an important chemical and process industry that sold its product all over the world was established at Hull, Quebec. This was the Eddy Match Company, which in 1854 was still producing matches in blocks by the old hand system. Later it became the world's largest mass producer of wooden matches."[34]

been built, and peopled by the operatives—land rises rapidly in value—the neglected swamp is cleared and the timber is converted into all sorts of wooden "notions"—tons of vegetables, grains, or grasses, are grown where none grew before—the patient click of the loom, the rushing of the shuttle, the busy hum of the spindle, the thundering of the trip-hammer, and the roaring of steam, are mingled in one continuous sound of active industry.[33]

The opening of the Welland Canal. Why would this canal be important to the economy of British North America?

9

The road to rebellion

WHY DID IT HAPPEN?

"Elementary, my dear Watson," were the suave, calculated words of Sherlock Holmes, the master detective of Sir Arthur Conan Doyle's Victorian novels. No matter what the problem, Holmes' answer was predictably the same. Audiences everywhere were comforted by his talent for bringing forth a ready and often simple answer for the most complicated mystery.

What about problems in real life? Can they usually be explained by a simple, or single, cause? It is tempting to believe that a single person or certain condition is responsible for an event. Doing so, however, can mean ignoring many alternative, plausible explanations and possible interrelationships among them. Too often it is assumed that if event "B" follows action "A", then "A" must have caused "B".

Determining *causation* is one of the more difficult, as well as fascinating, activities facing the student of history. Some would even say that causes cannot be identified, that history is "just one damn thing after another." Generally, though, historians seem to agree that it is possible to analyze causes, recognizing that a historical phenomenon is normally the result of several interacting causes.

As you study the rebellions in Lower Canada and Upper Canada, you will have a chance to examine some of the circumstances and

242

events leading up to the troubled times of 1837. In trying to answer the question, "Why did it happen?", you may not find the explanation to be "elementary". However, applying the questions provided later should help you to sharpen your skills in analyzing real-life issues.

BACKGROUND

From 1791, the year of the Constitutional Act,* Upper Canada (later Ontario) and Lower Canada (later Quebec) each developed in unique ways. Yet there were certain common features, at least in the political situation, in both colonies, as well as in the other colonies of British North America. *Representative Government* had been established; each colony had an elected assembly, which provided the population at large with some political voice. Actual decision-making, however, rested with the Governor who was appointed by the British Government, and appointed advisory councils. These advisory councils came to be dominated by small cliques, giving a minority of businessmen influence over the majority of the population which was made up mainly of small farmers.

*See page **281**.

These governing cliques, known as "Family Compacts",* or "Tories" dominated not only the governments but all other phases of life in the colonies. Members of the Compacts controlled land companies, owned the banks and loan companies and dominated transportation, i.e. shipping, canals, stage-coach companies. They used their position on the councils to influence government policy and to control **patronage**. Since no laws could be passed without the approval of the councils, the Assemblies had little power to limit the privileges of the Compacts.

*The Family Compact in Lower Canada was often called the Château Clique.

political favours, usually in the form of jobs or contracts

Leading churchmen and educators were often influential in the Compacts. For example, the Church of England (Anglican Church) obtained large land grants, called "clergy reserves" in Upper and Lower Canada. As a result, the Church of England had additional financial support and status as the dominant Protestant denomination. In Upper Canada, Bishop John Strachan, the spokesman of Anglicanism and a member of the Legislative Council, advanced Anglican-controlled education at all levels in an age when churches provided whatever formal education there was.

Members of the Compacts saw themselves as the protectors of the ties between the colonies and Britain. The Tories often yielded to the temptation to brand their opponents disloyal. To label a man "republican" was an effective tactic. It could raise suspicions that he held "American" attitudes, the like of which led the American colonies to break away from Britain. In colonies where the Loyalist tradition was strong, appeals to loyalty carried a great deal of weight.

Bishop John Strachan

Soon after the War of 1812, discontent with the "establishment" began to grow in both Upper and Lower Canada. Various groups whose common interest was opposition to the government began to cooperate. They came to be known as "Reformers", because they wanted to reform, or improve, the governments and conditions in the colonies for the average settler. Land, they believed, should be more easily and cheaply available. They wanted money spent on roads that would connect the pioneer family with the "outside world." They wanted more schools and other improvements, but their only hope for reform lay with the Assemblies, and the Assemblies generally had a limited say in government decisions.

FAMILY COMPACT NOT A FAMILY

Many years ago (in 1915), a historian noted that the term "Family Compact" was not an accurate label:

This clique came to be known as the Family Compact. The term, drawn from the alliances between the crowned heads of Europe during the seventeenth and eighteenth centuries, was not only absurd as applied to Canadian party politics, but was even less appropriate than party designations usually are. 'There is in truth,' confessed Lord Durham, 'very little of family connection among the persons thus united.' The Rev. John Strachan, for instance, one of the leading spirits in the Family Compact for many years, had no family relationships in York until his son married in 1844 the daughter of John Beverley Robinson. Nor was there the nepotism among the Family Compact that has been commonly imagined. 'My own sons,' testified John Beverley Robinson, 'have never applied, and I have never applied for them, to the Government for any office of any kind, and they none of them receive a shilling from the public revenue of the country in which I have served so long.' But however inappropriate the term Family Compact may be, it has become part and parcel of Canadian history; ... [1]

OR WERE THEY?

If members of the Family Compact were not blood relatives, they were "related" in a different way, according to another historian:

... York in the eighteen-twenties had the population of a village, and socially was divided into two classes—the governing circle, which with the members of the learned professions and a few wealthy merchants, constituted society, and the others. The former were exclusive and their pretentions were magnified by the fact that they were all members of one religious communion, the Church of England. The propriety [correctness] of the term Family Compact has often been questioned, but whether or not there was a blood relationship within the group so designated, there is no question at all of the existence of a spiritual family compact comprising the whole group. The aggressive arrogance of this group was the cause of more ill-feeling than all the other factors of the colonial life combined. . . . [2]

CONTRASTING VIEWS OF THE FAMILY COMPACT

(A) The Governor, Sir Francis Bond Head:

The 'family compact' of Upper Canada is composed of those members of its society who, either by their abilities and character have been honoured by the confidence of the executive government, or who, by their industry and intelligence, have amassed wealth. The party, I own, is comparatively a small one; but to put the multitude at the top and the few at the bottom is a radical reversion of the pyramid of society which every reflecting man must foresee can end only by its downfall. . . . [3]

(B) William Lyon Mackenzie:

This family connexion rules Upper Canada according to its own good pleasure, and has no efficient check from this country to guard the people against its acts of tyranny and oppression. It includes the whole of the judges of the supreme civil and criminal tribunal (Nos. 6, 12, and 16)—active Tory politicians. Judge Macaulay was a clerk in the office of No. 2, not long since. It includes half the Executive Council or provincial cabinet. It includes the Speaker and other eight Members of the Legislative Council. It includes the persons who have the control of the Canada Land Company's monopoly. It includes the President and Solicitor of the Bank, and about half the Bank Directors; together with shareholders holding, to the best of my recollection, about 1800 shares. And it included the crown lawyers until last March, when they carried their opposition to Viscount Goderich's measures of reform to such a height as personally to insult the government, and to declare their belief that he had not the royal authority for his despatches. They were then removed; but with this exception the chain remains unbroken. This family compact surround the Lieutenant-Governor, and mould him like wax to their will; they fill every office with their relatives, dependants, and partisans; by them justices of the peace and officers of the militia are made and unmade; they have increased the number of the Legislative Council by recommending, through the Governor, half a dozen of nobodies and a few placemen, pensioners, and individuals of well-known narrow and bigoted principles; the whole of the revenues of Upper Canada are in reality at their mercy;—they are Paymasters, Receivers, Auditors, King, Lords, and Commons![4]

Lower Canada

In late November, 1837, rebellion broke out in Lower Canada outside Montreal. A number of battles followed, in which the rebels, calling themselves "Patriotes", violently expressed their resistance to the colonial government. The main period of fighting lasted only a few weeks. Looking back, one sees a desperate rebel action, unlikely to succeed against the authority of the British Crown (Empire). Yet the rebellion was not a sudden, isolated event; it had been building for a long time.

The name Louis-Joseph Papineau has become almost synonymous with the French-Canadian reform movement out of which exploded the Rebellion in Lower Canada. From a well-to-do family, and himself a seigneur, he was trained in the law and well acquainted with British parliamentary practice. He was first elected to the Assembly before the War of 1812, while in his early twenties. An eloquent and temperamental representative of French-Canadian interests, he was the Speaker (chairman) of the Assembly almost continuously from 1815 to 1837. His political career paralleled an age of expansion, change and conflict.

As we saw in the previous chapter, international events like the War of 1812 and the Napoleonic Wars had many effects on British North America: the decline of the fur trade, the rise of the timber trade, the great migration, and so on. Tensions had begun to show even earlier, when newspapers like *Le Canadien* were founded to express concern for French-Canadian rights. A lawyer, a farmer, a priest and a mill-worker may each have held a different view of rights, but all would resent and fear any threats to French-Canadian customs and institutions. During the 1820s and 1830s, one incident after another helped shape a growing discontent with the way things were going in Lower Canada. The resulting conflict meant pressure on, and within, the colonial government.

"To the Loyalist, Papineau was the root of all evil. A French loyal ditty [song] attributed every calamity of the era to him, cholera morbus, earthquakes and potato-rot included, each stanza finishing with the refrain, 'C'est la faute de Papineau.' [It's Papineau's fault.']'[13]

The Rebellion was not a "clear-cut conflict between the ethnic groups",[5] but the main division in the population of Lower Canada was ethnic (racial), that is, between the English minority and the French majority. Within each section there were, of course, different interest groups but English-speaking businessmen controlled much of the commercial life in the colony. The English-speaking merchants therefore had considerable economic power over the French-Canadian groups, of which the largest were the farmers and the most vocal (outspoken) were lawyers and other professionals.

Beginning with the fur trade in the 1760s, the English-speaking merchants seized opportunities for profit-making; as time went on, they moved into land speculation, banking, new industries, the timber trade, construction of roads and canals that would facilitate

A plan to "swamp the French"

Separating the English and the French, as the Constitutional Act (1791) only partly succeeded in doing, failed to solve the conflict between the two cultures. For one thing, a powerful English-speaking minority remained in Lower Canada, in Montreal. This group believed their business success was being held back by an unprogressive colonial government and the French-Canadian majority. They argued that the St. Lawrence-Great Lakes region would be more prosperous if it came under a single government.

On their behalf, friendly British politicians proposed, in 1822, a bill to join Upper and Lower Canada. Part of the plan was to eliminate, within fifteen years, the use of the French language in the elected assembly. Since English-speaking members would have outnumbered French-Canadian representatives in government, other French-Canadian rights could have been endangered.

The uproar in Lower Canada, in which English-speaking Canadians hostile to the schemes of the merchants joined with French Canadians, led to the bill being dropped. However, considerable damage was done, as suspicion of the motives of the English-speaking population grew in the minds of men like Papineau.

---

commerce and trade. They naturally used whatever advantages could be found, including their influence in government. The French, on the other hand, often felt exploited, at a disadvantage economically, and this feeling was deepened by the decline in farming that worsened with the depression of the 1830s. Outspoken French Canadians readily pointed the finger at "les Anglais" and accused them of being responsible for all that was wrong, including the changes which threatened the traditional French-Canadian way of life.

The cultures of the two racial groups were markedly different. In an age when church organizations were so influential, in political and other terms as well as in spiritual matters, and when religious faith was so central to the lives of most people, the fact that the greater part of the English-speaking people were Protestant and the French people were solidly Catholic meant a considerable gulf existed. Furthermore, language, family life, and traditions divided the two peoples.

The Government ultimately was the place where those dissatisfied with the **status quo** tried to bring about change. The *Patriotes*, the party of reform, worked over the years to use their domination of

the existing state of affairs

the Assembly to press their claims. One source of power was control of government spending. Certain revenues, of course, such as customs duties, provided for in the Quebec Revenue Act of 1774, were at the disposal of the Governor. But the Assembly had the right to approve or deny the spending of public money.

The wrangle over "voting supply", as the approval of spending was called, continued year after year. Nevertheless, the Assembly constantly faced the fact that the Governor and his councils, dominated by the Family Compact, had the last word on the passing of new laws. In other words, in the case of a showdown, it was clear that the part of the colonial government appointed by Britain had power over the part elected by the people of the colony.

A generation of struggle entered a crucial phase with the "Montreal massacre." During the election campaign of 1832, British troops called out to control a potential riot fired on the crowd. Three French-Canadians were killed, and what upset people even further was that charges against the commanding officers were dropped.

Relations between the ethnic groups were further strained by an epidemic of cholera spread by immigrants arriving at Quebec. Healthy immigrants were a sufficient threat to the French-Canadian majority; unhealthy ones spread suffering and burdened the colony. The assembly responded by passing restrictions on immigration.

In 1834, the Assembly took a bold step by adopting the Ninety-two Resolutions, drawn up under Papineau's guidance. They included (a) a list of complaints about and criticisms of the domination of the French-Canadian majority by the English-speaking Family Compact, (b) demands for the control of all government spending by the Assembly, (c) a demand for the control of the Executive, and thus of government policy, by the Assembly to make its function comparable to that of the British House of Commons. An admiration for American institutions and ideas shone through the Resolutions, and a veiled threat of force to gain reforms could be discerned.

The Ninety-two Resolutions frightened moderate supporters of reform, such as the English-speaking newspaper editor, John Neilson, and increased the opposition of the Church. But in the elections of 1834 Papineau and his followers won a sweeping victory. In 1835 Britain appointed a new governor who was instructed to make recommendations for increasing harmony within the government of Lower Canada. He was unsuccessful, and unrest continued; persistant economic depression hardened tempers in all parts of society.

The Colonial Office, that part of the British Government responsible for administering Britain's colonies, shifted to a hard line in 1837. Rejecting the Assembly's demands, the Colonial Office further empowered the governor to approve government spending without the authorization of the Assembly. The time for confrontation had

The first paid corps raised at Quebec was named the Porkeaters, a regiment some six hundred strong, able bodied, resolute fellows, mostly Irish labourers, mechanics and tradesmen, who did no discredit to their supposed diet. These bacon-fed knaves began by looking the awkward squad; but drill by the non-coms. of the regulars, aided by strict discipline, soon made them perform their revolutions with the regularity and precision of their instructors. It is easy to fancy this regiment going into action under Colonel Rasher, with the wholesome advice, *Salvum Larder*, floating to the breeze in the hands of Ensign Fitch—'Charge, Sausage, charge; On, Bacons, on,'.... [15]

248

arrived. Papineau, and especially his more militant supporters, saw no hope of gaining reforms by constitutional means. There was talk of armed force as the only way to convince Britain that the reformers were serious.

Throughout the hot summer of 1837, mass meetings, angry speeches, outbursts in the press all indicated a revolutionary spirit. The Assembly recessed at the end of August. The reform movement was now in the hands of impatient men. *Les Fils de la Liberté* were reminiscent of the Sons of Freedom of the Boston Tea Party of the American Revolution. *Les Fils* clashed in Montreal with members of the Doric Club, an organization of English-speaking extremists. The situation deteriorated into a racial struggle between two extremist groups. Could anyone, or anything, stop what seemed like an inevitable breakdown of order and descent into bloodshed?

In October the Patriotes organized the "Assembly of the Six Counties" at St. Charles, a town on the Richelieu River. Although they stopped short of any call to arms or "declaration of independence," they denounced the government and passed resolutions demanding many changes. Meanwhile, most of the troops from Upper Canada were dispatched to Lower Canada, and the governor, hoping to avoid open rebellion, suppressed the Doric Club and prepared to arrest the leaders of "Les Fils." Armed Patriotes obstructed the troops who were sent to carry out warrants for arrest. This led to a clash and bloodshed at St. Denis on November 23. Papineau fled to the United States. Two days later, resistance at St. Charles was broken. In December at St. Eustache, north of Montreal,

" . . . a good many French Canadians were made to join the rebel side by intimidation.

If the assurance of 'Je suis loyal' did not come quickly enough some inoffensive Frenchman would find himself popped into the guardhouse, and the results of jealousy and over-zeal have left many absurd stories. A county M.P., at the Chateau one sultry evening, seeing the rest all busy at ice-cream, asked for some. The Canadian Solon took a hugh spoonful, his first taste of such a delicacy. With a feeling of rage at what he thought an insult, or at least neglect, he cried out what is translated into, 'You abominable rascal, had this been for an Englishman you would have taken the chill off.' "[14]

The Battle of St. Eustache, Lower Canada, 1837

249

*In the "October Crisis" of
1970 in Quebec, the FLQ
members who kidnapped and
killed Pierre Laporte called
themselves the "Chenier cell",
after Dr. O. J. Chenier.

a rebel group led by Dr. O. J. Chenier* was crushed by a combination of soldiers and militia. The rebellion was virtually over. While there were skirmishes the following year, the authorities were fully in command, and mass trials sent hundreds to jail. Twelve rebels were sentenced to death by hanging, and fifty-eight were deported to penal colonies in Australia.

On the first page of the chapter, under the heading "Why did it happen?" it was mentioned that questions would be provided to help you analyze the causes of the rebellions of 1837. Consider the following,[6] which can be used for *either* rebellion:

1. What was the immediate cause for the event?
2. Had there been a background of agitation?
3. Did the actions of personalities on either side influence the outcome?
4. Were any new and potent ideas influencing the thinking of a considerable number of people?
5. How did the economic groups line up on the issue?
6. Were religious forces active?
7. Did any new technological developments influence the situation?
8. Can the events be partially explained by weakened or strengthened institutions?
9. Was the geography of the area a factor in the situation?

Upper Canada

In contrast with the uprising in Lower Canada, the Rebellion in Upper Canada was small in scale, with both rebels and defenders acting "in the best traditions of comic opera."[16] Montgomery's Tavern, then north of Toronto, was the scene of a battle lasting less than half an hour on a mild winter morning in early December. The rebels were scattered, the tavern burned, and instigators of the affair were rounded up for trial. To the people of that day, however, the event was no comic opera, nor were the conditions leading up to it.

The central figure among the rebels in 1837 was William Lyon Mackenzie. He had come from Scotland in 1820 at the age of twenty-five, and set himself up as the fiery and fearless editor of a newspaper called the *Colonial Advocate*. His vigorous attacks, often of a personal nature, on the Family Compact and their privileges soon led to the destruction of his print shop. The result of its destruction was widespread public recognition, which Mackenzie turned into votes. He was elected to the Assembly of Upper Canada in 1828.

The agitation for reform in Upper Canada had actually begun before Mackenzie arrived in the colony. Shortly after the War of

Why had the rebellion failed?

The following are newspaper headlines that *could* have appeared after the collapse of the Rebellion. Which one would be most convincing to (a) the Governor of Lower Canada, (b) one of the Patriote leaders, (c) the Roman Catholic Bishop of Montreal, (d) an English lord visiting the colony after the Rebellion, (e) a Canadian student in the 1970s?

> WEAK LEADERSHIP SINKS REBEL CAUSE: MASS UPRISING FAILS THROUGH LACK OF PLANNING
>
> CATHOLIC CHURCH CONVINCES MAJORITY THAT REBELLION IS WRONG
>
> REFORM MOVEMENT SPLIT; RADICAL REFORMERS A SMALL MINORITY
>
> LOYAL MILITIA TOO MUCH FOR REBELS
>
> PAPINEAU'S FLIGHT DOOMS THE REBELLION

1. Which headline do you think is *most* accurate?
2. Which do you think is *least* accurate?
3. Would a combination of the headlines present the best explanation? What are some of the things a student of history could do in order to arrive at his own interpretation? How would your study of causation help you to understand why the rebellion failed?
4. Do you think that two historians in the 1970s, one French-Canadian and one English-Canadian, might differ in their interpretations? How?

Papineau: traitor or cautious hero?

What impressions of Louis Papineau and his situation do you get from the following documents?

Historian and novelist, Joseph Schull, describes Papineau's role in the events of 1837:

Passionate, eloquent, and electric, alight with his dreams and angers, he had stirred the depths of the parishes and unloosed a rising wind. He had transformed squalor and misery into the living anguish of conquest, and he had wakened a sense of destiny that would never be stilled again.

Yet he had been carried to the heights of a prophet while he remained a politician. He thundered against the oligarchy, but he did not expect to change them. His one hope was to rouse opinion in England by the spectre of an aroused colony. The cheers of his

Louis-Joseph Papineau

country meetings were to be heard across the Atlantic, over the heads of his enemies and impressing his distant friends. He spoke of war to arouse those cheers, but he did not think of war; he was still the man of parliaments who was thinking of minds and votes. The habitants were less subtle. They saw a war with weapons in the way of the Thirteen Colonies. They saw a free people, a nation under Papineau, *la nation canadienne* at last in being. Papineau saw it too, glimmering along the horizon, but he still looked down on huddles of helpless men. He had no arms for them, no plan for them, and even the ultimate goal was still obscure. He was shrewd enough to be aware of it and wise enough to fear it, but there could be no stopping now. He had paralysed colonial government to sway a British Parliament, and it remained his only hope. He must go on or go down.[7]

A comment about Papineau's departure at the height of the rebellion:

It may have been that Papineau, the undisputed chief of the movement, felt obliged to preserve himself from capture—it is said to have been agreed among the *Patriote* high command that Papineau should keep apart from all fighting, in order to be free to negotiate later with the government—or he may have been unwilling to participate in the open insurrection which he had always opposed. In any case his action at Saint-Denis, imitated later by most of the chiefs of the *Patriotes*, created a breach between the leaders and their followers which played no small part in the rapid collapse of the movement.[8]

Although eight of the most prominent leaders of the rebellion were deported to Bermuda, many others who took part in the rebellion were not so fortunate:

In Montreal, following the rising of 1837, 501 were imprisoned; at Quebec, five. After the second rising, at the end of 1838, 116 were jailed on charges of treason in Montreal, 18 at Quebec, 19 at Sherbrooke and two at Three Rivers. Of 108 brought to trial by court-martial, nine were acquitted, 27 freed under bond, 58 deported to Australia . . . and 12 were executed.[9]

Papineau had great difficulty in deciding about the use of rebellion as a means of bringing about change:

The exact attitude of Papineau during these months of agitation is difficult to determine. He does not seem to have been quite clear as to what course he should pursue. He had completely lost faith in British justice. He earnestly desired the emancipation of Canada from British rule and the establishment of a republican system of government. But he could not make up his mind to commit himself to armed rebellion. 'I must say, however,' he had announced at St. Laurent, 'and it is neither fear nor scruple that makes me do so, that the day has not yet come for us to respond to that appeal. . . . '

In later years he was always emphatic in denying that the rebellion of 1837 had been primarily his handiwork. 'I was,' he said in 1847, 'neither more nor less guilty, nor more nor less deserving, than a great number of my colleagues.' The truth seems to be that Papineau always balked a little at the idea of armed rebellion, and that he was carried off his feet at the end of 1837 by his younger associates, whose enthusiasm he himself had inspired. He had raised the wind, but he could not ride the whirlwind.[10]

E. B. Taché, later a Father of Confederation, noted:

M. Papineau is certainly a great speaker and a man of first-rate talent, but ambition and vanity have made deep ravages in his fine and powerful intelligence, and discontent has embittered his naturally good heart. . . . [11]

Fernand Ouellet, a historian who is an authority on Papineau, wrote in the 1960s:

Was Papineau a great man? There is no doubt that he represented the very model of a great man for a good number of his contemporaries, and he has not lacked later admirers. Thanks to the brilliant and dramatic personality concealing his deep-seated weakness, he did exert a unique influence on the French Canadians. He awakened them to ideas of nationalism and liberty. He was a striking incarnation of their aspirations. But in his actions the appeal he made was more to negative sentiments. Of these, a persecution complex and racial hatred stirred up useless agitation and reinforced the passive attitude of a people who had taken refuge in their own past and really had no great wish to change it.[12]

1. If Papineau had been a more decisive leader, how different might the history of Lower Canada (Quebec) have been?
2. Do you think Papineau was right or wrong to leave for the United States during the Rebellion? Had he already contributed all he could to the reformers of Lower Canada?
3. Was Papineau a hero or a traitor? Explain.
4. Do you think you need more information before you can reach a conclusion about question #3? What *kinds* of information might be helpful?

Upper Canada	Lower Canada

1817

| Agitation over land problem; the story of Robert Gourlay | Early leadership of Louis Papineau |

1822

| | Union of Upper and Lower Canada proposed; successful opposition in Lower Canada |

1827-28

| Growing strength of Reformers | Clash between Reformers and the Governor; Papineau's influence increased |

1832

| Rise of William Lyon Mackenzie to leadership | "Montreal massacre" |

1834

| Mackenzie expelled from Assembly, re-elected; also elected mayor of York (re-named Toronto) | 92 Resolutions: demands for change by the Reformers; increased influence of radical reformers; moderates' withdrawal of support |

1835

| Seventh Report of Grievances: radicals more powerful, moderates declining support | |

1836-37

| | Rising tension between Reform Parties and Compacts; British Government's decision to take a "hard line" with Reformers; severe economic depression |

1812 the reform movement arose in opposition to the privileges established by the Constitutional Act of 1791. Reformers wanted the same powers for the Assembly, the only elected part of the government, as the House of Commons enjoyed in Britain. They also called for a fair policy of distributing land, improved roads and other public works, and wider educational opportunities.

Open criticism of the Family Compact's control of the colony began with one Robert Gourlay. Unable to secure the land grants he sought, Gourlay stirred up considerable indignation in 1817-18 among pioneer farmers and aroused the attention of the Family Compact. This oligarchy, or tightly-knit ruling group, succeeded in getting Gourlay banished from Upper Canada on a charge of libel. Other critics were similarly stifled, even if they had been elected to the Assembly, for the Family Compact's control extended to that body. Barnabus Bidwell, for example, was disqualified from elective office because he was an American; so was his son, Marshall. Through the 1820s, however, the grievances of ordinary people, especially the newly arrived immigrants, became more evident and the pressure for reform increased.

Robert Gourlay

*See page 222.

As the Gourlay case demonstrated, the distribution of land grants was an important issue in the frontier colony of Upper Canada. The practice was for the government to allocate large areas of land to companies, such as the Canada Land Company,* which in turn advertised and sold farm-sized parcels of land to prospective farmers. The companies were expected to attract immigrants to the new territory and provide them not only with land but also roads, bridges and other necessary public works. The system, if such a term is appropriate, was open to abuse, since a company might try to hold land back from sale for purposes of speculation.

Another issue involving land as well as other concerns was that of clergy reserves.* The Church of England (Anglican), led by Bishop John Strachan, claimed exclusive right to these lands as a means of providing revenue for its work in education, charity and other functions in addition to religious. Contesting this claim were the Methodists, the fastest growing Protestant denomination.* Their leader was Egerton Ryerson, editor of the Methodist newspaper, *The Christian Guardian*, and he threw his support to the Reform Party in the election of 1828, when William Lyon Mackenzie was coming to the fore.

*See note, p. 158.

*In Lower Canada, French Canadians were Catholic; the majority of English-speaking people were Protestant. In Upper Canada the religious differences were *between* different Protestant groups.

Issues such as land, religious rivalry and conflict between the financial elite and the majority of the population could only be solved by the action of government. However, as in Lower Canada, power rested with the Family Compact, who generally had the favour of whatever governor was resident and who dominated the appointed councils. Events of the early 1830s showed the Family

Why might Mackenzie's print shop have been destroyed?

*In the bargain Mackenzie became a kind of folk hero. When York was renamed Toronto in 1834, he was elected its first mayor.

*See the next chapter for his leading role in the struggle for Responsible Government.

Compact's control and the weakness of the elected Assembly, for even the Assembly had a majority who supported the status quo. When Mackenzie continued his attack on monopoly, in his newspaper and in speeches in the Assembly, he was expelled from office. In fact, he was expelled four times, each time to be re-elected.*

The year 1835 was a kind of turning point in the Reformers' struggle to wrest political and economic changes from the system. The Reformers had returned to a majority position, and a committee of the Assembly went to work under Mackenzie's direction to draw up a provocative report for submission to the British Government. The so-called *Seventh Report on Grievances* included complaints about the clergy reserves, the disposition of public lands, the privileges of the Church of England, the Canada Land Company, and the power of the banks. The Report demanded two basic constitutional reforms: an elective Legislative Council and an Executive Council responsible to the Assembly.

Mackenzie's demand for an elected Legislative Council, comparable to the Senate in the United States, sounded like "Americanization" and a departure from British-style government. Robert Baldwin,* a moderate Reformer, realized that the British Government would not willingly consent to surrender control over the colonial government in the way Mackenzie proposed. He stressed instead the need to reform the colonial government to resemble the British Government.

In 1836, Britain moved to avert a possible crisis by appointing a new governor, Sir Francis Bond Head. For a brief time he succeeded

Not all rebellion

The *Colonial Advocate*, published by William Lyon Mackenzie, was primarily a voice for Mackenzie's criticisms of the government. It was also, though, a local paper which appealed to its rural audiences. Mackenzie, it is said, had a sense of the curious which his readers appreciated, and the paper had its share of amusing stories. Here are a few of them:

> A short time since, in an adjoining town, a happy pair were joined in wedlock by a facetious [whimsical] squire whose fees totally exhausted the funds of the bridegroom. Not many days had elapsed before the parties who had been joined till death should them part, became mutually dissatisfied with their lot, and returned to the squire with their many tales of woe, beseeching him with all their eloquence to *unmarry them*; which he agreed to do, provided he was previously paid the sum of three dollars, double the fee of their first ceremony. This sum the bridegroom paid by a week's labour on the squire's farm. Then came the ceremony of the parting. The squire placed a block on the floor, on which was put a live cat; one pulled the head and the other the tail, while the squire with an axe severed the cat in twain, at the same time exclaiming 'Death doth you part.' The couple departed with the firm belief that the performance was strictly legal, and have not lived together since.[17]

> [Mackenzie told of] . . . 'an old curmudgeon [miser] whose brains were made of sawdust, hog's lard and molasses, but who on account of the spaciousness of his farm had been for years head of the school committee in his district,' and of his daughter who tricked the old man into hiring her lover as schoolmaster.

> For those who had not heard the man in person, Mackenzie printed a description of the Rev. Lorenzo 'Crazy' Dow, a Methodist preacher, whose parish was North America, 'wherein he itinerates [travels] at will, preaching by appointment from the tops of rocks.' The Rev. Mr. Dow told every congregation he preached to that they were hearing his best sermon, and at least one congregation that he needed a wife and would a lady please rise, upon which he married the first volunteer.

> Mackenzie watched, and then interviewed, the famous Mr. Sam Patch who specialized in leaping off things. On this occasion he had hurled himself 160 feet down into the whirling waters of the Niagara gorge, with the Falls for a backdrop and several thousand people looking on. Mackenzie's readers were gratified to learn that he 'inhales when he leaps and says it does not hurt him in the least.'[18]

There were other prominent reformers, such as Marshall Bidwell, the former American, and Robert Baldwin, later so effective a spokesman for "responsible government." But it was the fiery Mackenzie, hammering away in his newspaper editorials and his endless speeches in the Assembly, who championed the case of the common man against the power of the Family Compact.

in carrying out instructions to pacify the Reformers; he even appointed two of their leaders, Baldwin and Dr. John Rolfe, to his Council. However, he was soon making decisions without consulting his advisers, and he and the Assembly were at loggerheads. The governor dissolved the Assembly and one of the most bitter elections in Canadian history followed.

The Governor personally entered the campaign in the hope of getting an assembly that would support him. And he had some distinct advantages. He accused the Reformers of preferring American ways over British, thus endangering the ties with the mother country. Bond Head had the support of Egerton Ryerson, who believed Mackenzie had lost his senses and who used his considerable influence to urge Methodists to oppose the Reformers. Furthermore, it was only the hardy voter who risked the anger of the Governor and his supporters in the days before the secret ballot. The Reformers were overwhelmingly defeated.

A committee including Mackenzie issued the following on August 2, 1837:

The Declaration of the Reformers of the City of Toronto to their Fellow Reformers in Upper Canada.

THE time has arrived, after nearly half a century's forbearance under increasing and aggravated misrule, when the duty we owe our country and posterity requires from us the assertion of our rights and the redress of our wrongs.

Government is founded on the authority, and is instituted for the benefit, of a people; when, therefore, any Government long and systematically ceases to answer the great ends of its foundation, the people have a natural right given them by their Creator to seek after and establish such institutions as will yield the greatest quantity of happiness to the greatest number.

Our forbearance heretofore has only been rewarded with an aggravation of our grievances; and our past inattention to our rights has been ungenerously and unjustly urged as evidence of the surrender of them. We have now to choose on the one hand between submission to the same blighting policy as has desolated Ireland, and, on the other hand, the patriotic achievement of cheap, honest, and responsible government.

The right was conceded to the present United States, at the close of a successful revolution, to form a constitution for themselves; and the loyalists with their descendants and others, now peopling this portion of America, are entitled to the same liberty without the shedding of blood—more they do not ask; less they ought not to have.[19]

PROCLAMATION.

BY His Excellency SIR FRANCIS BOND HEAD,
Baronet, Lieutenant Governor of Upper Canada, &c. &c.

To the Queen's Faithful Subjects in Upper Canada.

In a time of profound peace, while every one was quietly following his occupations, feeling secure under the protection of our Laws, a band of Rebels, instigated by a few malignant and disloyal men, has had the wickedness and audacity to assemble with Arms, and to attack and Murder the Queen's Subjects on the Highway—to Burn and Destroy their Property—to Rob the Public Mails—and to threaten to Plunder the Banks—and to Fire the City of Toronto.

Brave and Loyal People of Upper Canada, we have been long suffering from the acts and endeavours of concealed Traitors, but this is the first time that Rebellion has dared to shew itself openly in the land, in the absence of invasion by any Foreign Enemy.

Let every man do his duty now, and it will be the last time that we or our children shall see our lives or properties endangered, or the Authority of our Gracious Queen insulted by such treacherous and ungrateful men. MILITIA-MEN OF UPPER CANADA, no Country has ever shewn a finer example of Loyalty and Spirit than YOU have given upon this sudden call of Duty. Young and old of all ranks, are flocking to the Standard of their Country. What has taken place will enable our Queen to know Her Friends from Her Enemies—a public enemy is never so dangerous as a concealed Traitor—and now my friends let us complete well what is begun—let us not return to our rest till Treason and Traitors are revealed to the light of day, and rendered harmless throughout the land.

Be vigilant, patient and active—leave punishment to the Laws—our first object is, to arrest and secure all those who have been guilty of Rebellion, Murder and Robbery.—And to aid us in this, a Reward is hereby offered of

One Thousand Pounds,

to any one who will apprehend, and deliver up to Justice, WILLIAM LYON MACKENZE; and FIVE HUNDRED POUNDS to any one who will apprehend, and deliver up to Justice, DAVID GIBSON—or SAMUEL LOUNT—or JESSE LLOYD—or SILAS FLETCHER—and the same reward and a free pardon will be given to any of their accomplices who will render this public service, except he or they shall have committed, in his own person, the crime of Murder or Arson.

And all, but the Leaders above-named, who have been seduced to join in this unnatural Rebellion, are hereby called to return to their duty to their Sovereign—to obey the Laws—and to live henceforward as good and faithful Subjects—and they will find the Government of their Queen as indulgent as it is just.

GOD SAVE THE QUEEN.

Thursday, 3 o'clock, P. M.
7th Dec.

☞ The Party of Rebels, under their Chief Leaders, is wholly dispersed, and flying before the Loyal Militia. The only thing that remains to be done, is to find them, and arrest them.

R. STANTON, Printer to the QUEEN'S Most Excellent Majesty.

PROCLAMATION

BY WILLIAM LYON MACKENZIE,

Chairman pro. tem. of the Provincial Government of the State of Upper Canada.

INHABITANTS OF UPPER CANADA!

For nearly fifty years has our country languished under the blighting influence of military despots, strangers from Europe, ru ing us, not according to laws of our choice, but by the capricious dictates of their arbitrary power.

They have taxed us at their pleasure, robbed our exchequer, and carried off the proceeds to [illegible] lands—they have bribed and corrupted ministers of the Gospel, with the wealth raised [illegible] industry—they have, in place of religious liberty, given rectories and clergy reserves [illegible]ign priesthood, with spiritual power dangerous to our peace as a people—they have [illegible]ed millions of our lands on a company of Europeans for a nominal consideration, and left them to fleece and impoverish our country—they have spurned our petitions, involved us in their wars, excited feelings of national and sectional animosity in counties, townships and neighbourhoods, and ruled us, as Ireland has been ruled, to the advantage of persons in other lands, and to the prostration of our energies as a people.

We are wearied of these oppressions, and resolved to throw off the yoke. Rise, Canadians, rise as one man, and the glorious object of our wishes is accomplished.

Our intentions have been clearly stated to the world in the Declaration of Independence, adopted at Toronto on the 31st of July last, printed in the Constitution, Correspondent and Advocate, and the Liberal, which important paper was drawn by Dr. John Rolph and myself, signed by the Central Committee, received the sanction of a large majority of the people of the Province, west of Port Hope and Cobourg, and is well known to be in accordance with the feelings and sentiments of nine tenths of the people of this state.

We have planted the Standard of Liberty in Canada, for the attainment of the following objects:

Perpetual Peace, founded on a government of equal rights to all, secured by a written constitution, sanctioned by yourselves in a convention to be called as early as circumstances will permit.

Civil and Religious Liberty, in its fullest extent, that in all laws made, or to be made, every person be bound alike—neither shall any tenure, estate, charter, birth, or place, confer any exemption from the ordinary course of legal proceedings and responsibilities whereunto others are subjected.

The abolition of hereditary honours, of the laws of entail and primogeniture, and of hosts of pensioners who devour our substance.

A Legislature composed of a Senate and Assembly chosen by the people.

An Executive to be composed of a Governor and other officers elected by the public voice.

A Judiciary to be chosen by the Governor and Senate, and composed of the most learned, honourable, and trustworthy of our citizens. The laws to be rendered cheap and expeditious.

A free trial by Jury—Sheriffs chosen by you, and not to hold office, as now, at the pleasure of our tyrants. The freedom of the Press. Alas for it, now! The free presses in the Canadas are trampled down by the hand of arditrary power.

The vote by ballot—free and peaceful township elections.

The people to elect their court of request commissioners and justices of the peace—and also their militia officers, in all cases whatsoever.

Freedom of Trade—every man to be allowed to buy at the cheapest market, and sell at the dearest.

No man to be compelled to give military service, unless it be his choice.

Ample funds to be reserved from the vast natural resources of our country to secure the blessings of Education to every citizen.

A frugal and economical government, in order that the people may be prosperous and free from difficulty.

An end forever to the wearisome prayers, supplications and mockeries attendant upon our connexion with the Lordlings of the Colonial Office, Downing St. London.

The opening of the St. Lawrence to the trade of the world, so that the largest ships might [illegible] up to Lake Superior, and the distribution of the wild lands of the country to the industry, [illegible]al, skill, and enterprise of worthy men of all nations.

For the attainment of these important objects, the patriots now in arms under the standard of Liberty, on NAVY ISLAND, U. C. have established a Provisional Government of which the members are as follows, (with two other distingnished gentlemen, whose names there are powful reasons for withholding from public view,) viz:

WILLIAM L. MACKENZIE, Chairman, Pro Tem.

NELSON GORHAM,	ADAM GRAHAM,
SAMUEL LOUNT,	JOHN HAWK,
SILAS FLETCHER,	JACOB RYMALL,
JESSE LLOYD,	WILLIAM H. DOYLE,
THOMAS DARLING,	A. G. W. G. VAN EGMOND.

CHARLES DUNCOMBE.

We have procured the important aid of Gen. Van Rensselaer of Albany, of Colonel Sutherland, Colonel Van Egmond, and other military men of experience; and the citizens of Buffalo, to their eternal honour be it ever remembered, have proved to us the enduring principles of the revolution of 1776, by supplying us with provisions, money, arms ammunition, artillery and volunteers; and vast numbers are floating to the standard under which, heaven willing, emancipation will be speedily won for a new and gallant nation, hitherto held in Egyptian thraldom by the aristocracy of England.

Brave Canadians! Hasten to join that standard, and to make common cause with your fellow citizens now in arms in the Home, London and Western Districts. The opportunity of the absence of the hired red coats of Europe is favourable to our emancipation. And short sighted is that man who does not now see that although his apathy may protract the contest, it must end in INDEPENDENCE, freedom from European thraldom for ever!

Until Independence is won, trade and industry will be dormant, houses and lands will be unsaleable, merchants will be embarrassed, and farmers and mechanicks harrassed and troubled; that point once gained, the prospect is fair and cheering, a long day of prosperity may be ours.

The reverses in the Home District were owing, 1st, to accident, which revealed our design to our tyrants, and prevented a surprise, and 2dly, to the want of artillery. 3500 men came and went, but we had not arms for one in twelve of them, nor could we procure them in the country.

Three hundred acres of the best of the publick lands will be freely bestowed upon any volunteer, who shall assist personally in bringing to a conclusion the glorious struggle in which our youthful country is now engaged against the enemies of freedom all the world over.

Ten millions of these lands, fair and fertile, will, I trust, be speedily at our disposal, with the other vast resources of a country more extensive and rich in natural treasures than the United Kingdom or Old France.

Citizens! Soldiers of Liberty! Friends of Equal Rights, let no man suffer in his property, person or estate—let us pass through Canada, not to retaliate on others for our estates ravaged, our friends in dungeons, our homes burnt, our wheat and barns burnt, and our horses and cattle carried off; but let us show the praiseworthy example of protecting the houses, the homes, and the families of those who are in arms against their country and against the liberties of this continent. We will disclaim and severely punish all aggressions upon private property, and consider those as our enemies who may burn or destroy the smallest hut in Canada, unless necessity compel any one to do so in any cause for self defence.

Whereas, at a time when the King and Parliament of Great Britain had solemnly agreed to redress the grievances of the people, Sir Francis Bond Head was sent out to this country with promises of conciliation and justice—and whereas, the said Head hath violated his oath of office as a governor, trampled upon every vestige of our rights and privileges, bribed and corrupted the local legislature, interfered with the freedom of elections, intimidated the freeholders, declared our country not entitled to the blessings of British freedom, prostrated openly the right of trial by jury, placed in office the most obsequious, treacherous and unworthy, of our population—and sought to rule Upper Canada by the mere force of his arbitrary power, imprisoned Dr. Morrison, Mr. Parker, and many others of our most respected citizens, banishing in the most cruel manner the highly respected speaker of our late House of Assembly, the Honorable Mr. Bidwell, and causing the expatriation of that universally beloved and well tried eminent patriot, Dr. John Rolph, because they had made common cause with our injured people, and setting a vast price on the heads of several, as if they were guilty persons—for which crimes and misdemeanors he is deserving of being put upon his trial before the country—I do therefore hereby offer a reward of FIVE HUNDRED POUNDS for his apprehension, so that he may be dealt with as may appertain to justice.

In Lower Canada, divine providence has blessed the arms of the Sons of Liberty—a whole people are there manfully struggling for that freedom without which property is but a phantom, and life scarce worth having a gift of. General Girard is at the head of 15,000 determined democrats.

The friends of freedom in Upper Canada, have continued to act in strong and regular concert with Mr. Papineau and the Lower Canada Patriots—and it is a pleasing reflection that between us and the ocean a population of 600,000 souls are now in arms, resolved to be free!

The tidings that worthy patriots are in arms is spreading through the Union, and the men who were oppressed in England, Ireland, Scotland and the continent are flocking to our standard.

We must be successful!

I had the honor to address nearly 3,000 of the citizens of Buffalo, two days ago, in the Theatre. The friendship and sympathy they expressed is honorable to the great and flourishing republic.

I am personally authorised to make known to you that from the moment that Sir Francis Head declined to state in writing the objects he had in view, in sending a flag of truce to our camp in Toronto, the message once declined, our esteemed fellow citizen Dr. John Rolph openly announced his concurrence in our measures, and now decidedly approves of the stand we are taking in behalf of our beloved country, which will never more be his until it be free and independent.

Canadians! my confidence in you is as strong and powerful, in this our day of trial and difficulty, as when, many years ago, in the zeal and ardour of youth, I appeared among you the humble advocate of your rights and liberties. I need not remind you of the sufferings and persecutions I have endured for your sakes—the losses I have sustained—the risks I have run. Had I ten lives I would cheerfully give them up to procure freedom to the country of my children, of my early and disinterested choice. Let us act together; and warmed by the hope of success in a patriotic course, be able to repeat in the language so often happily quoted by Ireland's champions,

> The nations are fallen and thou still art young,
> Thy sun is but rising when others have set;
> And tho' Slavery's cloud o'er thy morning hath hung,
> The full tide of Freedom shall beam round thee yet.

Militia-men of 1812! Will ye again rally round the standard of our tyrants! I can scarce believe it possible. Upper Canada Loyalists, what has been the recompense of your long tried and devoted attachment to England's Aristocracy? Obloquy, and contempt.

Verily we have learnt in the school of experience, and are prepared to profit by the lessons of the past. Compare the great and flourishing nation of the United States with our divided and distracted land, and think what we also might have been, as brave, independent lords of the soil. Leave then, Sir Francis Head's defence to the miserable serfs dependent on his bounty, and to the last hour of your lives the proud remembrance will be yours—"we also were among the deliverers of our country."

Navy Island, December, 13, 1837.

The radical reformers, like their counterparts in Lower Canada, were now faced with the choice of accepting defeat or turning to violence. Mackenzie swung between despair and the hope of change through an armed attack on "the system." Discontent was widespread in the countryside; the economic depression that had lasted for months showed no signs of ending. The outbreak of rebellion in Lower Canada was encouraging, partly because British troops had been dispatched there, leaving York unprotected.

Mackenzie had a half-formed plan of seizing city hall, with its store of arms, and having the government fall into his hands. On December 7, 1837, he gathered his supporters at Montgomery's Tavern, north of Toronto. The march on city hall, however, was so badly organized that volunteer militia drove the rebels back and the uprising collapsed. Some were captured; most of the rebels fled, including Mackenzie, who made his way to an unhappy decade of exile in the United States.

The rebellion, like the one in Lower Canada, had been crushed. The losers who had fallen into the hands of the authorities received rough "justice," while the British government was shocked into a thorough investigation of the Canadian situation.

William Lyon McKenzie's daughter Isabel, the last-born of thirteen children married John King in 1872. They became the parents of William Lyon Mackenzie King who would someday be Canada's 11th Prime Minister.

William Lyon Mackenzie: traitor or man of the people?

William Lyon Mackenzie

What was William Lyon Mackenzie's role in the rebellion of 1837? He was a newspaperman, famous—or notorious—for his biting editorials. He was a politician, elected several times to the colonial assembly and to the post of mayor of Toronto. Most of all, Mackenzie was a central figure in the reform movement, a controversial agitator against "the establishment". To some people, he was a kind of folk hero; to others he was a buffoon or worse, a traitor.

In the early days of the conflict, Mackenzie became interested in, and then committed to, the idea of government reform. He wanted the power of the Family Compact reduced and more representation placed in the hands of the people. Mackenzie used the editorial pages of his newspaper to speak out against the wrongs that he saw all around him. He gained a vast following among the common people and a growing list of enemies from among the politically influential.

As the conflict increased, the ranks of supporters and enemies grew. The more controversy that arose, the more Mackenzie gloried in it. It seemed that his position was being reinforced from both sides—the citizenry believed in him and the "establishment" challenged him. The reformers' campaign intensified, until the most radical reformers staged the rebellion on December 7, 1837. The rebellion was quickly dispersed, and Mackenzie fled to the United States where he continued his fight against the injustices.

Mackenzie wanted honest, efficient and representative government, and he campaigned to achieve it in Upper Canada. He had no master plan, however, and he was no organizer. He was caught up in the wave of reform, a part of which seemed to move quickly and with little thought to strategy or method. Whether because the feeling of power and influence overcame him, or because he felt no long-term plan was possible, Mackenzie's rebellion could never have been anything but small scale. Good intentions and moral principles are sometimes not enough.

CONTEMPORARY OPINIONS ABOUT MACKENZIE

Egerton Ryerson, the Methodist leader and former ally in the movement for reform, wrote of Mackenzie in 1833, after Ryerson had decided that Mackenzie was becoming too radical:

... we have conversed, freely and friendly, in years past, with both Mr. Mackenzie and his opponents, and have always found Mr. Mackenzie as a man open, generous, ardent, punctual, and honourable to all his engagements; and have believed, that however exceptionable much of his proceedings and writings were, their *general* tendency would be to secure rigid economy in the public expenditure, and remove abuses which candour must admit have gradually grown up in some parts of the administration of public affairs; . . . Mr. Mackenzie's great strength and merits, . . . consist in eliciting *facts* and useful state documents, in which, we think, they have rendered important service to Upper Canada; but Mr. Mackenzie, . . . fails in the employment of his facts, and applies many of them to purposes of abuse, irritation, and excitement, . . . So notorious is Mr. Mackenzie's incapacity to make a judicious use of his facts, and his rashness and imprudence, and violence, . . . that a distinguished legal gentleman, . . . and Member of the House of Assembly, known as a sincere friend of the people, never would *identify* himself with Mr. Mackenzie, nor commit himself into Mr. Mackenzie's hands; nor become responsible for his statements or measures; nor defend Mr. Mackenzie, nor advocate any of his measures. . . . [20]

Sir Francis Bond Head writes of William Lyon Mackenzie:

. . . Mr. M'Kenzie's exertions for many years were really almost superhuman. Every hardship, whether of wood, wind, or weather, which the settler encountered in his lonely residence in the forest, was, by some falsehood or other, ingeniously shown to proceed indirectly from Downing Street, or directly from the Government House, or Legislative Council, at Toronto. Every magistrate, militia officer, postmaster, or schoolmaster, who in any way misbehaved himself, either in public or private, was declared to be an especial favourite of the Government; . . .

After these mischievous misrepresentations (which lowered, if it were possible, Mr. M'Kenzie in the estimation of every honest, intelligent man) had sufficiently shaken the loyalty of those who . . . had unfortunately listened to his tales, he considered that the time had arrived for getting up some vague petition to the Colonial Secretary for the general correction of 'grievances.' In order to obtain sufficient signatures for this purpose, . . . the most barefaced deceptions were practiced. In various directions agents were employed who, themselves, affixed the names or marks of all who could be induced to acknowledge that they had any one thing to complain of; indeed, several worthy individuals were added to the list, who actually believed they had joined in a loyal address. The names and signatures thus collected in batches, on separate pieces of paper, were then all pasted together, and, with scarcely anything but these credentials in his wallet . . . this low adventurer . . . returned to his mother-country, to introduce himself in Downing Street to her Majesty's Secretary of State for the Colonies. . . . [21]

Mackenzie was beaten

" . . . Mackenzie was present at a public meeting in the Tory community of Hamilton. It degenerated into a stormy debate on procedure. The next day rumours were heard of a plot to take his life, or at least to maim him. . . .

"That evening, as he sat upstairs in a friend's house writing, two men came into the room. One of them, William Kerr, was justice of the peace, a member of the Assembly, and a government canal manager. He appeared friendly enough . . . [and] suggested that they go downstairs, as he wanted to say something personal to Mackenzie. . . .

"When they reached the ground floor Kerr opened the front door. Pointing to Mackenzie, he called out: 'This is your man!' Immediately Mackenzie was seized by his coat collar and grabbed from the other side by Kerr. His candle was dashed to the ground and several assailants struggled to pull him towards the greater darkness of the street. Mackenzie shrieked 'Murder!' He was struck a blow with a cudgel [a club or thick stick], kicked, and dragged off into the night. Only the timely appearance of friends saved him from further harm. . . . The victim bled profusely from a cut in the face and a bang on the head, and his chest hurt. . . .

"Mackenzie's frequent charges about the corruption of the judiciary were borne out when Kerr was brought to trial, for he escaped with only a small fine and a reprimand. . . . "[29]

LATER VIEWS OF MACKENZIE

Mackenzie-biographer William Kilbourn dismisses the theory that Mackenzie acted out a kind of revenge on the power figures of the colony:

One has heard it said that if Mackenzie had been admitted even to the outer circle of the colony's ruling class he would have never founded a newspaper: if the Robinsons could have seen fit to pay him a call, there would have been no rebellion in Upper Canada. Such propositions are tempting but untenable. In later years Mackenzie looked on several well-intentioned offers of favour or public office as little short of insulting. He rejected them all as subtle attempts to buy him off or to deprive him of the total liberty of expression which he considered proper to every free man, and most of all to a Mackenzie.[22]

Historian William Smith describes another side of Mackenzie's character:

That Mackenzie was, in all ordinary relations, a good man, no person who has studied his life can doubt. He was an affectionate, devoted husband and father, was honourable in all his business dealings, and a good friend. You could safely put your life in his hands—but not your secret. If it had a point, beware! He would have exploded, if he had attempted to keep it to himself. A friend in New York had in his possession a letter he received from Henry Clay, and Mackenzie quarrelled violently with him, because the latter refused to allow him to publish it. That the letter would have been 'good readin' justified, to him, any breach of privacy.[23]

Historian David Flint sees Mackenzie as a negative influence on society in the 1830s:

Perhaps because historians before and after the turn of the century glorified or glossed over his role in Canadian history, Mackenzie used to be thought of as a noble idealist, a public-spirited rebel against . . . authority, and a prophetic exponent of responsible government. . . .

[However], Mackenzie was not a political theorist and had no plan. In writing about the need for a representative system of government he was very vague. He was a gadfly whose main concern was to attack . . . power in the interests of the people: it did not matter (or was not clear) to him that he did this inconsistently. His grab-bag of suggestions for change . . . made him a radical in the context of the times he lived in. But from a modern point of view his ideals of cheap government, low taxes, and the non-intervention of government in society make him rather conservative and even 'right-wing.' The events he brought about in 1837 damaged the economy, caused many 'useful and respectable citizens' to emigrate, and led shortly afterwards to American raids on Canada and tension between Britain and the United States.[24]

Another historian, Charles Lindsey, explains why Mackenzie was not a good leader:

[Mackenzie was] a wiry and peppery little Scotchman; honest, brave, energetic; but ruthless in his exposure of wrong and wrong-doers: a man of strong personality, but unsafe in council, and oftentimes intemperate [extreme] in word and action.... Elected a radical member of the Assembly in 1828, he was again and again expelled by the influence of the 'family compact' only to be reelected by a devoted and enthusiastic constituency. His vituperative [abusive] pen, also, aroused against him bitter enemies: at one time it lost him the public printing; at another it led to the sack and destruction of his printing press. He was ... a born agitator, a man more suitable to engender strife and augment revolt than capable of exercising the patience and tact necessary to command large forces of men, or the judgment essential to political reorganization and true statesmanship.[25]

1. What impression do you have of Mr. Mackenzie?
2. If Mackenzie had been more effective as a rebel leader, how different might the history of Upper Canada have been?
3. Did Mackenzie do the right thing by fleeing to exile in the United States? Why or why not?
4. Was Mackenzie a traitor or a man of the people?
5. What similarities and differences can be noted between Mackenzie and Papineau according to: (a) temperament; (b) charisma; (c) organizational ability; (d) tactics; (e) degree of success in changing conditions which they believed to be wrong in their society?

Capital punishment 1837-style

Samuel Lount, a blacksmith, came to Canada from Pennsylvania in 1811. Known for his generosity and kindness to fellow-settlers, Lount was encouraged by them to run for parliament in the election of 1834. Successful in the election, he became a member of the Reform Party, led by the aggressive and temperamental William Lyon Mackenzie.

The Reformers seemed to be heading for some success in their efforts to curtail the power of the Family Compact until the setback in the election of 1836. Samuel Lount was one of the defeated. He joined with Mackenzie and others who had come to the conclusion that armed revolt was the only resort left. Secret meetings were held in the countryside and a "farmers' army" of several hundred began collecting what weapons could be found and making other weapons.

By December, 1837, Mackenzie's unpredictable temper had

made him a danger to the cause of reform and had driven many of his would-be supporters away. But Samuel Lount was one of those who followed "Little Mac" unswervingly into a haphazard attempt at rebellion. When the rebels were scattered at Montgomery's Tavern, Mackenzie and many of his leading co-conspirators managed to make their way to exile in the United States.

Peter Matthews

One who did not escape was Samuel Lount. In March, 1838, he and Peter Matthews were convicted of treason. In spite of petitions for clemency which reflected Lount's widespread popularity, the new Governor, Sir George Arthur, refused clemency. Lount was offered his life provided he would turn informer and reveal the names of his associates in the attack on Toronto. Lount refused, and on the morning of April 12, 1838, Samuel Lount and Peter Matthews were publicly hanged in Toronto on a charge of high treason.

According to a contemporary, "at their execution they manifested very good composure. Sheriff Jarvis burst into tears when he entered the room to prepare them for execution. They said to him very calmly, 'Mr. Jarvis, do your duty. We are prepared to meet death and our judge.' They then, both of them, put their arms around his neck and kissed him. They were then prepared for the execution, (sic) they walked to the gallows with entire composure and firmness of step."[26]

1. Was Samuel Lount a scapegoat for the Reform Party?
2. Should Samuel Lount have given the names of his associates in exchange for his life?
3. Did the Governor have any reason to listen to public demands for clemency or was he right in insisting on the letter of the law? What further information would help you to decide?
4. Are there times when a man's moral obligations supercede the law of the land? Should Mr. Jarvis have refused to perform the execution?
5. What is the function of the ombudsman in Canada today in protecting people from unjust laws?
6. Lount was hanged publicly as a deterrent to potential rebels. Does the principle of deterrence justify the taking of a person's life?

Ideas from the social sciences: rebellion, revolution and social change

---

Throughout Chapter 9 you have investigated the causes of two rebellions in Canadian history. Have times changed significantly, or were the 1960s in Quebec, for example, similar to the 1830s in Upper and Lower Canada? What causes men to rebel or revolt?

Sociologists, whose job it is to study man's behaviour in groups, have given us some information about society and man's ability or desire to change it.

Society is composed of people and institutions devised to maintain and pass on from generation to generation laws, customs, traditions and values which the majority of people feel are beneficial. Government is one example of an institution through which society can control its members. The laws a government makes may order the people to do some things (e.g. to pay taxes) and forbid them to do others (e.g. take someone's life, property, and so on) so that we may have an orderly, stable society. At least in a democratic country, government may be thought of as successful if it remains responsive to the wishes of the people.

If, however, people become dissatisfied with the way institutions are being run, they sometimes try to change what they think is unjust or unfair. If there are orderly, organized ways for the dissatisfied to express their views and to obtain adequate change, without disrupting the social order, then the reasons for discontent may diminish. On the other hand, if institutions are so rigid and unresponsive that people feel they are oppressed, then the idea of rebellion may arise.

A rebel group may form, believing that oppression can only be relieved by putting into power new rulers who are sympathetic to the ideas of the rebelling group. Thus there may be an attempted overthrow of the existing powers and the establishment of a new system of social control. Social control is always present; what is necessary is a balance between control and freedom so that man may live in harmony with others.

1. What were some of the social controls which the governments of Upper and Lower Canada were placing upon the people?
2. What were some of the tactics the people used to effect social change?
3. How effective were the Reformers' methods of bringing about desired change?
4. Could you suggest mistakes the Reformers made or ideas which they might have tried but did not?
5. Could a Reformer have been just as interested as any member of the Family Compact in personal power?
6. Were the people right in turning to rebellion to effect social change in 1837? Why?
7. Is armed rebellion or revolution ever justifiable? Why?

What is a revolution?

A revolution may be defined simply as the overthrow and replacement of a government or political system by groups acting on behalf of those governed. A revolution, however, is a complex phenomenon, and is much easier to define than to analyze.

In his book, *The Anatomy of Revolution*, historian Crane Brinton analyzed a number of major revolutions in history. He was trying to discover if there is a way to describe revolutions in general. The following are based on "uniformities" he found often applied to any revolution.

How many of the following conditions were *absent* in the rebellions of 1837? How does a *rebellion* differ from a *revolution*?

—Class conflict is a major cause of revolution, especially if one class feels exploited and looked down upon by another.
—Leading thinkers switch their loyalty from the "establishment" to the reformers.
—Government institutions are outdated and inefficient.
—Government leaders are inept and ineffectual in using the power that is available to them.
—Revolutions begin moderately and grow more violent in their later stages.
—Leaders of a revolution are generally men who are reasonably well off and educated but feel cut off from opportunity for real success.

10

Responsible Government: The ongoing quest

The term "Responsible Government" in the Canadian political tradition as well as in the British, means broadly that the government is answerable to the Canadian people. If it is acting against the wishes of most Canadians, they can express their disapproval openly in various ways. If a government continues with unpopular actions and policies, Canadians can decide to defeat it by voting at election time. Then another government takes office.

This chapter deals with the origins of Responsible Government. The basic principles, or ideas, are the same today as they were more than 100 years ago. By studying the struggle for Responsible Government, you have the chance to gain an understanding of one of the fundamental parts of modern Canadian government.

A. Aftermath of rebellion: the Durham investigation

The Rebellions of 1837, coming in the first months of Queen Victoria's reign, caused shock waves in Britain. The Prime Minister, Lord Melbourne, found himself under great pressure because of his government's handling of colonial matters. He responded by doing what prime ministers in trouble have often done—he appointed a commission to investigate. The commission's assignment was to find out what the trouble was in Canada and recommend some solutions.

The man chosen to head the investigation was John George Lambton, Earl of Durham. Lord Durham was a prominent aristocrat in his middle forties. He had more than twenty years experience in politics and the foreign service. A strange mixture of a man, Durham was proud, pompous, temperamental, opinionated—but highly intelligent and farsighted. In the unstable state of British politics, he might have aspired to be prime minister.

Though he was a wealthy member of British nobility and a son-in-law of a former British prime minister, Lord Grey, Durham was sympathetic to democratic ideas. He also proved to have imaginative views about the administration of the Empire as a whole, as his far-reaching recommendations for the Canadas would show.

Lord Durham arrived at his headquarters in Quebec City at the end of May, 1838. His title was Governor-General of British North America. The situation was tense and complicated, following the suppression of rebellion. All eyes were on the new man. Durham hardly had time to enjoy the prestige of his position. Almost immediately he was meeting with delegations about conditions in the colonies. He set up inquiries into laws, education, land problems and local government, and took tours to Montreal and Upper Canada as far as Niagara.

In five months, Durham and his assistants gathered the information that would form the basis of his report. He would later be criticized for lack of thoroughness. But he was working under severe handicaps of time, lack of support from the British government and some delicate issues in Lower Canada.

Durham dealt successfully with border troubles with the United States, one being a dispute over the New Brunswick-Maine boundary. He also obtained the United States' agreement to help restrain raids into Canada by Americans sympathetic to the unsuccessful rebels of 1837. Within British North America, however, Durham was faced with a problem that finally drove him to resign.

The issue was the large number of men who had been jailed for taking part in the rebellion. Something had to be done about the more than 150 prisoners. However, a fair trial by jury seemed impossible. Durham decided to order the release of all but the eight most serious offenders. They were exiled to Bermuda, under the threat of serious penalty if they returned.

For various reasons, the order of exile caused an uproar in Britain. The wavering government protected itself against the opposition attacks by disallowing Durham's decision. The governor, who learned of the developments from American newspaper reports, felt that his authority had been compromised. He resigned from office and returned to England.

The Earl of Durham

Durham at first refused the request that he go to Canada. His health was not strong, and he had just returned from representing Britain for two years in St. Petersburg (then the capital of Russia). It was only after a personal request from Queen Victoria that Durham agreed to undertake the mission to Canada.

"Radical Jack" was the nickname given to Durham by his opponents. His controversial behaviour was well illustrated by his selection of assistants. Among those who accompanied Durham to Canada was Gibbon Wakefield, a man who was noted for his schemes to strengthen the British Empire through emigration from the mother country to the colonies. Wakefield was also well-known for his three-year jail sentence, received for abducting a fifteen-year-old heiress. Thus Durham was risking criticism for appointing a controversial aide.

The Durham Report

The Durham Report was prepared under Durham's direction with the assistance of his leading advisers. It was submitted to the Colonial Secretary on January 31, 1839, approximately two months after Durham's return to England. The Report fulfilled two main purposes. It gave an analysis of conditions in British North America, and made proposals for dealing with the bases for discontent. The first part, consisting of four sections, discussed Lower Canada at great length, Upper Canada more briefly, the Eastern provinces and Newfoundland, and disposal of public lands and emigration. In the second section, Durham put forth his ideas for reform.

Observations

LOWER CANADA

Durham had arrived with certain expectations about what he would find. He was shocked by the different kinds of problems he discovered. He expected to deal with groups whose views about the running of government conflicted. Nevertheless, he felt there was a deeper issue:

> "I expected to find a contest between a government and a people: I found two nations warring in the bosom of a single state: I found a

struggle, not of principles, but of races. . . . every contest is one of French and English in the outset, or becomes so ere [before] it has run its course."[1]

His description of the French Canadians contains a hint of the recommendations he would make later in the Report:

"They clung to ancient prejudices, ancient customs and ancient laws, not from any strong sense of their beneficial effects, but with the unreasoning tenacity of an uneducated and unprogressive people. . . .

They are mild and kindly, frugal, industrious and honest, very sociable, cheerful and hospitable, and distinguished for a courtesy and real politeness, which pervades every class of society. The conquest has changed them but little. . . . the continued negligence of the British Government left the mass of the people without any of the institutions which would have elevated them in freedom and civilization . . . that would have assimilated their character and habits, in the easiest and best way, to those of the Empire of which they became a part."

By contrast, Durham found the English Canadians to be progressive:

"The English population, an immigrant and enterprising population, looked on the [British] American Provinces as a vast field for settlement and speculation, and in the common spirit of the Anglo-Saxon inhabitants of that continent, regarded it as the chief business of the Government, to promote, by all possible use of its . . . powers, the increase of population and the accumulation of property. . . . "

The conflict of races, Durham believed, was the root problem. The system of government made that problem worse. In his opinion, the French Canadians used their majority in the Assembly to block the progress of the English. This resulted in increased racial conflict.

Durham believed that the Quebec Act had been a mistake. In contrast to Sir Guy Carleton, who, some seventy years earlier, had predicted that the French Canadians would predominate "to the end of time,"* Durham wrote:

*See page 148.

" . . . it was quite impossible to exclude the English race from any part of the North American continent. It will be acknowledged by every one who has observed the progress of Anglo-Saxon colonization in America, that sooner or later the English race was sure to predominate even numerically in Lower Canada, as they predominate already, by their superior knowledge, energy, enterprise and

271

wealth. The error, therefore . . . is the vain endeavour to preserve a French Canadian nationality in the midst of Anglo-American colonies and states."

Assuming the inevitability of an English-speaking majority, Durham believed that the culture of the French Canadians was ultimately doomed. For their sake, as well as for the efficient management of the colony, Durham believed that the French Canadians should be assimilated. Thus he wrote:

". . . it must henceforth be the first and steady purpose of the British Government to establish an English population, with English laws and language, in this Province, and to trust its government to none but a decidedly English Legislature."

At great length, Durham wrote about the disadvantages of French-Canadian culture. Whereas English Canadians had the benefits of close ties with the mother country, and thus had the prospects of ongoing benefit from what was to him an advanced or British civilization, the French Canadians were isolated from France and cut off by language from "the enjoyments and civilizing influence of the arts."

1. (*a*) Match the following with the statements each would have been most likely to have made:

(A) A French Canadian lawyer
(B) An English Canadian merchant
(C) Lord Durham

>   1. "The French Canadians are basically inferior to English Canadians; they are a troublesome people who don't deserve the same status as the English majority."
>   2. "The French Canadians have a unique culture and lifestyle, which promises to flourish in spite of its isolation on the North American continent."
>   3. "The French Canadians have been left on their own for too long, and must be given the opportunity for assimilation into a more advanced (British) civilization."

(*b*) Which of these statements seems most convincing to you? Why?
2. (*a*) Suppose Britain had consistently followed a policy after the Conquest of allowing French Canadians to live entirely by their own language, customs and laws.
>   1. How different might Quebec be today?
>   2. How different might the relations between Quebec and the rest of Canada be?

Anglophone vs. Francophone culture

One of Lord Durham's premises was that since French Canadians were cut off from France, its insititutions and its culture, they were "a people with no history and no literature." Regardless of whether this is true or not, consider the following:

> Which of the following Canadians prominent in the arts and entertainment can you identify?

Gratien Gelinas	James Reaney
Michel Tremblay	David Freeman
Pauline Julien	Harry Hibbs
Ginette Reno	Ann Murray
Robert Charlebois	Murray McLachlan

> How many of the ones you could identify are French-Canadian? English-Canadian?
> Which ones are most typically Canadian?
> Do you think that French Canada or English Canada has the more distinctive culture in the 1970s? Why?

Does it seem ironic that the French Canadian culture, despite its severance from France, has an identity which is growing stronger as the months and years pass whereas English-Canadians seem forever to be trying to define theirs? Why do you think as you do?

(b) Suppose Britain, at the time of the Conquest, had decided on a policy of assimilation and stuck to it.
1. How different might Quebec be today?
2. How different might the relations between Quebec and the rest of Canada be?
3. Was assimilation more, or less, feasible at the time of the Conquest than when Durham recommended it?

(c) To what extent would present-day issues between Quebec and other parts of Canada *still* exist, regardless of which policy Britain chose?

UPPER CANADA

Durham had spent most of his five-month stay as Governor in Lower Canada. Consequently his analysis of conditions in Upper Canada was less complete. Furthermore, it was based mainly on

INTERESTING SIMPLICITY — CANADIAN REVOLT EXPLAINED.
A new short-hand method of reporting a parliamentary speech

reports made to him by his assistants. They had been strongly influenced by the Reform Party.

The troubles in Upper Canada, Durham concluded, were mainly due to the power of the "Family Compact" and the frustration of the Reformers. Durham described the situation:

> " ... Upper Canada ... has long been entirely governed by a party commonly designated as the 'family compact,' a name not much more appropriate than party designations usually are, inasmuch as there is, in truth, very little of family connexion among the persons thus united. For a long time this body of men, receiving at times accessions [additions] to its numbers, possessed almost all the highest public offices, by means of which, and of its influence in the Executive Council, it wielded all the powers of government. ... Successive Governors, as they came in their turn, are said to have either submitted quietly to its influence, or, after a short and un-availing struggle, to have yielded to this well-organized party. ... "

Against this entrenched group of powerful people, a reform movement developed. Even when they had control of the elected Assembly, the Reformers found they were powerless. They could neither influence the decisions made by government, nor remove the people behind them. Therefore, Durham wrote:

> "It was upon this question of the responsibility of the Executive Council that the great struggle has for a long time been carried on between the official party and the reformers."

274

Recommendations

For all its description, analysis and suggestions for reform, the Durham Report was notable for its three major recommendations. These were the union of Upper and Lower Canada, the granting of responsible government, and the division of powers between the British imperial government and the local governments of the colonies.

(1) Union of Upper Canada and Lower Canada

For Durham, the union of the central Canadian colonies—created as separate areas by the Constitutional Act—was a necessary first step, before other changes could be made. He explained that he first believed a federal union* of British American colonies would be best. He had concluded, however, that Confederation was not yet workable. Of more immediate importance was a joining of Upper and Lower Canada that would serve to assimilate the French. In the words of Durham:

*See page 364 for an explanation of the nature of federal union.

> " . . . I believe that no permanent or efficient remedy can be devised for the disorders of Lower Canada, except a fusion of the Government in that of one or more of the surrounding Provinces."

He explained further that an English majority, necessary to efficient government, would be brought about by union, with additional English population provided by immigration. The expected result would be that:

> "the French, when once placed . . . in a minority, would abandon their vain hopes of nationality."

It was very important, according to Durham, that the elected Assembly be set up on the basis of "Rep by Pop" (representation according to population). Equal representation for the two former colonies of Upper and Lower Canada would serve to extend the influence of the French Canadians. "Rep by Pop" would soon "swamp" them.

(2) Responsible Government

Once Upper and Lower Canada had been joined, Responsible Government, which Durham thought to be an essential step in restoring harmony in government, would be possible. Such a step would not be so difficult. In fact,

> "It needs no change in the principles of government, no invention of a new constitutional theory, to supply the remedy which would, in my opinion, completely remove the existing political disorders. It needs but to follow out consistently the principles of the British constitution."

Durham did not explain precisely how "the principles of the British constitution" would be put into operation in the colonies. In commenting on Responsible Government, he recommended that "the Colonial Governor ... be instructed to secure the co-operation of the Assembly in his policy, by entrusting ... administration to such men as could command a majority."

If this recommendation were accepted by the British Government, there would be a good deal of room for interpreting the meaning, *in practice*, of Responsible Government. As it turned out, the months and years ahead were to be filled with struggle before the modern meaning and practice of the term were established.

(3) Division of Powers

Responsible Government in the colonies was feasible only if the British government limited its own powers to imperial (Empire-wide) concerns. These included changes in the constitution, foreign affairs, external trade and the management of public lands.

All other matters should be handled by the colonial governments. Residents of a colony could best advise the governor on local needs, such as public works (for example, roads, canals and railways), education, and law and order.

Durham advised such a division of powers to reduce the likelihood of conflict between the imperial and colonial governments. He had an answer for those who feared that local self-government would mean a weakening of ties between Britain and the colonies. The result would be the opposite. Durham insisted "that the predominant feeling of all the English population of the North American Colonies is that of devoted attachment to the mother country".

He continued:

> "They value the institutions of their country, not merely from a sense of the practical advantages which they confer, but from sentiments of national pride; and they uphold them the more, because they are accustomed to view them as marks of nationality, which distinguish them from their Republican neighbours [the United States]."

1. In what way was the form of government Durham recommended the same as governments of present-day Canada? In what way was it different?
2. Why was a division of powers between the British Government and the colonial governments so important in Durham's time?
3. Does "national pride" mean the same thing as "Canadian identity"? In Durham's time, was it possible to have a "Canadian identity" different from "British identity"? Why or why not?

The Durham Report contained a wide range of recommendations in addition to the major ones. Some of these were:

1. Municipalities should be organized. This organization would help to prevent too great a concentration of political power, and involve the citizens in civic affairs.

2. Emigration from Britain to the colonies should be promoted "on the greatest possible scale."

3. The distribution of public lands should be reorganized. Money should be spent on improving roads and other public works. The clergy reserves should be abolished.

4. An intercolonial railway should be built between Canada and the Maritimes. This would promote trade and encourage an eventual union of British North American colonies.

5. The post office should be organized as a single system.

RECEPTION OF THE REPORT

When the *Durham Report* was made public, the reaction was swift and generally negative. This was not surprising. He had severely criticized many different groups, and they were all on the defensive —including the British Government, which had commissioned the Report.

Criticisms, which have come forth for years, even generations, after the Report, have included:

1. the assessment of the French-Canadian way of life was unfair; in condemning the lack of material progress among French Canadians, Durham had failed to note many positive qualities of their culture;

2. he overestimated the importance of racial conflict as a cause of discontent in Lower Canada; otherwise, it is hard to explain the success of Baldwin and Lafontaine in creating the Reform Party and fighting for Responsible Government;

3. he overestimated the influence of Anglicization as a way of bringing French Canadians into full participation in Canadian life;

4. his judgements about Upper Canada were biased and formed second-hand.

Defenders of Durham replied:

1. that he had prepared his report under impossible pressures of time, workload and interference;

2. that the report was remarkably comprehensive, and provoked a great deal of thought about a host of colonial problems;

3. that Durham's recommendation of Responsible Government contributed to the improvement of government in British North America;
4. that his ideas for dividing power between imperial and colonial governments pointed the way for evolution of the Empire into the British Commonwealth.

B. The meaning of Responsible Government

The rebellions of 1837 were short-lived and unsuccessful efforts to bring about radical changes. They did, however, start a decade of struggle for more "responsible government". The two sides in the struggle were: (1) the Tories, allied with the British colonial secretary* and appointed British governors, and (2) the Reformers.

*The British cabinet minister in charge of the colonies.

Basically, the Tories tried to maintain the pre-rebellion system, which had been set up by the Constitutional Act. In this system, government was *representative*, but not *responsible*. In other words, each colonial government included an assembly, to which members were elected by citizens having the right to vote. However, the assembly was the weakest part of the government. The making of policy and major decisions took place "at the top."

The key man was the governor, whom the British government appointed and whom only the British government could remove. The governor was advised, on decisions concerning matters *within the colony**, by Councils. Their members were drawn from the Family Compacts, and were answerable to the governor since they were appointed by him, rather than to the Assembly and the voters.

*On defence, import and export trade, changes in the constitution and other subjects of concern to the British Empire as a whole, the Governor received his instructions from the British Government.

The goal of the Reformers was "responsible government" in colonial matters (see Diagram B). Essential to this form of government are the following principles:

1. the governor, representing the British Crown, is above politics; that is, he does not take sides;
2. the governor must accept the advice of his Executive Council, or "Cabinet." One way he does so is to sign into law any bills proposed by his Council and approved by the legislature (in practice, the Assembly, or House of Commons);
3. the Executive Council is chosen from among members of the legislature by the leader of the largest group. In modern terms, this means the leader of the "majority party" in the elected Assembly, who is known as "premier" or "prime minister";
4. the Executive Council stays in office only so long as it is supported by the majority in the Assembly. For example, if the Executive Council introduces a bill and the majority vote against (defeat) the bill, the Council is expected to resign.

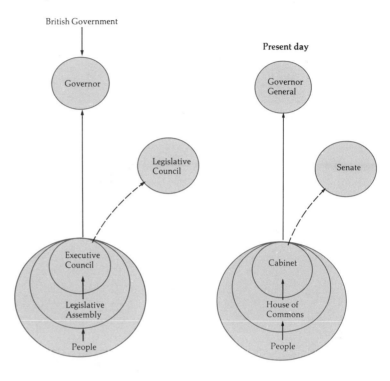

Diagrams A and B show the basic structure and relationship among the parts of colonial government "before and after" Responsible Government. The arrows suggest who held power in each case.

What *similarities* can you find between the two systems?
What *differences*?

The principles of responsible government may be more understandable through a comparison of Diagrams B and C. What similarities can you identify between the kind of government established in 1849 and the kind of government in Canada now? Differences?*

C. The achievement of Responsible Government in Canada

> Student: Responsible Government is about a lot of governors who came out to Canada and died, except one who signed 'the Bill' which meant Responsible Government was in and they threw rocks and eggs at his carriage.

The decade between 1839 and 1849 was a testing time in British North America for the political directions outlined in the Durham Report. Some of its recommendations were put into effect. Some

*Remember you are looking at only the simplest form of comparison and contrast. The *practice* of responsible government has varied in many ways down through the years, and is much more complicated now than it was in the mid-nineteenth century.

279

were acted upon in sharply modified form. Others were abandoned entirely. There would be many instances of "two steps forward, one step back" and some strange political twists before the establishment of a form of Responsible Government that has endured to the present.

A CANADIAN REFORMER URGES RESPONSIBLE GOVERNMENT

The question of how to give control of local affairs to the colonies without weakening the connection with Britain was not easily answered. The Canadian Reformer, Robert Baldwin, wrote a letter to Lord Durham on August 23, 1838. Baldwin had no doubts that Responsible Government was a NECESSARY *step to preserving Britain's ties with the colonies:*

... It is the genius of the English race in both hemispheres to be concerned in the Government of themselves—I would ask Your Lordship, would the people of England endure any system of Executive Government over which they had less influence than that which at present exists? Your Lordship knows they would not.— Can you then expect the people of these colonies with their English feelings & English sympathies to be satisfied with less—If you do Your Lordship will assuredly be disappointed—They can see a reason why their relations with foreign countries should be placed in other hands; but none why their domestic concerns should not be managed upon similar principles to those applied in the administration of the Imperial Government. ... [2]

THE PROVINCE OF CANADA CREATED

The British government decided that the two Canadas could best be governed as one colony, as Durham advised. There were several possible advantages. One government could be simpler and more efficient to maintain than two. The St. Lawrence trading system would be under a single system, not divided as before. The absorption of the French-Canadian way of life would be more likely, even though there was bound to be some initial protest.*

*See page 247, "A Plan to Swamp the French."

The man chosen to succeed Lord Durham as governor, and to bring about the union was Charles Poulett Thomson, Lord Sydenham. A man of practical outlook, with an extensive background in both politics and business, Sydenham would need all his talents. He was to gain approval for the union from all the main Canadian groups.

Sydenham succeeded, in a manner of speaking, in obtaining the desired Canadian consent for union. The opposition of French Canadians was automatic, since they saw the union as part of Lord Durham's plan to assimilate them. But Sydenham bypassed the French Canadians. He won approval for the plan from the Special

The power of patronage

Filbert Grog, a recently elected politician, has the power to fill a number of government jobs. He is perplexed over one in particular— supervisor of government horse barns. There are two applicants. One is Slade Barnaway, a tall stranger. He is a graduate in veterinary medicine who has spent much of his 30 years horsing around. The other is Silas Steale, who scarcely knows one end of a horse from another, but who happens to be Filbert Grog's first cousin, and who has bullied him since childhood. Whom should Mr. Grog appoint to the position?

This case is fictitious, but the problem of political appointments is probably as old as government itself. *Patronage* is the term for the power to grant government jobs to people for reasons other than merit or special training. One of the political facts of life is that governments have many favours to dispense among their supporters. This is true today, though patronage was a more general practice in the days before civil service commissions existed.

Certainly patronage was part of the system during the 1830s and 1840s, during the struggle for reform. As long as the Family Compact remained in power, its members were in a privileged position to maintain wide support through appointments and the granting of contracts for public works.

Robert Baldwin

The Reformers who challenged the Family Compact were striving for the *principles* of Responsible Government. However, the members of the Family Compact knew that Responsible Government would open up the possibility of the Reformers' gaining office. The Reformers were realistic about the fact that getting political power would mean the opportunity to reward their followers. In other words, patronage was one of the possible prizes of Responsible Government being established.

When the first Baldwin-Lafontaine ministry was formed in 1842 under Sir Charles Bagot, the Reformers were able to secure appointments for many supporters. Included among the jobs to be filled were such positions as judges, postal clerks, customs inspectors, school supervisors, and many more.

Louis Lafontaine

When another Governor, Sir Charles Metcalfe, arrived, he made appointments without consulting Baldwin and Lafontaine. They resigned over the challenge to their "power of patronage", which they regarded as a fundamental right of the party in power. Thus, the issue of patronage was an important part of the struggle for Responsible Government.

1. Were Baldwin and Lafontaine right in resigning over the "power of patronage"? Why or why not?
2. Should a political party *in modern times* have the right to reward campaign supporters with jobs, appointments, contracts or other favours? Why or why not?
3. Should there be positions in government which are not "political" appointments but which are filled solely on the basis of merit? If so, what might be examples of some of these?

Ignoring Lord Durham

Durham believed that the Assembly in the government of a united Province of Canada should be elected according to "Rep by Pop" (representation by population). This seems contradictory at first, since the French Canadians had a definite majority at the time, and would apparently have more representatives than English Canada. However, Durham was counting on massive English immigration to outnumber the French in a short time. A temporary French-Canadian majority, he thought would be a small price to pay.

The British government decided against the "small price" and assumed that an immediate English-Canadian majority could succeed in "swamping the French".

The assumption was wrong. The English Reformers were less opposed to French Reformers than they were to English Tories.

Only 40 years old when he came to Canada in 1839, Sydenham had already achieved high status in Britain. He had amassed a fortune in business, the Baltic lumber trade being one of his profitable operations. Knowledgeable in practical politics and well-known as an organizer, he had served as a cabinet minister in Lord Grey's government and as vice-president of the Board of Trade. If anyone could put Canadian government in working order, Sydenham seemed to be the man.

Council which had handled the affairs of Lower Canada since 1837 when the constitution was suspended. The Special Council, of course, wore the colours of the English-speaking merchants. These men expected new opportunities for commercial progress.

In Upper Canada the task of gaining acceptance of the proposed union proved to be more difficult. The Tories saw in the plan the disappearance of their privileged position and the loss of their effective control of government. But Upper Canada was deeply in debt. It suffered from a severe depression and needed funds for rapid development in order to keep pace with the United States. With the promise of a British loan of £1 500 000 Sydenham was able to win enough Tory support for the proposed Union.

The Reformers of Upper Canada, liked the prospect of the return of prosperous times. They saw in the union the end of Family Compact rule. Union would enable them to unite with the Reformers in Lower Canada for the purpose of winning responsible government. Sydenham readily secured the support of the Reformers of

Upper Canada. Thus, the Act of Union, passed by the British Parliament in 1840, came into effect in February, 1841.

The British plan was to create a **legislative union**. There would be one governor, one executive council, one legislative council and one assembly. The united colony was to assume the public debts of the two Canadas, although the debt of Upper Canada, where so much new territory had been opened for settlement, was far larger than that of Lower Canada.* Official records were to be kept in English, although French could be used in Assembly debates. All revenues with the exception of a limited civil list—guaranteed incomes for key government officials—were to be placed under the control of the legislature. In addition, the laws of Upper and Lower Canada* were to remain as before.

A crucial question was the composition of the United Assembly. The British Government had decided upon equal representation from the two "halves" of the united colony, even though the population of Canada East (formerly Lower Canada, later Quebec) exceeded that of Canada West (formerly Upper Canada, later Ontario) by some 200 000. However, English-speaking Canadians would have a majority, since 25% of Canada East's population was English-speaking and all Canada West representatives would be English-speaking.

The beginnings of party politics in Canada

WHAT IS A POLITICAL PARTY?

A political party is an organization of like-minded people who have the objective of gaining control of government. Once its leaders are in power, it seeks to implement its ideas through policies, laws, regulations, public relations and whatever tools are available to the state.

Political parties are vital to the maintenance of a democratic system. Otherwise power becomes concentrated in the hands of a group, differences of opinion are not tolerated, and minority elements are suppressed. In a democratic country, two or more parties exist to represent the various interests and to provide alternatives on a regular basis through elections. If one party is defeated, power passes peacefully to the party successful in the election.

Party systems vary from time to time and from place to place, but Responsible Government, on the British model of Parliamentary, or Cabinet, government requires well-organized political parties in order to work smoothly.

Why are political parties essential to Responsible Government?

The Act of Union was followed by some results quite unexpected by its creators. Instead of diminishing the role of French Canadians in

A union in which the previous separate governments were abolished and replaced by a new, unitary one for the combined area.

*The debt of Upper Canada exceeded £1 000 000; Lower Canada's debt was negligible.

*After the Union, called Canada West and Canada East respectively. Even though they were now united under one government, they retained the character of separate divisions.

What are true friends for?

It was ironic that Lafontaine was named a representative of York (Toronto) on the day before Sydenham was buried at Kingston. The man whom the late governor had kept out of the assembly now entered it through the courtesy of Robert Baldwin, who had been elected in both Hastings and York, and had asked his friends in the latter constituency to choose Lafontaine in his place. The incident was a proclamation of the alliance between the Reformers of the two provinces, and of that collaboration between French and English which was to create a different Canada than Durham had envisaged. A former lieutenant of Papineau, a man against whom a warrant for high treason had been issued four years before, a Catholic French Canadian, was elected from the stronghold of Protestant English Canada. The times had indeed changed.[3]

*See page 278.

*Lafontaine had been twice jailed for his part in the Rebellion of 1837 in Lower Canada.

public life and fostering "anglicization," it encouraged French Canadians to take part actively in politics to preserve their threatened culture. Brought together in the same Assembly, French Canadian Reformers, led by Louis Lafontaine,* and their English Canadian counterparts led by Robert Baldwin, found common cause in their struggle for Responsible Government.

The forging of bi-racial political links laid the basis for the Reform Party. While it never quite became an organized party in the modern sense, it was a coalition of political groups which combined to achieve common goals.

The Baldwin-Lafontaine partnership, an important combination in Canadian politics for the next ten years, was an answer to the methods of Lord Sydenham. He appeared to reject three of the four principles of Responsible Government,* in that he

1. acted as his own prime minister;
2. regarded his Executive Council as an advisory committee, not as the people who made decisions;
3. picked his Executive Councillors from all political groups in the Assembly. (This would be roughly equivalent to the present Governor-General picking a Cabinet from Liberals, Progressive Conservatives, New Democratic Party, and Créditistes.)

Only on point 4, the importance of maintaining the support of a majority in the Assembly, did Sydenham seem to be acting according to the principles of Responsible Government. But as long as he initiated much needed reforms and improved Canadian prosperity, he had support for *his* interpretation of Responsible Government.

In fact, Sydenham was not opposed to the idea of local self-government. But, he was convinced that Canadian politicians needed training before they could handle it. He also believed it necessary to settle several old issues and make many changes in the system before Responsible Government would work. Consequently he settled the long-standing problem of clergy reserves by dividing them among the various Protestant churches. The money from them was to be used for schools. He organized a system of municipal government, which was the basis for Ontario's present counties. And he encouraged the development of the St. Lawrence trading system through the building of roads and canals.

Sydenham's premature death in September, 1841, cut short a brilliant career. Injuries received when he fell from his horse were too much for his frail health, severely weakened by overwork.

1. In what ways might one say that Sydenham resisted Responsible Government?

Baldwin and Lafontaine

Robert Baldwin (1804-1858) was born in York (Toronto) and studied law under his father, William, a licensed lawyer *and* doctor, and one of the early leaders of the Reform Party. The younger Baldwin, first elected to the Assembly of Upper Canada in 1829, was a well-known, moderate reformer by the time of the rebellion of 1837, which he did not support. He was one of the first to advocate Responsible Government, and is known to have influenced Lord Durham's thinking about the subject.

Lafontaine (1807-1864), born the son of a farmer in Lower Canada, was a Montreal lawyer. He was a member of the Assembly from 1830-1837, and was inevitably an ally of Papineau. Though Lafontaine did not support armed rebellion in 1837, he was arrested, but released without trial.

After the rebellions of 1837, Baldwin was the principal leader of the English-Canadian Reformers, Lafontaine, of the French-Canadian Reformers. From 1841 to 1851, they were in and out of the Executive Council of the Province of Canada. In their persistent campaign to achieve Responsible Government, they twice resigned (1841, 1843) when governors refused to concede.

Together they formed the "Great Ministry" of 1848, under which the principles of Responsible Government were finally established. After this achievement, they found themselves out of touch with other issues, and both resigned from politics in 1851.

2. In what ways might one say that he had made important contributions toward its achievement?

RESPONSIBLE GOVERNMENT BECOMES REALITY

For nearly eight years following the death of Sydenham, the struggle for Responsible Government dragged on. During the time of his immediate successor, Sir Charles Bagot, the formation of the first Baldwin-Lafontaine ministry was an important step forward. In other words, these two leaders of the Reform Party acted for a time as "co-prime ministers." They headed the Executive Council, and the Governor generally followed their advice.

Bagot did not go so far as to appoint the Executive Council entirely from the Reform Party, which had a majority of the members in the Assembly. Thus, he did not go all the way to "Cabinet government" as we know it. In Britain, however, the attitude was

Charles Bagot

The Burning of Montreal, 1849

that Bagot had given up too much authority, and the next governor was instructed to regain control.

Sir Charles Metcalfe, in trying to regain control, was bound to have trouble with the Lafontaine-Baldwin ministry. An early dispute* led to the calling of an election in 1844. When the smoke cleared, the Tories, with Metcalfe's active help, had succeeded in branding the Reformers as disloyal to the British connection. With a Tory majority in the Assembly supporting him, Metcalfe seemed to be in charge. His triumph was short-lived, however, as incurable illness led to his retirement and death.

*See page 281.

A dramatic development in Britain suddenly overshadowed events in the colonies. Free trade was adopted in place of the policy of mercantilism.* Britain's swift industrial development had given its manufactured goods a great advantage in world markets. Down came the Navigation Acts and other regulations which had given the raw materials from the colonies a protected market in Britain.

*See page 165.

The empire was no longer to be a closed trading area. Foreign countries now had the chance to compete on an equal footing with the colonies. Suddenly the colonies were on their own in the vital matter of trade. They could no longer be denied the right to be on their own politically as well.

Metcalfe was accustomed to "running the show." He had spent 37 years in British India as an administrator, and he had recently served a tour of duty as Governor of Jamaica. Metcalfe was experienced, able, and tough—but incurable cancer made him a tragic figure in his last days in Canada.

The men who were responsible for the change in the Province of Canada were Lord Grey, the Colonial Secretary, and Lord Elgin, the new Governor of Canada (1847-1854). When the Reformers won a large majority in the election of 1848, Lord Elgin called on Lafontaine and Baldwin to form an Executive Council (Cabinet) as he had been instructed to do.

A first for Nova Scotia

A similar but less turbulent struggle was taking place in the Maritimes. It was here, not in the Province of Canada, that Responsible Government was first put into practice. In Nova Scotia, Joseph Howe, editor of the *Novascotian*, led the Reform Party, which kept up the pressure on the Governor. The latter reacted by relying on the Tories—in effect, on the Tory *party*, which had a majority in the Assembly.

If the Tories lost their majority, the Governor was instructed to accept the Reformers as the "government party." Lord Grey, the Colonial Secretary, wrote in November, 1846, to the Governor of Nova Scotia with such instructions.

In the election of 1847, the Reformers were victorious. Thus in January, 1848, the Governor called on the Reformers to fill the Executive Council, or "Cabinet." The first official Responsible Government in British North America had taken office.

In 1849 came the test of Responsible Government, the Rebellion Losses Bill. The purpose of the bill was to compensate people in Canada East (formerly Lower Canada) who had suffered property damage during the Rebellion of 1837. The Tories charged that rebels would be among those receiving money, and thus would be paid for their past disloyalty!

Even though Elgin doubted the wisdom of the bill, and knew that trouble might result, he signed the Rebellion Losses Bill. He was following the "advice" of his ministers, who had submitted the bill to the Assembly, where the bill had been passed.

Elgin's decision touched off a riot in Montreal, where the Governor was personally attacked by a mob. His carriage was bombarded with eggs and rocks as he left the parliament buildings, which were burned to the ground. Prominent Tories, including some of Montreal's leading businessmen, issued the Annexation Manifesto. This statement called for the end of ties with Britain and the annexation (takeover) of Canada by the United States.

As the months passed, however, Responsible Government became generally accepted as part of the Canadian system of government. On the eve of Confederation, in the 1860s, there were many controversial issues to debate. Responsible Government, however, was not one of them.

Lord Elgin was Lord Durham's son-in-law, and determined to bring about Durham's recommendation of Responsible Government. Elgin believed such a step would enshrine Durham as one of the great statesmen in Britain's history. He was right.

Lord Elgin

Violence and Protest in Montreal, 1849

The year 1849 was a year of triumph and frustration, especially in Montreal. Elgin's acknowledgement of Responsible Government signalled victory for the Reformers, an alliance of English and French Canadians. The Tories, the majority of whom were English, were furious, however. The economy had been in a slump since Britain's introduction of free trade in 1846 had ended the protected market in Britain long enjoyed by colonial producers. Now the Tories seemed to have been excluded from political power as well.

Two events illustrate the tension:

(a) THE MONTREAL RIOT

An eye-witness to the riot, a Montreal shop-keeper, wrote the following account of the attack on Lord Elgin and the burning of the Parliament Buildings:

Business is *terrible dull* and nothing is now talked of but a *republican government*. Today the Govn [Governor Elgin] came to town on horseback attended as usual by an aid and his Groom, went home about 3 o'clock and every one supposed the business of the day concluded and that his excellency had gone to dinner. But in about an hour more he came again to town *in state* attended by his officers and a Guard more than usually numerous. What is all this about? was at once the inquiry. It was not supposed that it could be to give the Royal Sanction to any bill, for before such a sanction is given it is customary to give public notice to that effect and call out the soldiers in front of Parliment house and fire a salute with much more parade etc, but on this occasion there was no notice given and no display nor anything to indicate that the Royal Sanction was to be given to any measure, but it was rumored that the Bill for indemnifying the Rebellion losses was now to be sanctioned tho the members said it was the *New Tariff Bill*, but on the report spreading thru town (which it did like wildfire) an immense mob assembled and sourounded the Parliment house to see what his Excellency intended to do—and when it was finally announced that he had really given the Royal Sanction to the Bill, then there was *trouble*—as his Excellency left the House for his carriage at the door he was assailed with stones, clubs & rotten & good eggs by thousands, and he was struck in the face with an egg, his carriage windows broken etc. but by the speed of his horses, he was enabled to escape with no injury except to his carriage and his equipage—I stop here for the cry is raised that the *Parliment House* is on fire—fire—fire is the cry—and from my shop door I see the red flames light up the Heavens—I go—more after I see what the row is—April 26th. Tis too true—Last night about 8 o'clock while Parliment was still sitting a mob (it can be called nothing else tho' composed of some our most worthy citizens) assembled around the House, and commenced the distruction of the building, by breaking windows etc. Soon the doors were broken open and a stout fellow sprang into the speakers chair with the exclamation *"I disolve Parliment"* This was the Signal—and immediately in the face of the members, and an immense multitude of spectators the Gas Pipes were fired in a dozen places, and the building wraped in flames—the "Golden Mace", sacred emblem of Royalty, was seized by the infuriated mob and borne into the street amid shouts of derision & scorn. The Members barely escaped with their lives, and that splendid Building with its rare paintings, all the records of the Provinces from the first settlement, all the acts of Parliment, that Library, worth alone, £100,000, all, all, are distroyed. That splendid portrait of the Queen, which you may remember was droped into the street, and torn into a thousand pieces, All was lost, nothing saved, and the structure now is but a heap of smoking ruins. The loss to the city cannot be less than £300,000 The fire Engines were not allowed to play upon the fire at all, and it was only on the arrival of General Gore with a body of soldiers that the engines were allowed to approach for the protection of other property.[4]

(b) THE ANNEXATION MANIFESTO

The Manifesto contains brief consideration of several alternative solutions to Canada's state of "ruin or rapid decay." Each of these, including Confederation, an independent republic of Canada, and free trade with the United States, is rejected. Finally, the Manifesto, signed by Canadians who either were or would become prominent in business and/or politics, called for union of Canada with the United States:

The reversal of the ancient policy of Great Britain, whereby she withdrew from the Colonies their wonted [accustomed] protection in her markets, has produced the most disastrous effects upon Canada. In surveying the actual condition of the country, what but ruin or rapid decay meets the eye! . . .

———————

Whilst the adjoining States are covered with a net-work of thriving railways, Canada possesses but three lines, which, together, scarcely exceed 50 miles in length. . . .

———————

The bitter animosities of political parties and factions in Canada, often leading to violence, and, upon one occasion, to civil war, seem not to have abated with time; nor is there, at the present moment, any prospect of diminution [decrease] or accommodation. The aspect of parties becomes daily more threatening towards each other, and under our existing institutions and relations, little hope is discernible of a peaceful and prosperous administration of our affairs. . . .

———————

Of all the remedies that have been suggested for the acknowledged and insufferable ills with which our country is afflicted, there remains but one to be considered. It propounds a sweeping and important change in our political and social condition involving considerations which demand our most serious examination. THIS REMEDY CONSISTS IN A FRIENDLY AND PEACEFUL SEPARATION FROM BRITISH CONNECTION AND A UNION UPON EQUITABLE TERMS WITH THE GREAT NORTH AMERICAN CONFEDERACY OF SOVEREIGN STATES.[5]

D. Reform and Responsible Government in the Maritimes

As part of British North America, the Maritimes were generally subject to the same British imperial policies as the Canadas. They all were colonies, maintained, in part, for the commercial and strategic advantage of a world-wide Empire. Furthermore, developments in the Canadas affected the Maritimes and vice versa. Nevertheless there were differences in the treatment given the Maritimes by the British Colonial Office. The struggle for reform and Responsible Government took a different path there than it did in the Canadas.

In the first place, the change from "Family Compact" rule to Responsible Government was peaceful and free from the agonies of rebellion. Such explosive issues as racial differences and large-scale expansion on the frontier were absent. The battle over revenue*— including patronage—was never marked by confrontation as it was in Upper and Lower Canada.

*Remember that the struggle for Responsible Government was more than a matter of principle; it involved control of appointments to government jobs, awarding of contracts, and so on.

The Reformers could not be charged with disloyalty and republicanism. Such claims, used at different times to defend the existing situation in the Canadas, would have seemed out of place in a region where many Reformers could claim the same Loyalist background as the Tories. Moreover, the British Colonial Office paid more heed to the moderately expressed Maritime demands for "the rights of Englishmen".

NOVA SCOTIA

*The word "oligarchy"— meaning a small, close-knit group holding power—is the more accurate term often used to describe such a group. Related terms are "power structure" and "power elite."

In Nova Scotia, as in the Canadas, a "Family Compact"* dominated public life. The wealthy merchants in Halifax, retired army and navy officers and government officials not only received appointments to the Councils but were elected to the Assembly. The Church of England, part of the "power structure", controlled religion and education. Thus the backwoods farmers and coastal fishermen had been ruled from Halifax by a firmly-entrenched oligarchy ever since 1758, when Nova Scotia was granted *representative* government.

Joseph Howe was the central figure in the reform movement in Nova Scotia. He first made a name for himself through his newspaper, the *Novascotian*. In it, he attacked the privileges and high-handed politics of the Family Compact.

In 1835, Howe was charged with **libel** for publishing in his newspaper a letter accusing Halifax magistrates of corruption. In conducting his own defence, he made a speech that lasted more than six hours! Howe was acquitted. The verdict was widely cheered among the people, to whom he had become a hero.

making false accusations, damaging to people's reputations

The next year he was elected to the Assembly. Now he could promote the movement for reform as a politician and as an editor.

JOSEPH HOWE SPEAKS TO THE JURY

Howe's incredible speech was filled with evidence, discussion of legal principles and appeals to ideals of British justice. The following brief excerpts are taken from the "finale":

[Gentlemen of the jury] Will you, my countrymen, the descendants of these men, warmed by their blood, inheriting their language, and having the principles for which they struggled confided to your care, allow them to be violated in your hands? Will you permit the sacred fire of liberty, brought by your fathers from the venerable temples of Britain, to be quenched and trodden out on the simple altars they have raised? Your verdict will be the most important in its consequences ever delivered before this tribunal; and I conjure you to judge me by the principles of English law, and to leave an unshackled press as a legacy to your children....

If for a moment I could fancy that your verdict would stain me with crime, cramp my resources by fines, and cast my body into prison.... Even then I would not desert my principles.... I would toil on and hope for better times.... Nor is there a living thing beneath my roof that would not aid me in this struggle: the wife who sits by my fireside; the children who play around my hearth; the orphan boys in my office, whom it is my pride and pleasure to instruct from day to day in the obligations they owe to their profession and their country, would never suffer the press to be wounded through my side. We would wear the coarsest raiment [clothing]; we would eat the poorest food; and crawl at night into the veriest hovel [most wretched hut] in the land to rest our weary limbs, but cheerful and undaunted hearts.... Yes, gentlemen, come what will, while I live, Nova Scotia shall have the blessing of an open and unshackled press....[6]

1. You are a member of the jury. Judging from this excerpt, what do you think would have been your reaction to Howe's speech in his own defence?

2. Which statement in this excerpt do you think might have had the most appeal to members of the actual jury?

Shortly after the publication of the *Durham Report*, Joseph Howe wrote his famous *Letters to Lord John Russell*. Russell, the Colonial Secretary at the time, had stated publicly his belief that Responsible Government as recommended by Durham was unworkable in a colony. In Howe's "open" letters, which were published as a pamphlet, he protested this denial of British rights. Why refuse loyal British subjects in the colonies the form of government enjoyed by people in Britain?

HOWE CHALLENGES THE COLONIAL SECRETARY

These excerpts are taken from Howe's first letter, several pages long, to Lord John Russell:

... for the honour of the British name ... let us manage our own affairs. ...

... a responsible Executive Council as recommended by Lord Durham would be preferred. ... the principle of responsibility to the popular branch must be introduced into all the colonies without delay. ... It is mere mockery to tell us that the Governor himself is responsible. He must carry on the government by and with the few officials whom he finds in possession when he arrives. He may flutter and struggle in the net, as some well-meaning Governors have done, but he must at last resign himself to his fate; and like a snared bird be content with the narrow limits assigned him by his keepers. ... [7]

It was only a matter of time before Howe and two other Reformers were appointed to the Executive Council in Nova Scotia. This was progress, since the Governor, Sir Colin Campbell, had at least appointed someone other than a member of the Family Compact. In Howe's opinion, though, the Reformers were token members, with no real say in the government. Eventually he resigned.

*See page 287.

Then Lord Grey*, in 1846, instructed the new Governor, Sir John Harvey, to be prepared to follow the principles of Responsible Government. The following year, the Reformers won a clearcut victory in the election. Thus in January, 1848, J. B. Uniacke, the official leader of the Reform Party, became the first premier of Nova Scotia.

Responsible Government was, therefore, achieved in Nova Scotia before it was achieved in Canada. As for Joseph Howe, although he was not the first premier, he remained the colony's most influential Reformer and public figure, a status he held until after Confederation.

Evolution not revolution

Canada, unlike most countries, is said to lack a revolutionary tradition. The system under which we live came about through "evolution", or gradual change. No political revolutions erupted to alter, in some dramatic way, the course of Canada's development.

Although revolution may be more exciting, it is also more drastic and violent in its effects. Where revolution is seen as a necessary activity, government may be unstable. Divisions among groups may be bitter and long-lasting. Order may be possible only through the use of military police or armed forces. One or more groups may use force to suppress others. The loss of individual rights may be the price paid for the stability of "the state".

Canadians live in a country where political changes have come gradually. Canada became a nation, but for a long time it was a British colony, and several generations passed before full self-government was attained. The system of government is democratic, but many groups or types of people—labour, women, ethnic minorities, to name some of the more obvious—have travelled a long road to full participation in the system.

As times have changed, our system has been adapted through evolution. The enduring question in an age of dramatic change is whether or not this method will always be adequate.

THE OTHER ATLANTIC COLONIES

In New Brunswick and Prince Edward Island, the main dispute between the Assembly and the Councils was about control of land. Neither colony had developed the clear-cut political divisions between Tories and Reformers that existed in Nova Scotia and Canada.

In New Brunswick, the Assembly wanted control of Crown lands, on which so much valuable timber stood. These lands were being exploited by a small group of wealthy businessmen who dominated the Councils.

In Prince Edward Island, much of the rich farm land was owned by absentee landlords who lived in England, but whose agents in the colony influenced both the Councils and the Assembly. Those who led the reform movement were trying to break the hold of the absentee owners, and to open land for ownership and speculation by local residents.

Newfoundland's situation was different again from that of any other colony in British North America. The social classes there were sharply divided. The St. John's merchants, generally English-speaking, Protestant and wealthy, dominated the great mass of fishermen, of whom half were Irish and Catholic, and all were poor.

A system of Responsible Government was introduced into each of the colonies: New Brunswick (1848), Prince Edward Island (1851) and Newfoundland (1855). The issues that gave rise to the need for reform, however, were not settled by the introduction of Responsible Government.

Responsible Government has been taken for granted by Canadians for a long time, since it was "achieved" in 1849. However, it is not something concrete that was "made" once and operates by itself. If Canadians fail to appreciate its underlying ideas and to help them work, Responsible Government is not likely to function in the best interests of all the people.

1. Besides voting, in what ways can Canadians participate in the governing of our country?

11

The Eve of Confederation

Even in the 1970s a Canadian travelling from one coast of Canada to the other is struck by the variety, the differences from one region to the next. And in spite of the influence of mass media, rapid travel, urbanization and education, Canadians in the Maritimes exhibit traits different from those of Canadians in Quebec, Ontario, the Prairies, British Columbia or the North.

It is hard to imagine, nevertheless, the variations among the colonies in British North America on the eve of Confederation. They had many things in common, of course, since every colony was governed by British officials according to British practices and influenced by the customs, manners and literature of the Mother Country. Yet British ways were modified by the isolation, geography, population and other circumstances of each colony.

To get a "bird's-eye view" of the colonies from which Canada eventually grew, picture yourself aboard a helicopter. Imagine a fantastic flight from St. John's, Newfoundland, to Victoria, British Columbia, on the eve of Confederation. Looking down, you get impressions about the land, the communities where people lived and worked, the ways they travelled, the opportunities and difficulties they experienced. In important ways, Canadians on the eve of Confederation lived lives very different from ours. In important ways also, their lives were very similar.

The land: a regional view

THE ATLANTIC COLONIES

The Atlantic Provinces, Newfoundland and the Maritimes, had much in common in the 1860s, as they do now. All were affected by nearness to the sea and by close ties to Great Britain, for example. Other Canadians, though, are likely to be surprised to learn that each has a long history of separate development and the pride that goes with occupying a special place within a larger scheme, whether British, Canadian or North American.

NEWFOUNDLAND

> "I'se the b'y that builds the boat,
> And I'se the b'y that sails her!
> I'se the b'y that catches the fish
> And takes 'em home to Lizer.*"
> (Newfoundland Folk Song)

*Eliza or Liza

Newfoundland has undergone dramatic changes in the last few years, perhaps more than any other province. In 1949, after more than 200 years of being a British colony, Newfoundland joined Canada. Developments in hydro power and other heavy industries have created a variety of new occupations, and fishing has become less central to the life of the province. The standard of living, in general, has risen sharply; medical care, education and other services are more readily available. Radio and television, as well as improved transportation by air and sea, have helped establish connections with the rest of Canada. Newfoundland is now a natural part of Canada and North America, rather than a British outpost as it was for most of its history.

MONEY IS NOT EVERYTHING

The changes in Newfoundland have been beneficial, but a way of life has been severely disrupted:

Nobody starves to death anymore, not even children. Nobody, or at least not many people, die because of a lack of medical services. For the first time, every child can learn to read and write, even if the educational standard is much lower than on the Mainland. Men who never had anything to lean on except their own strong muscles can now draw unemployment insurance, sick benefits, or relief assistance, while their wives gather in the baby bonus cheques. Old people, who used to survive (or try to) on a government pension of $120.00 a year are now so relatively affluent that they hardly know what to do with their money. The population is exploding; not because more children are being born, but because a lot more of them are surviving.

It all looks very good indeed. And yet there is a shadow over the paradise created by Confederation. Having tasted the fruits of the

Canadian way of life, more and more and more Newfoundlanders are turning their backs on the pitiless grey sea which made them what they were. The truly vast Newfoundland merchant marine, mostly under sail, as late as 1939 had about five hundred sailing vessels operating out of Newfoundland ports, many of them engaged in the trans-Atlantic salt fish trade, while others carried cargo to and from Canadian and Caribbean ports. But employment in the fisheries has fallen sharply as, indeed, it must. Where once fifty men, working for starvation wages, could land a certain weight of fish, now four or five men, better paid and operating a modern dragger, do the same job.

Standards of living go up, and the number of acceptable jobs at these new standards, go down. The birth rate goes up, and there are not enough jobs available even for those presently employable. And so Newfoundland, once noted as the greatest exporter in the world of salt fish, is now exporting men and women as its major produce. They go because they must, and because the new generation will not accept the kind of life their fathers knew.[1]

From our helicopter overhead, now that the early morning fog has lifted, we can see pre-Confederation St. John's below in a valley, surrounded by rocky cliffs that plunge steeply into the sea. The green grass of the valley beyond the settlement contrasts brilliantly with the grey-black rock of the coast.

A closer view reveals the harbour, busy with the ships of many nations, although the majority carry British flags. Away from the water and the rather dingy harbour area, most of the houses are small and simple. Larger residences, surrounded by well-kept grounds, no doubt belong to community leaders; there must be a few people who are wealthy and powerful. A striking feature of the town are the churches, of which there appear to be a large number. Their varying sizes and the shapes of their steeples indicate that the population is a mixture of Protestant and Catholic.

The roads in the port are obviously well-used, but their rutted tracks don't go much beyond the settlement. As the helicopter heads away from the capital and along the coast, over the Burrin peninsula on the way to Port-aux-Basques, tiny hamlets appear tucked away in isolated inlets, some not yet quite clear of fog. Each village is surrounded by rocky wilderness; little effort has been made to clear the trees, since no one is going to make a living by farming. Fishing boats of many sizes ride the waves at each of these outports. There is no doubt about the way people support themselves and their families. How isolated these villages, or fishing stations must be; how dependent on the sea for communication and travel, as well as for a livelihood.

St. John's Newfoundland. Why do you think this site was chosen for a settlement?

[[There are many things about Newfoundland that an aerial view does not reveal. For example, most children, especially in the outports, have little chance for education. The churches provide some basic schooling, but only the merchants of St. John's can afford to send their children to a private academy or to school in Boston, New York or London.

Another fact is the high degree of British control in the colony. Although the leading residents obtained a certain amount of responsible government by 1855, Britain's domination of the government and economy of Newfoundland is greater than it is in the other colonies.]]

CLASS STRUCTURE IN NEWFOUNDLAND

... the 'Fishocracy' of St. John's exert a great influence over all the other classes of the community. Society in St. John's is composed of four classes—

First.—The principal merchants, high officials of Government, and some of the lawyers and medical men.

Second.—The small merchants, large shopkeepers, some of the lawyers and doctors, and secondary officials.

Third.—Grocers, master mechanics, and schooner holders; and the

Fourth Class is the fishermen.

The first and second classes rarely, if ever, hold any social intercourse with the others. There is no colony belonging to the British Empire where influence and name tend so much to form caste in society, and where it is more regarded than in St. John's. This distinction of caste has a very pernicious influence.[2]

NUMERICAL STRENGTH OF RELIGIOUS DENOMINATIONS IN NEWFOUNDLAND IN 1857[3]

Church of Rome	57,214
Church of England	44,285
Wesleyans	20,229
Presbyterians	838
Congregationalists	347
Baptists and others	44

NOVA SCOTIA

"You can tell a Nova Scotian by the fragrance of the ocean,
For they always wear the perfume of the North Atlantic spray."

———

"You'll always know a **Bluenose** by his diet right away."

———

"You ain't a Nova Scotian if you don't like fish."[4]

These lines from a song written by Jim Bennet , popular Maritime broadcaster and entertainer, suggest a way of identifying a true Nova Scotian. While he is speaking whimsically, he is pointing out something very true about the people of Nova Scotia—their sense of identity.

A nickname for the people of Nova Scotia (and at one time of New Brunswick) popularized in the nineteenth century by humourist Thomas Chandler Haliburton.

The helicopter veers sharply to the left, and after crossing open water for more than an hour, you are looking down on Cape Breton. Are you surprised to see such deep valleys and hills that look almost mountainous? Along the coast of the mainland you see signs of new farms and villages on the rivers. Suddenly it is hovering over the deep harbour of Halifax.

The star-shaped fortress indicates that Halifax is a military garrison; so do the British navy vessels, for which Halifax is one of the important bases of the Empire. Presumably the British officers are influential in the economic and social life of the town.

Merchant vessels crowd the harbour too; overseas trade is important. No doubt the large homes in Halifax belong to businessmen who export fish and import rum from the West Indies or manufactures from England. Perhaps their neighbours include owners of shipyards, where the swift clipper-type ships are built. Clearly this is the capital and the dominant settlement in the colony.

The variety of buildings is striking. Right below us is the place where the government of the colony meets. Could that building over there be Dalhousie University? The Anglicans seem to have the greatest number of churches—not surprising in a centre where the British presence has been growing for a century. Perhaps you notice that print shop, where a certain Joseph Howe publishes the *Novascotian*.

Following the coastline, the chopper passes over the smooth white rock of Peggy's Cove, the attractive German settlement of Lunenberg, and around the "French coast" on the south of the colony. On the Bay of Fundy side, you swing up the Annapolis Valley, over the village of Truro, and sharply west to Amherst, near the border of New Brunswick.

On a circle tour, Nova Scotia appears to be much like an island. The larger settlements are close to the sea, which exercises a profound influence on the lives of most Nova Scotians.

[[If you had the time to have the helicopter land from place to place, you would, of course, learn much more. e.g. that prominent Nova Scotians, Tories and Reformers alike, revere the British connection; ambitious citizens aspire to a career in the British navy, a London business, or even the political life of the mother country; that the "old" families, especially the descendants of Loyalists, dominate the colony, even though they have been outnumbered by the thousands of Irish, Scottish and other immigrants; and that formal education is highly valued in the colony. A public school system had evolved by the 1860s. The churches continued to provide schools, though, and operated most of the colleges, such as St. Francis Xavier in Antigonish (Catholic), Acadia in Wolfville (Baptist), and King's College in Windsor (Anglican).]]

THE IMPORTANCE OF FISHING TO NOVA SCOTIA

Nova Scotia had been aptly named, for the land was as rugged as the people. There were fertile lowlands, but much of the province was quite unfit for cultivation. Although agriculture still stood at the head of its industries, it was under the necessity of importing grain from the United States. Second in extent but first in significance stood the fisheries. Here its maritime position gave to Nova Scotia a decided advantage over all competitors, with the possible exception of Newfoundland. Its long coastline with its innumerable bays and inlets gave it an exclusive control of almost limitless inshore fisheries. Its position on the Bay of Fundy, on the Gulf of St. Lawrence, and on the Atlantic facing the Grand Banks, gave it

TOP: *Halifax, from Dartmouth*; BOTTOM: *the Citadel, Halifax*

equally extensive facilities for deep-sea fishing. Unlike most of the fishermen of Newfoundland, these cautious Nova Scotian fishermen were farmers in their spare time, gaining economic stability. In no other part of British North America, if we except Newfoundland, did fishing occupy so large a place in the economic life of the people. Not by chance did a codfish appear on the coat of arms of Nova Scotia.[5]

THE INN AT ST. PETER'S (1856)

The driver of the stage-coach lays down the ribbons, after a sixty-mile drive, to say: 'This is St. Peter's.'

Now so far as the old-fashioned inns of New Scotland are concerned, I must say they make me ashamed of our own. Soap, sand, and water, do not cost so much as carpets, curtains, and fly-blown mirrors; but still, to the jaded traveller, they have a more attractive aspect. We sit before a snow-white table without a cloth, in the inn-parlour, kitchen, laundry, and dining-room all in one, just over against the end of the lake; and enjoy a rasher of bacon and eggs with as much gusto as if we were in the midst of a palace. . . . [7]

DESCRIPTION OF A NOVA SCOTIAN SETTLER (1859)

There, too we may see the pride of the colonies, the brave and hardy settler, who has laboured night and day at digging, draining, fencing, and manuring, at felling trees and clearing away stones, who has conquered the wilderness and succeeded in turning the desert into a garden, and has enriched his country while he has made himself independent. He is lord of the soil, pays no rent to landlord, has a comfortable and tasteful wooden cottage, with a pretty garden around it, keeps his own little vehicle, and has probably been over at the markets at Halifax, where he has business once or twice a week, and where he has a snug balance at his banker's. . . . a true Anglo-Saxon in speech, features and character. He looks a little rough at first, but this is only the effect of the out-door, somewhat rugged life he has led; and on conversing with him, you will find him . . . quite wide-awake, well informed, and intelligent, perhaps a little puritanical in his ideas.[8]

PRINCE EDWARD ISLAND

"I'm Bud the Spud
From the bright red mud
From good ol' Prince Edward Island"[9]

The refrain from a song written and performed by country singer Stompin' Tom Connors pays tribute to a product that has long been a staple of Prince Edward Island's prosperous agricultural industry. The "Garden of the Gulf" is still known for its lush green fields and its pastoral landscape, but tourism *now ranks well ahead of potatoes in the province's economy. Prince Edward Island enjoys its heritage as the birthplace of Confederation* and the home of "Anne of Green Gables," but it still faces the problem of retaining its distinctive lifestyle in an age when new sources of income are needed to maintain a living standard comparable to that of other provinces.*

*The first Confederation Conference was held in Charlottetown, Prince Edward Island in September, 1864.

From Amherst, the helicopter drifts due north and across the choppy Northumberland Strait. Soon an island of brilliant green growth and astonishingly red soil comes into view. Agriculture must be the main industry; most of the island is rural, even though the impression you get is that different groups have settled in the various regions of the colony. Are all those crops below really potatoes? Near the middle, on the south, is a concentration of people—this must be the capital of Charlottetown.

[[You cannot tell, from your airborne point of view, that Prince Edward Island has many problems. First of all, the island is quite cut off from the mainland, by turbulent water in summer and treacherous ice in winter. The population is divided among Loyalists, early settlers from the United States, Acadian French, and recent Scotch and Irish immigrants.

More serious, much of the land is owned by "absentee land owners," since large tracts of land had been granted to political favourites in England as early as the 1760s. Therefore, many of the farmers who are working the land are really "squatters", liable to be forced off, with nothing to show for their efforts. Even by the time of Confederation, the land question was an issue.

Charlottetown, 1843

303

Nevertheless, whether they hold the title to their land or not, the farmers of Prince Edward Island are blessed with fertile soil. Though many of the Islanders leave to seek their fortunes in the lumber camps of New Brunswick or Maine, the farms of the colony produce potatoes and cereal grains for export.]]

EDUCATION ON PEI

The following excerpt is from a lecture delivered in the Mechanics' Institute at Charlottetown by John A. Stark, Esq., Inspector of Schools, 1855.

An educational machinery has been set in motion, admirable in many of its external provisions. There are upwards of 260 schools, in which from eleven to twelve thousand children are in attendance. An excellent series of school books has also been provided, but one thing is yet lacking. The great increase in the number of schools, the large proportion of the revenue voted for education will never improve and elevate the education of the people, unless the standard of qualification for the teacher be raised, and a provision made for his special training, in the art of communicating. But I would indulge the hope that, ere long, there will not only be a Normal School established, but that every school will be provided with a play-ground, or *uncovered school room*, for the children, and a house and garden for the teacher. When this is accomplished, Prince Edward Island will be a model and example to the North American Colonies.[10]

THE HAZARDS OF MAIL DELIVERY IN PEI (1855)

In the winter, mail is carried by steamboat from Cape Traverse to Cape Tormentine. Often the voyage is extremely hazardous as this document suggests.

During the winter of 1854-5, the mail boat, in endeavoring to effect a passage, got into the midst of masses of floating ice, and could not work her way to either shore; a violent snow storm, accompanied with wind, arose, and she was driven for a distance of forty miles in the direction of Pictou. After four days' exposure to the storm and to piercing cold, the crew succeeded in landing at Wallace. The result of this melancholy occurrence was the death of one of the passengers from starvation, and consequent exhaustion; and several of the others were so seriously frozen that amputation of the legs of one, and part of the feet and toes of others, was rendered necessary.[10]

Well, come on to New Brunswick,
The unspoiled country, where eastern hospitality's the style,
When you get there you will find the picture province of Canada,
The gateway to the Maritimes that greets you with a smile.

The "picture province" is blessed with some of Canada's most scenic landscape, winding river valleys, beautiful parks and historic towns and landmarks. The first-class highway system provides easy access for the booming tourist trade which is a major part of the province's economy. The celebration of traditions dating back to pre-Loyalist times, along with the development of a modern economy, enables New Brunswick to combine some of the best of the past and the present. An Acadian, Louis Robichaud, was premier through the 1960s and the French language Université de Moncton was founded in that decade. Public education has been organized to equalize educational opportunity throughout the province. Fredericton, the capital, has become the home of some of Canada's most able poets.

The flight plan takes us back across Northumberland Strait over the Chignecto Peninsula into New Brunswick. The town of Sackville, noted for its ship-building, is now the home of the new Mount Allison University, founded by the Methodists (1859). Although the North Shore beckons, the journey follows the south shore, washed by the tides of the Bay of Fundy. Passing over Moncton and Sussex eventually brings us to the sprawling port of Saint John.

Saint John is the timber capital of the Maritimes. Ships in various states of completion are visible, but the most striking sight is the timber floating down the Saint John River, and the many sawmills. The clearings visible at various points in the interior are lumber camps, where many immigrants earn a living.

Inland on the bank of the Saint John River is Fredericton. Smaller than Saint John, Fredericton is home to the provincial Parliament buildings, where major decisions are made. Northward lies the border with Lower Canada (Quebec).

[[To get a more complete picture of New Brunswick, it would be necessary to fly back along the North Shore. During the Great Migration, many newcomers have settled on rivers like the Miramichi and the Restigouche. There the Acadian French share the arable land with these immigrants, most of them Irish or Scotch.

Much of New Brunswick is rugged, timber country. Life for the settlers is simple and harsh on the frontier, and rum provides relief after long hours of work. The churches work hard to bring religious comfort. A strong temperance movement, aimed at prohibiting the sale of liquor, has developed, as it has done across the border in the neighbouring state of Maine.

TOP: *Saint John, N.B.*; BOTTOM: *Fredericton, N.B. How do Fredericton and Saint John differ? Why?*

Like the other Atlantic colonies, New Brunswick had church-run schools and the beginnings of a public school system. The University of New Brunswick was founded in 1859.

Unlike the other Atlantic colonies, New Brunswick has a long border with the United States. There have been many quarrels about the border, even after it was officially settled in 1842. Better connections with Canada, including a railway, would seem to offer a feeling of security.]]

FARMING IN NEW BRUNSWICK

Alexander Munro writes in 1855 about the lack of scientific farming methods.

Farming in this Province is carried on, with some few honorable exceptions, in a most slovenly and unscientific manner; and when we contrast the number of persons who are comfortably sustained by this pursuit and the quantities of agricultural produce raised, with the system, or rather the absence of any system, applied to the raising it, we must be struck with astonishment at the capability of the soil and the geniality of the climate, which produce, with so little scientific labor such large quantities of food for the sustentation both of man and beast.[11]

1. What positive comment is made about New Brunswick land?

A CASE FOR NEW BRUNSWICK-MADE CLOTH

Alexander Munro writes in 1855 about the preference for any goods which are imported over homemade goods regardless of the quality.

A country which raises as fine sheep as any can be found on this continent, and in which no less than 168,038 were kept in 1851, while it could profitably maintain more than twice the number, ought certainly to make its own cloth. Hemp has been successfully raised in many parts of the Province; and no one can call in question the capabilities of our soil for the production of flax. Notwithstanding these advantages, and the abundance of water power and of coal, the manufacture of these raw materials is principally confined to the females of our country, who make what is here called 'homespun cloth,' prepared in a variety of ways, according to the purpose for which it is intended; and it is only due to them to say that for uniting the qualities of durability, appearance, warmth, and real utility it is hardly exceeded by the manufacture of any country. Still, it appears that we have such a predilection for the productions of other countries, however good our own may be, however capable our artizans may be of working up our raw materials, (and they are hardly inferior to any in quickness of apprehension and ingenuity) as to prefer exporting our own produce, and often reimporting it, manufactured into articles for our own domestic consumption.[12]

In 1852, the pressure of the temperance groups was felt in the Assembly, where Leonard Tilley was their spokesman. The man who would later lead New Brunswick into Confederation was behind a bill to prohibit the importing of liquor. The bill passed, but it stirred up such a reaction that an election a few months later returned an anti-temperance majority. "Prohibition" was promptly repealed.

1. What characteristic, sometimes attributed to the Canadian identity, is shown in Munro's comment about preference for anything which has been imported?

2. Do you think that Canadians today still prefer goods manufactured elsewhere? Can you give any examples?

EMIGRANTS TO NEW BRUNSWICK

There were certain rules which an emigrant had to obey.

All emigrants are, on their arrival in New Brunswick, detained at the quarantine station until they have been examined by the proper medical officer. The tax on each emigrant is 2s 1d. sterling... which the master of the ship has to pay; and in addition to which, if there are any lunatic, idiot, maimed, blind, aged or infirm person, not belonging to an emigrant family, a bond must be executed that such person shall not become chargeable to the Province for three years.... [13]

*For more information about the topic of immigration see pages 215-221.

1. Why might the colony of New Brunswick make rules governing immigration?*

THE PROVINCE OF CANADA

"Maître chez nous."

"A place to stand,
A place to grow,
Ontario."

Since Canada's centennial year in 1967, the province of Ontario has been publicized as "a place to grow," and growth of all kinds is associated in the minds of Canadians with this prosperous province. Quebec, too, has experienced dramatic growth in economic, industrial and cultural terms, where the French-Canadian majority increasingly live by the slogan, "Maître chez nous" (masters in our own house).

The Province of Canada, created by the union of Upper and Lower Canada in 1841, was the equivalent of the modern provinces of Quebec and Ontario. Today they contain more than 60% of Canada's total population and more commerce and industry than the rest of the country combined. Upwards of 80% live in urban areas, which include Ottawa, the national capital, and the metropolitan areas of Montreal and Toronto-Hamilton. Powerful mass media, such as the national television network, broadcasting out of central Canadian studios, focus much of the time on Ontario and Quebec. Here many of the great newsmaking issues of the nation such as biculturalism, urbanization and problems of the economy seem to have their roots, and many of the decisions that affect all Canada are made in these two provinces.

Across the border in the Province of Canada are thick, uninhabited forests. The lower St. Lawrence is so wide as to seem like an open

Percé, Lower Canada

Lower Town, Quebec

sea. For some 240 km along the north shore, the long, thin farms which originated in the days of the seigneurial system are laid out.

Suddenly you spot the Ile d'Orleans, and then the river narrows and the heights of Quebec are right below you. You know immediately why Champlain chose this site for his habitation and why the town of Quebec was so crucial to the defence of New France.

Quebec has not been a capital city since the union of Upper and Lower Canada, but the fortifications atop Cape Diamond leave no doubt of its continued military importance. The Bishop's palace and the Seminary of Quebec, also located in the Upper Town, are indicative of the power of the Roman Catholic Church in this part of Canada.

A second look reveals the Lower Town below the heights. Here is dockside Quebec, where timber ships depart for the long haul down the St. Lawrence and across the Atlantic—and where they return with their "cargoes" of immigrants. In every direction, new ships are under construction.

Upriver the farmhouses and villages form an almost unbroken line of settlement along the water's edge. One centre is Trois Rivières, a town of 3 000; to the south, out of sight, lies Sherbrooke,

What can you learn about Montreal from this picture?

the centre for British immigrants pushing back the frontier in the
Eastern Townships.

Two hundred and fifty km upstream is Montreal, a city of
40 000, the largest in Canada. This business metropolis is the most
inland port, and a vital centre of exchange. Here the crops exported
from the farms of Canada West are loaded for overseas markets.
Imports are landed for distribution to the expanding population of
the city and the many growing centres to the west.

The city is famous for its "mountain". It lies at the junction of
two important rivers, the St. Lawrence and the Ottawa, which flows
from Bytown (renamed Ottawa in 1855). In Bytown, rival lumbermen battle for control of the lucrative lumber trade. Also at Bytown
is the start of the Rideau Canal, built as a military water route to
Kingston.

The other route to Kingston is upriver along the Lachine Canal.
This is a town of only 6 000, but important in spite of its small size
because of the decision, in 1841, to name it as the capital of the Province of Canada. About 280 km further along the north of Lake Ontario is the growing town of Toronto. Some 15 000 inhabitants dwell
in "muddy Toronto," where you can see evidence of sharp contrasts.

Toronto, Canada West

Typical of the frontier towns of Canada West are the impressive commercial buildings and the dingy taverns, large estates and ramshackle slums.

Around the west end of Lake Ontario lies Hamilton, a town of 4 000, and even further, Niagara Falls. Providing a continuous waterway to Lake Erie is the famous Welland Canal, a short distance to the west. Northward in all directions is evidence of rich farming country. The towns below could be London or Galt or any of a number which originated during the Great Migration of the 1830s and 1840s.

[[The Province of Canada, with more population than all the rest of British North America, enjoys an economic "boom" at mid-century (early 1850s). New people, the new staples of timber and wheat, and the new technology based on steam attract investment and stimulate business.

Under a single government, the two major population groups— Protestant English-speaking and Catholic French-speaking—attempt to co-exist. Separate school systems are supported by government grants. New colleges service the rising English population—the University of Toronto (1848), Queen's University in Kingston, McGill University in Montreal. Newspapers are becoming important, both to the people at large and to their operators; for example, the *Christian Guardian* (Egerton Ryerson), *Le Canadien* (Etienne Parent) and the *Globe* (George Brown).]]

TOP: *Tweed, Ontario.* BOTTOM: *The Gore, Hamilton, 1862. What interests you most about this view of King Street?*

"It's a moody Manitoba morning,
And I like it that way."

It had been a backward spring. The roads were blocked, and the home-made thermometers were still registering nightly low temperatures of sixty-eight to seventy-five below zero. Suddenly the voice of Sarah, Sarah Binks, the Sweet Songstress, [of Saskatchewan] burst upon them with its message of hope and cheer. Spring was coming; the burbank would be back and the return of the snearth was imminent. No wonder Saskatchewan took her to its broad, flat bosom. Two weeks later a delayed chinook melted the Saskatchewan snows and Sarah awoke to find herself, if not exactly famous, at least something of a local celebrity."[13a]

The White Hatter Pledge:
"We, havin' pleasured ourselves considerable in
the only genuine cowtown in Canada, namely Calgary, . . .
solemnly promise to communicate this here Calgary
brand hospitality to all folks and critters who
cross our trail thereafter, Honest Injun."

The provinces of Manitoba, Saskatchewan, and Alberta are home to some six million people of diverse ethnic background. Although the economy is based mainly on agriculture, petroleum and light industry, only in Saskatchewan does the number living in rural areas compare with the number of urban dwellers. More than half the residents of Manitoba live in the capital city of Winnipeg, and the Alberta cities of Edmonton and Calgary are the fastest growing urban centres in Canada.

"Westerners" are known for the fierce pride about their region and for a certain feeling of "alienation" from the power centres in the East, meaning Ontario and Quebec. These provinces have often been regarded as taking advantage of the West through control of commerce and finance and through their domination of the policies of the Federal Government.

From the east side of Lake Huron, it is necessary to travel more than 1080 km "as the crow flies" to reach the nearest settlement to the West. Even the fur traders have abandoned their posts along the "Trans-Canada canoeway" since the merger of the Hudson's Bay Company and the North West Company in 1821.

Imagine flying along the shores of Georgian Bay, the miles of connecting waterways, and then the cliff-like north edge of Lake Superior. Throughout your journey, you see a landscape unmarked by the presence of man. On the left, endless bodies of water; on the

TOP: *The* Anson Northrup
BOTTOM: *Métis camp on the prairies*

Saskatchewan River near Fort Carleton

right, vast stretches of rock, lakes and pine of the pre-Cambrian shield.

Beyond the Lakehead, several hundred miles of wilderness stretch before the junction of the Red and Assiniboine Rivers is reached. There the twin spires of St. Boniface Cathedral come into view. Established as a mission in 1818, St. Boniface has become the centre of a French-speaking district where the majority of the population are Métis. North of the forks, in Kildonan, lie the farms of the Scotch settlers who first arrived with Selkirk half a century ago. The hub of the settlement is Upper Fort Garry, near which are a hotel and about a dozen wooden frame buildings. One of them is the location of *The Nor'Wester*, the first newspaper in the colony (1859).

On the Red River, a small steamboat makes its way south. Perhaps it is the Anson Northrup heading for St. Paul, since the Red River is now replacing the overland trail to the fast-growing American centre. A band of Métis on horseback are heading into the countryside, perhaps heading off to a buffalo hunt?

Further west along the Assiniboine, are occasional signs of habitation, possibly the remains of trading posts. On the plains a huge dust cloud appears, an indication of a herd of buffalo so numerous you cannot begin to count them. Indian horsemen cannot be far behind; to them the buffalo is the source of their survival.

The prairie passes below. Tall grasses wave; there are more rivers and patches of trees than one might expect. Perhaps one day, settlers from the east will believe they can make a living here. Suddenly the flatness ends, and the Rocky Mountains appear.

[[The vast Indian domain stretching from the Great Lakes to the

In 1862, the first store was built at the corner where two fur-trader's trails met—now the corner of Portage and Main. By the time Winnipeg was incorporated in 1874, this new location had become the business centre of the town. Upper Fort Garry was torn down in 1881 in order to extend Main Street; only the gate stands today as a reminder of the time when Red River was a "company town" of the Hudson's Bay Company.

Prairie landscape

The Red River settlement survived for some forty years in isolation after the fur trade rivalry ended in 1821. Free from the conflict that had plagued its early years, Red River endured drought, grasshopper plagues, and a flood in 1826 that engulfed the settlement. The buffalo hunt, fur trading and farming were the keys to existence. A curious venture into industry, the Buffalo Wool Company, failed to change the pattern.

Rockies is governed by the Hudson's Bay Company. Men like Sir George Simpson maintained the Company's hold well into the 1860s, although the "Sayer incident" was a sign that times are changing—at least in the south. In 1849, Sayer, a Métis trader, was found guilty at Red River of selling furs to American traders, in defiance of the Hudson's Bay Company's monopoly. The Company did not imprison him, however, recognizing that the advance of the frontier meant competition was unavoidable.

In the 1850s, in fact, the West once more began to enter the thinking of Easterners. Settlement was reaching the limits of the good farmland in Canada West, and there was growing interest in a new frontier beyond the Great Lakes and Canadian Shield. George Brown, soon to be one of the most influential "Fathers of Confederation", used his newspaper, the *Globe*, to promote settlement of the West.]]

A BUFFALO HUNT NEAR CALGARY, JULY 1858

We were now ... more than two miles' distance from the buffalo. ...they were in such numbers that their peculiar grunt sounded like the roar of distant rapids in a large river, and causing a vibration also something like a trembling in the ground.

We had scouted the animals pretty well, so that all that remained for us was to eat our breakfast and make for the point of attack.... Having ascended the slightly elevated ridge, we then beheld our game, four or five thousand buffalo, some lying down, some grazing with the old bulls in the outskirts. At our appearance the wolves, who almost invariably accompany bands of buffalo, sneaked about and around eagerly watching our movements.... Soon after seeing us the buffalo were in motion at a steady lope, crowding gradually into a thick black mass.... The run was magnificent.... We killed 17 cows, generally speaking in good condition, and were now not only provided with meat for our present wants, but also enough to dry and preserve for expeditions contemplated in the mountains.[14]

BRITISH COLUMBIA

The trees continue to grow, the fish return to the rivers, the earth is still rich in natural gas and minerals. The wealth is there (in B.C.)[15]

It is often said tongue-in-cheek, that, for British Columbians, Canada ends at the Rocky Mountains—meaning either that Canada is a place on the other side of the mountains or that British Columbia is Canada. Whatever the truth in such whimsy, Canada's Pacific province is physically separate from the rest of the country. Many of its cultural ties are with the western United States, and

Fort Yale. Why would people come to a location like this?

economically British Columbia has an important, and growing, involvement with the United States and with countries across the Pacific Ocean, especially Japan. Yet British Columbia's place in Confederation is deeply rooted in Canadian history.

Long before you reach the Rocky Mountains, the "sea of rock" looms before you. Where the clouds do not obscure them, the snow-topped peaks glisten in the sun. The approach seems endless over the remaining miles of prairie, and the foothills that eventually give way to the mountains themselves.

The vast rock barrier that divides the Pacific Coast from the rest of Canada can be penetrated by Kicking Horse Pass and other breaks. The whole region might be nothing but mountain peaks and deep valleys and wild rushing rivers.

Between mountain ranges is a broad valley, the valley of the Columbia that drains southward. Across another mountain chain, is yet another valley. Somewhere to the south off the flight route is the Okanagan. A westerly course traces the Thompson River to the plateau where the Thompson joins the Fraser.

Victoria, Vancouver Island

You have already noted steamboats on the Thompson, and as you turn down the Fraser River, cut deeply into the mountain rock, you see a trail on the left of the canyon. Along this route, the Cariboo Road, mule trains make their way north in search of gold.

The gold rush, having spread north from California, has brought thousands of fortune hunters to the Fraser Valley. Southward and west along the turbulent river are many small settlements. No doubt they have sprung up short years, or months, before. The steamboat heading north is probably carrying supplies to Yale, where merchants will make gold their own way from the miners.

The valley widens and the Fraser delta spreads below, not yet cleared of trees. There are farms and ranches now, the first signs of the rich agricultural development of the future. At the mouth lies New Westminster, an important port for the exchange of goods from ocean vessels to riverboats. Just to the north, a new town, Vancouver, will eventually boom when the Canadian Pacific Railway locates its terminal there.

Across the Strait of Georgia lies Vancouver Island, established as a British Crown Colony in 1849. Victoria, at the southern end, is a boom town of some 3 000—4 000 people. The Pacific headquarters of the Hudson's Bay Company are here, and so are the shipping companies, the saloons, and the stores—many of them American-owned—which cater to the sudden influx of population.

You have now come to the end of your journey which began some 9 000 km away at St. John's, Newfoundland. Such a journey could only be described as a rare treat—a century ago or today. What better way to feel the rich variety of Canada, truly one of the main strengths of the nation?

[[For a half century, the Pacific Coast had been the scene of rivalry for furs between the Hudson's Bay Company and companies from the United States and Russia. In 1825, Russia's agreement to restrict its activities to territory north of latitude 50° 40′ relieved pressure from that direction. From the south, however, the pressure continued to build.

In 1818 the United States and Great Britain had agreed to occupy jointly the territory north of the Columbia River. By 1846, growing numbers of Americans had followed the "Oregon Trail" to settle in the region, and the international boundary was set at the forty-ninth parallel.

The Hudson's Bay Company, which had represented the British presence on the Pacific for decades, was being forced back. As part of an attempt to resist further United States' advances, Britain established Vancouver Island as a Crown Colony in 1849.

Yet the gold rush of the 1850s attracted thousands of immigrants, especially from the United States, to Vancouver Island, and to the mainland. Consequently, British Columbia was created a colony in 1858, and joined with Vancouver Island in 1866. There was strong concern in Canada, however, that American encroachment could soon mean the loss of the territory, and thus of the western coast which was essential to building a nation from sea to sea.]]

HOTEL ACCOMMODATION, VICTORIA, 1860s

An Englishman describes his first night in Victoria:

I was not a little surprised, on asking in the conventional manner for a bed for the night, to be shown by the energetic proprietor (in his shirtsleeves, ready for any emergency) into a billiard saloon, upon the floor of which he kindly pointed out a space about three feet wide, where I might, in company with forty or fifty others provided with similar accomodation, spread my own blankets, and sleep upon them, for a trifling fee of fifty cents. . . .

. . . The only drawback I found . . . was that a pair of gentry, who came in rather late, requested permission of the . . . occupiers of the floor to play a game of billiards, as a bet of a hundred dollars depended upon it; promising, at the same time, to 'step clear and not disturb anybody.' This arrangement succeeded well enough for some time, till one of the players began to lose the game and his temper, and, heedless for the moment of the position of affairs, brought down the butt-end of his cue on what he fondly imagined was the floor. It happened, however, to be the stomach of a burly young Englishman, who, having the bad taste not to see the joke, jumped up and struck the man with the cue a considerable blow in the eye, knocking him down on the top of a few more of us, including myself. This caused a great row, in which everybody hit out at everybody else; the lights were put out. somebody [sic] fired a pistol, and amidst great confusion the two players somehow got hustled out into the street, there to settle anew, in some other place, their hundred-dollar bet.[16]

Development of a Canadian literature: pre-Confederation

BACKGROUND

From the time of the British Conquest until the 1860s, British North America was adjusting to the business of settling the new land. Apart from the times of strife such as the War of 1812 and the rebellions of 1837, much of a settler's life was spent clearing the land and making a home for his family. As the years passed, these jobs became more routine, and a pattern was established. Communities and villages were beginning to emerge. Because people now felt more "at home" in their new land, they had more leisure time than they did a century ago. More immigrants arrived in the 19th century, and more people took up the business of writing. Some of the most famous descriptions of clearing the land were written by novelists of this period, and it was in 1836 that Canada saw its first satire, the famous *The Clockmaker; or The Sayings and Doings of Samuel Slick, of Slickville*. Literature was coming alive in British North America.

Literary Time Line

1806   Establishment of *Le Canadien*, one of the most influential newspapers in Quebec.

1806   Henry Alline, *Life and Journal*

1807   George Heriot, *Travels through the Canadas*

1810   Stephen Miles publishes the *Kingston Gazette*

1812   John Richardson, *War of 1812* (a ballad)

1825   Oliver Goldsmith, *The Rising Village*

1828   John Richardson, *Tecumseh*

1832   Tiger Dunlop, *Statistical Sketches of Upper Canada*

1836   Catherine Parr Traill, *The Backwoods of Canada*
        Thomas Chandler Haliburton, first series of *The Clockmaker; or The Sayings and Doings of Samuel Slick, of Slickville*

1837   A. Gerin-Lajoie, "Un Canadien Errant"

1846   George Warburton, *Hochelaga*

1848   Anna Jameson, *Winter Studies and Summer Rambles*

1852   Susanna Moodie, *Roughing It in the Bush*

1853   Toronto *Globe* becomes a daily newspaper

1858   D'Arcy McGee, *Canadian Ballads*

1863   P. A. de Gaspé, *Les Anciens Canadiens*

Highlights

OLIVER GOLDSMITH

This first native-born Canadian poet was born and raised in the Maritimes. Oliver Goldsmith was a grand-nephew of the famous Anglo-Irish poet (also named Oliver Goldsmith) who wrote "The Deserted Village" in 1825. "The Rising Village" is a poem in three parts: the first talks of the growth of Nova Scotia and the third of the prosperity it enjoys, but the second (of which this excerpt is a part) tells the story of Flora and Albert, a couple who are about to be married when this tragedy occurs.

"The day was fixed, the bridal dress was made,
And time alone their happiness delayed,
The anxious moment that, in joy begun,
Would join their fond and faithful hearts in one.
'Twas now at evening's hour, about the time
When in Acadia's cold and northern clime
The setting sun, with pale and cheerless glow,
Extends his beams o'er trackless fields of snow,
That Flora felt her throbbing heart oppressed
By thoughts, till then, a stranger to her breast.
Albert had promised that his bosom's pride
That very morning should become his bride;
Yet morn had come and passed; and not one vow
Of his had e'er been broken until now.
But, hark! a hurried step advances near,
'Tis Albert's breaks upon her listening ear;
Albert's, ah, no! a ruder footstep bore,
With eager haste, a letter to the door;
Flora received it, and could scarce conceal
Her rapture, as she kissed her lover's seal.
Yet, anxious tears were gathered in her eye,
As on the note it rested wistfully;
Her trembling hands unclosed the folded page,
That soon she hoped would every fear assuage,
And while intently o'er the lines she ran,
In broken half breathed tones she thus began:
   'Dear Flora, I have left my native plain,
And fate forbids that we shall meet again:
'Twere vain to tell, nor can I now impart
The sudden motive to this change of heart.
The vows so oft repeated to thine ear
As tales of cruel falsehood must appear.
Forgive the hand that deals this treacherous blow.
Forget the heart that can afflict this woe;
Farewell! and think no more of Albert's name,
His weakness pity, now involved in shame.'

Ah! who can paint her features as, amazed,
In breathless agony, she stood and gazed!
Oh, Albert, cruel Albert! she exclaimed,
Albert was all her faltering accents named.
A deadly feeling seized upon her frame,
Her pulse throbb'd quick, her colour went and came;
A darting pain shot through her frenzied head,
And from that fatal hour her reason fled!

Flora, with one slight mantle round her waved,
Forsook her home, and all the tempest braved.
Her lover's falsehood wrung her gentle breast,
His broken vows her tortured mind possessed;
Heedless of danger, on she bent her way
Through drifts of snow, where Albert's dwelling lay. . . . "[17]

To find out what happens to Flora as she sets
out for her lover, Albert's, house, try
reading "The Rising Village."

CATHERINE PARR TRAILL

Catherine Parr Traill, born in London, England, migrated to Upper Canada where her elder sister (Susanna Moodie) and her brother (Samuel Strickland) had settled. Catherine Parr Traill and her husband had a difficult life in Canada. They lost their farm several times through court action over a debt incurred by helping a friend, and they were forced to live with their son after their newly-reconstructed home was destroyed by fire.

Throughout these ordeals, Catherine managed to write several children's books and books about settling the new colony. Her most famous, *The Backwoods of Canada* (1836) was an account of her life in the woods with practical advice on building a home, importing groceries, attending "bees" and so forth.

After her husband died, Catherine returned to Britain and received enough money from the British Colonial government for her service in the colony, to live until her death in 1899.

In this excerpt from her book *The Backwoods of Canada*, Catherine Parr Traill relates a conversation between a well-to-do lady settler and a neighbour. The lady, appalled that her neighbour would allow his son to "degrade himself" by doing manual labour such as chopping wood, asks the man what Canada is good for.

"It is a good country for the honest, industrious artisan. It is a fine country for the poor labourer who, after a few years of hard toil, can sit down in his own log-house and look abroad on his own land and see his children well settled in life as independent freeholders. It is a grand country for the rich speculator who can afford to lay out a large sum in purchasing land in eligible situations; for if he have any judgment he will make a hundred per cent as interest for his money after waiting a few years. But it is a hard country for the poor gentleman whose habits have rendered him unfitted to his situation; and even if necessity compels him to exertion, his labour is of little value. He has a hard struggle to live. The certain expenses of wages and living are great and he is obliged to endure many privations if he would keep within compass and be free of debt. If he have a large family and brings them up wisely so as to adapt themselves early to a settler's life, why he does well for them and soon feels the benefit on his own land; but if he is idle himself, his wife extravagant and discontented, and the children taught to despise labour, why, madam, they will soon be brought down to ruin. In short, the country is a good country for those to whom it is adapted: but if people will not conform to the doctrine of necessity and expediency, they have no business in it. It is plain Canada is not adapted to every class of people."[18]

SUSANNA MOODIE

The sister of Catherine Parr Traill, Susanna Moodie and her husband emigrated to Canada one week before the Traills. Susanna's literary career, like that of her sister, was begun in Britain and continued in the new land. She wrote in order to give some financial help to her husband who became lame after an accident in 1837. Her novel, *Roughing It in the Bush* (1852), which was serialized in the magazine, *The Literary Garland*, was similar to Catherine's *The Backwoods of Canada* except that it was much more personal, subjective and light than was Catherine's attempt at describing life in Canada. Susanna also wrote *Life in the Clearings Versus the Bush* (1853) which was a kind of handbook on Canadian manners, dress, and customs, intended for the British reader.

> *Mrs. Moodie gives her comment on Canadian families:* "The harmony that reigns among the members of a Canadian family is truly delightful. They are not a quarrelsome people in their own homes. No contradicting or disputing, or hateful rivalry, is to be seen between Canadian brothers and sisters. They cling together through good and ill report, like the bundle of sticks in the fable; and I have seldom found a real Canadian ashamed of owning a poor relation. This to me is a beautiful feature in the Canadian character. Perhaps the perfect equality on which children stand in a family, the superior claim of eldership, so much upheld at home, never being enforced, is one great cause of this domestic union of kindred hearts."

> *On beauty and Canadian women:* "The rosy face of the British emigrant is regarded as no beauty here. The Canadian women, like their neighbours the Americans, have small regular features, but are mostly pale, or their faces are only slightly suffused with a faint

blush. During the season of youth this delicate tinting is very beauti-ful, but a few years deprive them of it, and leave a sickly, sallow pallor in its place. The loss of their teeth, too, is a great drawback to their personal charms, but these can be so well supplied by the den-tist that it is not so much felt; the thing is so universal that it is hardly thought detrimental to an otherwise pretty face."

On drinking: "Alas, this frightful vice of drinking prevails throughout the colony to an alarming extent. Professional gentlemen are not ashamed of being seen issuing from the bar-room of a tavern early in the morning, or of being caught reeling home from the same sink of iniquity late at night. No sense of shame seems to deter them from the pursuit of their darling sin. I have heard that some of these regular topers place brandy beside their beds that, should they awake during the night, they may have within their reach the fiery potion for which they are bartering body and soul. Some of these persons, after having been warned of their danger by repeated fits of *delirium tremens*, have joined the tee-totallers; but their abstinence only lasted until the re-establishment of their health enabled them to return to their old haunts, and become more hardened in their vile habits than before."

On education: "A few years ago schools were so far apart, and the tuition of children so expensive, that none but the very better class could scrape money enough together to send their children to be instructed. Under the present system, every idle ragged child in the streets, by washing his face and hands, and presenting himself to the free school of his ward, can receive the same benefit as the rest.

"What an inestimable blessing is this, and how greatly will this education of her population tend to increase the wealth and prosper-ity of the province!"[19]

THOMAS CHANDLER HALIBURTON

A humorist whose popularity rivalled that of Charles Dickens, T. C. Haliburton was the first native-born Canadian to achieve interna-tional recognition in both Britain and the United States. Born in Nova Scotia in 1796, Haliburton studied law, was appointed to the Halifax House of Assembly and later to the Supreme Court of Nova Scotia as a Judge.

In 1826 Haliburton joined Joseph Howe's "Club" where mem-bers wrote witty satires on politics, literature and society. *The Clock-maker; or, The Sayings and Doings of Samuel Slick, of Slickville,* was first serialized in Joseph Howe's newspaper, *The Novascotian* and won Haliburton fame. The character of Sam Slick was created to be a mouthpiece for Haliburton's social criticism and economic recom-mendations. Sam Slick quickly won international fame, and the book eventually had 70 editions as well as translations into other languages.

Haliburton wrote other works, but *The Clockmaker* remains his most famous.

In this passage, the Clockmaker talks about politics in Nova Scotia.

> "Politics makes a man as crooked as a pack does a peddler; not that they are so awful heavy neither, but *it teaches a man to stoop in the long run.* Arfter all, there's not that difference in 'em . . . for if one of them is clear of one vice, why, as like as not, he has another fault just as bad. An honest farmer, like one of these Cumberland [a Nova Scotia county bordering on New Brunswick] folks, when he goes to choose atwixt two that offers for votes, is jist like the flying-fish. That 'ere little critter is not content to stay to home in the water, and mind its business, but he must try his hand at flyin', and he is no great dab at flyin', neither. Well, the moment he's out of water, and takes to flyin', the sea fowl are arter him, and let him have it; and if he has the good luck to escape them, and dive into the sea, the dolphin, as like as not, has a dig at him, that knocks more wind out of him than he got while aping the birds, a plaguy sight. I guess the Bluenoses [nickname for people of Nova Scotia] know jist about as much about politics as this foolish fish knows about flying. *All critters in nature are better in their own element.*
>
> "It beats cock-fightin', I tell you, to hear the Bluenoses, when they get together, talk politics. They have got three or four evil spirits, like the Irish Banshees, that they say cause all the mischief in the Province: The Council, the Banks, the House of Assembly, and the Lawyers."[20]

The people: a social view

Although each of the colonies of British North America on the eve of Confederation was unique and had many distinct features, the daily lives of the people had much in common. Regardless of location and class, colonists in that pioneer time shared many day-to-day concerns of work and play. Whether it was for establishing a homestead or settling in one of the growing towns, the Canadian of a century or so ago had available to him a technology which was very limited by the standard of the 1970s: not only did he have much less choice of goods and services, but he also often found it necessary to make do with homemade articles, from soap to whiskey. If he were a newcomer, he probably lacked many of the advantages that were taken for granted in the "old country," including cultural and recreational activities. There were only certain ways in which he could provide schooling for his children, practise his religion, and enjoy his usually rare amounts of leisure time.

The documents which follow are grouped according to religion, education, arts and letters, recreation and daily living. The selection of documents is intended to give you a few impressions of what it was like to be a colonist in the 1850s and 1860s in British North America.

RELIGION

RELIGION AND BUSINESS

What connection might there be between religion and successful businessmen?

[The case of Toronto demonstrated] that there is a close connexion between the Protestant ideals of individualism, energy, and plain living and the process of capitalist accumulation. Protestantism both gives a religious sanction to vigorous business enterprise and at the same time fosters a simple, moral way of life. Strengthened against the temptation to dissipate his energies and his resources in the pleasures of this world the Protestant businessman devotes more of both to the extension of his business.... A canvass of church records demonstrates that the men who were establishing Toronto's economic supremacy were at the same time building its churches.... [21]

RELIGION IN UPPER CANADA

The social side of religion was also important.

Church services were early held in courthouses or other government building, in taverns, stores or private homes, until it was possible to erect a church building by the subscription and labour of the members.

In most denominations the service was most informal, though a sense of decorum was apparent in the custom of men and women sitting in separate sections of the room. Sometimes the men removed their coats in warm weather, and people frequently walked in and out during the course of the service; while often the week's mail was distributed at the church door at the close. There were Sunday schools for the children in connection with most churches, and in some cases they had a few books to be distributed among those whose education was sufficient to enable them to read. In fact the social life of the pioneer community centred in the church and the school, the clergyman and the teacher being not infrequently the same person. [22]

THE ITINERANT PREACHER

There were many hardships endured by the preachers who travelled the country.

Imagine ... the experiences of Rev. Nathan Bangs, in the early days of the nineteenth century, on those lonely journeys throughout the

peninsula of Niagara, with its settlements scattered from Lake Erie to Lake Ontario. To complete one round and preach daily to the isolated groups of people meant a tour of six weeks, during which he many a time simply tied his horse to a tree and slept where he could. When transferred to the region of the Bay of Quinte, his zeal was tireless, as he rode, visited and preached through the summer and on into the autumn, when with many others he was seized with typhus, which had become epidemic. Seven weeks of wasting disease used up his strength and so affected his voice that preaching was impossible for months, and his speech was marred for the rest of his life. And his remuneration in money was twenty dollars a quarter![23]

THE CAMP MEETING

Susanna Moodie, one of Canada's first authors, writes of the fervour of the religious camp meeting.

Towards the middle of his discourse, the speaker wrought himself up into such a religious fury that it became infectious, and cries and groans resounded on all sides; and the prayers poured out by repentant sinners for mercy and pardon were heart-rending. The speaker at length became speechless from exhaustion, and stopping suddenly in the midst of his too eloquent harangue, he tied a red cotton handkerchief round his head, and hastily descended the steps, and disappeared in the tent provided for the accommodation of the ministers. His place was instantly supplied by a tall, dark, melancholy looking man, who, improving upon his reverend brother's suggestions, drew such an awful picture of the torments endured by the damned, that several women fainted, while others were shrieking in violent hysterics.[24]

1. How does religion seem to be connected to both business enterprise and social intercourse in British North America? How might the personal characteristics of Reverend Nathan Bangs help him become a successful businessman?

2. What reasons might the colonists have for wanting to maintain their religions in the new land?

3. How were religion and education connected?

4. Were there hardships of living which might make the people turn more avidly toward religion? If so, what might some of them be?

5. To what extent might the "success" of a camp meeting be dependent upon the personalities of the ministers? Can you see any parallels between a camp meeting and (a) a rock concert; (b) a Stanley Cup hockey game; (c) a political rally?

EDUCATION

INFORMAL SCHOOLING IN NEWFOUNDLAND (1830s)

Not all education was carried on in organized classrooms of schools. Here are examples of other kinds of education:

. . . throughout the settlements educational work of a less organized nature was carried on by clergy and lay men and women [people not of the clergy]. Most of it was voluntary. An educated woman would undertake to give daily lessons in reading and writing to children of her neighbors. In another place a man or a woman would teach in the evening or in a Sunday school. In Fortune Harbor, a northern settlement, the Roman Catholic bishop in 1834 found the people exceptionally well instructed in their religion and virtuous in their ways, thanks to the fathers of three families, who took turns in assembling the whole populace at their respective houses on Sundays and holy days for a religious lecture and devotions.

Another interesting and not uncommon practice is illustrated by the story of the master of a fishing boat who had among his crew an Englishman of some education who was growing old for the work. The master, who had had no schooling when he came out from England in his youth, and who had been compelled to work hard to support a large family, said to his elderly employee: 'John, thee canst read. It seems a sad unchristian way for my boys to grow up without learning. Do thee stop ashore and teach the children and I'll pay thee the wages as thof [sic] thee went in the boat.' Not only was the bargain made, but arrangements were made also to include the children of a neighbor's family.[25]

SCHOOLS IN ONTARIO, 1849

A local Superintendent of schools describes what the average pupil endured:

The School Houses in many instances ... are miserable Shanties, made of Logs, loosely and roughly put together. . . . Under your feet are loose boards, without nails, across which, when one walks, a clatter is produced equal to that heard in a lumber yard. Over your head are the naked rafters, stained with smoke and hung with cobwebs and dust. Two or three little windows, generally half way up the walls, admit the light; and a rough door, which does not fit the opening, creaks upon its wooden hinges. . . . Desks are generally long, sloping shelves, pinned up against the walls, as high as the breasts of the Pupils who sit before them. The Seats are without backs and from eighteen inches to two feet high. . . . We have no Black Boards, no Maps, and no illustrative Apparatus of any kind. . . .

When we enter one of these Schools we behold a picture of discomfort and misery. The children are perched upon the benches before described; but as they have no support for their backs, and as only the taller of them can reach the floor with their feet, marks of weariness and pain are visible in their features and postures. . . . all avail themselves of every possible excuse to change their position and so obtain relief. Some asking permission to go out, others to get a drink, and many constantly flocking to the Teacher's desk with words to be pronounced, Sums to be examined and corrected, Pens to be mended, or difficulties to be explained in connection with Grammar lessons, etcetera. So that the place is filled with noise and disorder, rendering study impossible, and anything like the cultivation of cheerful and benevolent affections entirely out of the question.[26]

TORONTO ELEMENTARY SCHOOLS, 1859

As nearly all the children who attend the City Schools come from the industrial classes, the system of instruction pursued in the schools has been based upon practical considerations of utility, so as to impart to the pupils such a sound and useful English education as shall fit him or her to enter upon the daily pursuits of industrial or domestic life. . . .

According to the 'General Regulations for Common Schools,' as prescribed by the Council of Public Instruction, every alternate

Saturday is declared to be a holiday, and for some time this regulation was carried out in the City Schools; but it was not found to work well—the Saturday *going to School* was too often forgotten by the pupils—the alternate attendance soon became almost nominal —and, in consequence, the Schools are now not open at all on Saturdays. As regards other holidays, it has been customary to give a week at Easter—a month in summer, usually in August—and a fortnight at Christmas.[27]

Public Schools, City of Toronto.—Time Table, Male Department, Third Division—Hours of Study, from Nine A.M. to Noon; and from One to Four P.M.—Occupation of time.

From	To	Monday	Tuesday	Wednesday	Thursday	Friday
9.00	10.00	Reading, Scriptures with Sacred Geography	Reading-Derivations, 5th Book Dictation, 4th Book	Reading-Dictation, 5th Book; Science (Natural), 4th Book	Reading-History, 5th Book; Political Economy 4th Book	Repetition and Elocution
10.00	10.50	Writing-Small Hand	Writing-Large Hand	Drawing	Writing and Book-keeping	Writing of Figures; Revision of Euclid
10.50	11.00	Forenoon Recess				
11.00	12.00	Arithmetic-Examine Simple Rules	Arithmetic-Compound Rules	Arithmetic Proportion	Arithmetic-Fractions, &c	Arithmetic-Repetition
12.00	1.00	Noon Intermission				
1.00	2.00	Grammar-Letter-writing (Composition)	Analysis of Sentences-Comp. of Sim. Nominatives	Grammar-Composition; Des. of Objects; Abstracts	Analysis of Sentences-Written Parsing or Comp.	Repetition of Grammar and Analysis; Composition
2.00	2.50	Geography of America—Map Drawing	History	Geography (General)—Map Drawing	History	Repetition; Geography Object Lesson
2.50	3.00	Afternoon Recess				
3.00	3.55	Arithmetic, Algebra, Euclid	Arithmetic, Algebra, Mental Arithmetic	Arithmetic, Euclid, Science (Natural)	Arithmetic, Algebra, Mental Arithmetic	Singing and Recitation of Poetry, &c.

N.B. The School to be opened and closed with Scripture Reading and Prayer. Books from the Library will be given out each Friday afternoon.[27]

SOME FACTS ABOUT SCHOOLING IN PRE-CONFEDERATION CANADA

Because of the tremendous variation from colony to colony, general statements about schooling are difficult to make. However, the following points give impressions:

There were no compulsory attendance laws.

The school year was approximately six months long, assuming the teacher did not quit.

Memorization and recitation were the main activities through which children were expected to learn.

Most children spent the equivalent of approximately two years in school, and did not advance past elementary school.

The idea of public school education for *all* children was very new.

The well-to-do sent their sons, and occasionally their daughters, to private academies.

1. Financing public education was complicated by religious conflict. A big issue, one that would lead to more and more bitterness, was the meaning of the word "public" in public school education. "Public" did mean tax-supported schools. Would church-run schools, such as those of the Roman Catholic Church, qualify for government grants?[28]

1. What kind of inequalities in education might have existed in British North America at this time?

2. Why should education be important to the sons and daughters of the colonists?

3. Should public schooling for young girls have been encouraged during this time? If so, what kinds of skills or learning should have been stressed?

4. What problems might there be if education and religion were closely linked together? What advantages might there be?

5. What was the purpose of schooling in British North America? What do you think the purpose of education in British North America should have been? Should education have been controlled by the colonists, the colonial governments or the government of Great Britain?

6. What educational problems exist today which did not exist in the 1850s and 1860s? What problems existed then but do not exist now?

ARTS & LETTERS

The following documents are excerpts from some of the first books written by colonists in British North America:

from WINTER STUDIES AND SUMMER RAMBLES IN CANADA

Dec. 20, 1836

"What Toronto may be in summer, I cannot tell; they say it is a pretty place. At present its appearance to me, a stranger, is most strangely mean and melancholy. A little ill-built town on low land, at the bottom of a frozen bay, with one very ugly church, without tower or steeple; some government offices, built of staring red brick, in the most tasteless, vulgar style imaginable; three feet of

Settlers' log cabin, Tartique River, P.Q., c. 1865

snow all around; and the gray, sullen, wintery lake, and the dark gloom of the pine forest bounding the prospect; such seems Toronto to me now. I did not expect much; but for this I was not prepared. Perhaps no preparation could have *prepared* me, or softened my present feelings. . . . If I look into my own heart, I find that it is regret for what I have left and lost—the absent, not the present—which throws over all around me a chill, colder than that of the wintry day—a gloom, deeper than that of the wintry night."[29]

from ROUGHING IT IN THE BUSH

"After removing to the bush, many misfortunes befell us, which deprived us of our income, and reduced us to great poverty. . . .

While my husband was absent on the frontier during the rebellion, my youngest boy fell very sick, and required by utmost care both by night and day. To attend to him properly, a candle burning during the night was necessary. The last candle was burnt out; I had no money to buy another, and no fat from which I could make one. I hated borrowing, but, for the dear child's sake I overcame my scruples, and succeeded in procuring a candle from a good neighbour, but with strict injunctions (for it was *her last*) that I must return it if I did not require it during the night.

I went home grateful with my prize.[30]

from THE CLOCKMAKER, OR THE SAYINGS AND DOINGS OF SAMUEL SLICK OF SLICKVILLE

Any man that understands horses has a pretty considerable fair knowledge of women; for they are jist alike in temper, and require the very identical same treatment. Encourage the timid ones, be gentle and steady with the fractious, but lather the sulky ones like blazes."

"The only persons who duly appreciate it [Nova Scotia] are the Yankees."

"Give up politics. It's a barren field."

"An intemperate advocate is more dangerous than an open foe,"[31]

from THE CANADIAN SETTLER'S GUIDE

"It is a matter of surprize to many persons to see the great amount of energy of mind and personal exertion that women will make under the most adverse circumstances in this country. I have marked with astonishment and admiration acts of female heroism, for such it may be termed in women whose former habits of life had exempted them from any kind of laborious work, urged by some unforeseen exigency, perform tasks from which many men would have shrunk. Sometimes aroused by the indolence and inactivity of their husbands or sons, they have resolutely set their own shoulders to the wheel, and borne the burden with unshrinking perseverence unaided; forming a bright example to all around them, and showing what can be done when the mind is capable of overcoming the weakness of the body."[32]

The preceding documents are examples of some of the earliest colonial literature. These men and women were writing about life as they saw it more than 100 years ago.

Such first-hand materials may be referred to as "primary documents". Do they differ in content, style or tone from other documents in this chapter?

Are any of their comments "modern," that is, do they hold truths about life and/or people today?

The next two documents give a general impression of the arts and their development in British North America.

LITERATURE IN NOVA SCOTIA (1855)

Alexander Munro comments on the literature of the colony, and gives a warning about the novels.

This Province is in advance of many and much older countries in the character and ability of its literary productions. Every year adds new and more varied works to its stocks, and the facilities of obtaining books from other countries are continually increasing. One thing, however, should be guarded against, both in this and the adjacent Colonies, as injurious, more especially to the rising generation; we allude to the circulation of novels and other light trash of literature, which is now becoming so common. The principal part of these works impart no useful knowledge, but on the contrary, do much to corrupt the morals and retard the intellectual advancement of the people.[33]

1. What might be an argument in support of the colonists reading "novels"?

MECHANICS' INSTITUTES

"Prominent among associations which aimed at mutual improvement was the Mechanics' Institute. Joseph Bates, who had had experience in such societies in London, England, appears to have established the first in Upper Canada at York in 1831.... Many men of importance gave their time to provide an opportunity for improvement among 'the middle classes, working men and intelligent mechanics', who, in a day of social exclusiveness, had little chance to develop intellectually and culturally.... Mechanics' Institutes became very numerous in Upper Canada in the fifties and sixties, even small villages frequently having organisations. It was found in many localities that the societies languished from the lack of support of those whom they were formed to benefit; but upon the whole they were for half a century a very valuable contribution towards the provision of a broader life for tradesmen and labourers."[34]

1. Why might it be important for tradesmen and labourers to acquire a "broader life" or to become familiar with the arts?

RECREATION

AGRICULTURAL FALL FAIRS

Rural fall fairs today had early beginnings.

Agricultural fall fairs were held very early in Canada, and from the 1840's there is mention of ladies from the local church having a display table and selling 'pretty toys.' Possibly the first charity bazaar was that given under the leadership and patronage of Lady Colborne, wife of the Lieutenant-Governnor of Upper Canada in 1830. She introduced this old British custom to York to raise money to clothe the poor. Her friends and assistant used the substantial proceeds to purchase quantities of red flannel to make undergarments for the less fortunate. It was obvious that the ladies tried to make as much money as they could and that they felt they could pressure men acquaintances to purchase. So much

A barn raising.

so that etiquette books felt compelled to add this reminder: 'If you have a table at a fair, use no unladylike means to obtain buyers. Never appear so beggarly as to retain the change, if a larger amount is presented than the price, offer the change promptly, when the gentleman will be at liberty to donate it if he thinks best, and you may accept with thanks. He is under no obligation to make such a donation.'[35]

LOGGING BEES

Logging bees were extremely important and brought all the men from miles around. They brought not only their wives to help with the food and to gossip, but also their oxen and all the heavy chain they owned. In a well-organized bee the men were divided into teams which raced against each other to speed up the work. Generally four men and a yoke of oxen made a gang, and while the race was on the "Grog Boss" would go from team to team with his jug giving out the whisky allowance. When the day's work was over the cut logs would be set on fire and the young people would gather to roast corn, tell ghost stories, and dance.[36]

INNS AND TAVERNS

Whisky was early considered an antidote to the hardships and misfortunes of pioneer life, and a means temporarily to forget care and trouble....

The number of inns and taverns that existed in Upper Canada in former times would surprise the present generation. Every cross-road had one or more, and the main highways supported many dozens of them. The small city of Toronto had in 1850 a total of 152 taverns and 206 beer shops to supply a population of about 30,000 and such farmers as brought their produce thither to market. Distilleries were among the first establishments in most settlements, and provided large quantities of cheap liquor, usually

The Inn at Cramachi, Bay of Quinte

obtainable at 25¢ a gallon, or even less; and almost all taverns were maintained largely by the sale of strong drink.[37]

ETIQUETTE OF THE INN

The 'bar' of the tavern was the great attraction to many, and its great blazing fire, on which a cartload of wood glowed with exhilarating heat, to others. Every one on entering, after desperate stamping and scraping, to get the snow from the feet, and careful brushing of the legs with a broom, to leave as little as possible for melting, made straight to it, holding up each foot by turns to get it dried, as far as might be. There was no pretence at showing deference to any one; a laborer had no hesitation in taking the only vacant seat, though his employer were left standing. 'Treating' and being 'treated' went on with great spirit at the bar, mutual strangers asking each other to drink as readily as if they had been old friends. Wine-glasses were not to be seen, but, instead, tumblers were set out, and 'a glass was left to mean what any one chose to pour into them' [sic].[38]

SPORTS IN BRITISH NORTH AMERICA

...characteristic of Canada were the sports of winter. Snow-shoe and dog-sled had long been necessary for winter travel over Indian trail and along frozen lake and river, and they were supplemented in the days of settlement by sledge and carriole. Travel by carriole was just as pleasurable in winter as the canoe was in summer, and it was a time when travelling was but seldom pleasant. The settler's sleigh was usually home-made and its body ran very close to the

Sleigh Scene, Toronto Bay

Steeplechase, London, Canada West, 1843

ice; while that of the 'gentlemen' in the towns had runners, and was often a very elaborate affair. The carriole had no covering, so travellers were well bundled up in furs. Sleighing-parties have remained a characteristic Canadian winter pleasure. . . .

Skating, which originated in Holland, was also a favourite amusement, though it was frequently considered improper for girls to participate in such a form of pleasurable exercise.[39]

THE ART OF CURLING

Curling began in Canada at Quebec in the last years of the eighteenth century, though the first organised club was instituted in Montreal in 1807. Among the earliest curlers were Scotch officers of the garrisons, who relieved the monotony of military life by engaging in the game. . . .

French-Canadians did not know what to think of these activities of the Scotchmen upon the ice. One of them, a farmer near Quebec who had just seen the game for the first time, related

excitedly to his neighbour: 'Today I saw a band of Scotchmen, who were throwing large balls of iron like tea-kettles on the ice, after which they cried "Soop! soop!", and then laughed like fools. I really believe they ARE fools.'[40]

1. As a person your age and sex in British North America in the 1850s and 1860s, how might you have spent your leisure time?

2. "Bees" were examples of early forms of social cooperation. Are there modern parallels to the "bee", or is such cooperation a thing of the past?

3. About which of the following do you think you could argue effectively?

Be it resolved that:

> Whiskey was an effective and necessary antidote to the hardships and misfortunes of pioneer life.
>
>   OR
>
> Whiskey was surely the demon drink, and no one should have become dependent upon it to mask his troubles.

4. How might a foreigner today describe the game of hockey if he saw it for the first time?

5. Why do you suppose the colonists eagerly sought to develop various kinds of recreation?

DAILY LIVING

A MISCELLANY OF HOUSEHOLD HINTS FOR THE PIONEER WOMAN

Cheap as stockings are it is a good economy to knit them. Cotton and woollen yarn are both cheap; hose that are knit wear twice as long as woven ones; and can be done at odd moments of time not to be otherwise employed. Where there are children, or aged people, it is sufficient to recommend knitting as an employment. It is a foolish waste of time to tear cloth into bits for the sake of arranging it anew in fantastic figures; but a large family may be kept out of idleness, and a few shillings saved, by thus using scraps of gowns, curtains etc.

If you would avoid waste in your family, attend to the following rules, and do not despise them because they appear to unimportant: 'many a little makes a mickle.' Look frequently to the pails, to see that nothing is thrown to the pigs which should have been in the grease-pot. Look to the grease-pot, and see nothing is there which might have served to nourish your own family, or a poorer one.

Count sheets, towels, spoons etc. occasionally; that those who use them may not become careless.

Pioneer lighting equipment

Attend to all the mending in the house, once a week, if possible. Never put out sewing.

Buy your wollen yarn in quantities from someone you can trust.

There's no need of asking the character of a domestic, if you have ever seen her wash dishes in a little greasy water.[41]

NEWSPAPERS AS INSULATORS

A newspaper, folded several times and laid across the chest during a cold walk or ride, is a most excellent protector. If the bed-clothing is not sufficiently warm, especially at hotels, two or three large newspapers spread on the bed between the blanket will secure a comfortable night, as far as cold is concerned.[42]

SOAP-MAKING

Soap is made from a union of the lie of wood ashes, and any sort of grease, the refuse of the kitchen; even bones are boiled down in strong lie, and reduced. The lime of the bones are, by many soap-makers, thought to improve the quality of the soap. The careful Canadian housewives procure a large portion of their soap-grease from the inside, and entrails of the hogs, and other beasts that are killed on the farm. Nothing in this country is allowed to go to waste, that can be turned to any good account.[43]

TOILET FACILITIES

Reminiscing of his boyhood in the settlements of western Ontario, George Stanley says:

Most of them were content to put up with the very rudest accommodation and conveniences; one room, containing several beds, often holding not only the whole household, but any passing stranger. How to get in and out, unseen, was the greatest difficulty. I have often been in trouble about it myself, but it must surely have been worse for the young women of the family. As to any basin or ewer in the room, they were Capuan luxuries in the wild bush. 'I'll thank you for a basin, Mrs. Smith', said I, one morning, anxious to make myself comfortable for the day, after having enjoyed her husband's hospitality overnight. It was gloriously bright outside, though the sun had not yet shown himself over the trees. 'Come, this way, Mr. Stanley; I'll give it to you here,' said Mrs. Smith. Out she went, and lifted a small round tin pie-dish, that would hardly hold a quart, poured some water into it from the pail at the door, which held the breakfast water as well, and set it on the top of a stump close at hand, with the injunction to 'make haste, for there was a hole in the bottom, and if I didn't be quick the water would all be gone'. Luckily I was all ready; but there was no offer of soap, and so I had to make my hands fly hither and thither at a great rate, and finish as best I could by a hard rubbing with a canvas towel.[44]

DANCING

Of all the amusements of early times dancing was the most universal and appears to have given the greatest pleasure to the greatest number.... The music supplied at dances was not, however, the all-important matter in pioneer days: where a fiddler or a bag-piper was not obtainable the young people whistled, sang, or made music with a comb. In much of the dancing in the rural districts more exercise than grace was apparent. Waltzing was not generally popular, the square dance being most in vogue.[45]

RULES TO BE OBSERVED AT FASHIONABLE DANCING PARTIES OR SOCIABLES IN LARGE CITIES

When dancing a round dance, a gentleman should never hold a lady's hand behind him, or on his hip, or high in the air, moving her arm as though it were a pump handle, as seen in some of our western cities, but should hold it gracefully by his side.

Unless a man has a very graceful figure, and can use it with great elegance, it is better for him to walk through the quadrilles, or invent some gliding movement for the occasion.

If a lady waltzes with you, beware not to press her waist; you must only lightly touch it with the open palm of your hand, lest you leave a disagreeable impression not only on her *ceinture*, but on her mind.

The master of the house should see that all the ladies dance. He should take notice particularly of those who seem to serve as 'drapery' to the walls of the ball-room (or 'wall flowers', as the familiar expression is) and should see that they are invited to dance.[46]

CLOTHING

No lady should wear her dress so low as to make it quite noticeable or a special subject of remark....

The fashion of wearing low-necked dresses on certain occasions thus leaving the neck and the upper part of the chest bare, is fraught with evil consequences. It would be less objectionable in countries uniformly warm; but that our daughters here in frigid and changeable climate, should expose to the chilling winds a vital part of the body, is one of the evils of fashion which should be discountenanced by every mother, and father, and brother. Of the unseemliness and reckless immodesty often connected with this exposure, it is not necessary to speak in this discussion.[47]

1. What are some of the moral judgements made in "A Miscellany of Household Hints for the Pioneer Woman"?
2. What could Canadians in the 1970s learn about the use of resources from the example of soap-making by pioneer women?
3. How many of the Rules of Etiquette listed here are still "proper" with some modification?
4. Are there "unwritten laws" for women and men in Canadian society today as there were in the early days of the colonies? What are some of them? Which society might more strongly censure someone who dissented from what was "proper"? In which society might someone be more inclined to conform, especially socially? Why?

No. 144
FINAL
EDITION
****

The Washington Beacon

Shedding light on the nation's events

10¢
WITH
COMICS 15¢

TUESDAY, JUNE 1, 1970

DEVELOPMENT SET FOR NORTHERN STATES

Washington, D.C. (A.P.C.)—A roads to resources plan for developing the northern states was announced in Washington today. Secretary of State for Northern Affairs, Hiram Fludd, told reporters, "The time has come to raise the living standard of fellow Americans in the Canadian region. And let me emphasize that the results of this plan will benefit everyone in the United States of North America."

The most ambitious scheme involving the Federal Government since World War II will involve five of the nation's largest corporations in developing

—a nuclear power complex in Atlanticanada;

—large-scale farming in Centricanada's southern peninsula, to supply fresh produce to the densely populated area south of the Great Lakes;

—the petroleum industry of Wescanada, with pipelines running to the southern part of the nation;

—the technology for routing fresh water from the Canadian Rockies into waterways of the western states;

—an extension of the interstate highway system into the Canadian frontier.

Further details about the roads to resources plan will be released during the next few weeks, Fludd, said.

A spokesman for the state government in Centricanada was the first to praise the plan. "It will create thousands of jobs for unskilled Canadians who now receive welfare," declared an aide to the governor. "The personnel coming into our part of the country will pump millions of dollars into our economy."

Governments in the other Canadian states are expected to make statements later this week.

The United States of North America

CENTRICANADA REP NAMED TO HIGH POST

In a White House bulletin today, Mackenzie Marceau, Canadian-American congressman, was named commissioner for northern affairs. Mr. Marceau will have important responsibilities in the economic development plan to be implemented in the north.

Reached for comment at his home in Montreal, Mr. Marceau said he was pleased that a Canadian-American was being given the chance to serve the republic. It was proof, he said, that the annexation of Canada by the United States meant opportunities for Canadians which did not exist in "the old days."

Mr. Marceau indicated that he would be taking up permanent residence in the Washington area soon. "I can best perform my duties from the national capital," he explained.

"My family is looking forward to the move. Several of our friends have relocated in southern cities in order to give their families the opportunity to (continued on page 4).

(continued on page 4).

EDMONTON-TO-ATLANTA OR BUST

"Meeting people and sightseeing are two of my biggest thrills," says marathon cyclist Roberta Riley. Bicycling from Edmonton to Atlanta, Miss Riley is on her way to fame and fortune. If she makes it to Atlanta by the week's end, she will be the first woman to make the journey in less than 50 days. Chambers of Commerce in Edmonton and Atlanta are holding $2000 each for Roberta Riley if she can break the female marathon cycling record.

Among the problems Miss Riley has encountered have been a snow storm, tempera-

tures well above 30°C, tornadoes, a near collison with a Greyhound bus, and countless repairs to her bicycle. Her most vivid recollections are of people.

Although Miss Riley has cycled long distances in the northern states, this is her first trip through the south. She finds that Americans are as friendly in one region as in another. "An American is an American." she is fond of saying.

COME BACK LITTLE BEAVER

A contest is raging in six states today over who gets the beaver. This furry little creature has been the cause of arguments in three Canadian states as well as New York, Illinois and Oregon—each state wants the extinct beaver for its official state animal. Canadian state officials are appealing to history since beaver furs were once an important part of their economy. New Yorkers think the industrious beaver a

suitable symbol for their state and feel they have enough clout to win the nation-wide referendum some say will arise over the beaver.

NOSTALGIA FESTIVAL WINNER FROM DEUX RIVIERES

An old French Canadian ballad and a wistful style was the right combination for Danielle Verlaine at the annual Auldport nostalgia festival. The singer, dressed in native costume, took away the $10 000 first prize, singing of life in the days when French-speaking people lived along the St. Franklin River. Runner-up was Melvin Flit, playing a guitar-like instrument known in remote areas of the Midwest in the 1870s.

Miss Verlaine's song told of a French Canadian village on the St. Franklin, then known as the St. Lawrence River. A young hockey player had returned to (continued on page 6)

(continued on page 6)

12

Confederation

This page of an imaginary "Washington Beacon" may seem incredible to you now, but suppose Confederation had never happened. If the Dominion of Canada had not been created in 1867, as the first stage of a nation "from sea to sea", is it likely that the colonies of British North America would have been absorbed, sooner or later, by the United States? If the United States of North America had been the result, would not the stories and features in the "Washington Beacon" be plausible?

In the 1860s, the colonies of British North America were at a crossroads. A number of serious problems were coming to a head: fear of aggression by the United States, the threat of economic slowdown, a crisis in government in the Province of Canada.

At the same time, circumstances favoured some form of bold action. In a sharp reversal of policy, the British Government let it be known that it was favourable to some form of Canadian union. A sense of purpose appeared to be developing among British North Americans. Colonial leaders were looking for a scheme that would secure the future of a British North American nation.

Several choices appeared to be available. The Maritime colonies, for example, thought that a union of the colonies of their region would be a step forward. The Province of Canada, on the other hand, was looking for some form of wider union, including all British North America.

They called it Canada, eventually

The name, *Canada*, was not used to mean the country from coast to coast until after 1867, when the existence of the Dominion of Canada was proclaimed. From 1760, the time of the Conquest, until Confederation, the British colonies were referred to collectively as *British North America*.

This term included Newfoundland, Nova Scotia, New Brunswick, Prince Edward Island and the united *Province of Canada* (having two sections: Canada West, before 1840 known as Upper Canada, after Confederation as Ontario; Canada East, formerly Lower Canada, later Quebec). On the west coast, beyond the Hudson Bay Company's territory of Rupertsland, was British Columbia (known separately as British Columbia and Vancouver Island until united in 1866). In 1871 when British Columbia joined, Canada extended from sea to sea.

A. The United States: threat or example?

HISTORICAL BACKGROUND

The following portions of a speech by an eloquent member of the Canadian Assembly, D'Arcy McGee, may be overly dramatic. Yet they refer to facts about American expansion, which had encompassed vast amounts of territory in a few years.

Did American pressure force the creation of a transcontinental Canadian union?

Was fear of losing the West the main American "threat"?

Was the United States more influential as an *example* than as a *threat*?

THE THREAT FROM THE UNITED STATES

D'Arcy McGee's speech about the danger from the United States. CONFEDERATION DEBATES, *February 9, 1865:*

... These are frightful figures [referring to the numbers of soldiers and guns possessed by the United States] for the capacity of destruction they represent, for the heaps of carnage that they represent, for the quantity of human blood spilt that they represent, for the lust of conquest that they represent, for the evil passions that they represent, and for the arrest of the onward progress of civilization that they represent. ...

... They [the United States] coveted Florida, and seized it; they coveted Louisiana, and purchased it; they coveted Texas and stole it; and then they picked a quarrel with Mexico, which ended by their getting California ... had we not the strong arm of England over us, we would not now have had a separate existence. ... [1]

1. The United States expanded south and west to include Florida (1783), Louisiana (1803), Texas (1845), and California (1850). Did Canadian leaders seem to have reason to fear U.S. expansion to the north?

Relations between the United States and British North America had been improving. Anti-American traditions, originating with the Loyalists, were still alive, but a grudging admiration for American economic progress was gaining strength. Suddenly, in 1861, the American Civil War exploded. In Great Britain, sympathy for the South, the Confederate states, was very strong, since a divided United States would be less of a rival. From a business viewpoint, Southern cotton for the British textile industry was an important factor.

Canadians viewing the struggle in the United States were fearful. Residents of the northern states were angry with Britain, and this fact, it was felt, was ominous for Canada, far more so than for Britain.

The Trent Affair, the St. Alban's raid, and other incidents served to show Canadians that they were in danger of being caught in the middle. While the Civil War lasted, Americans, specifically in the Northern States, were preoccupied with the struggle at home. But with the end of the war in April, 1865, Canadians feared the intentions of the American leaders. Canada's political leaders spoke publicly of danger, because it was Canada, after all, that had reason to fear American expansion northward.

In fact, most Americans were primarily concerned with the job of rebuilding a country devastated by four years of war. Yet statements in American newspapers, and even in Congress, were enough to suggest the possibility that Canada could be invaded by a battle-hardened army.

More realistically, the Fenian raids in June, 1866 might have provoked an international incident. The Fenians, whose ranks included Civil War veterans, were Irish-Americans intent at striking a blow against "British tyranny" by conquering Canada. The raids along the Niagara River and the New Brunswick border, which the United States government did little to stop, could hardly be considered an invasion. Yet the fact that marauders, lacking both numbers and organization, could terrorize border communities was an indication of how vulnerable the British North American provinces were. Union could mean both a stronger and more efficient militia for home defence and a stronger voice in dealing with Washington.

Fear of losing the West to the United States by default was perhaps the most realistic reason for concern about American influ-

"Manifest destiny," a phrase introduced to Americans in the presidential election campaign of 1846, had caught the imagination of the country. According to this idea, the United States was intended, by God, to expand across North America—both in east-west and south-north directions. Could Canadians expect to escape this pattern?

The *Trent* affair in 1861 dramatized the predicament of British North American defence as the colonies became caught in the strife between the United States and Great Britain. Two southern (Confederate) agents were forcibly removed from the British steamer *Trent* in the Gulf of Mexico and taken captive aboard a ship of the Northern (Union) navy. Britain was furious over the interference with its shipping. Demands in the Northern States for annexation of British North America prompted the British to dispatch nearly 14 000 troops to Saint John, New Brunswick. With the St. Lawrence frozen and no railway connection to Canada, the troops had to make a difficult and time-consuming overland march; had an invasion occurred, the Province of Canada might have fallen before help arrived.

The Fenian Raid. What do the letters IRA stand for on the flag?

ence. The isolated prairie region, stretching for hundreds of miles between the Canadian Shield and the Rockies, was still held by the Hudson's Bay Company. Yet the Company's monopoly was no longer a guarantee of either law and order or of resistance to American advance. Settlers at Red River found the rule of a commercial company unsuited to the needs of a growing community, and began to demand changes, possibly union with Canada. But Red River was developing a dependence on the American centres of Minneapolis and St. Paul for supplies, trade and transportation. By the 1860s the possibility of annexation by the United States was very real.

Especially difficult was the problem of preserving the two British crown colonies on the Pacific Coast—British Columbia and Vancouver Island. The gold rush of the 1850s in the Fraser River valley had brought temporary prosperity to the area. Governor James Douglas of Vancouver Island extended his authority to the Fraser, where he maintained law and order and supervised such vital public works as the Cariboo Road. His policy was confirmed by the British decision to make British Columbia a crown colony in 1858. However, the cost of building roads and providing other essential services meant that the colonial governments accumulated considerable debts. These were still unpaid when the boom subsided and most of the gold-seekers departed.

The British government simplified administration and reduced its expense by joining the two colonies as British Columbia, with Victoria as the capital, in 1866. But the danger of the United States expanding northward through settlement, as it had done in Oregon Territory, was ever present.

American pressure was one side of the coin; American example was the other. Canadians were envious of the standard of living which seemed constantly on the rise in the republic to the south. Moreover, while Canadian leaders may have voiced fears about possible aggression from south of the border, they admitted a grudging admiration for the American political system. It was said that the United States had tried nobly to create that most difficult of political arrangements, a federal union. Though they had made serious mistakes, they had shown the way to those wise enough to adopt the successful features of the American system and avoid the faulty ones. In particular, the United States had made the tragic error of allocating too much power to the states and too little to the central government. The result was that the southern states had felt they could successfully challenge a government which claimed to act on behalf of all the states. Canadians had the opportunity to design a union which could prevent an outcome such as the Civil War.

The St. Alban's raid, carried out against the small town in Vermont, aroused Union anger in the fall of 1864. In October, while the Fathers of Confederation were meeting at Quebec for the second of the Confederation Conferences, a band of Confederate soldiers attacked and robbed the town of St. Alban's, Vermont. Fleeing to Canadian soil, they were arrested and tried in Montreal; but the magistrate set them free. Charging that Canada could not police its own borders, the Union government threatened such action as terminating the Rush-Bagot Treaty of 1817 and placing gunboats on the Great Lakes and Lake Champlain.

MILITARY DEFENCE AS A REASON FOR CONFEDERATION
George Brown, in the CONFEDERATION DEBATES, February 8, 1865:

... But not only do our changed relations towards the Mother Country call on us to assume the new duty of military defence— our changed relations towards the neighboring Republic compel us to do so. For myself, I have no belief that the Americans have the slightest thought of attacking us.... But ... there is no better mode of warding off war when it is threatened, than to be prepared for it if it comes. The Americans are now a warlike people. They have large armies, a powerful navy, an unlimited supply of warlike munitions, and the carnage of war has to them been stript of its horrors. The American side of our lines already bristles with works of defence, and unless we are willing to live at the mercy of our neighbors, we, too, must put our country in a state of efficient preparation. War or no war—the necessity of placing these provinces in a thorough state of defence can no longer be postponed.

... And how can we do this so efficiently and economically as by the union now proposed? ... [2]

1. Even if Canadian politicans doubted there was likely to be an American attack—as Brown admits—were they justified in exploiting the *possibility* in order to advance the cause of Confederation?

DOUBTS THAT CONFEDERATION WOULD HELP DEFENCE

Anti-Confederationist, A. A. Dorion, refuted the argument that Confederation would aid the defence of British North America:

It is said that this Confederation is necessary for the purpose of providing a better mode of defence for this country. There may be people who think that by adding two and two together you make five. I am not of that opinion. I cannot see how by adding the 700,000 or 800,000 people, the inhabitants of the Lower Provinces, to the 2,500,000 inhabitants of Canada, you can multiply them so as to make a much larger force to defend the country than you have at present. Of course the connection with the British Empire is the link of communication by which the whole force of the Empire can be brought together for defence (Hear, hear.) But the position of this country under the proposed scheme is very evident. You add to the frontier four or five hundred more miles than you now have, and an extent of country immeasurably greater in proportion than the additional population you have gained.[?]

1. Do you find Dorion's argument more or less convincing than the one stated by George Brown? Explain.

B. Economic conditions, economic hopes

TRADE

To what extent was the drive for Confederation the result of economic pressures?
What were the main economic groups, and which had the most influence?
Was Confederation a "Grand Trunk job"?

*See pages 286, 288.

The words "trade" and "railways" had powerful meanings in the 1860s. Trade, after all, was the basis of economic growth and an improved standard of living. Railways were vital to the movement of goods and people. The future looked gloomy, however. This was especially true for exports, which historically had been so important to Canadian producers, whether they dealt in furs, timber, wheat or other products. Some years before, Britain had decreased in value as a trading partner,* and now the United States seemed likely to go the same route.

How did the colonies come to find themselves in the position of having no trading partners outside British North America?

Traditionally, British North America had depended on selling exports like wheat and timber to British buyers for much of its income. Actually such exports could have been bought more cheaply from nearby foreign countries, in Western Europe, or from more industrially advanced countries, including the United States. However, the British government used laws and duties on foreign goods

The American Civil War: a lesson for British North Americans

The American Civil War (also called the War Between the States) is noteworthy to Canadians for a number of reasons. The War coincided with that period in Canadian history in which the provinces of British North America were trying to solve their own economic and social problems as separate colonies. One of the things that worried some British North Americans was the danger of an American invasion and secession of part of the British North American provinces to the United States. The American Civil War represented the breakdown of a Union, just as Canadians were moving toward the formation of one.

The Civil War has been the subject for much American literature, and it has given the American nation many of the myths and legends of its heritage. Among the known facts of the conflict are that it began at Fort Sumter, South Carolina in April, 1861, and ended four years later with the surrender at Appomattox Courthouse by General Robert E. Lee on April 9, 1865. During those four bloody years, Confederate (Southern) soldiers battled Union (Northern) soldiers for causes which they probably never fully understood. The differences in the way each geographical area had developed—the industrial North with its factories and towns vs. the agricultural South with its dependence upon the single crop of cotton and its ever-increasing need for pickers—were underlying reasons for the division between the North and the South.

Along with this division came different ways of living and different beliefs. One of the strongest of these differences was the South's belief in the institution of slavery. So the North's cry for the abolition of slavery became one of the catalysts for the secession of the Southern states from the Union. The founders of the **Confederacy** believed strongly in States' Rights—that a state government should have the right to ignore a federal law which was unpopular in the state. The election of President Abraham Lincoln and the newly formed Republican Party was a victory for those opposed to the expansion of slavery. Lincoln was seen in the South as a leader hostile to the interests of the South. Only by seceding from the Union, they believed, could they preserve the Consitution and the powers it granted to the States.

Canadians in the 1860s had much to observe from their American neighbours, and much to weigh in 1867 when it became our turn to unite a diverse people into one nation.

What lessons could Canadians learn from the United States' experiment with a federal union?

Also called the Confederate States of America, these were the eleven states (South Carolina, Georgia, Florida, Alabama, Mississippi, Louisiana, Texas, Virginia, Arkansas, Tennessee and North Carolina) which wished to secede from the Union.

Nova Scotia's first steam locomotive

The governor of the province
of Canada, Lord Elgin,
believed that public support
in the colony for annexation
had been exaggerated.
Nevertheless, he believed the
situation was serious. In his
view, the British Government
must act to give Canadians
hope for a brighter future. He
knew that Britain was not
going to restore
special markets in the mother
country for colonial products.
He also knew there was a
possible alternative—trade
with the United States.

to discriminate against others and give advantages to those within the Empire. Then, in the late 1840s, Britain adopted a policy of *free trade*, and the colonies lost their "protected" markets.

An economic depression followed. Colonial wheat and timber had to compete on an open market with products from other countries. Shrinking markets and declining prices made agriculture unprofitable, and many farmers abandoned their farms to start life anew in the American West. Newly-constructed flour mills fell idle, and the railway boom that started with the prosperity of the 1840s came to a halt. Canada's business leaders, most of whom were Tories politically and supporters of strong ties with Britain, felt abandoned by the mother country. Such men, in the decade before, had vilified their liberal opponents as republicans and traitors under "the American influence." Now, in 1849, Tory leaders joined in drawing up the Annexation Manifesto, urging union with the United States.

The American market looked inviting to Canadian businessmen. Yet the United States had a system of tariffs to protect its producers against foreign competitors. A way had to be found to get a special "deal" for British North America. The British, in the person of Lord Elgin, found a way—reciprocal trade, or reciprocity.

The United States was persuaded to allow natural products—the products of "farm, forest and fishery"—from British North America to enter the United States free of duties. In return, American fishermen gained extra privileges in British North American waters.

The year the Reciprocity Agreement was negotiated was a turning point in the financial fortunes of British North America. Consider the increase in trade with the United States shown by the following figures (figures for each year represent millions of dollars):[3]

1850—14.6	1857—46.2	1864—56.1
1851—17	1858—39.3	1865—62.0
1852—15.6	1859—47.3	1866—73.3
1853—18.9	1860—46.2	1867—46.0
1854—32.8	1861—44.4	1868—50.3
1855—42.8	1862—39.0	1869—52.6
1856—50.3	1863—45.1	1870—61.6

The Reciprocity Agreement (1854-1866) seemed like a dream come true for Canadian producers. Although it was really a very complicated treaty, the Reciprocity Agreement removed barriers to Canadain-American trade. Admitted duty-free for sale in the expanding American market were products like timber and lumber, fish, all kinds of farm products, and coal.

The boom in Canadian trade owed something to demands created by the Crimean War (1854-1856) and the American Civil War, but the Reciprocity Agreement was seen by many on both sides of the border as a significant benefit to British North America.

Though trade flourished, political relations did not. Unfriendly relations had developed between the United States and Britain during the Civil War, and troubles on the Canada—U.S. border made matters worse. American producers who wanted a return to protective tariffs played effectively on the situation, and, in 1865, the United States announced its intention to terminate the Reciprocity Treaty.

It seemed as though British North America was going to lose its second major market in twenty years and face another calamitous depression. Was there a logical alternative for the colonies?

A major goal in the lives of British North Americans, "old" residents and immigrants alike, was to get ahead financially. By and large they had the opportunity to do so, but periods of prosperity were short and offset by cyclical depressions. As time went on, economic progress seemed increasingly dependent upon the decisions of governments and businessmen in Britain and the United States. A transcontinental union of British North American colonies could mean economic growth and stability and thus more opportunities, individually and collectively, for financial independence.

RAILWAYS

Railways were needed, so the argument went, for the transportation of troops and supplies in the event of an American invasion. Yet the fundamental reason for railways was trade. As early as 1851, at the beginning of the next railway boom, there was talk of an intercolonial railway to link the Atlantic ports with commercial centres on the St. Lawrence River.

By the 1860s, the idea of a transcontinental railway was gaining support. Such a railway would provide a physical link with the isolated colonies at Red River and on the Pacific coast. Such a link was necessary to protect them from absorption by the United States, and to encourage settlement in the West. Ultimately, a transcontinental railway could be one of the "bonds of the British Empire," connecting the mother country with the trade of the Orient.

C. Changing British colonial policy

What was the attitude of British political leaders to Confederation by the mid-1860 s?
What interest did British investors have in Confederation?
What actions did the British Government take during the crucial stage of the movement to implement the Seventy-Two Resolutions?

Any important political development in British North America from the Conquest to Confederation, was largely influenced by the policies and actions of British governments. Think of the Quebec Act, the War of 1812 or the Rebellions and Responsible Government. None of these were entirely the result of circumstances in North America. Since the united Province of Canada, Newfoundland and the others were still *colonies* in the 1860s, Britain might be expected to have a hand in something as momentous as Confederation.

HISTORICAL BACKGROUND

Some Britons took great pride in having colonies all over the world, since they brought prestige, military advantage and, usually, financial gains. Other Britons regarded colonies as more of a burden than an advantage; if they were given independence, Britain could retain trade and other economic benefits and rid itself of the costs of defending and administering the colonies.

Two examples illustrate the British attitude toward British North America. One concerns railways, the other defence. In the 1850s there had been many discussions about building an inter-colonial railway between Canada and Nova Scotia. British businessmen, like Edward Watkin, an influential figure in the Hudson's Bay Company and the Grand Trunk Railway, were anxious to see an ambitious railway-building program, for it could sharply improve investment opportunities. However, railway projects were costly, and required either great risks on the part of private investors or backing by the British government.

Individually, the colonies could not inspire the necessary financial or political support. Negotiations to bring about cooperation among the colonies and between the colonies and Britain were complicated and frustrating. Confederation would provide a central colonial government. The British Government and businessmen would then have one government to deal with, instead of several.

The defence of British North America had become a much more serious matter by the 1860s. The strained relations between the United States and Britain during the American Civil War resulted in a heavy burden on the British treasury.

Confederation as a "Grand Trunk Job"

According to some critics of Confederation, there were many arguments put forward by pro-Confederation forces—but the *real* reason was the hope of saving the financially troubled Grand Trunk Railway.

The Grand Trunk Company had completed a rail connection between Sarnia and Rivière du Loup, west of Quebec City. Caught up in the optimism of the 1850s, the Company had underestimated costs and overestimated profits. The government of the Province of Canada, meanwhile had provided millions of dollars in loans to the Company.

If the Grand Trunk went bankrupt, British and Canadian businessmen would lose heavily. So would the Canadian government. A way had to be found to make the Grand Trunk Railway profitable.

In the *Confederation Debates* of February 16, 1865, A. A. Dorion spoke of one "project" involving E. W. Watkin, the British president of the Grand Trunk Company. In 1861, Watkin had tried to get government loans in order to finance an intercolonial railway. This railway would connect the Grand Trunk with Halifax, and hopefully, produce profits. When the intercolonial railway project fell through,

> ...some other scheme had to be concocted for bringing aid and relief to the unfortunate Grand Trunk—and the Confederation of all the British North American Provinces naturally suggested itself to the Grand Trunk officials as the surest means of bringing with it the construction of the Intercolonial Railway. Such was the origin of the Confederation scheme. The Grand Trunk people are at the bottom of it; and I find that at the last meeting of the Grand Trunk Railway Company, Mr. Watkin did in advance congratulate the shareholders and bondholders on the bright prospects opening before them, by the enhanced value to their shares and bonds, by the adoption of the Confederation scheme and the construction of the Intercolonial as part of the scheme. I repeat sir, that representation by population had very little to do with bringing about this measure [Confederation]. . . . [5]

Under pressure from British bankers and the promoters of the Grand Trunk, the British government indicated a willingness to guarantee a loan for the construction of an intercolonial railway between Canada and the Maritimes. A united Canada could turn such a possibility into a reality.

At the onset [of the Grand Trunk Railway], nine of its directors were members of the Canadian cabinet and later, six of the twelve directors had the dual roles of cabinet ministers and board members of the Grand Trunk. Also represented on the board were London bankers and the Bank of Montreal. By 1867, the Canadian government had 'loaned' the company $26 million, all of which was 'forgiven'.[4]

Many British leaders argued that troubles with the United States would diminish without British political and military involvement in a North American colony. If the colonies expected to enjoy responsible government and the right to establish their own tariffs, there was no reason why they should not assume an increasing proportion of the costs of their own defence.

By the 1860s, British policy was shifting away from the idea of controlling colonies to the idea of increasing their self-government, and the responsibilities that went with it. Confederation would improve the ability of British North America to undertake such responsibility.

HISTORIANS' NEGLECT OF BRITISH INFLUENCE

The paragraph below was taken from the book, British Attitudes Towards Canada, 1822-1849, *written in 1971. Although the author, Prof. Peter Burroughs, dealt with a limited time span in his book, his remarks in this paragraph clearly apply to the years leading up to Confederation:*

Because of an understandable preoccupation with indigenous North American forces and tendencies, Canadian historians writing about the century between the conquest and confederation have often paid insufficient attention to the character of British colonial policy and the nature of English opinion concerning overseas possessions. Yet every facet of Canadian economic and political development during these years, and many aspects of the country's social and religious history, were profoundly influenced by British attitudes and policies. The ideas and actions of politicians in distant Westminster and administrators in the recesses of Downing Street were significant for Canadians. This book is therefore written in the confident belief that Canadian history in the colonial period is not fully intelligible without some understanding of the wider imperial context, the changing nature of British policies, and the underlying opinions of Englishmen concerning the empire in North America.[6]

D. Canadian Identity

There was an opportunity for the "creation of a new Nationality," said the Governor-General, Lord Monck, in January, 1865. His remark was made in the Speech from the Throne opening the session of the Assembly of the Province of Canada. Lord Monck was helping to set the stage for the Coalition Government as it prepared to launch the Confederation Debates.

Was the Governor-General merely using grand phrases to add aura to the Confederation proposal, or was he genuinely anticipating a Canadian nation, with a way of life distinct from any other? By the same token, what did George Cartier mean when he said, in the Confederation Debates:

> The question for us to ask ourselves was this: Shall we be content to remain separate—shall we be content to maintain a mere provincial existence, when, by combining together, we could become a great nation?... Objection had been taken to the scheme now under consideration, because of the words 'new nationality.' Now, when we were united together,... we would form a political nationality with which neither the national origin, nor the religion of any individual would interfere. It was lamented by some that we had this diversity of races, and hopes were expressed that this distinctive feature would cease. The idea of unity of races was utopian—it was impossible. Distinctions of this kind would always exist. Dissimilarity, in fact, appeared to be the order of the physical world and of the moral world, as well as of the political world. But with regard to the objection based on this fact.... British and French Canadians alike could appreciate and understand their position relative to each other. They were placed like great families beside each other, and their contact produced a healthy spirit of emulation [rivalry]. It was a benefit rather than otherwise that we had a diversity of races.... [7]

The importance of a national literature is discussed in 1864 by E. H. Dewart, an editor, Methodist minister and poet:

> ... A National literature is an essential element in the formation of national character. It is not merely the record of a country's mental progress: it is the expression of its intellectual life, the bond of national unity, and the guide of national energy. It may be fairly questioned, whether the whole range of history presents the spectacle of a people firmly united politically, without the subtle but powerful cement of a patriotic literature....
>
> Our colonial position, whatever may be its political advantages, is not favourable to the growth of an indigenous literature. Not only are our mental wants supplied by the brains of the Mother Country, under circumstances that utterly preclude competition; but the majority of persons of taste and education in Canada are emigrants from the Old Country, whose tenderest affections cling around the land they have left. The memory of the associations of youth, and of the honored names that have won distinction in every department of human activity, throws a charm around everything that comes from their native land, to which the productions of our young and unromantic country can put forth no claim....
>
> ... If we cannot point to a past rich with historic names, we have the inspiring spectacle of a great country, in her youthful might, girding herself for a race for an honorable place among the nations of the world. [8]

George Brown

Historian P. B. Waite interprets the Canadians' feelings about national, or Canadian, identity:

> ... They wanted to be grown up, but they felt hurt at being pushed out of the house. They wanted the trappings of nationality, but they were ... only just able to put one foot before the other. 'Responsibility,' warned the *Times*, 'goes with power, and the [British American] colonies being now powerful, are also responsible.' British North Americans were purposive yet hesitant, surer of what they wanted than they were of themselves. They were still adolescent with high dreams and fancies; nationality was the most golden of them all. July 1, 1867 was the beginning of a long and difficult maturity.[9]

1. What are some of the ingredients that the documents suggest are necessary to the creation of a national identity?
2. Which were present in Canada at the time of Confederation? Which were missing?
3. How different is the situation in Canada now?

Political deadlock

By the spring of 1864, the Province of Canada, essentially present-day Ontario and Quebec, appeared to be ungovernable. The union, established in 1841, was plagued by such problems as:

> conflict between French-Canadians and English-Canadians;
> the lack of a clear-cut system of political parties;
> the lack of causes, or goals, which could raise the level of politics above local concerns.

John A. Macdonald

Confusion often arises over the use of the word "government." Used one way, it means the political *system*. Used another way, as a synonym for *ministry*, government means the party or group that is in charge of the system.

Political leaders such as John A. Macdonald, Georges Cartier and George Brown had tried to keep the government operating through a series of temporary alliances among political groups. However, after 15 **ministries** in 12 years, they seemed to have run out of combinations that could make decisions and get laws passed. Without a change in the system, there seemed to be no way out of the "political deadlock". The state of affairs was so hopeless that two old political enemies, John A. Macdonald and George Bown, agreed to work together to try to find a solution.

The alternatives

Politically, British North America was on the verge of change. There were a number of alternatives to choose from, each with advantages and disadvantages. As you read about each of the following, try to put yourself in the place of a "Father of Confederation" and (a)

You can't tell the players without a scorecard

In the 1840s, most politicians in the Province of Canada were either Tories or Reformers. On the eve of Confederation, the political situation was much more confusing. The following groups, however, could be identified:

Liberal-Conservatives: formed in 1854, this party drew its strength from the former Tories of Upper Canada, especially cities like Toronto and Kingston. John A. Macdonald was the dominant figure.

Bleus: the French-Canadian supporters, prominent in the business life of Canada East (Quebec). E. P. Taché and Hector Langevin were notable members.

Rouges: younger French-Canadians, mainly professionals from the Montreal area—although A. T. Galt was a prominent member for a time, as were some other English-Canadians. A. A. Dorion was the most influential.

Clear Grits: representatives of the English, mainly rural residents of Canada West. George Brown was the leader.

Independents ("loose fish"): in this category were many politicians, whose votes on any particular issue were unpredictable, who supported different groups at different times.

Was Confederation a scheme by central Canada to solve its problems of government?

Was Confederation the only possible form that a union of all Canada could take?

Did any alternative plan seem to have as many potential advantages as Confederation?

"brainstorm" the possible consequences of each scheme (b) separate, as best you can, the consequences into advantages and disadvantages (c) decide which of the alternatives you would choose, and for what reasons.

Before you start, you might decide which group from among the many in British North America you belong to; for example, a Nova Scotian, a French Canadian from Canada East, an English-speaking resident from Montreal, a person from Canada West (Ontario).

A. Regional adjustments

1. PROVINCE OF CANADA

(a) *Representation by Population ("Rep by Pop")*

Recommended by the Clear Grit Party of Canada West, "Rep by Pop" was intended to break the impasse in government by linking representation in the elected Assembly to the size of population. The

The story of the militia bill shows how serious "political deadlock" had become. Between 1861 and 1864, several different versions of a bill intended to provide some defence for the colony were introduced to the Assembly. Even though the American Civil War was raging and the Canadian fears of invasion were increasing, bill after bill was either defeated or "watered down". The British Government became convinced that Canadians would rather play at politics than face the most serious problem on their doorstep.

Act of Union (1841) provided for equal representation from Canada West (English-speaking) and Canada East (mainly French). However, the population of Canada West was growing much faster by the 1860s, and "Rep by Pop" would mean an increase in English-speaking representation.

1. What would be the drawbacks? Advantages? For whom?
2. Would "Rep by Pop" be fair to all groups affected?

(b) *Dual Federation*

One of the chief causes of political deadlock was the "stand-off" between Canada West and Canada East. Because the interests of each were often opposed, a law that benefited one would not interest the other. Since each half had the same number of representatives in the Assembly, the result was often a stalemate.

To allow each half of the Province of Canada some freedom to handle local problems, while keeping an overall government for matters of common concern, some politicians favoured two levels of government, as shown in the diagram.

1. What would be the advantages?
2. What would be the limitations?

2. MARITIME UNION

In the early 1860s a movement to unite the Atlantic colonies was encouraged by the British government and some local politicians. There was concern that individual colonies could not maintain prosperous growth or cope with problems in a changing world. However, by September, 1864, when the Charlottetown Conference was scheduled to discuss the issue, no particular plan for Maritime union had general support.

1. What would be the advantages?
2. What would be the disadvantages?

B. Confederation

The alternative to changing the political structure of parts of British North America was a union of the parts. What advantages might there be in the larger union, compared to the other alternatives, in relation to the following: (a) defence, (b) trade, (c) railways, (d) workable government? What drawbacks?

Union of all British North America was not a simple alternative since it could take different forms. Basically there were two possible types of union: legislative union and federal union.

None of these regional solutions had any reference to what is now western Canada, i.e. the vast area from Lake Superior to the Pacific Ocean. In the 1860s, most of this part of British North America was known as Rupertsland and belonged to the Hudson's Bay Company.

Leading figures in Confederation

John A. Macdonald: a Kingston lawyer, a veteran of twenty years in politics, Macdonald was the practical politician who steered the Confederation plan through its various difficult stages.

George Brown: publisher and editor of the Toronto *Globe*, Brown put Confederation ahead of his own political career. More a journalist and promoter than a politician, Brown made the Great Coalition possible by agreeing to work with Macdonald, his long-standing rival.

George Cartier: the French-Canadian lawyer and businessman who argued that Confederation was the way to preserve the French-Canadian way of life.

Alexander Galt: a prominent Montreal businessman and politician who promoted Confederation as the way out of Canada's economic difficulties. Galt worked out the financial arrangements involved in the plan.

D'Arcy McGee: the dreamer, a former Fenian, whose eloquence helped make the case for Confederation—and who died by assassination in the first months of Canada's existence.

Dr. Charles Tupper: the crafty and ambitious pharmacist, who carried Nova Scotia into Confederation against difficult odds.

Leonard Tilley: the skillful leader who turned defeat into victory in leading New Brunswick into Confederation.

THE LOSERS

Antoine Aimé Dorion: the prominent Rouge, Dorion fought unsuccessfully against Confederation as a plot to dominate French Canada.

George Dunkin: the determined crusader for the rights of the English-speaking minority in Canada East. He advanced some of the most critical—and lengthy—arguments against Confederation.

Joseph Howe: the chief Maritime anti-Confederate, Howe voiced the fears of Nova Scotians and fellow Maritimers that Confederation threatened their identity—and their property.

"Double Majority" had been discarded as an alternative. According to this practice, a bill could only become a law if it obtained a majority of votes in both the Canada West and Canada East "halves" of the Assembly. As a way of keeping harmony between French and English, double majority had been tried, but it was not satisfactory because it was slow and inefficient.

A legislative union is one in which two or more regions are joined under a unitary government, such as was the case with the united Province of Canada between 1840 and 1867. All sovereignty is originally vested in the top level of government; power to set policy, make decisions and pass laws may be delegated to lower levels, such as municipal governments, but the central government is supreme. This system is relatively simple, efficient and economical. It is also highly centralized and likely to be suitable for smaller, homogeneous countries.

A federal union, on the other hand, has at least two levels of government, in which (a) a central government has powers over matters common to the whole region e.g. currency, defence, foreign relations, while (b) regional governments (provincial, state) are responsible for matters of a more local nature e.g. roads, health services. Control is divided between the levels of government. In a "strong" federation, the regional governments are assigned limited, specific powers and the central authority has overall control. In a "weak" federal union, the central government has specific, or enumerated powers and the regions retain general, or residual, powers. Whatever the case, a federal union is more complicated than a legislative one. On the other hand, it may be the only way to join districts which are widely separated or differ in culture or other ways.

The difference between a legislative union and a federal union is not so simple as it may appear. A federal union may be set up so that very limited responsibility is assigned to the regional governments and vastly superior powers are given to the central government. If the latter has the authority to disallow laws passed by lower governments, then their position may differ little from what it would be in a legislative union.

1. Political changes were certain to be made in British North America in the 1860s. From the information presented so far, which of the following choices do you think was most probable:
(a) regional adjustment or union of all the colonies? why?
(b) if union of all the colonies, which type of union—legislative or federal? Why?
2. Compare your conclusion with what actually happened by the time the Dominion of Canada was created in 1867.
3. What are the main differences, if any, between your conclusion and what actually happened? Do you understand the reasons for the choice actually made in the 1860s? (Consider circumstances, personalities, etc.)

Confederation achieved

Confederation came about as a result of many kinds of decisions made over a period of three years in response to a problem situation. Taken together, these decisions represented a certain view of a Canadian future influenced by certain values and motives. A *policy decision* by the British Government to permit, even encourage, union among its North American colonies was necessary before Canadian leaders could take action.* The formation of the "Great Coalition" involved both *political* and *personal* decisions when long-standing political opponents agreed to join forces and work for the creation of a particular constitutional alternative—Confederation. The subsequent Confederation Conferences and related events were part of a network of decision-making which led to the proclamation of the Dominion of Canada on July 1, 1867.

*A. T. Galt's Confederation proposal to the Canadian Assembly in 1858 was killed when Britain declined to give approval.

As you read the following account of how Confederation was achieved, keep in mind the following questions:

1. To what extent was Confederation one alternative among many? What were the other *feasible* alternatives?
2. Did Confederation serve the interests of all groups of people in British North America? Equally, or some more than others?
3. Was Confederation achieved by a series of inevitable steps? Was it a scheme imposed upon British North America by a select group or combination of groups? If so, who were they?
4. What strategies were used by pro-Confederationists? Opponents?
5. To what extent was Confederation "the solution" to problems? Did it raise new ones? What were they?

THE GREAT COALITION

A dozen ministries in fifteen years, two elections and four ministries between 1861 and 1864 seemed to demonstrate the futility of government in the United Province. Sectional conflict, racial and religious division, the awkward practice of Double Majority and the unpredictable independent members all contributed to instability. Affairs of state had reached an impasse and government had bogged down in political dissension.

At this point of crisis, the Great Coalition, an event of far-reaching importance, came into being. Brown persuaded the Assembly to set up a committee to analyze the reasons for the political deadlock. As a result of the committee's findings and the constant encouragement of Lord Monck, the Governor, leaders of the Clear Grits and the Liberal Conservatives, in spite of their long-standing differences, agreed that they must co-operate in order to form a

Anyone familiar with lumbering operations in Canada knows the nature of a log jam. Timber dumped into a river floats down stream freely until it strikes an obstacle, when the logs pile up and make a blockade and seemingly hopeless confusion, only to be cleared when the 'key log' is removed. The events leading up to the early 'sixties in Canadian politics may be likened to a log jam. Political cliques and the dominance of small issues, quarrels and jealousies between leaders, stagnation in public business—all these created a hopeless situation that called for decisive treatment. . . . Where was the 'key log' of this confused situation? It was found in the idea of a coalition which was proposed and realized in 1864.[11]

[George Brown] has been described by a friend as a 'steam engine in trousers,' and had he lived in more recent times would no doubt be called 'a human dynamo.' He seemed never to stop working. His mind was ever on the alert, and his body was able to keep pace with it. Living before the advent of typewriters and the fashion of dictating, he laboriously wrote his editorials by hand, using a pencil never more than two inches long.[10]

*Hodge-podge was mutton boiled up with vegetables. Canadian reaction varied. The *Leader* thought it quite palatable. The *Quebec Mercury* thought it was flavoured with ashes! Chowder was "haddock sliced and boiled until a rather suspicious mixture is produced" (Toronto *Leader*). This description suggests the Canadian reaction to chowder.[15]

durable coalition government. George Brown again eased the way by entering into a coalition with Macdonald and Cartier, his bitter political opponents.

Macdonald's skillful diplomacy welded the coalition into a workable team. But Brown and Cartier were the men directly responsible for the creation of the coalition. Without the adherence of either the Grits or the *Bleus* a coalition would have been impossible. The Brown-Macdonald-Cartier government, in which the Grits were given three seats in the cabinet, was formed. This strong government, capable of commanding a majority in the Assembly, set out to make Confederation a reality.

CANADIANS AND MARITIMERS MEET

One of the many receptions given for the visiting Canadians in the summer of 1864 was the Royal Halifax Yacht Club's annual picnic, which they called their "Hodge-Podge and Chowder Party". Treated to Maritime dishes, quantities of wine, rousing speeches, and bagpipe concerts, the Canadians also joined in "manly and exhilarating games" such as the following:*

... leap-frog at once became the order of the day and a lively scene ensued.... Blue-noses sprang over Canadians with a shriek of delight. Canadians bounded over New Brunswickers and tripped over Nova Scotians. Editors and correspondents mingled in the fray and perilled their valuable persons by seeking the bubble reputation....

The effect of such encounters was described by a Halifax newspaper:

They [the Canadians] were strangers, they are now acquaintances, friends ... and let us hope, will aid materially in forwarding that grand scheme which all the more intelligent politicians of our common country seem to have at heart—a complete political consolidation of these British North American colonies.[14]

THE CHARLOTTETOWN CONFERENCE

At about the time the Great Coalition was formed in the Province of Canada, the Maritime colonies were considering some kind of Maritime union. The British government regarded Maritime union as a possible preliminary step to a wider union and, therefore, approved an initiative by Nova Scotia to arrange a conference. Favourable resolutions were passed by the legislatures of Nova Scotia and New Brunswick. The selection of Charlottetown as the site of the meeting helped to lessen Prince Edward Island's fears of any changes that might mean the loss of its autonomy.

When the delegates convened on September 1, 1864, they were joined by eight members of Canada's coalition cabinet, led by John

Forming a coalition can mean difficult decisions

In agreeing to participate in the Great Coalition led by John A. Macdonald, what risks were taken by such people as George Brown and George Cartier?

Professor Cornell, in The Great Coalition *writes (1966):*

George Brown's personal situation was quite precarious, for he had taken the initiative in bridging the gap between the Clear Grit Liberals and their most ardent opponents. Of the three parties involved, the Clear Grits were least given to following uncritically in the wake of a determined leader. Although it is now established that the highest public concerns drove Brown to his action, it was very possible that his party might at any time disown him, leaving his public career in ruins. Any miscalculation in June 1864, or in the next eighteen months might seem to give the Conservatives or Bleus a political advantage, and lead to his undoing. From his point of view it was a hazardous business. . . .

. . . A great convention of the Reform Movement, held in Toronto in late 1859, had, with Brown's strong intervention, hammered out a number of generally agreed goals. They would seek to implement the principle of representation by population, perhaps requiring the creation of some form of federal union. By these means they would secure control of their own destiny in Canada West, and the opportunity to benefit in opening the prairie west to settlement and economic development . . . the nature of the existing union frustrated the Clear Grits from achieving these aims by their own unaided efforts. The Great Coalition provided an agency by which these goals might be reached.[12]

Again in The Great Coalition *Professor Cornell writes:*

. . . The principals [leaders] who entered the coalition did so at some considerable risk to their careers. . . .

G. E. Cartier's entry into the Great Coalition was overshadowed by the possibility that the rank and file of his party would appraise his tactics as committing the French-Canadians to a full involvement with Anglo-Saxons in a situation where they would be a decreasing minority. The move to a general federation would mean giving up some of the security for language, customs and religion, that was built into the constitution of the Union. Even in the Great Coalition, the agency for change, Cartier and his French-Canadian supporters would be in a minority. He might be disowned by his people as a false leader. Today Cartier is not revered in Quebec as one of the great historic leaders of French Canada. It is considered that Dorion's policy of fighting the Great Coalition and all its works, was a much sounder policy in 1864 than the one pursued by Cartier.[13]

agreement by all members

1. What is the purpose of a coalition? If a coalition makes decisions on the basis of **consensus**, what sorts of situations could there be in Canadian government today, or in the future, that may call for the formation of a coalition?

2. Can you think of occasions on which coalitions may be desirable in provincial government? Local government?

A. Macdonald and George Cartier. Through the co-operation of Canada's Governor, Lord Monck, and the Colonial Secretary, the Canadian representatives had sought and obtained an invitation to state their arguments for a larger association of British North American colonies.

THE CHARLOTTETOWN CONFERENCE

George Brown's letter to his wife about the Canadians' arrival at the Charlottetown Conference and the sociable atmosphere in which the discussions were held:

Our party from Quebec consisted of Cartier, John A. [Macdonald], Galt, McDougall, Campbell, Langevin, McGee and myself.... We had great fun coming down the St. Lawrence—having fine weather, a broad awning to recline under, excellent stores of all kinds, an unexceptionable cook, lots of books, chessboards, back-gammon, and so forth....

.... Having dressed ourselves in correct style, our two boats were lowered man-of-war fashion—and being each duly manned with four oarsmen and a boatswain, dressed in blue uniforms, hats, belts, etc., in regular style, we pulled away for shore and landed like Mr. Christopher Columbus who had the precedence of us in taking possession of portions of the American continent....

[At the close of the first day of the conference we had a fine dinner] oysters, lobsters and champagne and other island luxuries. This killed the day and we spent the beautiful moonlight evening in walking, driving or boating, as the mood was on us. I sat on ... [the] balcony looking out on the sea in all its glory.

Cartier and I made eloquent speeches [on Saturday, September 3], of course, and whether as the result of our eloquence or of the goodness of our champagne the ice became completely broken, the tongues of the delegates wagged merrily....

The Charlottetown Conference, 1864

The evening [of Monday, September 5] I passed on board the steamer, playing chess and catching lobsters over the side of the steamer.[16]

1. Does Brown's comment that the Canadians "landed like Mr. Christopher Columbus" reveal anything about the Canadians' attitude toward attending the Charlottetown Conference?

They arrived in Charlottetown with hope of success aroused not only by the official British attitude, but also by the friendly reception they expected and received. A hundred Canadian politicians (including D'Arcy McGee), businessmen and journalists had completed a tour of Maritime centres in the preceding August. The social encounters between people of both regions had lowered barriers and made co-operation more likely.

The Canadians used well-prepared arguments to point out the advantages of the larger union over the Maritime plan. Economic growth through expanded markets and increased investment, aid for completing an intercolonial railway, improved defence and greater opportunity for Maritime politicians were attractive possibilities of the Canadian plan. In less than a week of meetings, the idea of

Maritime union was set aside, and the delegates agreed to meet at Quebec to examine more fully the advantages and problems of a union of all British North America.

Why had the idea of a Maritime union been so quickly replaced by the thought of Confederation? Here is an explanation from historian P. B. Waite, author of the booklet "The Charlottetown Conference":

> ... what was missing from the Charlottetown Conference was any effective progress toward Maritime union. It is clear that it reached the conference table by a strength not its own. It had never developed sufficient force to overcome the resistance of the men and the institutions it would abolish. By contrast, the federal union proposed by the Canadians guaranteed the continued existence of the provinces. ... Moreover, Confederation promised something that Maritime union could not: a transcontinental nation. It was true that this proposal had come from Canada, and things Canadian often had something sub rosa [underhanded] about them; but national glory was surely something about which even Canadians could be genuine. The idea of a British North American nation might be unrealistic, but it called up in the minds of the young, the energetic and the talented hopes and ambitions hitherto only dreamed of.[17]

THE QUEBEC CONFERENCE

The Quebec Conference, beginning on October 10, 1864 was attended by delegates from all the Atlantic colonies, including Newfoundland, and the Cabinet ministers of Canada's coalition government. To promote frank discussion and to prevent revealing, as far as possible, any serious divisions which might develop, the delegates decided to follow the practice of cabinet secrecy and closed the meetings to the public and the newspapers.

The politicians were only too well aware of the many obstacles to union, including the conflicting demands of the different regions, tariff barriers among the provinces, strong local pride and the fear of every colony or culture that it might lose more than it would gain. The pressures for union were immediate and forceful. But only a spirit of compromise and patience could make possible the creation of a national system of government that could accommodate the aspirations of French Canadians, the individuality of Prince Edward Island, the urge of Upper Canadians for westward expansion and all the other special interests.

1. You are to be a delegate to the Quebec Conference. Write a letter to a citizen in your home colony explaining why you agreed to holding the meetings in secret.

2. You are a newspaper editor from a town in one of the colonies. Write an editorial stating that the meetings should be open to the public and give your reasons.

The nature of the union was the fundamental question. John A. Macdonald was the principal advocate of a legislative union, which would provide one government sovereign over all affairs not under the jurisdiction of the British government. He was deeply concerned about the importance of a strong government that could ensure the endurance of the union. The United States, he believed, was suffering a terrible civil war because it had a federal system in which the states had too much power and the central government too little. French-Canadian spokesmen, such as Cartier, were opposed, however, on the grounds that their rights of law, language and religion would be in jeopardy. Prince Edward Island, and the other Atlantic colonies too, protested that their interests and ways of life could not be protected under a unitary system. Only a federation of provinces, each with its own government for local affairs and a central government to administer matters of common concern, held the promise of joining together an area so large and diverse as British North America.

The Seventy-Two Resolutions, sometimes referred to as the Quebec Resolutions, were finally approved by the conference as the basis of Confederation. They proposed a federal system, with authority divided between a new central government and the provincial governments.*

*See page 370.

THE NATURE OF THE UNION

John A. Macdonald argued for a union of all British North America, with the strongest possible central government:

... In framing the constitution, care should be taken to avoid the mistakes and weaknesses of the United States' system, the primary error of which was the reservation to the different States of all powers not delegated to the General Government. We must reverse this process by establishing a strong central Government, to which shall belong all powers not specially conferred on the provinces. ... A strong central Government is indispensable to the success of the experiment we are trying. . . . [18]

THE FATE OF THE CONFEDERATION PLAN

The delegates at the Quebec Conference had devised a plan generally acceptable to themselves, but they had no legislative authority.

That is, the Seventy-Two Resolutions were not law; they were not binding on any of the colonies represented at the conference. The Confederation plan would go no farther until the individual colonial governments—in particular, those of Canada, New Brunswick and Nova Scotia—had given their approval. Then Confederation would require the blessing of the British Government and the passage of an act by the British Parliament.

The Confederation Debates

PROVINCE OF CANADA

The Confederation plan was debated both in and out of governments for many months, but the most crucial debate was the one in the Assembly of the united Province of Canada. In the 1860s, the spotlight was on central Canada, where more than sixty per cent of the population of British North America lived.

John A. Macdonald opened the formal debates by putting forth the case in favour of Confederation. He confronted the Assembly with the possibility that it was Confederation "now or never". In his words, "It is an opportunity that may never recur."

For nearly six weeks, the Canadian Assembly debated over and over again the issues that had come up since the idea of Confederation was first proposed: the American threat, the economic problems, the need for railways, political deadlock, and the need for French-English harmony.

Opposition to Confederation came mainly from two groups. The English-speaking minority in Canada East feared for its future in a French-Canadian province. Alexander Galt was hard-pressed to assure his fellow members that minority rights would be safeguarded. French-Canadian Liberals (then called the "*Rouges*"), led by A. A. Dorion, claimed that Confederation would deprive French Canada of the means to preserve its way of life. It was possible to suspect that the whole plan was a thinly-disguised English-Canadian plot.

The coalition government, however, had the overwhelming support of Canada West. Its representatives, English-speaking, saw the opportunity of eliminating political deadlock, of acquiring the Northwest, of financing canals and roads, and of submerging French Canada in an Anglo-Saxon country. From Canada East came the support of French-Canadian Conservatives. Cartier, for example, defended their position by saying that Confederation, providing as it did for provincial control of provincial matters, was the best possible guarantee of cultural survival for French Canada.

The Great Coalition then, had an overwhelming majority. The opposition was badly divided, and could present no commonly sup-

Should the people have a say?

George Brown was against submitting the RESOLUTIONS *to the voters.* CONFEDERATION DEBATES, *February 8, 1865:*

. . . . An appeal to the people of Canada on this measure simply means postponement of the question for a year—and who can tell how changed ere then may be the circumstances surrounding us? Sir, the man who strives for the postponement of this measure on any ground, is doing what he can to kill it almost as effectually as if he voted against it. . . . [20]

The Hamilton TIMES *, a Reform newspaper, held a different view:*

If their [the people's] *direct* decision on the confederation question is unnecessary, we know of no question that has arisen in the past, we can imagine none in the future of sufficient importance to justify an appeal to them. The polling booths thereafter may as well be turned into pig-pens, and the voters lists cut up into pipe-lighters.[21]

A. A. Dorion insisted upon a vote by the people, CONFEDERATION DEBATES, *March 6, 1865:*

. . . . Everywhere [in Lower Canada] this scheme has been protested against, and an appeal to the people demanded; and yet, in defiance of the expressed opinions of our constituents, we are about to give them a Constitution, the effect of which will be to snatch from them the little influence which they still enjoy under the existing union . . . I shall oppose this scheme with all the power at my command, and insist that under any circumstances it shall be submitted to the people before its final adoption.[22]

Jean Charles Bonenfant in THE FRENCH-CANADIANS AND THE BIRTH OF CONFEDERATION *(1966) comments on the attitude of the French-Canadian population:*

. . . . The French-Canadian voters of Lower Canada could not express their views on the project of Confederation before it was adopted, but the fact remains that a large number of their representatives in both houses were opposed to it. . . .

Although we have no mathematical proof, it seems likely that the majority of French Canadians were favourable to Confederation during its formative stages from 1864 to 1867, and . . . even though the French Canadians wanted to preserve their identity, they never seriously thought of independence as a solution. . . .

A majority of French Canadians favoured Confederation a hundred years ago because it was the only realistic solution which presented itself to them, and even those who opposed it were content to say that it was premature but did not offer an alternative solution.[23]

Professor P. B. Waite (1962) comments on the government's justification for not consulting the Canadian public:

.... The Government took the view that an election was unnecessary.... Nothing could be gained from the turmoil of a general election; the Government had good reason to think an election could hardly strengthen its position and might conceivably weaken it. The public position of the Government was stated by two powerful government papers, the Conservative Montreal *Gazette*... and the Toronto *Globe*. As might have been expected, the *Gazette* said that in British practice the Canadian parliament would be perfectly justified in asking the Queen for constitutional changes without the prior consent of the Canadian electorate. "If there be a settled doctrine of the British Constitution it is that the people's representatives in Parliament are not mere delegates charged with certain specific duties, but are, in fact, the people in their political capacity...." The *Gazette* deprecated proposals for an election; it would be a plebiscite after the French mode, or "after the style of our democratic neighbours." The *Globe* agreed. The idea was "one of those dreadful American heresies against which we are so often warned now-a-days."[24]

---

ported alternative. The coalition leaders described Confederation as a political masterpiece which none but a fool or a knave would oppose. Moreover, the Seventy-Two Resolutions were to be considered and voted on "as a package," with no opportunity for changes. Opponents knew that even if they succeeded in showing that some of the Resolutions were ill-conceived, they had no chance to replace them, let alone to defeat the total Confederation plan.

In the end, the coalition ministry had its way, and the legislature voted 91—33 in favour of Confederation.

The STRATFORD BEACON *(March 17, 1865) observed the effects of the long intensive Confederation Debates in the Canadian Assembly. This account refers to the atmosphere just before the Assembly approved the Quebec Resolutions:*

... the House was in an unmistakably seedy condition, having, as it was positively declared, eaten the saloon keeper clean out, drunk him entirely dry, and got all the fitful naps of sleep that the benches along the passages could be made to yield.... Men with

the strongest constitutions for Parliamentary twaddle were sick of
the debate, and the great bulk of the members were scattered
about the building...impatient for the sound of the division bell.
It rang at last, at quarter past four [in the morning], and the jaded
representatives of the people swarmed in to the discharge of the
most important duty of all their lives.[19]

Totals	For	Against	No Vote
Canada West	54	8	3
Canada East	37 (27 French Canadian)	25 (21 French Canadian)	3

1. What do these statistics suggest regarding French-Canadian feelings about Confederation?
2. How does the English-Canadian vote differ?

THE ATLANTIC COLONIES

Reception in the Maritimes of the Confederation plan ranged from
indifference to open hostility. Neither Prince Edward Island nor
Newfoundland was essential to the union at this time, and their
failure to join could be accepted. New Brunswick and Nova Scotia,
however, were vital to the creation of a trans-continental Canada.
When organized opposition mounted in those two colonies, the
Confederationists were shaken.

In New Brunswick, Tilley decided to "go to the people." During
the election campaign, however, the critics played on the idea that
New Brunswick would be giving up some of its independence if it
joined the union. Charges that Maritimers were being sold out for
"80¢ a head"* to the Upper Canadians had a telling effect.

In March, 1865, just as the Confederation Debates were reaching
a successful conclusion in Canada, the news came that Tilley's government had suffered a crushing defeat. In Nova Scotia, meanwhile,
Premier Charles Tupper took his cue from the upset in the neighbouring colony. He decided to wait a while before presenting the
Seventy-Two (Quebec) Resolutions to the Assembly. Opposition to
Confederation was at least as great in Nova Scotia as in New Brunswick, since the highly respected and influential Joseph Howe was in
the forefront.

*Under the proposed plan, the
colony was to receive a grant
based on the sum of 80¢ per
person, as compensation for
giving up powers of taxation
to the central government.

CROSS ROADS.

SHALL WE GO TO WASHINGTON FIRST, OR HOW(E)?

ANTI-CONFEDERATION SENTIMENTS IN THE MARITIMES

W. H. Needham speaking in the House of Assembly of New Brunswick, April 3, 1865:

When I forget my country so far as to sell it for Confederation, may my right hand forget its cunning, and if I do not prefer New Brunswick, as she is, to Canada with all her glory, then let my tongue cleave to the roof of my mouth. When the day comes when we shall have...Confederation deposited in the grave, those that will be there will not be there as mourners, but as glorifiers, and they will sing, with hearts elate with patriotic joy:

> Then safely moored, our perils o'er,
>   We'll sing the songs of Jubilee,
> For ever and for ever more,
>   New Brunswick, Land of Liberty.[25]

A sample of Joseph Howe's "Botheration Letters," a mocking criticism of the Confederation idea, published in a Halifax newspaper a few months after the Quebec Conference:

Where there are no cohesive qualities in the material, no skill in the design ...*unite what you will and there is no strength....* Was there strength when the new wine was united to the old bottle, or the new cloth to the old garment? Is union strength when a prudent man, doing a snug business is tempted into partnership with a wild speculator? Was Sampson much the stronger when the false Delilah got him confederated, bound him with cords and cut off his hair?[26]

An anti-Confederation ditty current in Newfoundland:

Hurrah for our native isle, Newfoundland!
Not a stranger shall hold one inch of its strand!
Her face turns to Britain, her back to the Gulf.
Come near at your peril, Canadian wolf!

Ye brave Newfoundlanders who plough the salt sea
With hearts like the eagle, so bold and so free,
The time is at hand when you'll all have to say
If Confederation will carry the day.

Would you barter the rights that your fathers have won,
Your freedom transmitted from father to son?
For a few thousand dollars of Canadian gold,
Don't let it be said that your birthright was sold.[27]

Great Britain, however, gave its official blessing to Confederation in the fall of 1865, and took steps to ensure its success. The Lieutenant-Governor of New Brunswick was instructed to use his influence, and an election was called for the spring of 1866. A furious pro-Confederation platform was adopted by Tilley and his followers. Money poured into his campaign, from many sources—railway promoters, shipping and timber interests—even the Canadian government. The threat of Fenian raids was played up, to dramatize the need for union in order to strengthen defence. The predictable result: Tilley was returned to power, and the new Assembly approved Confederation.

In Nova Scotia, an unsympathetic governor was replaced by Sir Fenwick Williams,* a native Nova Scotian. With British backing, Charles Tupper was able to get Confederation approved in principle. He then joined Tilley in urging the Canadians to complete the work of union while conditions were favourable. In the fall of 1866, preparations were made for the final Confederation Conference.

*See page 300.

THE LONDON CONFERENCE

The London Conference began in December, 1866, under the chairmanship of John A. Macdonald. The representatives from Canada, Nova Scotia and New Brunswick had to revise the Quebec Resolutions for acceptance by the British government and passage as an

Act of Parliament. This accomplished, the delegates agreed on the name "Canada" for the new union. The only seriously considered alternative was "Kingdom of Canada," a name which Macdonald and others thought would properly suggest the continuation of strong ties with Britain and stress the importance of the monarchy in the new union's government. The British government vetoed the idea, however, because the word "kingdom" would have provoked strong reaction from the republican United States.

CANADA—NOWHERESVILLE OR ? ? ?

Even the very name Canada is open to the power of negative thinking. An eminent Canadian sociologist, a native of Austria, has pointed out that where he came from the word is pronounced *keine dah* and means "nobody there." The name Canada is supposed to derive from what the Indians kept yelling at our discoverer, Jacques Cartier, as they pointed up river, so that for what it is worth *"Kanata! Kanata!"* means "Yonder are our wigwams!" There was another view which held that the Indians must already have conversed with Portuguese fishermen drying the cod they had taken off the Grand Banks and who, unlike Cartier, did not realize they had discovered Canada. This view suggested that the Indians were really saying *"Aca nada"* in Portuguese, so that Canada means "There's nothing here." No matter that the story is discredited ("Wigwams," or "Village," is what we are, whether we like it or not), its intention points to the heart of things. This is a nothing place. Nowheresville. And here is the trick of it. If you are nothing you may also be anything. You may be a map or a model of everything. You might even hope someday to become something—
"a something possible, a chance," as a novelist once called Canada. The scholar and former diplomat Douglas LePan has found the Canadian passport a useful image for all this. The little blue booklet stamped in gold is one of the world's more precious commodities, the one most often used by those operating international rackets or spy systems. Its popularity lies not just in the fact one can travel almost anywhere with it, but that one can speak almost any language with almost any accent, be a member of almost any race, "English or French or Ukrainian or Polish or Chinese, and still be a Canadian. One can, in fact, be almost anyone and still be a Canadian. To be a Canadian is to have a passport to the whole world."[28]

The British North America Act

CANINES CAUSE MORE CONCERN THAN CONFEDERATION

Although Confederation had been hotly debated in the colonies, the BNA Act was a routine piece of legislation in the British House of Commons:

Except for Canadians themselves . . . and a few Britishers like the colonial secretary, Lord Carnarvon, nobody took it [Confederation] very seriously. The House of Commons at Westminister was three-quarters empty when it passed the British North America Act, though it filled up immediately afterwards for the debate on a dog tax bill. Oh, the English knew what they were doing, all right— their fits of absent-mindedness were for acquiring empires, not for sloughing them off. It was just that the idea of Canada bored them, as it has bored most Englishmen ever since.[29]

The British North America Act was passed by the British Parliament in March with a minimum of debate; not even the exertions of the tireless Joseph Howe had aroused any serious opposition. Queen Victoria signed the Act on March 29, 1867. The Dominion of Canada, consisting of Ontario and Quebec (formerly the Province of Canada), and Nova Scotia and New Brunswick, was to begin its formal existence on July 1, 1867.

End Notes

CHAPTER 1

1. Bruce Hutchison, quoted in John Columbo, *Columbo's Canadian Quotations*, p. 276. Edmonton: Hurtig, 1974.
2. From Edward De Bono, *Eureka! How and When the Greatest Inventions Were Made: An Illustrated History of Inventions from the Wheel to the Computer*, p. 71. London: Thames and Hudson, 1974.
3. From Barbara Brown, "Biofeedback: An Exercise in 'Self-Control' ", *Saturday Review*, Vol. 2, No. 11, February 22, 1975, p. 22. Copyright 1975 by *Saturday Review* and Barbara Brown. Reprinted by permission of *Saturday Review*.
4. From Mary J. Dunstan and Patricia Garlan, *Worlds in the Making: Probes for Students of the Future*, p. 289. Englewood Cliffs, New Jersey: Prentice-Hall, Inc., 1970. Reprinted by permission of Prentice-Hall, Inc.
5. From Edgar D. Mitchell, "Outer Space to Inner Space: An Astronaut's Odyssey", *Saturday Review*, Vol. 2, No. 11, February 22, 1975, p. 20. Copyright 1975 by *Saturday Review*. Reprinted by permission of *Saturday Review*.
6. "Duped, Experts Admit", *Winnipeg Free Press*, February 6, 1974. Copyright 1974 by Reuter Ltd. Reprinted by permission of Reuter Ltd.
7. From Samuel E. Morison, *European Discovery of America: The Northern Voyages*, pp. x-xi. New York: Oxford University Press, 1971. Reprinted by permission of Oxford University Press.
8. From J. H. Parry, "Introduction" to J. R. Hale, *Age of Exploration*, Great Ages of Man Series. New York: Time-Life Books, 1966. Reprinted by permission of Time Incorporated.
9. From Samuel E. Morison, *op. cit.*, p. 159.
10. From J. R. Hale, *op. cit.*, p. 15.
11. From Keith J. Crowe, *A History of the Original Peoples of Northern Canada*, p. 66. Montreal: Arctic Institute of North America. McGill-Queen's University Press, 1974. Reprinted by permission of McGill-Queen's University Press.
12. *Ibid.*, p. 65.
13. From J. R. Hale, *op. cit.*, pp. 80-82.
14. From Stephen Leacock, *The Mariner of St. Malo: A Chronicle of the Voyages of Jacques Cartier*, p. 112. Toronto: Glasgow Brook, 1914.
15. From Morris Bishop, *White Men Came to the St. Lawrence: The French and the Land They Found*, pp. 29, 31-32. London: George Allen & Unwin Ltd., 1961. Reprinted by permission of George Allen & Unwin Ltd.
16. From Samuel E. Morison, *op. cit.*, pp. xi, xii.
17. From Matthew Arnold, "The Future", in *The Works of Matthew Arnold in Fifteen Volumes*, Vol. II, p. 115. New York: AMS Press, Inc., 1970.
18. From Samuel E. Morison, *op. cit.*, p. xii.
19. From Arthur C. Clarke, *Profiles of the Future*, pp. 82-85. New York: Harper & Row, 1964. Bantam Books edition. Reprinted by permission of Harper & Row.
20. Louis Joseph Halle, "Why I'm for Space Exploration", *The New Republic*, April 8, 1968, p. 14. New York: The Republic Publishing Co., Inc.
21. Bertrand Russell, "Let's Stay Off the Moon", quoted in M. Ross & J. Stevens (eds.), *Images of Man*, p. 90. Toronto: MacLean's Magazine, 1958.
22. From Robert Stanfield, "Man and Government", in Stephen Clarkson, ed.,

Visions 2020: Fifty Canadians in Search of a Future, p. 119. Edmonton: Hurtig, 1970. Reprinted by permission of Mr. Stephen Clarkson.

23. Bruce Hutchison in John Columbo, *op. cit.*, p. 276.

CHAPTER 2

1. From J. S. Frideres, *Canada's Indians: Contemporary Conflicts*, p. 116. Scarborough, Ontario: Prentice-Hall of Canada, Ltd., 1974. Reprinted by permission of Prentice-Hall of Canada, Ltd.

2. From J. H. Kennedy, *Jesuit and Savage in New France*, pp. 97-98. Hamden, Conn.: Archon Books, 1971.

3. From *North/nord*, Vol. XXII, No. 6, Nov./Dec. 1975, p. 41. Ottawa: Department of Indian Affairs and Northern Development. Reproduced by permission of the Ministry of Supply and Services, Canada.

4. From Keith J. Crowe, *A History of the Original Peoples of Northern Canada*, pp 19-20. Montreal: Arctic Institute of North America. McGill-Queen's University Press, 1974. Reprinted by permission of McGill-Queen's University Press.

5. From Morris Bishop, *White Men Came to the St. Lawrence—The French and the Land They Found*, pp. 14-17. London: George Allen & Unwin Ltd., 1961. Reprinted by permission of George Allen & Unwin Ltd.

6. *Ibid.*, p. 18.

7. *Ibid.*, pp. 23-23.

8. From Keith J. Crowe, *op. cit.*, p. 21.

9. From *Relation de la Nouvelle France 1632*, Vol. 25, p. 106; *Relation de la Nouvelle France 1634*, Vol. VI, p. 228 in J. H. Kennedy, *op. cit.*, p. 106.

10. From *Relation de la Nouvelle France*, Vol. III, p. 74 in J. H. Kennedy, *op. cit.*, p. 107.

11. From *Breve Relazione*, Vol. XXXVIII, pp. 256-258 in J. H. Kennedy, *op. cit.*, p. 107.

12. *Ibid.*, p. 108.

13. From *Relation de la Nouvelle France*, Vol. VII, p. 176 in J. H. Kennedy, *op. cit.*, pp. 112-113.

14. From *Relation de la Nouvelle France*, Vol. III; *Jesuit Relations*, Vol. II, p. 78 in J. H. Kennedy, *op. cit.*, p. 113.

15. *Ibid.*, p. 111.

16. From *Relation de la Nouvelle France 1633*, p. 104 in J. H. Kennedy, *op. cit.*, p. 114.

17. From George W. Cronyn, *The Path on the Rainbow—An Anthology of Songs and Chants From the Indians of North America*, p. 158. New York: Boni and Liveright, 1918.

18. *Ibid.*, p. 116.

19. From Fr. Chrestien Le Clercq, "New Relation of Gaspesia" from *The Native Peoples of Atlantic Canada: A History of Ethnic Interaction* by Harold Franklin McGee, Jr., pp. 45-46. Toronto: McClelland & Stewart, New Canadian Library, 1974. Reprinted by permission of The Canadian Publishers, McClelland & Stewart Ltd., Toronto.

20. From Morris Bishop, *op. cit.*, pp. 23-26.

21. From Diamond Jenness, *Indians of Canada*, pp. 158-159. Ottawa: Government of Canada, Department of Mines, 1932. Reproduced by permission of the Ministry of Supply and Services, Canada.

22. *Ibid.*, p. 175.

23. From Selwyn Dewdney and Franklin Arbuckle, *They Shared to Survive—The Native Peoples of Canada*, pp. 41-42. Toronto: Macmillan of Canada, Ltd., 1975.

24. *Ibid.*, p. 92.

25. From Douglas Leechman, *Native Tribes of Canada*, pp. 83-85. Toronto: W. J. Gage, 1956. Copyright by Gage Educational Publishing Limited.

26. *Ibid.*, pp. 130-132.

27. From G. Lanctot, *A History of Canada, Vol. I*, pp. 13-14. Toronto: Clarke, Irwin & Co. Ltd., 1963-1965.

28. From G. R. Stevens, *The Imcompleat Canadian*, pp. 11-12. Canada: T. Eaton Co., 1965.

29. From Diamond Jenness, *op. cit.*, p. 176.

30. From Selwyn Dewdney and Franklin Arbuckle, *op. cit.*, pp. 168-169.

31. From Dr. Kaj. Birket-Smith, *Eskimos*, pp. 114-115. Denmark: Rhodos, 1971.

32. *Ibid.*, pp. 128-129.

33. From Selwyn Dewdney and Franklin Arbuckle, *op. cit.*, p. 172.

34. From Edward Moffa Weyer, Jr., *The Eskimos—Their Environment and Folkways*, p. 327. New Haven: Yale University Press, 1932.

35. From *People From Our Side*, a life story with photographs by Peter Pitseolak and oral biography by Dorothy Eber. Hurtig Publishers, Edmonton, 1975.

36. From Edward Moffa Weyer, Jr., *op. cit.*, pp. 234-235.

37. From Keith J. Crowe, *op. cit.*, p. 181.

38. From Nicholas Denys, *Description and Natural History of the Coast of North America (Acadia)*, ed. and trans. by William F. Ganong, pp. 440-443. Toronto: The Champlain Society, 1908. Reproduced by permission of The Champlain Society, Toronto.

39. From Keith J. Crowe, *op. cit.*, p. 100.

40. From Edward Moffa Weyer, Jr., *op. cit.*, p. 138.

41. From Keith J. Crowe, *op. cit.*, pp. 210-211.

CHAPTER 3

1. Based on William John Eccles, *The Ordeal of New France*, p. 38. Toronto: CBC International Service, 1969.

2. Eric Wilton Morse, "Voyageurs Highway" in William J. Megill, *Patterns of Canada*, pp. 52-53. Toronto: McGraw-Hill Ryerson Ltd., 1966.

3. From J. B. Brebner, *The Explorers of North America, 1492-1806*, p. 141. London: A & C Black Ltd., 1933. Reprinted by permission of A & C Black Ltd., London.

4. Jacques Cartier in H. P. Biggar (ed.), *The Voyages of Jacques Cartier*, pp. 49, 50-51, 60-61. Ottawa: F. C. Acland, 1924. Published by the Public Archives of Canada, a department of the Crown.

5. From W. A. McKay, *The Great Canadian Skin Game*, pp. 1-2. Toronto: Macmillan of Canada, Ltd., 1967.

6. From John Hopkins Kennedy, *Jesuit and Savage in New France*, p. 129. Hamden, Conn.: Archon Books, 1971.

7. For a full analysis of the Dollard controversy, see André Vachon, "Dollard des Ormeaux" in *Dictionary of Canadian Biography*, pp. 266-274. Toronto: University of Toronto Press. Copyright 1969 by University of Toronto Press. Reprinted by permission of University of Toronto Press.

8. John A. Irving (ed.), "The Development of Communications in Canada" in *Mass Media in Canada*, pp. 4-5. Toronto: McGraw-Hill Ryerson Ltd., 1962.

9. From J. B. Brebner, *op. cit.*, pp. 361, 262, 366.

10. Pierre Gaultier de Varennes, Sieur. de la Vérendrye in L. J. Burpee (ed.), *Journals and Letters of Pierre Gaultier de Varennes de la Vérendrye and His Sons*, pp. 451-452. Toronto: The Champlain Society, 1927. Reprinted by permission of The Champlain Society, Toronto.

11. From Raymond Douville and Jacques-Donat Casanova, *Daily Life in Early Canada—From Champlain to Montcalm*, pp. 25-31. London: George Allen & Unwin, Ltd., 1967. Reprinted by permission of Macmillan Publishing Co., Inc., New York.

CHAPTER 4

1. From G. Ferraro and B. Larkin, *The Invisible Castle: Institutions—A Concept Study*, p. 7. New York: Macmillan Publishing Co., Inc., 1975. Reprinted with permission of Macmillan Publishing Co., Inc., New York.

2. From W. J. Eccles, *The Ordeal of New France*, p. 103. Toronto: CBC International Service, 1969.

3. From Morris Bishop, *When White Men Came to the St. Lawrence—The French and the Land They Found*, pp. 74-75. London: George Allen & Unwin Ltd., 1961. Reprinted by permission of George Allen & Unwin Ltd.

4. E. C. Parson, "Micmac Folklore" in Walsh, *Indians In Transition*, p. 48. Toronto: McClelland & Stewart Ltd., 1971.

5. From W. J. Eccles, *op. cit.*, p. 26.

6. From G. M. Wrong, *The Rise and Fall of New France*, Vol. I, pp. 341-343. Toronto: Macmillan Company of Canada, Ltd., 1928.

7. From Mason Wade, *The French Canadians 1760-1967*, Vol. I, pp. 39-40. Toronto: Macmillan Company of Canada, Ltd., 1968.

8. "Marie de l'Incarnation" in W. S. Wallace, *Macmillan Dictionary of Canadian Biography*, 3rd ed., p 496. Toronto: Macmillan Company of Canada, Ltd., 1963.

9. From *The Beginnings of New France, 1524-1663* by Marcel Trudel, p. 250. Toronto: McClelland & Stewart Ltd. (The Canadian Centenary Series), 1973. Reprinted by permission of The Canadian Publishers, McClelland & Stewart Ltd., Toronto.

10. From Marcel Trudel, *op. cit.*, p. 260.

11. From W. J. Eccles, *op. cit.*, p. 97.

12. From Raymond Douville and Jacques-Donat Casanova, *Daily Life in Early Canada —From Champlain to Montcalm*, pp. 101-102. London: George Allen & Unwin Ltd., 1967. Reprinted by permission of Macmillan Publishing Co., Inc., New York.

13. From Hugh MacLennan, *Two Solitudes*, pp. 12-13. Toronto: Macmillan Co. of Canada, Ltd., 1945.

14. From G. R. Stevens, *The Incompleat Canadian*, pp. 29-30. Canada: T. Eaton Company, 1965.

15. From Mason Wade, *op. cit.*, pp. 36-37.

16. "Boucher, Pierre" in W. S. Wallace, *op. cit.*, p. 70.

17. From *Ideas in Exile: A History of Canadian Invention* by J. J. Brown, pp. 24-25. Toronto: McClelland & Stewart Ltd., 1967. Reprinted by permission of The Canadian Publishers, McClelland & Stewart Ltd., Toronto.

18. From G. Frégault, *Canadian Society in the French Regime*, CHA Booklet, No. 3, 1954, p. 14. Ottawa: Canadian Historical Association. Published by the Public Archives of Canada, a department of the Crown.

19. From W. J. Eccles, *op. cit.*, pp. 103-104.

20. Based on R. W. Winks, *The Blacks in Canada, A History*. New Haven, Conn.: Yale University Press, 1971.

21. From Raymond Douville and Jacques-Donat Casanova, *op. cit.*, pp. 84-85.

22. *Ibid.*, pp. 89-90.

23. From Benjamin Sulte, "The Captains of Militia" in *Canadian Historical Review*, September 1920, pp. 1-3. Toronto: University of Toronto Press. Copyright 1920 by University of Toronto Press. Reprinted by permission of University of Toronto Press.

CHAPTER 5

1. From F. Parkman, *A Half-Century of Conflict*, pp. 360-368, 381-382. Boston: Little, Brown & Co., 1969.

2. "Circular letter from Governor Lawrence to the Governors on the Continent", PAC Report, 1905, II, App. B.

3. From Andrew Clark, *Acadia: The Geography of Early Nova Scotia to 1760*, p. 360. Madison, Wisconsin; University of Wisconsin Press, 1968.

4. *Relation of the French Neutrals, 1758.* Pennsylvania Archives, 1758. First series, Vol. 3.

5. From L. H. Gipson, *The British Empire Before the American Revolution*, pp. 176-181. New York: Alfred A. Knopf, Inc. Copyright 1958 by Alfred A. Knopf, Inc. Reprinted by permission of Alfred A. Knopf, Inc.

6. From Edgar MacInnis, *Canada: A Political and Social History*, p. 114. Toronto: Holt, Rinehart & Winston of Canada, Ltd., 1959.

7. From Guy Frégault

8. From W. J. Eccles, *The Ordeal of New France*. Toronto: CBC International Service, 1969.

9. From I. K. Steele, *Guerillas and Grenadiers: The Struggle for Canada, 1689-1760*, p. 76. Toronto: McGraw-Hill Ryerson Ltd., 1969.

10. *The Centennial of the Settlement of Upper Canada by the United Empire Loyalists, 1784-1884* (pub. by the Centennial Committee), pp. 25-27. Toronto: Rose Publishing Co., 1885.

11. "Montcalm and Wolfe (1884)" in John Robert Colombo (ed.), *Colombo's Canadian Quotations*, pp. 464-465. Edmonton: Hurtig Publishers, 1974.

12. From Mason Wade, *The French Canadians 1760-1945*, pp. 48-49. Toronto: Macmillan Company of Canada, Ltd., 1955.

13. From Michel Brunet, *French Canada and the Early Decades of British Rule, 1760-1791*, CHA Booklet, No. 13, 1965, p. 5. Ottawa: Canadian Historical Association. Published by the Public Archives of Canada, a department of the Crown.

14. From Fernand Ouellet, "Le Nationalisme Canadien-français: de ses origins à l'insurrection de 1837", *Canadian Historical Review*, p. 128. Toronto: University of Toronto Press. Copyright 1964 by University of Toronto Press. Translation by George Rawlyk.

CHAPTER 6

1. From W. J. Eccles, *The Ordeal of New France*, p. 142. Toronto: CBC International Service, 1969.

2. From Adam Shortt and Arthur Doughty (eds.), *Documents Relating to the Constitutional History of Canada, 1759-1791*, Part I, pp. 191-192. Ottawa: King's Printer,, 1918.

3. From *Quebec: The Revolutionary Age, 1760-1791* by Hilda Neatby, pp. 49-50. Toronto: McClelland & Stewart Ltd., 1966. Reprinted by permission of The Canadian Publishers, McClelland & Stewart Ltd., Toronto.

4. From Adam Shortt and Arthur Doughty (eds.), *op. cit.*, pp. 233-234.

5. *Ibid.*, pp. 231-232.

6. From *The Old Province of Quebec, Vol. I, 1760-1778* by A. L. Burt, p. 90. Toronto: McClelland & Stewart Ltd. (Carleton Lib. ed.), 1968. Reprinted by permission of The Canadian Publishers, McClelland & Stewart Ltd., Toronto.

7. From Adam Shortt and Arthur Doughty (eds.), *op. cit.*, p. 284.

8. *Ibid.*, pp. 295-296.

9. From A. L. Burt, *op. cit.*, pp. 188-189.

10. *Ibid.*, p. 189.

11. From Adam Shortt and Arthur Doughty (eds.), *op. cit.*, pp. 589-590.

12. From Hilda Neatby, *The Quebec Act: Protest and Policy*, pp. 3-4. Scarborough, Ontario: Prentice-Hall of Canada, Ltd., 1972. Reprinted by permission of Prentice-Hall of Canada, Ltd.

13. From John Garner, *The Franchise and Politics in British North America, 1755-1867*, pp. 82-83. Toronto: University of Toronto Press. Copyright 1969 by University of Toronto Press. Reprinted by permission of University of Toronto Press.

14. From W. P. M. Kennedy, *The Constitution of Canada, 1534-1937*, pp. 84-85. Toronto: Oxford University Press, 1938. Reprinted by permission of Oxford University Press, Toronto.

15. Frances Brooke, *The History of Emily Montague*, quoted from Letter XLIX to Miss Rivers. London: Silleri, January 1, 1769.

CHAPTER 7

1. From W. P. M. Kennedy, *Documents of the Canadian Constitution, 1791-1915*, pp. 139-143. Toronto: Oxford University Press, 1918. Reprinted by permission of Oxford University Press, Toronto.

2. From R. Coupland, *The Quebec Act: A Study in Statesmanship*, p. 170. Oxford: Oxford University Press, 1925.

3. F. Ouellet, "Histoire economique et sociale du Québec, 1760-1850", pp. 121-122 in

George A. Rawlyk, *Revolution Rejected, 1775-1776*. Scarborough, Ontario: Prentice-Hall of Canada, Ltd., 1968. Reprinted by permission of Prentice-Hall of Canada, Ltd.

4. From J. B. Brebner, *The Neutral Yankees of Nova Scotia—A Marginal Colony During the Revolutionary Years*, p. 299. New York: Columbia University Press, 1937.

5. From *The Atlantic Provinces, The Emergence of Colonial Society, 1712-1857* by W. S. MacNutt, p. 76. Toronto: McClelland & Stewart Ltd., 1965. Reprinted by permission of The Canadian Publishers, McClelland & Stewart Ltd., Toronto.

6. Lady Tennyson in John Columbo, *Columbo's Canadian Quotations*, p. 581. Edmonton: Hurtig Publishers, 1974.

7. From Jo-Ann Fellows, *The Loyalist Myth in Canada*, p. 97. Ottawa: Canadian Historical Association (Canadian Historical Papers), 1971. Published by the Public Archives of Canada, a department of the Crown.

8. *Ibid.*, p. 100.

9. From G. N. D. Evans, *Allegiance in America: The Case of the Loyalists*, p. 22. Reading, Mass.: Addison-Wesley, 1969.

10. From Catherine S. Crary, *The Price of Loyalty—Tory Writings From A Revolutionary Era*, pp. 401-402. New York: McGraw-Hill, 1973.

11. From R. W. Winks, *The Blacks in Canada, A History*, pp. 28-29. New Haven, Conn.: Yale University Press, 1971.

12. From Catherine S. Crary, *op. cit.*, pp. 407-410.

13. From *Upper Canada: The Formative Years, 1784-1841* by Gerald M. Craig, p. 31. Toronto: McClelland & Stewart Ltd., 1963. Reprinted by permission of The Canadian Publishers, McClelland & Stewart Ltd., Toronto.

14. Thomas Jefferson in R. Reid, *The Canadian Style*, p. 307. Don Mills; Fitzhenry & Whiteside Ltd., 1973.

15. From Eric Nicol and Peter Whalley, *An Uninhibited History of Canada*. Toronto: Musson Book Company, 1965.

16. From Glenn Tucker, *Poltroons and Patriots*, Vol. I, p. 56. Indianapolis: Bobbs-Merrill Co., 1954.

17. From D. B. Read, *Life and Times of Sir Issac Brock*, pp. 125-127. Toronto: William Briggs, 1894.

18. Henry Clay in John R. Columbo (ed.), *op. cit.*, p. 115.

19. From William Wood, *Selected British Documents*, Vol. I, p. 352. Toronto: The Champlain Society, 1920-1928. Reprinted by permission of The Champlain Society, Toronto.

20. "Sir Issac Brock" in W. S. Wallace, *Macmillan Dictionary of Canadian Biography*, 3rd ed., p. 83. Toronto: Macmillan Company of Canada, Ltd., 1963.

21. From Glenn Tucker, *op. cit.*, p. x.

22. *Ibid.*, p. 24.

23. From *Tiger Dunlop's Upper Canada, Comprising Recollections of the American War, 1812-1814 and Statistical Sketches of Upper Canada for the Use of Emigrants by a Backwoodsman* by William Dunlop, pp. 34-35. Toronto: McClelland & Stewart Ltd., 1964.

24. *Ibid.*, p. 49.

25. From E. P. Patterson, II, *The Canadian Indian: A History Since 1500*, p. 86. Ontario: Collier-Macmillan, 1972.

26. From G. M. Craig, *op. cit.*, p. 85.

27. From W. S. MacNutt, *op. cit.*, p. 150.

28. From Mason Wade, *The French Canadians, 1760-1967*, Vol. I, p. 123. Toronto: Macmillan Company of Canada, Ltd., 1968.

29. From *Western Ontario and the American Frontier* by Fred Landon, pp. 42-43. Toronto: McClelland & Stewart Ltd. (Carleton Lib. ed.), 1967. Reprinted by permission of The Canadian Publishers, McClelland & Stewart Ltd., Toronto.

CHAPTER 8

1. From H. H. Langton (ed.), *A Gentlewoman in Upper Canada, The Journals of Anne Langton*, pp. x-xi. Toronto: Clarke, Irwin & Co., 1950.

2. John MacTaggart, "Three Years in Canada: An Account of the Actual State of

the Country in 1826-7-8" in B. Sinclair et al, *Let Us Be Honest and Modest, Technology and Society in Canadian History*, p. 38. Toronto: Oxford University Press, 1974.

3. From Brigadier General E. A. Cruikshank, *The Correspondence of Lieutenant Governor John Graves Simcoe*, Vol. III, 1794-1795, pp. 191-193. Toronto: The Ontario Historical Society, 1925.

4. *Ibid.*, pp. 191-193.

5. From Susanna Moodie, *Roughing It in The Bush*, pp. 111-112. Toronto: Maclear and Co., 1871.

6. From J. J. Talman (ed.), *Loyalist Narratives From Upper Canada*, p. 127. Toronto: The Champlain Society, 1946. Reprinted by permission of The Champlain Society, Toronto.

7. From Robin W. Winks, *The Historian as Detective: Essays on Evidence*, p. xvii. New York: Harper Colophon Books, Harper and Row, 1970.

8. From *Canadian Business History, Selected Studies, 1497-1971* by D. Macmillan, p. 265. Toronto: McClelland & Stewart Ltd., 1972. Reprinted by permission of The Canadian Publishers, McClelland & Stewart Ltd., Toronto.

9. G. M. Trevelyan' quoted in A. L. Rowse, *The Use of History*, p. 66. London: English Universities Press, 1963.

10. From E. H. Carr, *What Is History?* p. 111. New York: Alfred A. Knopf, Inc. (Vintage Books ed.). Copyright 1967 by Alfred A. Knopf, Inc. Reprinted by permission of Alfred A. Knopf, Inc.

11. From L. Gottschalk, *Understanding History, A Primer of Historical Method*, 2nd ed., p. 26. New York: Alfred A. Knopf, Inc. Copyright 1969 by Alfred A. Knopf, Inc. Reprinted by permission of Alfred A. Knopf, Inc.

12. Gotthold Ephraim Lessing, quoted in L. Gottschalk, *op. cit.*, pp. 29-30.

13. From D. G. Creighton, *The Commercial Empire of the St. Lawrence, 1760-1850*, pp. 72-73. Toronto: Macmillan Company of Canada, Ltd., 1956.

14. From W. Kaye Lamb (ed.), *Sixteen Years in the Indian Country: The Journal of Daniel Williams Harmon, 1800-1816*, pp. 27-28, quoted in P. B. Waite, *Canadian Historical Documents Series*, Vol. II, *Pre-Confederation*, p. 127. Scarborough, Ontario: Prentice-Hall of Canada, Ltd., 1965.

15. John Todd's description in A. S. Morton, *A History of the Canadian West to 1870-71*, (ed. version), quoted in P. B. Waite, *op. cit.*, pp 142-143.

16. From D. Macmillan, *op. cit.*, pp. 272-273.

17. Quoted in Edwin C. Guillet, *The Great Migration, The Atlantic Crossing by Sailing Ship Since 1770*, pp. 35, 39, 40. Toronto: University of Toronto Press. Copyright 1963 by University of Toronto Press. Reprinted by permission of University of Toronto Press.

18. *Ibid.*, p. 43.

19. *Ibid.*, pp. 71, 72, 75, 93.

20. From Joseph Schull, *Rebellion, The Rising in French Canada, 1837*, p. 25. Toronto: Macmillan Company of Canada, Ltd., 1971.

21. Quoted in Edwin C. Guillet, *op. cit.*, p. 3.

22. *Ibid.*, p. 230.

23. From H. M. A. James Coyne (ed.), *The Talbot Papers, Transactions of the Royal Society of Canada*, 1909, p. 54. Ottawa & Montreal: Royal Society of Canada.

24. From Robina and Kathleen Lizars, *Humors of '37, Grave, Gay and Grim—Rebellion Times in the Canadas*, pp. 327, 328. Toronto: William Briggs, 1897.

25. *Ibid.*, pp. 326, 327.

26. Gerald Tulchinsky, "The Montreal Business Community", quoted in D. S. Macmillan, *op. cit.*

27. Michael Katz, "The People of Canadian City: 1851-52" in *Canadian Historical Review*, December 1972, p. 425. Toronto: University of Toronto Press. Copyright 1972 by University of Toronto Press. Reprinted by permission of University of Toronto Press and Mr. Michael Katz.

28. For a fuller discussion of Canadian historical writing, see *Approaches to Canadian History*. Toronto: University of Toronto Press, 1967 and especially J. M. S. Careless, "Frontierism, Metropolitanism, and Canadian History".

29. From E. C. Guillet, *Pioneer Travel in Upper Canada*, p. 155. Toronto: University of Toronto Press. Copyright 1963 by University of Toronto Press. Reprinted by permission of University of Toronto Press.

30. From B. Sinclair et al (eds.), *op. cit.*, pp. 116-117.

31. *Ibid.*, p. 53.

32. From E. C. Guillet, *Pioneer Travels in Upper Canada*, pp. 97-98.

33. From B. Sinclair et al (eds.), *op. cit.*, pp. 74-75.

34. From *Ideas in Exile, A History of Canadian Invention* by J. J. Brown, pp. 61-62. Toronto: McClelland & Stewart Ltd., 1967. Reprinted by permission of The Canadian Publishers, McClelland & Stewart Ltd., Toronto.

CHAPTER 9

1. George M. Wrong and H. H. Langton, "Chronicles of Canada Series", quoted in S. W. Wallace, *The Family Compact*, pp. 2-3. Toronto: Glasgow, Brook and Co., 1915.

2. From William Smith, *Political Leaders of Upper Canada*, p. 91. Toronto: Thomas Nelson and Sons Ltd., 1931.

3. Sir Francis Bond Head, quoted in S. F. Wise (ed.), *A Narrative*, p. 213. Toronto: McClelland & Stewart Ltd. (Carleton Library ed.), 1969.

4. From W. L. Mackenzie, *Sketches of Canada and the United States*, pp. 405-409. London: E. Wilson, 1833.

5. From Mason Wade, *The French Canadians*, Vol. I, p. 152. Toronto: Macmillan Company of Canada, Ltd., 1955.

6. Based on Carl Gustavson, *A Preface of History*, p. 62. New York: McGraw-Hill Book Company. Copyright 1955 by McGraw-Hill Book Company.

7. From Joseph Schull, *Rebellion: The Rising of French Canada, 1837*, pp. 39-40. Toronto: Macmillan Company of Canada, Ltd., 1971.

8. From Mason Wade, *op. cit.*, p. 173.

9. From Stanley B. Ryerson, *Unequal Union, Roots of Crisis in the Canadas, 1815-1873*, p. 80. Toronto: Progress Books, 1973. Reprinted by permission of Progress Books.

10. From Alfred D. Decelles, *The 'Patriotes' of '37, The Chronicles of Canada*, Vol. VII, No. 25, pp. 66-68. Toronto: Glasgow, Brook & Co., 1916.

11. E. B. Taché, quoted in F. Ouellet, *Louis-Joseph Papineau: A Divided Soul*, p. 6. Ottawa: Canadian Historical Association. Published by the Public Archives of Canada, a department of the Crown.

12. *Ibid.*, p. 20.

13. From Robina and Kathleen Lizars, *Humours of '37, Grave, Gay and Grim—Rebellion Times in the Canadas*, p. 24. Toronto: William Briggs, 1897.

14. *Ibid.*, p 30.

15. *Ibid.*, p. 104.

16. From Arthur Lower, *Colony to Nation*, p. 245. Toronto: Longman Canada Ltd., 1964.

17. From W. Kilbourn, *The Firebrand, William Lyon Mackenzie and the Rebellion in Upper Canada*, p. 38. Toronto: Clarke, Irwin & Co., 1956.

18. *Ibid.*, pp. 38-39.

19. From Charles Lindsey, *The Life and Times of William Lyon Mackenzie, Vol. II*, p. 334. Toronto: P. R. Randall, 1862 (Toronto: Coles Publishing Co., 1971).

20. From C. B. Sissons, *Egerton Ryerson: His Life and Letters, Vol. I*, pp. 204-205. Toronto: Clarke, Irwin & Co., 1937.

21. From *Sir Francis Bond Head, A Narrative* by S. F. Wise (ed.), pp. 1-2. Toronto: McClelland & Stewart Ltd. (Carleton Library ed., No. 43), 1969. Reprinted by permission of The Canadian Publishers, McClelland & Stewart Ltd., Toronto.

22. From W. Kilbourn, *op. cit.*, pp. 20-21.

23. From William Smith, *Political Leaders of Upper Canada*, p. 122. Toronto: Thomas Nelson & Sons Ltd., 1931.

24. From David Flint, *William Lyon Mackenzie, Rebel Against Authority*, pp. 7-8. Toronto: Oxford University Press. 1971.

25. Charles Lindsey, "Life and Times of William Lyon Mackenzie", quoted in Orrin E. Tiffany, *The Canadian Rebellion of 1837-38*. Buffalo, N.Y.: Buffalo Historical Society, 1905. This excerpt from Coles Canadiana Edition, p. 17. Toronto: Coles Publishing Co., 1972.

26. From Stanley B. Ryerson, *op. cit.*, p. 128.

27. From Robina and Kathleen Lizars, *op. cit.*

28. From David Flint, *op. cit.*, p. 120.

29. *Ibid.*, pp. 84-85.

CHAPTER 10

1. All excerpts from Charles Lucas (ed.), *The Durham Report*, pp. 16-17, 30-31, 48, 70, 288-289, 148, 151, 303-304, 307, 277-278, 279-280, 284. Oxford: Clarendon Press, 1912.

2. Robert Baldwin letter to Lord Durham, August 23, 1838. *PAC Report, 1923*, p. 328. Published by the Public Archives of Canada, a department of the Crown.

3. From Mason Wade, *The French Canadians, Vol. I*, p. 234. Toronto: Macmillan Company of Canada, Ltd., 1955.

4. Josephine Foster, "The Montreal Riot of 1849", CHR, Vol. XXXII, 1951, pp. 62-63. Toronto: University of Toronto Press. Copyright 1951 by University of Toronto Press. Reprinted by permission of University of Toronto Press.

5. From Sir Arthur G. Doughty, *The Elgin-Grey Papers, Vol. IV*, pp. 1488, 1490. Ottawa: King's Printer, 1937.

6. From J. A. K. C. Chisholm, *The Speeches and Public Letters of Joseph Howe, Vol. I*, pp. 70-71. Halifax: The Chronicle Publishing Co., Ltd., 1909.

7. *Ibid.*, p. 230.

CHAPTER 11

1. Farley Mowat, "Newfoundland: 'T'ree Hunnert Year Gone By'", quoted in William Kilbourn (ed.), *Canada, A Guide to the Kingdom*, pp. 98, 99. Toronto: Macmillan Company of Canada, Ltd., 1970.

2. From P. Toque, *Newfoundland: As It Was and As It Is In 1877*, pp. 86-87. Toronto: John B. Magurn, 1878.

3. From J. Hatton, *Newfoundland: Its History, Its Present Condition, and Its Prospects in the Future*, p. 363. Boston: Doyle and Whittle, 1883.

4. From Jim Bennett, "Nova Scotia Diet".

5. From William Menzies Whitelaw, *The Maritimes and Canada Before Confederation*, p. 21. Toronto: Oxford University Press, 1934. Reprinted by permission of Oxford University Press.

6. From W. Stewart Wallace, *The Dictionary of Canadian Biography*, Vol. I, A-K, p. 711. Toronto: Macmillan Company of Canada, Ltd., 1945.

7. Frederic S. Cozzens, "Acadia: Or a Month With the Blue Noses", quoted in P.B. Waite, *Canadian Historical Documents Series*, Vol. II, *Pre-Confederation*, p. 190. Scarborough, Ontario: Prentice-Hall of Canada, Ltd., 1965.

8. Hugo Reid, "Sketches of North America", quoted in P. B. Waite, *op. cit.*, p. 191.

9. From Tom Connors, "Bud the Spud".

10. From A. Munro, *New Brunswick, With A Brief Outline of Nova Scotia and Prince Edward Island*, pp. 367, 369. Halifax: R. Nugent, 1855.

11. *Ibid.*, pp. 56.

12. *Ibid.*, pp. 118-119.

13. *Ibid.*, p. 381.

13a. From *Sarah Binks* by Paul Hiebert, p. 48. Toronto: McClelland & Stewart Ltd., 1971.

14. Irene M. Spry, "The Palliser Expedition, 1857-60", quoted in P. B. Waite, *op. cit.*, pp. 146-147.

15. From *Saturday Night*, June, 1974.

16. R. Byron Johnson, "Very Far West Indeed: A Few Rough Experiences on the North-West Pacific Coast", quoted in P. B. Waite, *op. cit.*, pp. 152-153.

17. From Oliver Goldsmith, *The Rising Village and Other Poems*, pp. 30-32. St. John N.B.: John MacMillan, 1834.

18. From *The Backwoods of Canada* by Catherine Parr Traill, pp. 149-150. Toronto: McClelland & Stewart Ltd., 1929. Reprinted by permission of The Canadian Publishers, McClelland & Stewart Ltd., Toronto.

19. From Susanna Moodie, *Life in the Clearings*, pp. 38, 40, 45-46, 53. Toronto: Macmillan Company of Canada, Ltd. (ed. by R. L. Dougall), 1959.

20. From Thomas C. Haliburton, *The Clockmaker*, p. 62. Toronto: McClelland & Stewart Ltd. (New Canadian Library ed.), 1958.

21. From D. C. Masters, *The Rise of Toronto, 1850-1890*, p. 30. Toronto: University of Toronto Press. Copyright 1947 by University of Toronto Press. Reprinted by permission of University of Toronto Press.

22. From E. C. Guillet, *Pioneer Days in Upper Canada*, p. 143. Toronto: University of Toronto Press. Copyright 1963 by University of Toronto Press. Reprinted by permission of University of Toronto Press.

23. From W. G. Smith, *Building the Nation: A Study of Some Problems Concerning the Churches' Relation to Immigrants*, pp. 44-49. Toronto: Issued by Canada Congregation Missionary Society, 1922.

24. From Susanna Moodie, *op. cit.*, p. 113.

25. From Charles E. Phillips, *The Development of Education in Canada*, pp. 52-53. Toronto: W. J. Gage, 1957. Copyright Gage Educational Publishing Limited.

26. From J. George Hodgins, *The Establishment of Schools and Colleges in Ontario, 1792-1910, Vol. II*, p. 84. Toronto: L. K. Cameron (Printer to the King's Most Excellent Majesty), 1910.

27. "Report on the Past History and Present Condition of the Common or Public Schools of the City of Toronto" in Douglas Lawr and Robert Gidney, *Educating Canadians, A Documentary of Public Education*, pp. 107, 110, 111. Toronto: Van Nostrand Reinhold, 1973.

28. Based on C. E. Phillips, *op. cit.*

29. From Anna Jameson, *Winter Studies and Summer Rambles in Canada*, p. 17. Toronto: McClelland & Stewart Ltd., 1965.

30. From Susanna Moodie, *op. cit.*, p. 121.

31. From Thomas C. Haliburton, *op. cit.*, pp. 40-41, 102, 73, 115.

32. From Catherine Parr Traill, *The Canadian Settler's Guide*, p. 24. Toronto: McClelland and Stewart Ltd., 1969.

33. From A. Munro, *op. cit.*, p. 319.

34. From E. C. Guillet, *op. cit.*, pp. 180-181.

35. From Una Abrahamson, *God Bless Our Home: Domestic Life in Nineteenth Century Canada*, p. 22. Toronto: Burns and MacEachern, 1966.

36. *Ibid.*, pp. 31-32.

37. From E. C. Guillet, *op. cit.*, p. 144.

38. From John C. Geikie, *Adventures in Canada; Or Life in the Woods*, p. 154. Philadelphia: Porter and Coates.

39. From E. C. Guillet, *op. cit.*, p. 151.

40. From Edwin C. Guillet, *Early Life in Upper Canada*, pp. 361-363. Toronto: University of Toronto Press. Copyright 1963 by University of Toronto Press. Reprinted by permission of University of Toronto Press.

41. L. Child, *The American Frugal Housewife*, quoted in Una Abrahamson, *op. cit.*, pp. 108-109.

42. Home and Health, quoted in Una Abrahamson, *op. cit.*, p. 113.

43. From Catherine Parr Traill, *op. cit.*, appendix.

44. From John C. Geikie, *op. cit.*, p. 147.

45. From E. C. Guillet, *Pioneer Days in Upper Canada*, p. 156.

46. Complete Rules of Etiquette, quoted in Una Abrahamson, *op. cit.*, pp. 28-29.

47. *Ibid.*, p. 113.

CHAPTER 12

1. Darcy McGee in *Confederation Debates*, February 9, 1865, pp. 130, 132.
2. George Brown and A. A. Dorian in *Parliamentary Debates on the Subject of Confederation*, pp. 107, 256. Ottawa, 1951.
3. From D. C. Master, *Reciprocity, 1846-1911*, CHA Booklet No. 12, p. 8. Ottawa: Canadian Historical Association. Published by the Public Archives of Canada, a department of the Crown.
4. From *The Canadian Corporate Elite, An Analysis of Economic Power* by Wallace Clement, pp. 60-61. Toronto: McClelland & Stewart Ltd. (Carleton Library ed.), 1975. Reprinted by permission of The Canadian Publishers, McClelland & Stewart Ltd., Toronto.
5. From A. A. Dorian, *op. cit.*, p. 251.
6. From Peter Burroughs, *British Attitudes Towards Canada, 1822-1849*, p. v. Scarborough, Ontario: Prentice-Hall of Canada, Ltd., 1971.
7. George E. Cartier, quoted in P. B. Waite, (ed.), *The Confederation Debates in the Province of Canada, 1865*, pp. 50-51. Toronto: McClelland & Stewart Ltd. (New Canadian Library Edition), 1963.
8. E. H. Dewart. From the introduction to "Selections From Canadian Poets", quoted in *Canadian Anthology* pp. 73-75, Revised ed., 1966.
9. From P. B. Waite, *The Life and Times of Confederation, 1864-1867*, p. 328. Toronto: University of Toronto Press. Copyright 1962 by University of Toronto Press. Reprinted by permission of University of Toronto Press.
10. From *Confederation and Its Leaders* by M. O. Hammond, p. 49. Toronto: McClelland & Stewart Ltd., 1927. Reprinted by permission of The Canadian Publishers, McClelland & Stewart Ltd., Toronto.
11. *Ibid.*, p. 120.
12. From R. G. Cornell, *The Great Coalition*, CHA Booklet No. 19, pp. 18-19. Ottawa: Canadian Historical Association, 1966. Published by the Public Archives of Canada, a department of the Crown.
13. *Ibid.*, pp. 18-19.
14. From P. B. Waite, *The Life and Times of Confederation*, pp. 70, 72.
15. *Ibid.*, p. 70 note.
16. From P. B. Waite (ed.), *Pre-Confederation*, pp. 216-217. Scarborough, Ontario: Prentice-Hall of Canada, Ltd., 1965.
17. From P. B. Waite, *The Charlottetown Conference*, 1864, CHA Booklet No. 15, pp. 23-24. Ottawa: Canadian Historical Association, 1963. Published by the Public Archives of Canada, a department of the Crown.
18. John A. Macdonald in Pope, *Memoirs*, V. I, pp. 269-270. J. Durie and Son, 1894.
19. From P. B. Waite, *Life and Times of Confederation*, p. 156.
20. George Brown in *Confederation Debates*, February 8, 1865, pp. 86-114.
21. From P. B. Waite, *Life and Times of Confederation*, p. 122.
22. A. A. Dorian, in *Confederation Debates*, March 6, 1865, pp. 694-695.
23. From Jean Charles Bonenfant, *The French Canadians and the Birth of Confederation*, CHA Booklet No. 21, pp. 8, 18-19. Ottawa: Canadian Historical Association. Published by the Public Archives of Canada, a department of the Crown.
24. From P. B. Waite, *Life and Times of Confederation*, pp. 121-122.
25. From K. A. MacKirdy et al (eds.), *Changing Perspectives in Canadian History*, p. 217. Toronto: J. M. Dent and Sons (Canada) Ltd., 1967.
26. From P. B. Waite, *The Life and Times of Confederation*, p. 212.
27. From Edith Fowke et al, *Canada's Story in Song*, pp. 106-107. Toronto: Gage Educational Publishing Co., 1970.
28. From *The Making of a Nation* by William Kilbourn, prologue, pp. 8, 9. Toronto: McClelland & Stewart Ltd. (Canadian Centennial Library), 1965. Reprinted by permission of Canadian Publishers, McClelland & Stewart Ltd., Toronto.
29. *Ibid.*, p. 6.

Index